PK

The Assassination of Gaitán

The Assassination of Gaitán

Public Life and Urban Violence in Colombia

Herbert Braun

The University of Wisconsin Press

Published 1985

The University of Wisconsin Press
114 North Murray Street
Madison, Wisconsin 53715

The University of Wisconsin Press, Ltd.
1 Gower Street
London WC1E 6HA, England

First printing

Printed in the United States of America

Library of Congress Cataloging-in-Publication Data
Braun, Herbert, 1948–
    The assassination of Gaitán.
    Bibliography: pp. 257–271.
    Includes index.
    1. Bogotá (Colombia)—History. 2. Riots—Colombia—
Bogotá. 3. Gaitán, Jorge Eliécer, 1902–1948—
Assassination. 4. Colombia—Politics and government—
1930–1946. 5. Colombia—Politics and government—
1946–1974. I. Title.
F2291.B6B73 1985   986.1′063.1′0924   85-40362
ISBN 0-299-10360-9

Colombia is divided, so to speak, into two nations: Bogotanos and provincials, the latter being the victims of the former. . . . For it is here [in Bogotá] that the politicians have always hatched the wars that we provincials have had to fight for them to further their fortunes, while they stay here enjoying themselves, chatting delightfully among enemies.

Rafael Uribe Uribe (1898)
Liberal general, politician, and intellectual

[To] Bogotá . . . gentle, insular, and Mediterranean city, has fallen the task, since colonial times, of forming a nation around her, guiding it, defining its destiny, maintaining it united and compact . . . and of being at all times the ancestral home to which come Colombians from the most remote places of the country in search of a culture, a great national prestige, the fulfillment of an ambitious dream, or, simply, a comfortable and tranquil existence under the shelter of her hospitality.

Rafael Azula Barrera (1956)
Conservative politician and intellectual

Contents

Illustrations

Preface

Year after year a story is told in Bogotá and throughout Colombia. It re-counts the life of one man and the experiences of those who lived through the day of his death. So much has been added to and taken from the story that it now has a fictional, almost fantastic, character. "Novels aren't written to recount life," the realist Peruvian author Mario Vargas Llosa has told us, "but to transform it by adding something to it."[1] As people remember their past, however, they often transform it without the help of the novelist. I have sought to recover an assassination in Bogotá for history, and present it as part of a secular process so that we may build upon the past. Colombians of an entire generation and from all social classes were unable to freely exercise their public rights after that death on April 9, 1948. This book is for them, with the hope that their children will be able to participate openly and actively in politics.

As we turn events into words and years into pages, historians unavoidably add to history by drawing connections and making inferences that the actors themselves may not have. But in these pages there is much more that is missing and that I have not recovered. I am profoundly grateful to Luis Eduardo Ricaurte and all the other men and women who talked to me about their experiences. This history can only be less than theirs, for life is at its fullest when it is lived, rather than when it is told, whether as fiction or as history.

Something in this book comes from the experiences of those who were living on the Calle 10 on April 9, 1948, and from Tránsito, a domestic servant in a petit bourgeois home in Bogotá whose life crossed on that day with that of a common drifter named El Alacrán. They are not protagonists in this book because they are fictional characters given to us by Manuel Zapata Olivella and by José Antonio Osorio Lizarazo,[2] who is also one of the first historians of the events I reconstruct in these pages. I turned to fiction as I began to inquire about the events of that day, for the literary imagination was the best entry into the world of those who destroyed the center of Bogotá in a few afternoon hours.

No two novelists want to tell the same story; no two historians can. This book is very much the result of my interaction with the oral and written testimony on which it is based. Fortunately for both myself and the reader, however, I did not write it alone. Thomas E. Skidmore worked with me on every page as he guided this work through its first stages. Charles W. Bergquist's trenchant commentary helped me place the narrative within a wider historical context. I gained a growing sense of the richness of Colombian political history in conversations with Marco Palacios as we both taught Latin American history at the Colegio de México. I have been inspired by William B. Taylor, who helped uncover what the sources were telling me, nudged me to ask additional questions of them, and tried to restrain me from saying more than my work with them would sustain. Yet these pages are mine, and I am responsible for the weaknesses and errors that remain.

Many others gave of their time and knowledge. Christopher Mitchell, Richard E. Sharpless, Peter H. Smith, and Alexander W. Wilde were helpful as I was beginning to do research. Steve J. Stern read this work with a discerning eye when it was a dissertation for the University of Wisconsin and offered many valuable suggestions for revision, as did Rodolfo Pastor at the Colegio de México. A reader for the University of Wisconsin Press kept me from many an error. At the University of Virginia, William B. Taylor was joined by Gary D. Allinson, Edward L. Ayers, Dorothy Ross, and Alexander Sedgwick, other colleagues in the History Department, and graduate and undergraduate students, who offered comments and words of encouragement as my work drew to a close.

I have been trained in American universities and now teach in the United States. From here the Latin American republics are perceived through many cultural and ideological blinders. Colombia is best known in the United States through the fantastic literature of Gabriel García Márquez as a distant world doomed to cyclical devastation. I hope that this story of civilian politics and urban violence will help dispel some of the myths, and that the reader will come to appreciate the search for order, the love of laws, the depth of convictions, and the strength of collective purpose which characterize the conflicts that make for historical change in Colombia.

The translations from Spanish to English are my own. But here also I received assistance. Cecilia Zárate-Laun and William B. Taylor, as well as Jane Barry, who went through my prose with respect and grace, suggested many a change. Peter Givler brought the manuscript to the University of Wisconsin Press, and Jack Kirshbaum, my editor, saw to its well-being.

This book was made possible by Barbara Forrest and my friends in Madison, Wisconsin, and by my family in Bogotá, and by those who became my friends in Colombia as we shared historical interests. The research was made possible by Fulbright–Hays and Social Science Research Council fellowships. I was aided by the staffs of the Casa Museo Jorge Eliécer Gaitán, the Cruz Roja Colombiana, the Biblioteca Nacional, and the Biblioteca Luis Angel Arango in Bogotá, the Inter-Library Loan department of Memorial Library at the University of Wisconsin in Madison, and the archives of the International Red

Cross, the National Archives, and the Library of Congress in Washington, D.C. Francisco Sáenz Arbeláez gave me permission to use the files of the Junta de Daños y Perjuicios, which he had carefully stored in his private law office, and Daniel Martínez Quijano found the Red Cross files on the *bogotazo* in the basement of the old Red Cross building in Bogotá.

Cecilia Brown Villalba made the last stages of this work the most promising, as together we finished typing the manuscript two months before the birth of our daughter, Emilia Braun Brown. We hope Emilia finds inspiration in novels, for Vargas Llosa has told us also that "regimes that seek to exercise total control over life mistrust works of fiction and subject them to censorship. Emerging from one's own self, being another, even in illusion, is a way of becoming less a slave and of experiencing the risks of freedom."[3] The conflicts through which we struggle for a better life make the dreams of fiction historically possible.

The Assassination of Gaitán

Introduction

This is the story of the violent death of Jorge Eliécer Gaitán, and of the crazed, fleeting passions of the crowd that took to the streets of Bogotá, Colombia, on the afternoon of April 9, 1948, to avenge his murder. In a few hours downtown Bogotá was in flames, its public buildings bombed and ransacked, its stores looted.

I chose to study the *bogotazo*, as the riot has come to be known, to remove myself from the conventions of macrohistorical, social science-dominated thinking about the Latin American past and future. I had grown distrustful of the many models through which scholars of various political persuasions deduced the causes of Latin American tradition and backwardness. These models pointed to inevitable decay, continuous stagnation, or a telescoping of history into a socialist future, and often told us more about scholars' preconceptions than about the history of the Latin American people. I therefore decided to study something exceptional, and small, in order to learn about what then seemed to be significant deviations in a teleological process. By looking at Colombian history through an accidental and unpredictable event, I came to perceive historical patterns that are not contained in the traditional dichotomies of developed and underdeveloped, advanced and dependent, societies.

Historians have passed the riot by. Throughout my youth I heard quiet rumors that the riot had split the nation's history in two. I wished to give life

3

to the rioters, not necessarily by justifying their actions, but by giving them a place in the history of Colombia. For the crowd of the *bogotazo* has been dismissed as an expression of a barbarous underside of Colombian society. Elias Canetti's anthropologically informed work provided many insights into its behavior.[1]

The realization came quickly, however, that I was in for a long haul on a short subject. The more people I interviewed and talked to in Bogotá, the less comprehensible the events became. It was not the behavior of the crowd that confounded me. What seemed bizarre were the actions of the politicians on that afternoon and evening. To better understand them and Gaitán, I draw on Alexander Wilde's rich study of Colombian politics and on Richard Sharpless's thorough biography of Gaitán.[2] Although the behavior of the politicians is placed within a wider cultural and economic context in these pages, and Gaitán is not portrayed as either a populist or a socialist, both works were instrumental in shaping this study.

The politicians of Colombia compelled me, through their beliefs and their behavior, to look to the culture through which they, Gaitán among them, explained their reality. I seek to bring them, also, to life in these pages. Historians who have searched among cultural and behavioral changes for explanations of the Latin American past are close to my concerns. Too often, however, they perceive too little change, and their writings have a deterministic hue. They derive individual and collective behavior from a pervasive Catholic and Iberian tradition whose paternalistic and corporatist strands tend to envelop Latin America in hierarchical and authoritarian societies.[3]

Too often, also, those who concern themselves with the political culture of Latin America do so with pity for its alleged irrationality. Latin Americans are seen as acting within narrow personalistic circles rather than in the broad aggregates where the objective, social needs of society can best be fulfilled. The masses are apathetic, distrustful of leaders and alienated from society. A major college textbook describes a culture without political participation, plagued by a "client population yearning to receive benefits from the government, but unable, short of rebellion, to modify local conditions."[4] Mauricio Solaún sees the Colombian political culture we will be studying as imbued with a "traditional normlessness," "familism," "friendism," and a distrust of others that can only lead to violence.[5] According to James Payne, the politicians of Colombia pursue personal and political "status" with an abiding disregard for the social and economic conditions of their society, while the nation's people seek political affiliations for the narrow prospects of employment rather than from a commitment to ideology, political programs, or class interests.[6]

According to Glen Caudill Dealy, there is an underlying rationality to Latin American and other Catholic societies, but it is antithetical to the private rationality of economically enterprising individuals. He argues that these societies cannot pass through a bourgeois-capitalist stage of history because they have not experienced and cannot experience the Protestant ethic. The driving force of people in Catholic societies, he suggests, is the search for power, for a separate public realm above private concerns, rather than the quest for material gain. In his pages a distinct culture determines their beliefs and actions regardless of time. Dealy draws much of his evidence from a secondary literature on the behavior of selected individuals in small towns and villages in various parts of Latin America. His otherwise perceptive comments are placed within an ahistorical context in which it seems that Latin America has not been part of the world capitalist economy.[7]

Historians and social scientists with more materialistic assumptions have also directed most of their efforts to studying permanence and continuity, the lack of change. They have searched for reasons why the societies and nations of Latin America have not achieved a fully articulated capitalist mode of production. Such concepts as a tenacious colonial heritage, the traditionalism of aristocratic landed elites, the incomplete transition from feudalism to capitalism, imperialism, unequal exchange, and dependency have been used to explain the poverty and class exploitation that characterize the region.

Scholars on the left and the right converge on the notion that Latin America has not fully experienced the market structures and mentalities of capitalism. From the perspective of the wealth, productivity, and homogenization produced by the market in advanced societies, they have reified capitalism as a necessary—albeit harsh, uneven, and exploitative—vehicle of progress in Latin America. The emphasis has been on what has not yet taken place. These approaches have a strong deterministic bent, with Latin American history conceived of as the recipient or the residue of world transformations.

Only in the last few years have leftist scholars been able to address the changes in Latin American societies that result from the rub of their own tensions.[8] As historians we have more often been angered by that which has not yet been accomplished, or that which changes just to stay the same, than we have been inspired by the conflicts that surround us—the calm demeanor behind which some wish to preserve their power, the passion of those who struggle to make themselves felt, and the rage of those who lose power and influence.

We will be asking about conflict and change in the realms of culture and politics as seen in the behavior of Colombia's public figures within a growing, export-oriented capitalist economy. We begin with the beliefs of the individuals and groups who participated in public life in Colombia from 1930 to 1950. I have taken those views and put them together with the ways in which leaders and followers acted in public to reach my conclusions about the patterns of their lives. Their history was filled with action, and I have attempted to narrate it in such a way that the reader may come to an understanding of the actors themselves, the often uncertain choices they faced, and the decisions they took in circumstances that were only rarely of their own choosing.

As I focused on the relationship between the beliefs and the behavior of the actors in this book, I became interested in the boundaries through which they gave meaning to their lives. Leaders as well as followers distinguished between public and private realms in Colombia. They felt that there were appropriate forms of comportment within each, and that only a select minority of public figures could perform in both. Gaitán captured the dichotomy when he divided Colombia into a *país político*, a country of politics, and a *país nacional*, a country of nationhood.

After 1930 the distinction between these two realms began to be questioned. I perceive the behavioral confusion that ensued in politics as an expression of a society undergoing profound changes. This book is a study of those changing forms of behavior in public. It begins with a description of the politicians of Colombia, focuses on the controversies that swirled around the figure of Gaitán, and ends with a spontaneous riot, the *bogotazo*, in which the behavioral roles of leaders and followers were reversed and none of the actors had time to prepare their performances.

The interpretation of Gaitán that unfolds in these pages comes from his writings and speeches, from his actions, and from what I learned of him in interviews with some of his closest followers. They agreed to speak with me about their past in the hope that I would produce an objective rendering of his life and thereby restore them to their just place in history. For Jorge Eliécer Gaitán is the most maligned public man of Colombia, and his followers are publicly derided to this day. Their views led me to an understanding of Gaitán, but the portrait of him that is presented in these pages cannot be theirs. I have wrestled with some of the differences and hope that I have done justice to the leader they describe, even though he has been rendered in my own way.

I have attempted to allow the leaders of the Liberal and Conservative parties, Gaitán's opponents, to speak for themselves, without, however, handing my pages over to them. They have conventionally been seen by scholars as the representatives of an exploitative ruling class, or as mere oligarchs whose conservative or reactionary views are knowable a priori. The leaders of the traditional parties of Colombia were all much quieter and more reserved than Gaitán, but they were prolific on paper and nuanced in their public behavior. They were men who strove not to draw a mass following. I hope that I have depicted the complexity of their views, the depth of their fears, and the historical potential of their public lives.

Finally, I use oral and written accounts of the riot to portray the urban crowd that destroyed Bogotá upon Gaitán's assassination. The crowd emerges historically out of the experiences of Gaitán's followers as he struggled for power against the Liberal and Conservative leaders. I have immersed myself in the riot in an effort to present a narrative that approximates the views and feelings of the rioters.

In order to understand how the actors conceived of their lives, I went in search of thinkers who might have similar views of history. I found connections, not among theorists who look to what capitalism has not accomplished in Latin America, but among those who are critical of the triumph of capitalism in the United States and Western Europe, and look back, as do Hannah Arendt, Richard Sennett, and, more ambivalently, Albert O. Hirschman, at what has been lost.[9] They lament the loss of the distinction between the public and the private, the fall of community and shared purpose, the rise of private, quotidian concerns into the realm of the public, and the alienation and excessive individualism that have emerged in the historical transition to capitalism. This is precisely the process which the historical actors in this book felt that they were living through. The concepts of private and public life resonate in their lives.

In this book we will be asking about the privatization of social life that comes with the expansion of market relations. Our focus will be on public life in Bogotá. The historic shift toward the private is a secular trend of capitalist societies, whether they are advanced or dependent, early or late industrializers, developed or underdeveloped, central or peripheral in the world economy. The transition is historically diverse, rich, and nuanced. Within each society the tensions between public and private interests play themselves out first and foremost in urban areas. The capital city is the center of public life, the seat of national government, and the place where politics is performed before a growing, anonymous audience.

In 1930 Colombians were embarking upon uncertain times. An enduring public tradition with precapitalist and Catholic roots, conceived of as the embodiment of abstract reason, morality, and the collective good, and performed by selected political elites in Bogotá as the nation's center of high culture and civilized comportment, faced a society increasingly mobilized around the individualizing, competitive values of market structures. Overtly, the controversies that define the period revolve around the issues of political legitimacy and the place of the individual in society and politics: who was and who was not to be a participating member of the emerging Colombian nation. These controversies were stirred by Gaitán. The democratizing potential they contained came to an end when Gaitán was killed and the crowd and the politicians shattered the relationship between leaders and followers in Colombia. Thereafter the nation broke apart into the anomic civil war known generically as *la Violencia,* the violence.

A premise of this book is that the privatizing trend can be seen in the changing behavioral relationship between leaders and followers. In a society where, as Gino Germani has put it, "there is a predominance—or at least a very vast area—of behavior regulated within the normative framework of elective actions or by individual choice, rather than by prescriptive action,"[10] leaders must reach out directly and intimately to their individualized following to fulfill their increased demands and aspirations. That changing relationship is a conflictual process that carries within it the makings of a new community—the rise of democracy—and the growth of a new terror, as leaders seek ever more sophisticated means to control their newly mobilized followers.

Gaitán was one of the many powerful political figures to emerge in Latin America during the industrializing years of the 1930s and 1940s. Leaders like Víctor Raúl Haya de la Torre of Peru, Juan Domingo Perón and Eva Duarte de Perón in Argentina, Getúlio Vargas in Brazil, and Lázaro Cárdenas in Mexico, among others, have generally been studied as urban populists who built upon traditional forms of paternal authority held to be widespread in Hispanic and Catholic cultures. In the Latin American context the term "populism" has been applied to various broad, multiclass urban coalitions of diverse ideology and composition that arise from the ephemeral character of those classes in the face of the enduring power of landed interests and international capital. Populist movements rise above social classes and are led by personalistic leaders with a wide popular appeal and authoritarian tendencies, who are usually seen as helping to preserve the established social order. According to Steve Stein, "The primary impact of most populist movements in terms of political development has been to increase popular participation while at the same time directing it into paternalistic forms that have served to bolster an exploitative status quo."[11]

Gaitán's politics shares features of populism. To regard him as a populist, however, is to make him appear uniquely Latin American, rather than the actor he was in a secular process that is part of the expansion of the market. If we focus on Gaitán as the historical product of a Latin American cultural ethos, and on his ability to control his followers and preserve established social structures, the historic changes that were taking place in Colombia may elude us. For a status quo is constantly changing, not only because of the rising levels of urbanization and industrialization to which leaders respond and the struggle between the challengers and the established political leaders, but in a deeper, cultural sense as well. To treat Gaitán as a populist, finally, is to remove him from the class context in which he fashioned his acitivity.

Gaitán represented a new social class that was emerging from the economic growth of the first three decades of the century. He was a petit bourgeois whose thinking was shaped by his own place in society and by his nation's subordinate place in the international capitalist order. He embodied the concerns of a small and insecure class of professionals, small property- and shopowners, and private and public employees who were shut out of high office in public life and were unable to compete economically against a bourgeoisie of landholders and financiers whose strength was bolstered by the narrow development of an export-oriented market.

Gaitán imaginatively expressed his social class in politics. He attempted to lead other social groups—artisans, carpenters, stonemasons, barbers, bus drivers, prostitutes, and others who serviced the needs of the rapidly urbanizing nation, and especially of his own city, Bogotá—and, when possible, to address the interests of other social classes, workers and peasants, that were also beginning to make themselves felt in society. His aim was to bring himself and his class to power at the head of a broad amalgam he called the *pueblo*, the people. He advocated those changes that would make his society correspond more closely with his own outlook. Gaitán's life demonstrates the multiple connections that exist in a Latin American nation between politics and social and economic interests.

Gaitán's politics were personalistic. But this was as much the result of the epoch in which he lived, and the changes he attempted to bring about, as of the culture of his society. All leaders are personalistic, regardless of time and culture. The nineteenth century in Latin America witnessed the rule of many *caudillos* on horseback who established intimate relations with their followers that obligated them to deliver on their promises or face death. The rise of the neocolonial order after 1870 called forth leaders who attempted, quite understandably, to be as impersonal as possible.

The rulers of Colombia during the first three decades of this century were a dour group rarely if ever seen in public. The Brazilian leaders of the Old Republic from 1899 to 1930 ruled through their machinations at the upper reaches of their party apparatus, and the aristocratic Conservatives in Argentina until 1943 lived at a disdainful distance from the people of their nation. Even Porfirio Díaz, who ruled Mexico from 1876 to 1911, was far removed from the mass of Mexicans and surrounded himself with men who espoused a scientific, dispassionate outlook on life. The Latin American past is filled with relatively stable, slow-moving, and remote civilian leaders.

The rule of all these leaders was personalistic in the sense that their decisions usually carried more weight than the law or the constitution. This personal form of rule was largely the result of economics: a narrow circle of oligarchs could maintain power over societies that still managed to satisfy many of their needs by exporting agricultural products and mineral resources. Their relationship to their followers, which is the key ingredient of leadership,[12] was far different from that of the rural *caudillos* who came before and the modern politicians—widely seen as new, urban *caudillos* —who came after.

Gaitán, like other Latin American leaders of his generation, introduced personality into mass politics. Like them, he presented the private side of his life as a focal point of public life and as a means of obtaining a following. When he spoke of his personal struggles in front of the crowd in the public plaza, Gaitán was perceived by other politicians and by established society as a vulgar man who was demeaning the high traditions of public life. Yet by doing so he was vividly expressing the ideals of his social class and bridging the distance between leaders and followers in Colombia. His leadership was constantly in flux, for the promises he had to make created obligations that he could fulfill only with difficulty.

Gaitán's personalistic style was a symptom of the subjectivity and intimacy that increasingly characterize the relationship between leaders and followers in advanced capitalist societies, where the people seek in authenticity and sincerity, in personal, intimate attributes rather than in statecraft, the indicators of the abilities of their leaders. In these societies politicians unabashedly speak of their private lives, and rarely is their informal behavior perceived as vulgar. Instead, politicians who do not reveal their innermost feelings are perceived with suspicion. These personalistic features of Gaitán's leadership are less a traditional Latin American phenomenon than they are an expression of a Latin American society turning bourgeois, or, as Germani puts it, a society becoming modern. Gaitán was part of that change. As a major actor in the historic shift toward a society defined by private concerns, he helped shape the cultural and social changes about which we wish to inquire.

In chapter 1 we meet the characters of this story, set the historical stage on which they practiced their political art, and look at how the political leaders of Colombia perceived their followers. I demonstrate how the traditional distinction between the public and the private was undermined with the growth of capitalism, opening the way for Gaitán. Chapter 2 describes Gaitán from his birth in 1898 through his university years in Bogotá and establishes the class basis of the politics he pursued during his lifetime. Chapter 3 follows Gaitán from his studies in Rome through his early political career in the late 1920s, to the start of his presidential campaign in early 1944. I show how he built a new space within the body politic during those years. Chapter 4 examines Gaitán's behavior within that space as he campaigned for the presidency. In chapter 5 we analyze Gaitán's experimental relationships with the traditional politicians and with his new followers and end with his achievement of the height of his power as April 9, 1948, approaches. In the next three chapters time is condensed. They deal with the few short hours of the afternoon of April 9, 1948, and with the days following the *bogotazo*.

Chapter 6 traces the steps through which social order came to an end. Chapter 7 looks at the crowd that destroyed Bogotá. The final chapter concludes with the destruction of peace in Colombia as the nation's leaders relinquish their public place. In the conclusion I reflect on how those who lived through the events remember them.

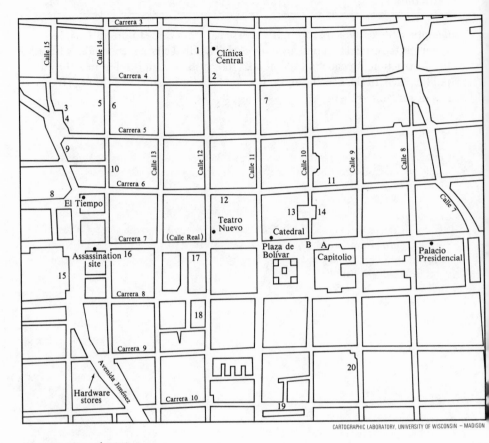

Downtown Bogotá, 1948.

A   Site of first attack of Presidential Guard
    on the crowd
B   Site of tank that shoots on crowd
    in the Plaza de Bolívar

1   Ministerio del Interior
2   Palacio de la Nunciatura Apostólica
3   Jornada
4   El Espectador
5   Ministerio de Justicia
6   Universidad Javeriana Femenina
7   Palacio Arzobispal
8   Jockey Club

9   Ministerio de Educación
10 Palacio de Justicia
11 Museo Colonial
12 Notary Public nos. 1 and 2
13 Teatro Colón
14 Palacio de San Carlos
15 Gobernación de Cundinamarca
16 Café Windsor
17 Palacio de Comunicaciones
18 U.S. Embassy
19 Mercado Central
20 Policía

1

The Dialectics of Public Life

Public life is not solely political, but equally and primarily, intellectual, moral, economic, religious; it comprises all our collective habits, including our fashions both of dress and of amusement.

José Ortega y Gasset (1930)

It just so happens that politics is the only intellectual activity in our country. Politics is an intellectual minimum, and all of us who would have preferred a humanistic career go into it. . . . Whether victors or vanquished, we Colombian intellectuals cannot live outside politics.

Juan Lozano y Lozano (1944)
Liberal politician and intellectual

The Rise to Power

Alfonso López rose slowly. Standing before his Liberal colleagues, he declared that in just one hundred days, on February 9, 1930, one of their own would be president of Colombia.[1] Bemused, the older statesmen of the party must have recalled their own naiveté and the brash statements of their younger years. They had been out of power since before they lost the War of the Thousand Days (1899–1902), the last of the nineteenth-century civil wars between Liberals and Conservatives, and had been unable to unseat the Conservatives in five elections of the ensuing peace. The Conservative Republic had been in place since 1885, before López was born. But the younger Liberals listened expectantly. They felt the stirrings of change. To a man they believed that they would orchestrate the nation's first enduring peaceful transfer of power. The civil wars were a thing of the past. Even many young Conservatives shared their ideals. The generation that had not made the wars felt that it would at last bring progress and democracy to Colombia. Its members would serve their nation as no others had done before.

In neither war nor peace had politics been democratic. It rested on a wide cultural chasm between leaders and followers. It had been, traditionally, a sporadic affair. Since the origins in the 1830s and 1840s of two political parties, leading Liberals and Conservatives had successfully mobilized large

13

numbers of their followers for only limited periods of time. More often in the nineteenth than in the twentieth century, these affairs revolved around military campaigns called by the leaders of one party against those of the other. Temporary resolution of these civil wars, or exhaustion, brought a measure of peace, a calming of the party *mística*, the fervor among the masses that fueled the wars, and a return to an atmosphere of statesmanlike conciliation among the leaders. These interludes were all-important, for they allowed the leaders to measure their distance from their followers and bring each affair to an end.

Periods of military quiescence were filled with political activity. Although the electoral campaigns, which were more the norm in the twentieth century than they ever were in the nineteenth, were often as passionately contested as the wars themselves, they were less costly and convulsive. In war and in peace, the parties tied entire regions, towns, and hamlets to their large, multiclass, and long-distance clientelistic networks, bringing Colombians of all walks of life into their folds. More than ideology, the life and livelihood of individuals was at stake. In war the victorious side found protection, and in peace small and large local political positions, credit facilities, and even land could come to those who lived in areas defended by their party. The party that won the presidency in Bogotá enhanced the position of its followers throughout the land, for they could easily recognize their party's accession to national power as the moment to obtain their own. At times they were encouraged by the leaders, who saw their own strength reflected in their followers.[2]

López was the son of a rich man, don Pedro A. López, who had built a huge commercial entrepot in Honda, on the Magdalena River near Bogotá, and was the founder of one of the nation's first banks, the Banco López. Throughout his rise to riches he groomed his eldest son to follow in his footsteps. Some of the leading Conservative and Liberal thinkers of the age became his tutors; he was sent to England to study at Brighton and later attended the Packard School in New York.[3]

In 1904, at eighteen, he became the director of Pedro A. López y Cía. Ten years later he resigned because of disputes with his three younger brothers. Without a job, López turned to politics and ended up in Congress in 1915, where he struck up a close friendship with a young Conservative star by the name of Laureano Gómez. He was also named director of the New York-based Mercantile Bank of the Americas. His superiors in New York considered him one of the ablest of Latin American bankers, yet he was forced to resign after accusations that he used his seat in Congress to favor his employers.[4]

As his fortune dwindled, López's passion for public life grew. He became notorious in Bogotá. He could be seen everywhere, in the dark cafés that lined the Calle Real (Carrera 7), in the private clubs, and in the editorial offices of the major newspapers. He attended endless *tertulias*, informal gatherings of intellectuals, always talking politics. He pursued few other topics; whether this was because he lacked confidence, having never attended a university, or because no other subjects interested him is not known. He seemed never to work or follow a regular schedule, and he showed up at the most unexpected moments. He developed a reputation as a respectable bohemian, a master of leisure time.[5]

López did not propose that he become president. He argued instead for Enrique Olaya Herrera, an established Liberal figure who had been minister of foreign relations in 1914 and, since 1922, ambassador to the United States. The defiant young Liberal showed himself to be a pragmatist. He was concerned that the Liberals promote individuals "who are not frightening." Confidently and coyly, the upstart leader of his party rejected all Conservative overtures for a compromise.[6]

The Conservatives were hopelessly divided among José Vincente Concha, Guillermo Valencia, the renowned poet from Popayán, the nation's most conservative city, and Alfredo Vázquez Cobo, the still vital general of the War of the Thousand Days. Concha had recently been president, and the other two had previously run for the highest office of the land. Unfortunately, the Catholic Church, which traditionally endorsed the Conservative candidate as its own, was of little help. Ismael Perdomo, the recently named archbishop of Bogotá and head of the church in Colombia, was unable to decide which of the candidates was the most Catholic.[7] In desperation, the Conservatives turned to Mariano Ospina Pérez, a young engineer from Medellín. He was the nephew of the recent president Pedro Nel Ospina, and came from a highly respected landowning family with a long tradition in Conservative politics. But none of the candidates were willing to bow to the younger sectors of their party.

The leaders of the new generation were heard from daily. During the decade before the 1930 election, they were the new men of the city and did much of the thinking, talking, and writing in Bogotá. They took over the city's dingy cafés, held loud conversations, declaimed sensual poetry, read works prohibited by the church, wrote prose and poetry for the daily papers, and even dabbled in socialist ideas.

The young men shocked Bogotá's traditional elite with their disrespectful attitudes and obstreperous behavior. They wore colorful clothing and poked fun at the *cachaco*, the upper-class Bogotano who took leisurely walks on the streets of the city sporting a black three-piece suit, a top hat, and a red carnation on his lapel, rhythmically swinging his umbrella. They satirized the world of young debutantes and the late-afternoon gossip sessions known as the *chocolate santafereño* in the homes of the elite. The tradition came from the colonial period, when the city was known as Santa Fé de Bogotá.[8]

The young iconoclasts felt that they had little in common with the old and stodgy politicians who quietly went about their public tasks, shunning the limelight as much as possible. The elders had participated in the Quinquenio, the first coalition government of the century. In 1909, calling themselves "centenaristas" because their action came one hundred years after the proclamation of Colombia's independence from Spain, they quietly overthrew Rafael Reyes, the general who had been the architect of the Quinquenio, when his rule turned dictatorial. In 1910 they formed the Unión Republicana, a bipartisan movement that hoped to supplant the old parties with new republican ideals.

These moderate Liberals and Conservatives believed in conciliation. They gained a majority in the Congress and elected one of their own to the presidency. The movement did not survive Carlos E. Restrepo's administration. Yet its ideal of compromise found expression in the subsequent Conservative governments of José Vicente Concha (1914–1918), Marco Fidel Suárez (1918–1921), Pedro Nel Ospina (1922–1926), and Miguel Abadía Méndez (1926–1930).[9] President Suárez was a noted philologist who spent most of his time poring over obscure texts. When he made his daily early-morning trek to church, few Bogotanos even noticed their president. Abadía Méndez, the last president of the Conservative Republic, was an expert on the classics. He was rarely heard from, and few saw him on the streets of the city as he walked to the university to teach a course in public law.

The younger generation spent much of its time in public. The most famous group gathered in the Café Windsor, owned by two Liberal *centenaristas*, Agustín and Luis Eduardo Nieto Caballero.[10] They appropriately called themselves *los nuevos*, "the new ones," after a short-lived magazine they had published a few years earlier. They were Liberals and Conservatives who prided themselves on their ability to calmly and rationally discuss issues over which previous generations had gone to war. The avid conversationalists were a microcosm of the nation's future rulers.

López showed up rarely, for he was older and more serious than most. He was usually elsewhere making sure that power would not escape him. After Olaya Herrera's transitional government came to an end in 1934, López himself became president. His four years at the helm witnessed the period's most significant agrarian, fiscal, labor, and constitutional reforms, known as the Revolution on the March. Constitutionally unable to succeed himself, López became president again in 1942.

The brothers Alberto and Felipe Lleras Camargo were leading members of the Windsor group. They moved into opposing factions of the Liberal party after 1930. Alberto, the younger of the two, rode on López's coattails and became president for a brief year in 1945. Felipe followed another Liberal, Jorge Eliécer Gaitán, but was less committed to public life than his brother.

Gaitán himself occasionally visited the Windsor but found the conversations frivolous and unconstructive.[11]

Some of the Windsor Liberals were leftists. Gabriel Turbay, for example, was enamoured of communism and the ideals of the Russian Revolution. After 1930, however, he became a stalwart member of the Liberal party. He filled virtually every cabinet post, became ambassador to the United States, and by the mid-1940s, seemed on his way to the presidency.[12] Others, like José Mar, Luis Tejada, and Luis Vidales, moved leftward even before the victory.

Leading Conservative intellectuals were also part of the Windsor group. Four of them, Augusto Ramírez Moreno, Silvio Villegas, Eliseo Arango, and José Camacho Carreño, formed their own group and aggressively called themselves *los leopardos,* "the leopards."[13] They were gripped by an intellectual Christian concern over the growth of materialism and would become the Liberals' most acerbic critics after 1930.

As time-consuming as their studies and café conversations was their devotion to newspaper offices. As early as 1913 Eduardo Santos, a self-described man of letters and an omnivorous reader, mortgaged a small inherited home to buy the fledgling and financially troubled *El Tiempo* from his uncle, Alfonso Villegas Restrepo.[14] Santos turned the newspaper into a financial success and through his evenly written editorials built a powerful position that brought him the presidency in 1938. Alfonso López also invested in a newspaper, the *Diario Nacional,* but with less success. In the early 1920s Villegas Restrepo again tried his luck with journalism and started *La República.* The Liberals Fidel and Luis Cano brought their family newspaper, *El Espectador,* to Bogotá from Medellín. In 1929 the *leopardos* founded *El Debate,* a Catholic journal that supported the presidential aspirations of Guillermo Valencia. Guillermo Camacho Carreño broke with his old friends in May of that year to found *El Fígaro* and support the candidacy of José Vincente Concha.

The most important journal of the second half of the decade was *Universidad,* edited by the Liberal intellectual Germán Arciniegas. In the lively pages of this weekly, the nation's future leaders freely expressed their ideas on the state of the nation, cultural and intellectual life, and their own responsibility as the next generation of leaders. Alfonso López called for efficiency in public office. Laureano Gómez worried whether a Colombian culture could ever be produced. Carlos Lleras Restrepo, a diminutive, prematurely balding, chain-smoking economics student, wrote about the need to restructure the country's financial institutions. Gabriel Turbay and many others expressed the need to reform Congress. Gaitán wrote about penal law and let his contemporaries know that their ideas were less original and advanced than they believed them to be.[15]

This gentlemanly bipartisan sparring was often marred by Laureano

Gómez and Gaitán. They introduced themes that would haunt their colleagues throughout the years of their rule. Gómez was the oldest son of a family of modest means that had moved to Bogotá in 1888. In Ocaña, Norte de Santander, they had been known as a respectable Conservative family. Laureano was born the year after the move, in downtown Bogotá, just blocks away from the Presidential Palace and the cathedral, the two institutions that were to dominate his life. He received his education at the Jesuit Colegio de San Bartolomé and at the Universidad Nacional, the public university, where he obtained an engineering degree in 1909. Gómez was a reserved and shy student who only came into his own when he entered public life. He never practiced his profession. Two years out of the university he was already a congressman, and by 1915 he had been elected to the Senate from the department of Boyacá. He was too young, however, to take his seat legally.[16]

Gómez would later earn a reputation in Congress for his oratorical abilities. He had a penchant for saying the unexpected and soon came to be regarded as the grand inquisitor of the public realm. Friends and foes called him *el monstruo*, "the monster," for his implacable struggle against the presidents of his own party and for his campaign against laxity, immorality, and corruption in high office.

In 1921 Eduardo Santos and Fidel Cano were called to the *palacio*, the Presidential Palace, to mediate a conflict created by Gómez's oratorical diatribe against President Suárez. The Conservative had accused Suárez of seeking a small loan from some foreign businessmen who had come to see him about entrepreneurial possibilities in Colombia. The sum involved was insignificant, and apparently the president had not even made a deal contingent on the loan. Suárez had incurred some debts, it seemed, and his meager presidential salary was insufficient to support even his spare, intellectual style of life. Brokenhearted and publicly humiliated, Suárez acknowledged his guilt, resigned, and then fainted on the floor of the Senate.[17]

The younger generation organized public conferences to delve into the problems that faced Colombia. López invited Gómez to offer his views at one. On June 8, 1928, talking to the city's cultural and political elite at the Teatro Municipal, he shocked his listeners by informing them that Colombia had little chance of ever becoming a civilized nation. In his view, the racial mixture of fanatical Spaniards, savage Indians, and primitive Negroes, combined with climatological and geographic handicaps, had proven fatal.[18]

The city responded with dismay, even though Gómez had said nothing that they had not heard before. In 1928 he was contradicting the growing optimism of the *nuevos* as well as the very idea underlying the conferences. *El Tiempo* wrote that Gómez's words "fell on this happy city as if on a funeral pyre."[19] Eduardo Santos agonized over the Conservative's message, for if it was right there was no purpose to politics. "How can we tell the people they must struggle . . . so that each stage in their lives is better than the one before, if no one believes this task can be achieved [for] without a people, it is not possible to construct even a relative state of culture."[20]

Gómez's ideas were ridiculed in the city's cafés and salons as simple, unscientific, and pessimistic. On August 3 he returned to the Teatro Municipal to retaliate against those who had mocked him. The politicians of Colombia, he exclaimed, were like fish. They were cold and mute. "They cannot exercise their slimy ability . . . without the water . . . . out in the sun, where there is fresh air, they will die."[21] This time it was Gómez's acrid tone and his unprecedented personal attack on the nation's leaders that shocked the city's elite.

Gaitán shared Gómez's concern for morality in government. In June 1929 he and the *leopardo* Silvio Villegas led Bogotá crowds in protest against malfeasance in municipal offices with such unexpected success that they came close to overthrowing President Abadía Méndez.[22] Three months later Gaitán launched a two-week attack against the government and the military for the massacre of banana workers in Ciénega who had gone on strike against the U.S.-owned United Fruit Company. Gaitán's daily speeches were the first defense of the people of Colombia from within the halls of Congress that Bogotanos could recall.[23] The debate catapulted Gaitán into the limelight and made him a key figure in the fall of the Conservative Republic.

Olaya Herrera returned to Colombia from Washington to preside over a brief campaign that filled the plazas of Bogotá, Medellín, and Cali. The Liberals were pleasantly surprised at their sudden popularity, but the young Conservatives worried that politics was changing too rapidly. They wondered how they would fare with the Liberals in power. Would generational and behavioral ties allow them to rule together?

Olaya Herrera won over the divided Conservatives with only 44.9 percent of the vote.[24] The ploy had worked for the fledgling Liberals, and the new president began a coalition government of National Concentration with both Conservatives and Liberals, young and old, in his cabinet.[25] The writers of *El Debate* were not overly distressed at Olaya's victory. They saw him and their own candidate, Guillermo Valencia, as men of peace who represented their ideals, and the other Conservative candidate, Vázquez Cobo, as a throwback to the *caudillos*. They rapidly decided that little would change. "The centralist republic will remain intact; the constitution will be unchanged; relations between the church and the state will remain unmodified; order, liberty, and justice will not be disturbed."[26] The Conservatives reminded their readers that "Doctor Olaya is as much an enemy of tumult, unruliness, and license as we are."[27] The generation, it seemed, would hold together.

After February 9, 1930, the young Liberals and Conservatives ushered in a prolonged period of electoral campaigns. Peace was to bring order and respect for life and the constitution. Looming on the horizon was a long-term, stable mobilization of the people. By the mid-1940s four national elections and twice as many congressional contests had dramatically undermined the traditional separation between leaders and followers. If a social contract was not exactly in sight, neither was one of those traditional respites that allowed the leaders to keep their place.

The Ideals of Public Life

The Liberal and Conservative leaders called their form of rule *convivencia*, the politics of civility. In the term they revealed their commitment to a distinct public life and to peace. They meant more than an orderly sharing of politics among the leaders of the traditionally warring parties. Their aim was to *convivir*, to live together in a realm of power they felt ideally suited to inhabit. These *convivialistas*[28] saw themselves as *civilistas* defending the civilian institutions of the nation, rather than as *caudillos* leading the nation into war.

In the midst of *convivencia*, the Liberal politician Juan Lozano y Lozano expressed it best. "For those of us," he wrote of the leaders of both parties, "who are natives of tropical lands, who are without culture, without tradition, with so little visible glory, who live in such primitive conditions, it is the sensation of being born, growing up, developing, coming together and clashing, of reciprocally knowing our lives, being present in the moments of sorrow and happiness, in a word, living together with (*convivir*) a group of people, that ties us to our concept of nationhood."[29]

Contrary to their optimistic statements and their critical appraisals of the politicians who preceded them, the past weighed more heavily on their hearts and minds than they would willingly admit. The peace set the *nuevos* apart. Yet they were the carriers of deeply held cultural traditions that flourished in peacetime. The political order they inherited was built on a precapitalist ethos. It rested on the belief that public figures were uniquely qualified to lead the people, whose base, individual lives continuously threatened social order and civilization. Social life depended on the curtailment of individual needs in favor of collective ones, the public good. Political order in Colombia was not based on the bourgeois notion of a society of private citizens whose aggrandizement led to economic welfare and whose rights were the groundwork of liberty. Its utopian vision pointed to a social organism in which a vast majority of individuals with enclosed lives and little in the way of status or position respected the civil duties that came with their place in society and were allocated to them by the public men. The basis of social life was more moral than economic.

These political ideals remained viable well into the twentieth century because of the narrow development of market relations based on traditional exports and the selective importation of manufactured goods. This typically Latin American participation in an international division of labor served the interests of exclusive elites without having to incorporate large sectors of the rest of society. In addition, Colombian elites managed to keep their nation relatively insulated from the international network of trade and investment until the first decades of the century. By 1913 Colombia ranked behind every major Latin America country, including Guatemala, Venezuela, and Costa Rica, in British investment.[30] Likewise, by 1914 U.S. investments in Colombia did not exceed $21 million,[31] and total foreign investment stood at approximately $60 million.[32]

As the economic and political elites of most other Latin American nations were avidly opening their economies to the neocolonial order after 1870, the Colombians in 1885 initiated La Regeneración, a prolonged experiment in a centralist, closed, and hierarchical social order led by Rafael Núñez, a Liberal turned Conservative, which sought to limit contact with the outside world. The effort was not as successful as its leaders might have hoped,[33] but Colombia witnessed little of the foreign investment or migration that helped change the face, culturally as well as economically, of nations like Brazil, Argentina, Chile, Mexico, and the United States. During the 1880s fewer than a hundred migrants came to Colombia per year. The number doubled during the following decade. Between 1908 and 1919 only about four hundred foreigners immigrated to Colombia each year.[34]

Sharply divided at the end of the nineteenth century about the national benefits of coffee exports and foreign capital and the place of government in the marketplace, the elites initiated the War of the Thousand Days, the longest and most devastating of the conflagrations that wracked the nation throughout the first century of its independence.[35] The war was won by National Conservatives, staunch nationalists and Catholics ideologically opposed to the secularization and materialism they felt would infiltrate Colombia through international capital from largely Protestant countries.

Under the aegis of the victorious Conservatives, Colombia's integration into the world market was slow and methodical. Until the 1920s the peasantry was held under the landlord's sway, the artisan and working classes remained small and unorganized, and the internal market was contained by small, wealthy elites. In 1877, when the tobacco trade began to decline precipitously, coffee represented only 13.54 percent of the total value of Colombian exports. By 1905, however, that figure had risen to 39.15 percent, and the boom continued, reaching 65.99 percent, the highest level prior to *convivencia*, in 1928.[36] Without serious conflicts between landed power and rising entrepreneurs, the politicians were able to rule in the name of an entire society spearheaded by the traditional power of landholders. In addition, land tenure in coffee was quite diffuse. During the Conservative Republic between a fifth and a fourth of the rural population became tied to the coffee market economy.[37] And coffee remained king. In 1946 fully three-quarters of the total value of Colombian exports came from coffee.[38] Coffee was the key to the progress of the nation.

The political order also obtained its strength from a cultural tradition that enhanced the division of society, morality, and individual behavior into separate public and private spheres and from social conditions that drove the politicians to further that division in order to differentiate themselves from the mass of their followers. From a Catholic culture emerged an organic, hierarachical view of society that defined individuals by their rank and duties. It gave little room to the individual and envisaged the public arena as the place where social order was paternalistically fahioned through the rational *vita contemplativa* of public figures. Their distance from the immediate reality of social life allowed them to think of the present in terms of the future needs of the entire society. Governance was perceived as the molding of the anarchic lives of followers, the encouragement of civilized comportment, and the raising of the masses above the necessities of daily life so as to ease their integration into society.[39]

The Liberal and Conservative politicians who engendered the peace after 1930 understood their roles in this manner. The Liberal Carlos Lleras Restrepo, who would become famous for his fiscal and economic reforms, believed that "It is the task of the government to make individuals aware of necessities in the spirit, and form in them the habit of adequately attending to them. It seems paradoxical, but practical sociology demonstrates . . . that the more backward a people . . . the less attracted [it is] by a better life. It is important to teach it the value of each change, to sow through our examples the seed of the ambition to better its life, to form it each time more nobly rebellious, to teach it the value of a home life, which is the supreme refuge. . . . To civilize a people is in sum nothing more than to give birth to new needs in it."[40] The Conservatives did not see their function much differently. According to Ramírez Moreno, "We aspire to awaken in the Colombian people those elemental virtues, the sentiment of honor, the notion of duty, the passion for justice, the cult of heroes, the love for Colombia, its religion, its land, and its fathers. We wish to make a passionate poem of our national history."[41]

The clear distinction between the two spheres of society also grew out of the social traumas that came with political independence and nationhood in the early nineteenth century. After the formal break with Spain, the cultural minority of *criollos*, white Spaniards born in the New World who sought to reap the benefits of independence, faced a densely populated land of largely uneducated, culturally distinct *mestizos*, the offspring of whites and Indians, without clear hierarchical principles through which to rule. They fought the wars against royal absolutism in the name of liberal ideals and republican institutions. The *criollos* did not have a feudal tradition, inherited public positions, or a tradition of courtly behavior from which to fashion a new legitimacy. Independence broke down the old corporate-like structures of the Spanish empire and raised the expectations of the masses that had participated and offered their lives in the quest for nationhood.

In the midst of the wars of independence against Spain, the Liberator Simón Bolívar had already attempted to solve the problem of governance, without recourse to monarchy, over a people that had not "been able to acquire knowledge, power, and civic virtue" and was unprepared for liberty. He proposed a hereditary senate "that would not owe its origin to appointment by the government or to election by the people" and would be filled by men who had been taught "the arts, sciences, and letters that enrich the minds of a public figure. From childhood they should understand the career for which they have been destined by providence, and from earliest youth they should prepare their minds for the dignity that awaits them."[42]

Such a hereditary senate never developed in formally republican Colombia, or anywhere else in newly independent Latin America, but learning, culture, wealth, and family background did serve as the vehicles toward a distinct public life. By the civil wars of 1876, social distinctions were sufficiently well drawn in Bogotá to allow the young leaders of both sides to leave the battleground behind and return in the evenings and on weekends to joust amicably in the urban salons for the favor of the city's young ladies. This behavior led one chronicler to exclaim, "Blessed be the school that taught the Bogotano to place the interests of the fatherland and of art above death."[43] In the midst of the wars, the nation's elite learned to *convivir* in a world of its own making.

The distinct public world developed in the nineteenth century to counter what the politicians who came to power after 1930 still considered the premature granting of democratic rights to the people.[44] It could not be entirely undemocratic, for no one could be legally or constitutionally excluded from seeking public office. The upper reaches of politics were open to anyone who cultivated certain cultural and behavioral traits. Social class, wealth, and family background, as well as racial heritage, were important, but only insofar as they led to the flowering of a public personality. Indeed, most of the public men of Colombia after 1930 came from relatively obscure backgrounds. Many were from the provinces, the promising sons of aspiring middle-class families or brokers tied to the parties who were sent to Bogotá to pursue an education in the nation's finest institutions of learning.

Yet public life was also a rarefied domain, for only a select few could obtain the necessary educational background, let alone have the intelligence, wit, and social skills to keep their hard-earned places. Some seemed to come naturally to public life, while others struggled all their lives but never quite made it. Learning and knowledge, a measure of culture, and a concern for the state of society were all prerequisites, but the ability to demonstrate these attributes at all times was the *sine qua non* of public life. It was therefore a constant performance, an act that could only be made real through continuous examples of what a public figure was. The *vita contemplativa* was a life of ceaseless action. The politicians referred to themselves as the *jefes*, the leaders, the chiefs, and as the *jefes naturales*, the natural chiefs, of society. Each wanted to be the *jefe único*, the sole chief of his party, the first among equals. The *jefe único* named a Directorio Nacional, a national directorate made up of representatives of the diverse tendencies of the party, to become its nominal leaders. The higher their rank, the more distinctive they appeared, and the more certain it was that they would not fall from public life.

Those from Bogotá seemed to have an advantage over those from the provinces, as did politicians who came from an intellectual background. The Lleras Camargo brothers and Lleras Restrepo were second cousins from Bogotá who stemmed from a long line of teachers. The Liberal politician Alfonso Araújo's father was the renowned Simón Araújo, founder, rector, and owner of the Colegio Araújo, where many middle-class Liberals sent their sons. The Bogotanos Juan, Carlos, and Fabio Lozano y Lozano were sons of a famous Liberal politician. Carlos studied law under Enrico Ferri in Rome, and Juan went to Cambridge to study finance. Some had once been rich but, like the conservative Camilo de Brigard Silva, the nephew of the noted literary figure José Asunción Silva, were considered self-made men when they turned to politics.

All the *leopardos* came to Bogotá to study. There they became involved in politics. Eliseo Arango was from the far-away town of Quibdó, from which he went to Manizales before arriving in the capital. Silvio Villegas was from Manizales, at the time one of the most fervent of Conservative towns. Augusto Ramírez Moreno came from Medellín, also a Conservative stronghold. Some of the most important Liberals were also from the provinces. Gabriel Turbay's foreign-born parents settled in Bucaramanga just before he was born. Darío Echandía was from Chaparral, a sleepy hamlet in Tolima. Plinio Mendoza Neira came from Boyacá. He built his political career there and then traveled to Bogotá just before López became president in 1934. Most became lawyers, some studied medicine, and a few became engineers. Regardless of profession, all turned their eyes to public life. Regardless of origin, they stayed in Bogotá once they had reached the capital city's highland plateau.[45]

Before and after 1930 the politicians insulated themselves from the voting power of their followers; they did not feel accountable to the people. Leadership worked from the top down, not from the bottom up. Only a candidate for the presidency, the highest office in the land and thus the most removed from the people, stood alone before the voters. All others were hierarchically placed on lists by party *jefes* for seats in the Senate, the House of Representatives, or the departmental assemblies. Governors, mayors, and all members of the judiciary were appointed. A politician's chance of winning a seat depended on his place on the list and the proportion of votes the list obtained. The first politician on each list was virtually assured of victory. The list was thus above all an indicator of the esteem in which a politician was held by his colleagues and the influence he wielded with them. When rival factions existed within a party, voters had a choice of two or more lists. If both parties participated, followers chose between Liberal and Conservative lists. A single list was not uncommon. Candidates for national office did not need to have any tie to the department the *jefes* selected them to represent and were moved around from election to election. In addition, each candidate had a deputy, who figured opposite him on the lists and stood in for him when he was otherwise engaged in public life. Often a politician's chances of advancement or election were better as a deputy high on the enumeration than as a main candidate further down. No politician could be held accountable to a specific group of voters for his performance in office.[46]

The *convivialistas* took an elevated view of their roles. Laws, for example, were "the noble spurs of man's will to govern."[47] Politics was conceived of as an indirect action on behalf of the people. Public life was a matter of intellectual creativity: thought, not action; meditation, not public spectacle. According to the *convivialistas*, thought endured, while actions did not. In thinking, "the means and the goals are clearly separated in such a way that once the [thinking] activity is over, its result, its goal, survives beyond the creative process." With action, on the other hand, the means and the goals were seen as indistinguishable. Once the "spectacular action is finished . . . its importance is over."[48] Neither demagogues, those who appealed directly to the crowd, nor public spectacles had much of a place in public life.

Through oratory in Congress and in the public plaza, the politicians attempted to forge a sense of community by instilling moral virtues and noble thoughts in their listeners. They felt that the people were to be moved by flowery language, by cadences and intonations and the ebb and flow of their words. Abstract themes offered their listeners principles around which to organize their lives, and high language served as an example of the Spanish that one day the Colombian people would collectively speak. The rhetoric of the plaza was also a means to speak to other politicians in the public forum, and as often as not they addressed their colleagues rather than the masses that stood before them. Oratory was for many the road to power, and they looked to the Roman Republic for examples to follow. But by the time the *convivialistas* came to power, many felt that oratory was a dying art.[49]

The distinct public tradition blossomed with the peace. The *convivialistas* became consumed by the pursuit of public life. Neither the quest for political power nor the search for economic wealth and social prestige can explain their determination to be public figures. In their eyes public life was an end in itself. In fact, power was corrupting, wealth was vulgar, prestige the concern of lesser men, and ideology mentally stultifying. At most, public life was a means toward a better society, but only because in their behavior, in their manners and tastes, and in the examples they set for their followers, public figures were the very expression of the good society.

They were extraordinary individuals with a remarkable ability to call attention to themselves, to turn everything around—history, culture, politics—and make each a reflection of themselves, their personalities, and their behavior. As public figures they had an abiding need to control their surroundings and influence others, lest they be molded and influenced. They lived with a passion to cultivate their inner lives, to be men of complex convictions, and to surprise others with the breadth of their knowledge.

Political ideologies, social and legal reforms, and contrasting visions of the past, present, and future were above all forms of self-expression and the means with which to maintain a public life. They were symbols of the politicians' belief in such abstract notions as progress or order, change or stability, modernity or tradition. Clear and persuasive arguments, deep thought, and reason were cherished independently of the positions they were marshaled to defend. Consistency and the espousal of predictable ideas were the signs of an ideologue. A public figure worthy of the name was able to roll with the punches, look at old issues with new eyes, advocate differing and even contradictory solutions to problems that appeared similar, yet base each on principle, and thereby represent the interests of the entire society rather than those of one group.

Public life was founded on the *convivialistas'* conception of their own nature. They felt within themselves the stirrings of two personalties. Carlos Lozano y Lozano seemed surprised to discover his distinctiveness. "I suppose that the same thing happens to many public men. They have two completely separate lives, their own and that which the public sees."[50] Few saw it quite as dramatically as Ramírez Moreno: "I have no intimacy. In my life there is no place for that vulgar condition. I am in everything a public man. Not once has anyone surprised me in a single activity that has not been carefully formed, prepared, arranged. I am an arrogant gentleman, even when I am buttoning my pants."[51] Juan Lozano y Lozano saw Olaya Herrera as an "exotic sort of man completely removed from that great human emotion which is the love of neighbor. . . . He is intellectually interested in people . . . but after ten years, after twenty years of polite friendship . . . every individual is for him still a strange being."[52] One of Gómez's biographers did not know which was his real subject, "the cunning public man, or the quiet conversationalist of private clubs."⁵³ Public personality allowed the reasoned dialogue, the compromises, and the quiet conversations on which the peace was built.⁵⁴

The politicians resembled other-worldly men, curates of public life. Politics, like religious life, called on its practitioners to withdraw from society in order to avoid its corrupting influences. As in the case of men of the cloth, following the ideals of *convivencia* required a life of abnegation in the service of others. Silvio Villegas wrote that he was a "philosopher for me, a priest for the people" (*el vulgo*).⁵⁵ They believed that there were two kinds of people: those who lived for themselves and those who lived for others. According to Abel Naranjo Villegas, politicians were imbued with a gentlemanly, *hidalguista* tradition of life from oneself (*desde sí*), rather than the bourgeois ideal of life for oneself (*para sí*).⁵⁶ The politicians were willing to sacrifice their own interests because it was in their nature to do so. "I feel that a cultured citizen in a backward country like ours," said Carlos Lozano y Lozano, "has responsibilities to society. In nations with long histories and immense mental talent, intelligence may be used for purely abstract tasks. But not among us; here each has a duty to serve in a more direct fashion."⁵⁷

As before 1930, all those outside the public realm were referred to as the *pueblo*. The *convivialistas* saw a few distinctions within this broad grouping. The most obvious were between *campesinos*, peasants, or *labriegos*, rural laborers, and *trabajadores*, *obreros*, or *proletarios*, urban factory workers. Peasants and workers were not always seen as part of the *pueblo*, and the terms usually had a roughly positive connotation. But most of the distinctions were subjective and pointed to an underlying unity. Leaders referred to *lo mejor del pueblo*, the best within the pueblo, *lo más avanzado, los cultos del pueblo*, the most advanced, the cultured *pueblo*, or *el pueblo sano*, the good, the healthy *pueblo*. They also talked of *el populacho*, the rabble, *el pueblo bajo*, the low *pueblo,* and *el pueblo raso*, the common *pueblo*. The last term was used for those within the *pueblo* who had been little exposed to the leaders. When the *convivialistas* spoke of *el pueblo puro*, the real, the pure *pueblo*, it was unclear whether they were romantically extolling or denigrating their followers. Context and intonation offered clues to the meaning.

The *convivialistas* kept their most graphic terminology for the urban multitude. The anonymous masses that congregated in the streets of the nation's cities were at times thought of as *ciudadanos*, citizens, as *colombianos*, or more often as *liberales* or *conservadores*. More often still, however, they did not fit any of these categories. They were *la gente torpe*, the rough and awkward folk, *la chusma*, the rabble, the riffraff, *la gleba*, the glebe, *la plebe*, the plebs, *las turbas*, the mob, *la canalla*, the canaille, *los truhanes*, the rogues. The most meaningful term of all, for Colombians both in and out of public life, was *los guaches*, the hoodlums.

The politicians did not share the romantic and utopian vision of the *pueblo* that filled the hearts of Nicholas Bonneville and Jacques-René Hébert, orators who addressed *le Peuple* in the midst of the French Revolution.[58] French revolutionaries searched for a term that symbolized their novel idea of nationhood. They borrowed the idealized Germanic notion of *das Volk* and translated it into French while keeping the capital letter in the German fashion. The *convivialistas* saw the *pueblo* more as *plebs* than as *populus*, more as laborers than as the soul of the nation.

Such a large and ill-defined entity as the *pueblo* made little empirical sense. It can be more validly used for those historical periods before capitalism encouraged the division of labor, before workers became differentiated from peasants, peasants turned into farmers, and the unemployed became distinct from both, and before middle sectors were spawned, perennially unsure of where they belonged. The continuing use of the term in Colombia after 1930 symbolizes both the relatively limited impact of market relations and the reluctance of the leaders to recognize the changes that the market was in fact wreaking in both city and countryside.

Public Life and Capitalism

In the contemporary world the private and the public have become nearly undifferentiated. According to Richard Sennett, eighteenth-century urban England and France were dignified by a delicate balance between easily distinguishable private and public realms. Industrial capitalism and the rise of the bourgeoisie in the nineteenth century brought overwhelming pressures toward privatization and the superimposition of the private on the public. Sennett laments the "tyranny of intimacy" that characterizes present-day social and political relations, and the death of public space.[59] Other social critics who have taken up this issue generally agree that the present age can be defined by the breakdown of the barriers between the two realms and by the increasing place of the private.[60] The trend is logical. A capitalist society in which the private, self-seeking efforts of the individual are not seen as actions in the public good is hardly possible.[61]

The Colombian politicians' concern with maintaining a clear distinction between the two spheres seems curiously outdated. It speaks to a formal adherence to social inequalities, a concern with social place and the reproduction of strict hierarchies that anonymous market structures have largely eliminated. In a society where the two realms are formally separated, we find a concern with proper, supposedly traditional forms of comportment, and we may expect, as Mary Douglas has put it, "less smacking of lips when eating, . . . less mastication, . . . less sound of breathing and walking," and "more carefully modulated laughter . . . more controlled signs of anger."[62] The struggle to keep individual and group behavior within clearly acceptable bounds was one of the major sources of conflict during *convivencia*.

Colombia's integration into the world economy brought the consensus between Liberals and Conservatives that made the politics of civility possible. At the same time, the expansion of market relations elicited the contradictions of *convivencia*. Peace called on the nation's leaders to build a new relationship with the *pueblo*. It undermined their conception of rationality, made difficult the sacrifices that gave the political order its moral purpose, and routinized public life, forcing the politicians into the roles of mere administrators of a complex society of conflicting private interests.

Many of the issues that had divided Liberals and Conservatives in the past were much attenuated when the *convivialistas* came to power. The Conservatives had lost some of their fear that contact with the secular and materialistic tendencies of foreign capitalism and Protestantism would undermine the centralized, hierarchical, and moral order they believed essential to the civilizing process in Colombia. Their abiding fear that the competitive and individualistic instincts of the *pueblo* would be unleased to threaten the established power of landowners, who they felt were the bulwark of the nation, eroded as those landed interests, represented by the Sociedad de Agricultores de Colombia and the Federación Nacional de Cafeteros, became tied to a growing national market and the export sector. Both organizations could claim to represent the national, public interest of an agricultural nation that depended on its primary exports.

By 1930 the religious question no longer elicited as much controversy. During the election, Liberals carefully reassured the church and the Conservatives that they were not about to nationalize the schools and confiscate church lands. Left vague were their plans for the reform of the Concordato, the formal relationship with the Vatican that established Catholicism as the state religion. All the *convivialistas* knew that the *pueblo* was more religious than any of them were, and that the church had established networks among the *pueblo* that helped maintain order and morality.[63] The Conservatives, in any case, were no more Catholic than their Liberal opponents. They were all married by the church, and never questioned baptizing their children into it. Liberals did not avoid Catholic schools and universities. They attended the Colegio Mayor de Nuestra Señora del Rosario, and Conservatives studied in the Universidad Nacional and the Universidad Libre, the public, state-run universities.

The 1920s were a period of unprecedented economic growth known as the Dance of the Millions. It was fueled by fiscal reforms, the reorganization of financial instititions, surging coffee prices on the international market, which reached an all-time high in 1928, a $25 million indemnity received from the United States for the loss of Panama in 1903, and the first major expansion of U.S. investments and public loans. A closer economic relationship with the United States was spurred by the Conservative presidents. Suárez's policy of attracting investment from the giant to the north was known as the Polar Star.

President Ospina and his ambassador in Washington, Enrique Olaya Herrera, aggressively sought loans and investments, and the Abadía Méndez regime used foreign loans to initiate large-scale public works, especially railroad construction. Colombian exports rose from $60 million in 1924 to $133 million in 1928.[64] During the five years preceding the Great Depression, almost $200 million entered Colombia in loans,[65] and the nation's capacity to import almost doubled in that period.[66]

Liberals also found many of their own traditional ideas outdated. They discovered that few liberals elsewhere still believed in laissez-faire economics. Indeed, the Colombian state had undergone a dramatic transformation in the past decade. State revenues nearly doubled from 44 million pesos in 1923 to 75 million in 1928.[67] The Banco de la República could now regulate currency, credit, and investments, and the state could be used to intervene in the economy.

The Liberals actually had little choice but to abandon their traditional economic ideas and adopt interventionist policies. They came to power at the height of the Wall Street crash. Traditional exports found no easy outlet on the world market, and tariffs were necessary to protect nascent local industry. During the 1920s Alejandro López, the foremost Liberal economic thinker, had already declared that state interventionism and economic centralism did not curtail the freedom of the individual, but could actually be used to enhance it.[68]

Before him, Rafael Uribe Uribe, the landowning Liberal hero of civil wars since 1876 and an architect of the twentieth century peace, argued for a vigorous coffee economy supported by the state. As a representative of those economic interests, Uribe Uribe increasingly saw liberty itself as restricted by professional politicians far removed from the material realities of the nation and more concerned with matters religious and philosophical than economic. In 1911, three years before he was assassinated in downtown Bogotá, the political arena seemed to him like a relic from a distant past. "This habit of erecting government as an entity superior to the nation springs from the ancient notion of divine right and hereditary power; but in a modern nation where human laws and suffrage are the basis of power, of democratic institutions, the government is nothing more than a delegate of the nation."[69]

Yet some issues still divided the young Liberals and Conservatives, and many of these went to the very core of public life. They largely agreed on their place in society, but felt quite differently, at least at the beginning of *convivencia*, about the relationships they could establish with their followers. To what extent could those in public life actually organize those outside? If the *pueblo* was to be mobilized in peacetime, through what kinds of institutions could this be accomplished, and how were they to be tied to the political parties? How could an organized *pueblo* be controlled? How were the hierarchical principles of social life to be preserved?

Differences made themselves felt quickly. The Liberals, by and large, felt more comfortable in the changing nation they sought to rule. They had more of an urban outlook, whereas the Conservatives' ideals continued to be illuminated by pastoral images. For them, the noise of the city, its density, and the heterogeneity of its population represented the decline of authority and principle. Bogotá grew from a city of 235,000 in 1928 to one of 628,000 in 1951.[70] After Villegas and Gaitán's exploits on the streets of Bogotá in 1929, Liberal and Conservative leaders never again faced the crowds of the city together. Even before the Liberals won the election, Villegas warned against the "messianic" fervor the Liberal candidate was arousing,[71] and Camacho Carreño called for the "intellectual, economic, and moral restoration of the nation."[72]

The Conservatives could only worry that the Liberals were becoming demagogues, losing their principles by drawing too near the crowd, all in an effort to win the hearts of workers. When the Liberals captured 61.5 percent of the vote in the congressional election of 1933, these fears seemed confirmed. Thereafter Ramírez Moreno warned against the "dictatorship of the tumult," and Villegas yearned for the end of the proletariat. "We must aspire to keep Colombians in the countryside, giving rural work advantages similar to those of urban work."[73] For the Conservatives, their opponents' growing popularity with the urban mass was turning governance into a mundane exchange of votes for full stomachs, power for workers' salaries and fringe benefits. The new Colombia was being increasingly dominated by material concerns. The Conservatives could now live neither with nor without the city: it was the center of civilization and culture around which they wished to build a nation, yet the city itself was becoming less cultured and civilized.

Many of the Conservatives nevertheless agreed with the Liberals that the confrontations that the Abadía Méndez government had provoked with labor would have to end. The last years of the Conservative Republic had witnessed the heightening of labor unrest, primarily among workers in foreign-owned banana and petroleum enclaves, which were becoming increasingly important export earners, and among workers along the Magdalena River, the nation's primary transportation network.[74] These industries were considered to be in the public sector because of their importance to the national economy. During the 1920s the only major labor conflict in private industry occurred in Bavaria, the largest brewery.[75] The onus was on the government to establish new labor laws that would ease the tensions of the past. A bipartisan consensus for these reforms was difficult to obtain, however, for the Liberals had as much to gain from them as the Conservatives had to lose.

Convivencia went through three phases. The first of these, the eight years of transition and reform during the administrations of Olaya Herrera and López, was the most progressive. The period saw clearly defined partisan conflicts and wholesale opposition to López's Revolution on the March, even though the reforms he sponsored were actually rather timid. It was only after 1946, when the Conservatives returned to power, that the politicians began to seriously consider the advantages of nationalizing certain sectors of the economy. In 1935 López's opposition formed the Acción Patriótica Económica Nacional (APEN), aimed at removing professional politicians from public life and replacing them with individuals actually concerned with the management of Colombia's economy. Industrialists opposed López's progressive tax, landowners sought to undermine his agrarian reform, and coffee interests curtailed the influence of the government in the Federación de Cafeteros. It seemed that the entire society, including important sectors of the Liberal party, opposed the very existence of the Confederación de Trabajadores de Colombia (CTC), the national labor federation that López had promoted. Yet close to the end of *convivencia*, only 4.7 percent of the labor force had been unionized.[76] Within the Liberal party the newspaper *La Razón* was formed to represent industrialists and landowners, and Gómez started his own newspaper, *El Siglo*, in 1936. The church, moreover, vigorously opposed the constitutional reform of the Concordato and all attempts to secularize the school curriculum.

López's intention was to regulate from above the growing tensions among private interests in a class society. Under his administration it became the task of public life to pursue the public good by teaching the capitalist that he could no longer survive without cooperating with other social classes. His aim was to rid the capitalist of "the ingenuous bourgeois illusion that it is still possible to avoid the strife and struggle of economic interests, and to attempt to persuade him to become part of the new world that has been born without his consent."[77] López wished to change prevailing customs and attitudes toward social life, to produce a more harmonious and organic relationship between the politicians and the *pueblo*. He attempted to convince his country people that the *pueblo* had an untapped, innate intelligence and the ability to act out its own destiny. Within the emerging class society, the *pueblo* could no longer be considered a mere spectator, for it too was developing its own interests.[78]

May Day 1936 symbolized the height of reform and reaction. Liberals staged a parade of worker delegations in front of the Presidential Palace, with López proudly standing on the balcony of the *palacio* next to labor leaders, leftist Liberals, and well-known communists. For Armando Solano, one of the left-leaning Liberals, the public spectacle demonstrated that much had changed in Colombia. "We have a democracy!" he exulted. The Conservatives were shocked and complained that the president of the republic was familiarly called *compañero* by the *pueblo*, while individuals who had no place in public life were intruding upon it.[79]

The second phase was a retreat initiated by President Eduardo Santos's self-described "pause" in the reforms, the rhetoric, the informality, and the mass demonstrations of his predecessor. The Santos presidency signified a return to a more distant relationship between leaders and followers as the Liberals began to lose much of the optimism that had characterized their first years at the helm. The period culminated in 1945 when López was forced to resign from his ineffectual second term. After a slow but steady recovery from the depression during the 1930s, the period was marked by a quickening pace of economic growth, the establishment of an industrial base, the formation of the Asociación Nacional de Industriales (ANDI), and a growing consensus among *convivialistas* on social and economic matters.

After 1938 even the mildest criticism of politicians called forth unexpected reactions. The period is symbolized by the controversies that surrounded the Third Labor Congress, held in Cali early in 1938. When Liberal labor leaders called for a resolution to congratulate Santos on his upcoming birthday, many who opposed the moderate president-elect refused, invoking the already traditional argument that labor matters had nothing to do with public life and that the congress should deal only with economic issues affecting the livelihood of workers.[80] Liberal leaders, and probably Santos himself, found the refusal scandalous and perceived the hidden actions of extremist infiltrators. Once the congress was over, a "Yugoslavian communist agitator in the service of the Comintern" was expelled from Colombia.[81] A few days later the Senate considered a law empowering the government alone to call labor congresses, forbidding foreigners to participate, and ensuring that they did not engage in "militant" activity.[82]

The crisis of *convivencia* began with the start of Gaitán's presidential campaign in 1944, while López was still in office, and coincided with the economic spurt at the end of World War II. Gaitán reintroduced partisan conflict into public life. He called for a campaign of the *pueblo* in the name of the Liberal ideals of the early 1930s and against the traditional leaders of both parties. The period was marked by governmental repression of the strike by the Federación Nacional del Transporte Marítimo, Fluvial, Portuario y Aéreo (FEDENAL), the powerful labor federation of river workers. The action, by interim President Alberto Lleras Camargo, was the first time during *convivencia* that the Liberals failed to mediate a strike in the public sector. The end of the strike came with the institutionalization of the labor movement, through Law 6 of 1945, into small enterprise unions that served the interests of the now more powerful industrialists.[83]

In 1946, in the first presidential campaign of *convivencia* in which the Conservatives participated, Mariano Ospina Pérez defeated a Liberal party divided between Gaitán and Gabriel Turbay: 1930 had come again, but the tables had been turned.[84] On April 9, 1948, the assassination of Gaitán, then the *jefe único* of the Liberal party, and the actions of his followers, heralded the death of *convivencia*. The end came eighteen months later, when Lleras Restrepo, the new Liberal *jefe*, declared on October 28, 1949: "We will have no relationship from here on with members of the Conservative party; as long as they do not offer us a different republic, with guarantees that put an end to this infamy, the relations between Liberals and Conservatives, already broken in the public sphere, must be suspended in the private sphere as well."[85]

The Controversies of Consensus

Even before 1938, the consensus among *convivialistas* outweighed their differences. This underlying unity proved to be a more disruptive force than their partisanship. As early as 1932, Villegas, who aggressively opposed most of the Liberal reforms, warned that the essential unity of the two parties was leading to the "decadence of national life."[86] For the *convivialistas* needed two parties and a clearly definable partisanship in order to rule. Without them the leaders could not display their use of reason and appeal to their followers in the name of the broad, underlying principles of social life. Unless Liberals and Conservatives could establish differences between themselves, their rule would resemble a one-party dictatorship rather than the civilizing process they felt it to be. *Convivencia* was the difficult art of coming together to serve society, not a being together. The search for compromise was the *raison d'être* of public life.

The economic changes that took place during *convivencia* undermined the moral basis of public life. The worst epithet, *oligarca*, was used to characterize not a government of the few, but those public figures who used their offices for private gain.[87] An *oligarca*, in essence, ceased to be a public figure. While both the *pueblo* and the capitalist lived narrow, unintellectual lives in the pursuit of money, they at least had little choice but to do so. They could be honest in their pursuit; the *oligarca* was unscrupulous. By failing to uphold the standards of public life and taking advantages others could not seek, the *oligarca* destroyed the fundamental differences in society by reducing the public to the private.

As the economy expanded, the line between private and public interests blurred. It became difficult to determine whether public policies benefited one interest group or the entire society. As the economy grew increasingly complex and economic interests sought laws, import licenses, and tax benefits, public men's opportunities for private gain multiplied. As economic elites amassed private fortunes, public men saw their own exalted position decline.[88] In the competitive market many were called on to represent national and international companies in court or as public relations advisors. The ideal of public morality thus opened the public realm to charges and counter-charges of corruption, which followers began to accept as inevitable. These new inequalities and the charges of corruption were all the more bitter because urban salaried groups and the urban *pueblo* were suffering. Inflation rates rose precipitously, and real wages remained level throughout the 1940s.[89] By the mid-1940s the word *oligarca* filled the air. It was as an *oligarca* that López was driven from office.[90]

By then public life was in disarray. As issues and principles receded, politics became increasingly acrimonious, unstable, and personalistic. The more threatened their distinct place in society was, the more the *convivialistas* struggled to maintain it. The leaders spawned ideologies without content or consistency that gained strength and meaning over time: around López something called *lopismo* grew up; Gómez created a *laureanista* wing of the party, which was loyal to any stand he took; the followers of Santos proudly called themselves *santistas;* and their moderate counterparts among Conservatives were the *ospinistas,* the rather unenthusiastic followers of Ospina Pérez. By 1944 these were the main distinctions around which public life was organized. Lleras Camargo despaired at the situation: "Our democracy fails . . . because the opposition does not allow us to govern; it obstructs; it fights everything from every doctrinal and political angle; it is a civil war, but without any of the grandeur of war, that is, without any of its dangers."[91]

But Lleras Camargo was farther from the truth than he might have imagined. As they felt the society beyond their public sphere increasingly impinge upon them, the politicians called on their followers to support them regardless of the consequences, whether through violent or orderly forms of partisanship, and in the name of a Liberal or a Conservative society. Emboldened by the prospects of a return to power against the divided Liberals, the Conservatives called for rebuilding a Conservative Republic, which could only be possible through the elimination of Liberals from offices large and small throughout the country. After the Conservative victory, followers of the party set upon their opponents and unleashed a civil war worse than any the nineteenth century had ever witnessed. Only through such a reaction could the Conservative leaders ensure their own place in a society that history was otherwise turning aginst them. Thus began *la Violencia,* a struggle with none of the dangers of war, for the leaders stayed within the city and did not place their lives on the line, but with grandeur nevertheless, for now again the *pueblo* was fighting for them, and once again the distance between leaders and followers was growing. In the short run, the more the *pueblo* fought itself in the name of Liberalism and Conservatism, the less threatened and more powerful the leaders were.[92]

Slowly but surely the *convivialistas* began to remove themselves from the public plazas. Politics was practiced within closed circles, in the Jockey Club or the Gun Club, where they could comment frankly and openly on their public animosities. They began to see politics more as an empty performance than as the art of imparting civilizing examples and moral principles to their followers. The basic decisions of public life were made in highly ritualized, formal, and secluded conversations in which they attempted to replicate in miniature their embattled art of reason, moral sacrifice, and compromise. Finally, they became more ponderous, carefully considering their every move and weighing the short- and long-term consequences of their behavior. They acted self-consciously and constantly strove to keep their emotions under control, both because they still wanted to keep the demeanor of rational men and because they no longer quite knew what they were about.[93]

Laureano Gómez and Jorge Eliécer Gaitán, the two politicians who had so strongly criticized the *nuevos* back in the 1920s, were also the *convivialistas* who brought the uncertainties of their colleagues to the fore. They were opposed to the underlying consensus of *convivencia*. The Conservative remained a pessimist, and ceaselessly called for a sharply divided, hierarchical society in which the *pueblo* would have little or no influence on public life. In the compromises of *convivencia* he saw only petty opportunism, instead of the leadership of men of intelligence and Christian moral values. He did more than any other politician to inflame the passions that fueled *la Violencia*. In that struggle he found the exalted values he missed in day-to-day politics. In its excesses and random killing, he no doubt saw his own beliefs confirmed: Colombia would indeed never become a civilized society.

Gaitán, on the other hand, always impatient with the pace of reform, became *convivencia's* greatest optimist and the most subversive figure of the period. His ideology and his politics were rooted in his social class. As a petit bourgeois he shared many of the ideals of the politics of civility. From within *convivencia*, rather than as a socialist or a fascist outsider, he was able to demonstrate that his colleagues were both unwilling and unable to carry out those ideals. He showed that the practice of *convivencia* was ideology, a lofty public cover-up of the private, personal interests of the politicians. The *convivialistas*, in other words, could only be *oligarcas*, no matter what stance they took in public life.

By failing to bring the ideals of civility to the *pueblo* and failing to create new expectations and possibilities among their followers, the *convivialistas* allowed themselves to be used by the elites as both exploited the *pueblo's* traditional humility and deference. *Convivencia* abetted the hidden actions of the haute bourgeoisie, landowners, plutocrats, and financiers, products of the narrow development of market relations, who produced capital and wealth without working. For Gaitán, politics during *convivencia* ceased to be a distinct public realm of reason and morality. Gaitán's ideal was a capitalism from below, a society of meritorious individuals, hard work, and small-scale property ownership, with the family as the cornerstone. His argument was disarmingly simple: politics had to deal with the mundane, with the daily concerns of followers, for progress lay in the private lives of the *pueblo*. Gaitán baffled his contemporaries. Born in 1898 into a struggling lower-middle-class family with bourgeois pretensions, he stormed the heights of Bogotá society by being unpredictable and unknowable. This dark-complected man with the nation's unforgettable indigenous past written across his face did not coexist easily with *convivialistas* who prided themselves on their Spanish ancestry. He compromised with them by using their polished phrases behind closed doors; he castigated them for their compromises in the public plazas, using the vernacular of the *pueblo* in his vitriolic oratory. Neither a carrier of elite political traditions nor a man of the *pueblo*, he did not fit into the refined upper reaches of Colombian social life that he pushed his way into, or into the obscure life of the *pueblo* that he strove to leave behind.

To neither friend nor foe was it clear whom he represented. In the eyes of many Gaitán was a socialist; some saw in him the makings of a fascist; others perceived him as the ugly face of resentment aimed at a cultured society from which he felt alienated; still others saw him simply as an *arriviste* whose sole concern was his own career. For many, Gaitán was all of these at one time or another. For his followers he was the savior who would redeem them from all earthly ills.

In his public life Gaitán appeared to be what he was not, and not to be what he was. He confounded the leaders by being so much like them but attacking their every move, by wanting to live as they did but never accepting them. He confused the critics of *convivencia* by sharing many of their views but never making common cause with them. Adding to the ambiguity, Gaitán could not easily be rejected by either the proponents or the opponents of *convivencia*, for he was unquestionably a man of exceptional values and one of the exemplary figures of the generation. No matter how much they opposed him, they all, however grudgingly, had to respect him. The uncertainty Gaitán produced led many to conclude that he was a bundle of contradictory and uncontrollable impulses, rather than a credible human being.

Yet Gaitán was a remarkably consistent thinker and politician. The confusions he created did not arise from inner contradictions and character weaknesses. They arose because his ideas and his politics were a continuous experiment within an uncharted middle ground between the politicians and the *pueblo*. In his own passage from the reviled *pueblo* to respect and leadership, he bridged the chasm that separated leaders from followers. Gaitán represented the historic passage of his society from an order sharply divided between a select public few and an inchoate mass to one of bourgeois proportions, defined by the accomplishments and merits of individuals. He signified the movement toward a society increasingly defined by private concerns. He lived on the margins between the *pueblo* and the politicians, between the old and the new.[94]

Able to stand aside from his own and all other social positions, he played a greatly expanded set of roles. The implications of Gaitán's position were radical, for he could play with the relationship between leaders and followers: he threatened the *convivialistas* with the wrath of the *pueblo*, and the *pueblo* with the treason of the *convivialistas*. By laying bare the public world of the politicians, he demonstrated that the distinction between their private and public selves was a myth. By showing that Liberals and Conservatives were much the same, Gaitán subverted their daily politics. By lauding the *pueblo* he gave it the confidence traditional leaders could not afford to give it.

Gaitán eroded the distance between leaders and followers, suggesting all the while that a reversal was imminent: the *pueblo* would oust the politicians. Although his opponents realized the danger they were in, they were uncertain what to do about it, for it did not come from within their own system and neither did it come from without: it came from Gaitán, who was both.

The perception of his unique role did not come to Gaitán as early as his ideology. The 1920s and 1930s were decades of experimentation, and he was nearly crushed on various occasions by pressures from both sides. Gaitán began to understand the implications of his fulcrum position when he launched his presidential campaign in 1944. Thereafter he practiced politics as a masterful balancing act, creating his own space within Colombian society. From there he built a popular following of unprecedented proportions.

By bridging the gap between leaders and followers in Colombia, Gaitán unmasked the hidden contradictions in the daily practice of *convivencia*. The three decades of peace after the War of the Thousand Days had made the civilizing process feasible. But the *convivalista* ideal of public life was only worth keeping if politics remained a life of the few who could easily distinguish themselves from all others. Now, by leading, the politicians could only promote their own demise, for the more moral, civic, and participatory their followers became, the less exclusive was their own realm, the less exceptional each one of them, and the less relevant their form of rule.

2

The Making of a Man in the Middle

I am a demagogue with equanimity. . . . I am a demagogue who has read some books.

Jorge Eliécer Gaitán (1944)

Gaitán Agonistes

Jorge Eliécer Gaitán was born on January 23, 1898—a year before the War of the Thousand Days broke out—in Las Cruces, an impoverished Bogotá neighborhood known as the "barrio of the fallen aristocracy."[1] The once-respectable if not fashionable barrio was sufficiently close to the center of the city to allow Jorge Eliécer's proud parents to bypass their own parish of Santa Bárbara and have their first-born baptized in the cathedral of Bogotá, where the rich and powerful were received into the church.[2] Thus, Gaitán's introduction to the ritualized world of his society's well-bred leaders came before he was conscious of it. Shortly after Gaitán was born, the family's continued poverty forced them to move farther away from the center of Bogotá to the working-class barrio of Egipto, along the foothills overlooking the city.[3] Jorge Eliécer became well known there. For the rest of his life his contemporaries were uncertain whether he had a middle-class or a working-class background.[4] But there was little question in their minds that he was a man of the *pueblo*.

Gaitán's social origins were unlike those of most of the leading figures of his generation. Gaitán was born into a Bogotá family that could barely support him and lacked the political connections that could ease daily life. His father, Don Eliécer, regarded himself as a man of intellect and learning. He collected

39

books in order to write a history of Colombia, but instead ended up opening a small used-book store. He had little business sense, and few of his efforts to keep his family afloat were successful. Undaunted by the recent Liberal defeat, Don Eliécer founded two short-lived but combative opposition newspapers in 1903 and 1905, for which he received the lukewarm recognition of the Liberals and the lasting enmity of the Conservatives. Jorge Eliécer's mother, Doña Manuela Ayala de Gaitán, was a schoolteacher known throughout the city and surrounding towns for her progressive, even feminist, ideas. She earned the wrath of the Conservatives for the allegedly Masonic ideas she taught in the schools she founded for the children of Liberal homes. Doña Manuela, although penny-wise, modest, and dedicated to her husband and children, could contribute little to the family coffers from her meager salary as a primary school teacher, and she could not keep the family from lurching from one financial crisis to the next.[5]

Gaitán grew up in an atmosphere of conflict and tension. As the oldest son of a hierarchical family, he was caught between a father who was authoritarian and headstrong (all the more so because of his public failures) and five younger siblings, whom Gaitán in turn was expected to direct. In this uncomfortable role Gaitán received the open support of his mother, who took his side in most of the conflicts between father and son.[6]

Don Eliécer, ever anxious to lighten his financial burdens, insisted that his oldest son pursue a practical career that would soon bring another income into the family. His mother, however, saw in the son's obvious intelligence a road out of poverty. She dreamed of a university education for him, a secure income, and even a measure of social recognition. Doña Manuela kept the sickly and emaciated-looking boy at home, where she taught him everything she knew. It was not until age twelve that Jorge Eliécer was sent off to school.[7]

Gaitán had to make it on his own on the city's streets and in its many schools. His schoolmates knew the poverty in which he lived, and once he began to be accepted into better schools, they mocked him for hawking his father's used books on street corners during vacations. Gaitán spent little time with his classmates, whose devil-may-care attitudes, encouraged by the long and unexpected peace, made him uncomfortable. Lacking the money to share their diversions, he declined their company by sternly asserting that he had his studies to pursue.[8]

The material surroundings of his early years left an indelible imprint on Gaitán's personality and powerfully influenced his social thought. The Gaitán family lacked the means to better their lot and had no fixed place in the social order. Not of the working class, neither parent had the skills that might provide a constant salary in the growing industrial plants. Not bourgeois, they owned no property to speak of and had no capital. Neither parent produced goods that others needed and that might give them a niche in

society. They trafficked in ideas, Liberal pride, and books. The precarious-
ness of their situation made them constantly fear what the next day might
bring. Closer to falling into the proletariat than to rising into the bourgeoisie,
they strove desperately to keep up the outward appearance of respectability
that might distinguish them from the working class and from the rural folk
entering the city.[9] Their strongest social attachment was to the Liberal
party.

Like the rest of his generation, Gaitán could not remember the last war
between Liberals and Conservatives. But young Gaitán was nourished on the
lore of the past conquests by Liberal *caudillos*, who were to remain his heroes.[10] Gaitán's later struggle against the leaders of his party was motivated,
at least in part, by his belief that the politicians of his generation were betraying the progressive ideals for which Liberal *caudillos* had offered their lives.
Except for a short period from 1933 to 1935, he remained loyal to his party,
not only because of his conviction that it was the most effective vehicle for his
reforms, but also because of his emotional ties to the party of his youth.

At an early age Gaitán began to exhibit a driving ambition, no doubt fueled
by his mother, and an untamable rebelliousness certainly learned in his
continual conflicts with his obstinate father. Once out of the home and in
secondary school, Gaitán began to dream of becoming a lawyer, traveling to
Europe, being famous, even one day becoming president of Colombia and
solving all the nation's problems.[11] He resisted school discipline and rejected
the traditional pedagogical methods forced on him.

He was expelled from various schools until his father's work for the Liberal
party finally came to his rescue in the form of a scholarship to the Colegio
Araújo in 1913. The Colegio was a well-known but not officially approved
school founded by the energetic Simón Araújo, who had chafed under the
traditional methods of the Conservatives and the priests. Its classrooms had
produced many an aspiring young Liberal politician.[12] While there, Gaitán
came into daily contact with the lighter-skinned and confident sons of established Liberals. But his behavior did not change. He compensated for the
differences between himself and his fellow students through attention-get-
ting behavior: "He argued in a loud voice, contradicted his professors, led
[classroom] disruptions, sought to impose his own ideas, and fought with his
schoolmates when they taunted him with humiliating nicknames . . . or did
not render him the degree of importance he demanded."[13]

While still at the Colegio Araújo, Gaitán took his first steps in politics. He
praticed his oratory by going to rallies for leading politicians, climbing onto
the podium once the speakers had finished and the crowd was getting ready
to leave. At a school ceremony in 1916 commemorating the birthday of Simón
Araújo, he suddenly jumped up before the scheduled speaker could begin and
launched into an oration that received favorable comment.[14]

In the 1917 presidential campaign, he decided to support the Conservative poet, Guillermo Valencia, who headed a coalition of moderate Conservatives and Liberals against the entrenched Conservatism of Marco Fidel Suárez.[15] Gaitán campaigned at school, disrupting classes with his orations and impromptu rallies. He wrote letters to *El Tiempo* and *El Motín* urging Liberals to support Valencia as the patriotic and progressive candidate of the *pueblo*.[16] Finally, he offered his services to the leaders of the national campaign but was rebuffed. Not easily discouraged, he went on his own speaking tour of the surrounding towns in Cundinamarca, delivering orations in favor of Valencia and chastizing the Conservative regime, and arousing so much attention that the Liberals supporting Valencia decided to bring the high school student officially into the campaign. The Liberal *caudillo* Benjamín Herrera sent him on a more extensive speaking tour through the Conservative strongholds in western Cundinamarca and Tolima, where he rapidly made a name for himself as an orator.[17]

While still a high school student he ran unsuccessfully for the Cundinamarca departmental assembly as a member of the Liberal University Directorate.[18] At that time he proposed what would become one of the major themes of his public life: the need to build a permanent party organization to incorporate the *pueblo* continuously into politics instead of making sporadic efforts around election time.[19]

Wherever he went he provoked controversy and opposition. Gaitán soon learned the limits of his words. In one town he was nearly lynched. In another he was denounced for insulting local leaders and threatening "rivers of blood" should electoral fraud be practiced there.[20] He apparently backed away from the charges by calling on the local populace to engage him in rational discourse instead. After his oration he was carried from the plaza on the shoulders of the crowd.[21] He defended his behavior in a letter to *El Tiempo*, announcing that neither "attempts to assassinate me, nor affronts and slander" would stop his struggle for justice.[22]

It would be too much to expect Gaitán to have well-defined social ideas at this point. His few writings are imbued with a romantic view of change, a belief in justice and equality, and the conviction that progress was being blocked by the narrow interests of incompetent Conservatives. The Liberal party would defend the nation and bring progress. Gaitán believed in honesty in elections and in government and had a vague idea of nationalism.

Above all, however, Gaitán showed a strong social compassion coupled with a hatred for the perpetrators of injustice. On March 16, 1919, while still in high school, he rushed from one street corner to the next and, hoisted above the shoulders of the crowd and barely able to control his tears, denounced the violent police repression of the peaceful demonstration by Bogotá's tailors that he had witnessed moments before. The tailors had organized to protest against a government decision to buy police uniforms from abroad rather than from their own artisan shops. The high school student denounced the conspiracy of monopolistic commercial interests that he saw lurking behind the decision until the police forced an end to his inflammatory rhetoric and he returned home in a rage.[23]

Gaitán's admission in February 1920 to the law school of the Universidad Nacional was a personal triumph that few of his social class had ever achieved. During his last year in high school, he transferred to an officially certified school from which his entry into the university would be considerably easier.[24] His sights set on becoming a lawyer, he disciplined himself and became a successful student. But he reached the coveted classrooms of the university at great cost to family harmony: while his father forced him out of the house, his mother pledged her continued support.[25]

Hoping to find a way to alleviate the financial hardships that university study entailed, Doña Manuela asked the assistance of President Marco Fidel Suárez, who had once glowingly referred to the Liberal schoolmistress's accomplishments. The president, who must have known of young Gaitán's political prowess during the recent presidential campaign, offered him a minor post in the Colombian embassy in Rome to facilitate his studies there.

Gaitán was probably not overly surprised by the ease with which his educational expenses and a secure position, probably for the rest of his life, had been obtained for him. It must have offered him some comfort to know that traditional avenues of privilege might be open to him should the need ever arise. However, the offer must also have confirmed his feeling that corruption was prevalent in the highest circles of government. While showering his mother with gratitude, he defiantly rejected the diplomatic appointment. Years later Gaitán recalled that the appointment contradicted his wish to make the much sought-after trip on his own resources. "A great satisfaction," he recalled, "was to reach an objective by means of personal effort. What a poor taste of prior mastication life must have for those men who have not felt such a delicious sensuality."[26] Gaitán was determined to be indebted to no one and to know that his achievements had come to him through his own merit and work.

Gaitán was no ordinary law student. Although he did not excell in his studies, he read widely in history, sociological theory, the arts, and literature. He joined a literary group and wrote articles and published interviews in *El Espectador* and *Gaceta Republicana*.[27] Shortly after entering the university, he threw himself into organizing the University Center for Cultural Propaganda, an effort that revealed many of his views on the role of politics in social life, views that would change surprisingly little throughout the years. The idea was to enlist the support of the rich and the well-educated in taking education out of the classroom and directly to the *pueblo*. This "campaign of scientific vulgarization"[28] reflected Gaitán's belief in the primacy of education as well as his distrust of the vague theorizing and the cavalier use of abstract ideas he constantly encountered both at home and in school.

Gaitán organized a series of lectures held in the Teatro Colón and attended by some of the leading representatives of Bogotá society. The lectures were delivered by experts on various social and economic subjects. The first, by Dr. Julio Manrique, was on the role of contagious diseases like diphtheria, typhoid fever, tuberculosis, and leprosy in an urban environment like Bogotá.[29] The choice of subject indicates that the health of the *pueblo* was already one of Gaitán's major concerns.

The primary audience was not the elite, however, but students like Gaitán who, he wrote, "would take precise notes . . . and would later go to the workers in the barrios and present the conferences in a clear and simple manner." Instead of listening to the "vacuous theorizers" who spoke about the social conditions of the *pueblo* without any first-hand knowledge, Gaitán wanted the university students to fan out through the city, including the prisons, and later through the entire country, to share with the workers in their own homes "the juicy fruits of science."[30]

The center got off to a good start. Even President Suárez expressed his intention to attend the first lecture organized by the student who had turned down his offer to study abroad. Gaitán's efforts were profusely lauded in the local press.[31] However, the upper-class students proved less interested than Gaitán, who soon seemed to be the only member of the center. By the end of the first year, Gaitán had managed to get a new group to tour the western departments of Tolima, Caldas, and Valle. The students who persevered were more interested in politics than in public health, and soon their critique turned to the Conservative regime. By January 1921 suspicions had been raised about Gaitán's use of the center's funds. Although he defended himself plaintively, he abandoned the center in the face of growing controversy.[32] He became ill, perhaps conveniently, and turned his attention to other tasks. This would not be the last time that illness would save him from making decisions at difficult moments of his public life.

Gaitán continued, nevertheless, to be active in politics. By 1922 he was one of General Benjamín Herrera's most trusted lieutenants during the Liberal *caudillo's* campaign for the presidency. Gaitán was sent again into the Conservative bailiwicks of Boyacá. As had happened in 1917, his presence in Conservative towns produced untold commotion. In Ubaté a riot nearly broke out, and Gaitán was forced to leave the podium; he returned once the audience had been calmed down, delivering the rest of his oration to the acclaim of the crowd. His efforts were widely publicized in the Liberal press in Bogotá,[33] and his reputation spread sufficiently to allow the law student to be elected in 1923 to the Cundinamarca departmental assembly, with its seat in Bogotá. Gaitán was elected from the heavily Liberal riverport town of

Girardot. Thus, he came to his first elected public office in Bogotá as the representative of a provincial town. What he had failed to achieve as a high school student became his while he was still a university student.

The controversy caused by Gaitán's generally moderate efforts indicates that he could not help clashing with his social betters and with the established powers within both parties. Almost imperceptibly, even to himself, he transcended the bounds of accepted behavior in the most inconspicuous and routine of acts. Instead of learning the deferential style in order to move up the social ladder, as others of his station did, Gaitán developed a clear, even exaggerated, conception of himself, fueled by that driving sense of presence characteristic of those striving for power but unwilling and unable to compromise.

The Organic Metaphor

Gaitán's years as a law student from 1920 to 1924 were the most formative of his life. He developed an ideology based on legal positivism that would permit him to perform his tightrope balancing act on the margins of traditional politics for the rest of his life. At twenty-six, the irrepressible man of action had already found a coherent world view that he spelled out in a little-read and much-misunderstood law thesis entitled *Las ideas socialistas en Colombia*.[34]

The study and practice of law opened up a world for which Gaitán was ideally suited. In the courtroom he attacked society, but did so from within a prestigious institution; he defended the individual against social injustice, but did so through the very laws of an unjust society; he attacked the social order for its callous treatment of criminals, but did so in order to protect society from crime; and finally, as a solitary courtroom figure, he called attention to himself, but only by defending others.

Gaitán's ambition was always to become a lawyer. Along with medicine and the church, law was one of professions pursued by the sons of the elite to maintain their social place and by the middle classes as an avenue to that realm. The church was associated with the Conservative party, and medicine was too private a practice for the man of action. Moreover, law was the most common route into public life. Gaitán chose criminal law. The profession seemed ideally suited to his oratorical skills as well as to his deeply rooted sense of social justice. Through it he could protect the poor and displaced individuals who so often found themselves on the wrong side of the law. In one of his first cases he cried out indignantly that he "was asking for the wretched a defense against a society that produces monsters, only to destroy them."[35] Revealingly, he chose to defend those who had been rejected and castigated by the social order. Gaitán used the ideas of legal positivism to attack the injustices of the social order in order to gain minimal sentences for individuals who had admitted their guilt. As a law student he became a folk hero in the barrios of Bogotá and the nemesis of all self-respecting lawyers and upright bourgeois citizens.

In his first trial in July 1923, Gaitán defended a small retailer who had been found guilty by a lower court of stealing a considerable sum of money from a rich and highly respected man from Tolima who had been granted a liquor monopoly there.[36] Gaitán showed that the rich man had refused to pay back a debt he had incurred with the retailer. Once Gaitán had succeeded in highlighting the social context of the crime, the retailer was treated more leniently by the court.[37] The case must have especially appealed to Gaitán, for in the relationship between the monopolist and the salesman he could see the exploitation that he felt lay at the root of all of society's ills.

In his second case Gaitán defended one of the five accomplices of Delfina Martínez and her lover Alfredo Orjuela, who were charged with slitting open the belly of Eva Pinzón, an emaciated prostitute known throughout the city as La Ñapa. Martínez had accused Orjuela of having had an affair with La Ñapa and attempted to prove that she was pregnant. Not finding the evidence, the group left the body of the prostitute to rot in the foothills near the city. Gaitán was able to get the charges reduced to a minimum, and his unexpected victory made him immediately famous, especially in the city's poorer sections.[38] Little did it matter at the time that justice was not served. Gaitán had defended those whom society and the law had always disregarded.

When Gaitán began his law studies, he found that the ideas of the classical school were taught in all his classes. This school of legal thought had developed in England in the eighteenth century with the ideas of Jeremy Bentham and in Italy under the influence of Cesare Beccaria. It was a reaction against the capricious and sometimes barbarous nature of punishment under all-powerful monarchs. Bent on protecting the individual against the often arbitrary power of the crown, it sought to devise fair and objective criteria for punishment. The classicists believed that ethics was based on a universally applicable deductive system of a priori principles. Their task was to classify moral transgressions and categorize their treatment. They believed that the individual was responsible for his own actions and that the role of society was to deal equitably with the criminal.[39]

Gaitán rejected these ideas instinctively. In his view the classicists believed that man behaved according to "eternal truths, immutable moral and social principles, given by Divine Providence."[40] Theirs was an unchanging world in which "crime and sin are confused."[41] Beneath the idea that man was an isolated, rational creature with free will, morally responsible only to himself, Gaitán perceived the smug countenances of the aristocrat who left the unprotected individual to fend for himself and the bourgeois who subjected the worker to an uncertain salary.

Gaitán was immediately attracted to legal positivism when he entered the Universidad Nacional. This school of thought had become popular among Latin American criminologists as early as 1908, when Enrico Ferri, who along with Cesare Lambroso and Raffaele Garófalo was known as one of the "holy trinity of criminology,"[42] made the first of two trips to South America.[43] Ferri did not include Colombia on his tour, but his theories were hotly debated in the law faculties in Bogotá. Few of the nation's lawyers deviated from the classical school, however, and Gaitán, the maverick, soon became the leading exponent of the new school of legal thought.[44]

Legal positivism was a response to the growing crime rates in the increasingly complex and densely populated European cities of the turn of the century. Positivists believed that the modern era faced an acute dilemma: with affluence crime became more prevalent. The "social diseases," wrote Ferri in 1899, of "insanity, suicide, and crime . . . are growing apace."[45] Positivists argued that social convulsions and change affected both the development of the individual personality and crime rates. Consequently, well-planned social reforms might reduce law breaking. Once the factors that led a person to crime had been discovered, the remedies might be found. Positivists shifted the emphasis from punishment to prevention, from crime to the criminal, from individual rights to the defense of society. They based their model of society on the paradigm of organic life: society was an organism composed of intricately related parts that worked harmoniously to maintain life. Order and progress were described through the metaphor of health; conflict and destruction were diseases and epidemics.[46]

In positivism Gaitán found a conception of society as a coherent entity. It offered a cautiously optimistic view of social change even though it gave prominence to the inhibitory biological and climatological factors that were so much a part of his thinking and that of his generation. It put him in touch with the emotional, irrational, and subconscious side of people that his culture and the Classicists disregarded. It gave him, moreover, a philosophy of history: society progressed from a metaphsical to a religious epoch and culminated in the age of science with which Gaitán identified. And, finally, it allowed him to concentrate on a concept of social change based on altering individual behavior and attitudes. In the words of Ferri, "in social life, penalties have the same relation to crime that medicine has to disease." Society and the individual could be rehabilitated through the "miraculous power of hygiene."[47]

The Quest for Balance

The positivist metaphor that Gaitán learned in law school—society as an organism that tends to a state of equilibrium—provides the framework for his most important theoretical work. In *Las ideas socialistas en Colombia,*

Gaitán attempted to prove that, contrary to the opinions of both Conservative and Liberal leaders, a social problem existed in Colombia.[48] It was the result of the growth of capitalism, which had to be dismantled if an egalitarian moral order with dignity for all was to be achieved. Capitalism, according to Gaitán, had shattered the equilibrium of society (pp. 65–67).

In one of the many reversals that characterized his public life, Gaitán argued that Colombia had a capitalist economy and that capital would lead Colombia out of it (p. 91). Following Marx, he claimed that since capitalism had arrived, socialism was indeed possible. However, the socialists of the period mimicked impractical European theories and incorrectly defined Colombia as feudal, whereas Gaitán followed Marx's dialectical theory of history. Socialism, he argued, would restore the lost equilibrium (pp. 65, 199–200).

Gaitán offered a remarkably coherent, if highly personal, analysis of the causes behind Colombia's problems along with some creative suggestions for change. Nevertheless, the law thesis was more the product of deeply held convictions born during the author's youth and his initiation into politics than of a distillation of sociological and legal theory. His ideas on exploitation and injustice were more an expression of his distrust of the nation's elite than a theory of history that explained their existence and pointed to their elimination. Writing at such a young age, and with a full law program to pursue in addition to his sundry political activities, it could hardly have been otherwise. The thesis was written with the same aplomb that characterized the young *caudillo's* oratory and political behavior. He offered his analysis as though he were dealing with self-evident truths. Although it is filled with references to and quotations from European social thinkers, there is little to indicate that Gaitán was deeply indebted to them. Moreover, his use of Marxism was sufficiently cavalier that the was able to adapt it to his own views.

Gaitán may well have thought of himself as a socialist. Certainly, many of his contemporaries came to that conclusion, and his thesis was indeed inspired by a passionate egalitarianism. However, *Las ideas socialistas* presented an ideal society where a class of honest and hard-working small property owners, protected by the state, held sway.[49] This petit bourgeois class, located somewhere around the middle of society, closely resembled Gaitán's background.

To argue for such a society Gaitán turned Marx around. The author envisaged a society, to use the Marxist terminology Gaitán himself employed, based on handicraft, artisan, and manufacturing modes of production where workers still had control over the means of production. According to Marx, these precapitalist and early capitalist forms were historically doomed by the logic of capital accumulation and the birth of "free" salaried workers.[50] Gaitán, however, had a utopian vision in which the worker was not separated form the means of production. He did not advocate an end to property owner-ship but sought instead to abolish ownership without labor and profit without work in order to bring about a society of small urban and rural property owners who controlled their own labor and the fruits of their endeavors. Gaitán saw work as the motor force of society: it was the sole producer of capital and the mechanism by which social equilibrium was maintained (p. 85).

Gaitán did not see capitalism as a historically necessary and progressive force. For him it was instead a regression, a false step largely imposed from abroad by the imperialist interests of advanced nations and by a tiny local minority. Wage labor and the unlimited accumulation of capital broke what-ever reciprocity and balance could exist between rich and poor, the powerful and the weak. The poor, progressively transformed into "that modern type that is called the salaried worker" (p. 116), were worse off than before. "To-day the new master pays a wretched wage and never has to worry about the nudity, or the hunger, or the health, or the life of the worker" (p. 128). The modern worker was left at the mercy of the capitalist. In Gaitán's view, the laborer had been robbed of his dignity as a human being; he was "disinherit-ed" (p. 124).

While capitalism left the worker alone and unprotected, the capitalist also lost his ties to the society in which he stood to gain the most financially. By using the "absolute right to property," an "absurdly granted privilege of the bourgeois order" (p. 24), the capitalist avoided having to behave according to "social criteria." Without social controls, the capitalist was free to accumulate capital and amass a private fortune and to "exempt himself from directly productive work, to dedicate himself to the direction of businesses . . . and the exploitation of the majority dedicated to work" (p. 89). Thus, Gaitán looked on the capitalist much as he did the criminal: the decisions of neither were public but occurred according to purely individualistic criteria in the hidden recesses of their minds.

Gaitán's peculiar analysis of capitalism was made possible by his most dramatic departure from Marx. He made a radical distinction between capi-tal and capitalism. The former he regarded as "a fact of the natural order" (p. 85), the result of individuals working on their own land or in their own enterprises and selling the products of their labor on the open market. His conception of capital was inextricably tied to small property ownership: "It is small production that required the producer to own the means of production" (p. 114). Rarely having enough capital to employ others, the small owner had to work his own property. Thus, capital, as Gaitán defined it, was the "product of direct, personal work" (p. 86) that the producers did not themselves con-sume and that they could reinvest to produce more goods. The small owner could only survive by meeting consumer needs, thus ensuring a balance between production and consumption and a leveling between rich and poor. Small ownership was thus eminently "social" and a contribution to the harmony of society. It is in this context that Gaitán's statement that "socialism is not the enemy of capital" (p. 125) can best be understood.

Capitalism was quite the opposite. Rather than the result of individual work, it was a "means of speculation" (p. 83). The individual property owner turned into a capitalist when he no longer needed to produce for consumption but used his capital to produce more capital. By investing in real estate, financial institutions, and public corporations—assets he did not need for his survival—he lived off unearned income (rent, interest, and dividends) for which he did not have to labor. The world of capital had been turned upside down. In capitalism, as Gaitán put it, "for the most effort, the least profit; to the most profit, the least effort" (p. 94).

Capitalism divided society into two unbalanced groups: a minority of property owners and a propertyless majority. "Society has reached such a level of economic concentration," he wrote, "that capital no longer has value and significance." Once deprived of equal access to capital, the majority was left with nothing but its labor to sell. "In the natural form of capital, the individual sold the fruit of his work; in capitalism he has to sell his person, he must sell himself" (p. 90).

For Gaitán the unearned income of the capitalist was socially unproductive, for it did not add to the available consumer goods. Since it produced nothing new, it could end only in a zero-sum game: "what some gain is what others lose." Moreover, capitalism did not lead to the growth of the social organism. "Large individual units of capital cannot be considered a benefit to national wealth; quite the contrary, they implant an imbalance [*desequilibrio*] and an injustice that is the source of all social injustice" (p. 85). The capitalist class was a parasitical class that undermined society. It was "individualistic."

Gaitán was not a theorist in search of a bourgeoisie. His objection to capitalism was moral as well as economic. He was ethically opposed to a society in which the many could do nothing but work for the few who did not have to work. Deprived of the right to labor on its own property, the *pueblo* turned humble and dependent; without the need to labor, the bourgeoisie turned self-sufficient and arrogant. Gaitán saw bourgeois society as a hierarchical order based on deference in which the individual was not judged according to his individual merit, his production, and his contribution to society. Thus, Gaitán was not arguing that the Colombian capitalist was reactionary or that he was unable to remake society in his image. He was hostile to the very idea of a bourgeois order of unlimited fortunes, of greed and rapaciousness. Once established, "in contrast to capital, capitalism acquires a definite hold on morality, religion, and the state" (p. 89). Capitalism, according to Gaitán, sanctioned an immoral order.

Gaitán's solution to the social problem lay in reestablishing the lost equilibrium (p. 117). His sights inevitably turned to the past. He argued for a return to a social organization that preceded the unrestricted, individual accumulation of property, the centralization of wealth and power, and the monopolization of the means of production. Whereas Marx wrote within a society where capitalism had made its greatest advances, Gaitán wrote in a society where it was just getting off the ground. What appeared to the nineteenth-century European theorist as an encompassing and inevitable structure seemed a tantalizingly fragile edifice to the twentieth-century thinker in an underdeveloped country.

For Gaitán there was still time to dismantle capitalism. The bourgeoisie was small and relatively weak, and wage labor was more common in the city than in the countryside. The *pueblo* had not as yet been integrated into the nation. According to Gaitán, by the first quarter of the twentieth century, class conflict had not appeared in Colombia. Without the armies of workers produced by the growth of modern industry and the cyclical crises of overproduction, endemic to advanced capitalism, that made workers aware of their exploitation, class consciousness could hardly develop. Gaitán's prescriptions would ensure that it did not. He suggested an economic order in which modern industry would be controlled to create an equilibrium between production and consumption.

A New Class Society

Three conceptualizations implicit in *Las ideas socialistas* are critical to Gaitán's subsequent political activity. The first is his definition of socialism; the second, his view of the role of conflict in society; and the third, his notion of the *pueblo*. All three flow from positivism and point to a petit bourgeois society.

Gaitán's socialism was rooted in the organic metaphor of positivism. He juxtaposed it to the "individualistic" criteria of capitalism, in which the individual acted as an isolated unit to further his own needs (p. 97). For Gaitán socialism quite simply meant the cooperation of all for the betterment of society. Only when all the parts functioned together as integral parts of the social organism could there be health and progress.

The collectivist spirit that lies behind socialist doctrine and Marx's thoughts was alien to Gaitán. His solution lay in an increased role for the individual, for whom he sought protection in private property. Gaitán's socialism was based on the criminologist's paternalistic preoccupation with the plight of the individual in a society where the rights of the propertyless were callously disregarded, rather than on the alienating and exploitative character of private property itself, as in the Marxist perspective.

Nor could Gaitán have been a socialist and still practiced the politics that

would characterize his middle position in society. Socialism would have
turned this man of action into a political revolutionary frontally attacking the
society from outside the established political institutions. He would have
created little ambiguity and controversy, and little of the power he built
around him. Had he been a socialist, it is more than likely that he would have
traveled either the solitary path of those who never acquiesced to traditional
partisanship but who obtained little influence in public life, or the path of
those who gave up the struggle, gained some notoriety, but lost their independence and their vision of equality.[51]

There was much in *convivencia* that was an integral part of Gaitán's culture and experience. He believed in the political ideas of service and sacrifice.
He understood and could practice the distinction the politicians made
between their private and public selves. He agreed with the peace and with
the tempered partisanship between Liberals and Conservatives. He too felt
that the traditional parties could represent the *pueblo* and that elections were
the basis of democracy. He believed in the family, the church, and the state.
Thus, he was able to participate throughout his career in traditional politics
without betraying his ideas.

Gaitán also saw social conflict through the eyes of a positivist. His analysis
of the deleterious effect of capitalism was the same one that he would apply
later to the politicians. His notion of conflict was not one of two antagonistic
forces coming together in struggle. Quite the contrary, he saw conflict as
emerging from two separating forces. In Gaitán's view of strife in Colombia,
the capitalist had turned his back on the worker, leaving him with arms
stretched out, looking abjectly in the direction of the departed protector. It
was in the subsequent absence of reciprocity and cooperation that a conflict
between the capitalist and the worker ensued. Gaitán's inclination was to
bring the parts together to search for harmony rather than to pit them against
each other.

He preferred to operate within social institutions rather than to retreat to
obtain an abstract appraisal of the whole and offer a complete alternative. In
the practice and rule of law, Gaitán found the surgical knife for his interven-
tions into society; in the Liberal party and the *pueblo's* right to vote, he saw
the medicine to cure society and defend it from illness. More than a politician
leading a social movement, Gaitán was a doctor who informed the *pueblo* of
what was best for it and advised individuals on how to be healthy and productive cells of the social organism.

Gaitán's broad conception of the *pueblo* flows naturally from his analysis
of capitalism. It was composed of all those who owned no property and had
only themselves to sell, as well as those small property owners forced to compete at a disadvantage against the capitalist. He appealed to "all those that
work for others . . . without directly reaping the fruit of their efforts. That
includes the forgotten middle class" (p. 93).

Gaitán did not see society in terms of social classes. When he looked at the elite, he focused on the behavior of individual financiers, merchants, and politicians. When he looked down at the thousands of followers who thronged into the plazas to hear him, he saw a conglomerate of individuals. And when he looked at the class he was most closely associated with, he saw separate shopkeepers, artisans, employees, and professionals who occupied individual places in the labor force. Thus, Gaitán's appeal to the whole *pueblo* as the beneficiary of his politics was more than a demogogic ploy. It was rooted in his view of society. When he thought of social change, he could see only individuals reshaping their attitudes and taking charge of their lives. From that vantage point Gaitán made moralistic and emotional pleas to the *pueblo* to be honest, decent, hard-working, and proud, and offered it the assistance of the state in its efforts.

Although Gaitán's analysis was internally coherent, it was not without the tensions characteristic of his middle position. These tensions would inevitably make themselves felt in his politics and lead to charges of hypocrisy and opportunism. They arose most clearly in his ideas on meritocracy. Gaitán opposed all hierarchies that did not rest on work. He concluded *Las ideas socialistas en Colombia* by offering a hierarchy of merit. Once all individuals were offered equal economic opportunities, "then we shall know who the really able ones are . . . society will benefit, and the repulsive spectable of the adulteratedly strong triumphant over the falsely weak will be impossible" (p. 209).

Gaitán's meritocracy was an open world in which all citizens had an active place. They would be judged by how they carried themselves and by their contribution to the general welfare. They would be judged by their work, their responsibility to their families, and the moral reciprocity of their social relations. In Gaitán's ideal society, the life of all was open to public scrutiny. Gaitán's image of the perfect individual was based on the self-made man who had only himself to rely on, and did so proudly. Publicness was the safeguard of society: what could not be made public could hardly be in the public good. For Gaitán, secretiveness and privacy were suspect.[52] Thus, the investment decisions of the capitalist, the closed-room discussions of the corporate board of directors, and the private conversations of the politicians were all anathema to him. He rebelled against them by the same instinct that made him react against the classical school. Although Gaitán understood and practiced the division between private and public life that the politicians crafted, he also squirmed under its implications.

If capitalism made the *pueblo* deferential and the capitalist haughty, the transition from the closed hierarchy of capitalism to the open meritocracy of capital depended on a transformation of the daily attitudes and behavior of the *pueblo*. Gaitán's revolution could not come about violently or suddenly. It was an evolutionary process encouraged by law and made possible through mass education. "As long as the multitudes are not enlightened and educated . . . it will be vain and futile to think of equitable representation" (p. 205). Without the knowledge with which to defend themselves, individuals could not be socially productive and develop the self-esteem to stand on their own feet. Without education they would remain humble.

Gaitán's egalitarian ideal based on a meritocracy of work was seriously flawed. At one point he argued that this meritocracy was but a steppingstone to true equality: "For the moment, an equalization of abilities is impossible, but with equality, time will produce that equalization of abilities" (p. 201). Gaitán did not feel that there was something intrinsically wrong with ranking people. In fact, he rarely objected to the prevailing notion that people were innately unequal. He was arguing for a society ruled by those who produced the most.

Gaitán's analysis offers one social class clear advantages in productivity over another. This is reflected in his failure to give a precise definition of "small capital." Although he made the absolute claim that nobody should employ anyone else, the lines of his argument indicate that he preferred a small manufacturing firm with a few employees to a large industry with hundreds of workers. The worker who sold his labor to a small property owner with whom he worked closely could logically establish reciprocity and trust with the owner and be protected by him in ways not available to a worker in a large factory. Presumably there was a moral cut-off point somewhere between a manufacturing shop and a factory.

It is not clear whether Gaitán failed to perceive the inconsistency or whether he appreciated the conflicts of interest inevitable in a broad coalition. If he emphasized the moral ideal that no individual ought to work for another, he was led to support the interests of the propertyless. Given the impracticality of that ideal, however, Gaitán's analysis did not predispose him to support the poorest within the *pueblo*. If he stressed the notion that production should meet his social criteria—that is, be directed toward consumption—he was led to support the small propertied group in the *pueblo* and to legitimize the relationship between the worker and the petit bourgeois on the basis of the reciprocity that might be engendered within the small shop and the social balance that small production would ensure. The moral egalitarianism that runs through Gaitán's thesis justified the preeminence of small property owners over the proletariat. For the former inevitably played a greater role than did their workers in the production of consumer goods. *Las ideas socialistas en Colombia* is an argument for the petit bourgeoisie as the truly meritorious class in society.

Positivism underwrote Gaitán's class ideology. To prevent class conflict, he proposed a smoothly functioning society in a state of equilibrium. Rather than the dictatorship of the proletariat, he offered the social rehabilitation of the individual in a society where property was controlled. Positivism provided a theoretical model to justify his mediation between the bourgeoisie and the proletariat and to substantiate his search for a balance in the middle ground occupied by the social class with which he identified. It reflected, finally, the fears of that class of separate small producers and consumers about class solidarities above and, especially, below them.

Far from the small and transitory class Marx had predicted it would be, Gaitán saw the petit bourgeoisie as the largest and most progressive class to emerge from the new societies of the twentieth century. His politics was designed to bring that class to power and to transform the society in its image. For Gaitán, the petit bourgeoisie was to be the permanent class in history.

3

Encounters on the Middle Ground

Bogotá is the least tropical of tropical cities.

Jorge Eliécer Gaitán (1932)

The Rise and Fall

Gaitán set out in 1925 along a winding, often tortuous path. He rose confidently to powerful positions more than once, only to fall back silently into his private law practice, his reputation seriously damaged. When his public actions brought the crosscurrents of conflict swirling around him, he disappeared from public life to gather strength and surface anew once the storms had subsided.

After obtaining his degree in November 1924, Gaitán practiced law for a year and a half from a small, sparsely furnished office in downtown Bogotá until he fulfilled his dream of traveling to Rome to study with his mentor, Enrico Ferri, whose ideas he had championed for the past five years. He proudly relied on his family to pay for the trip. Gaitán invested his meager savings in a small pharmacy in downtown Bogotá run by his brother, who sent him money to pay his expenses. The trip moved him closer to the elite that looked to Europe for its origins and traveled regularly to the Old World. Gaitán was only the second Colombian lawyer—the first was the Liberal politician Carlos Arango Vélez—to study with the eminent jurist. But Gaitán's success was unparalleled.

Ferri and Gaitán became close friends. Dressed in dapper clothing that resembled Ferri's, Gaitán was often photographed with him in the streets of

Rome.[1] Gaitán was much taken with the older man. In Ferri he must have seen images of the future to which he aspired. Ferri had risen from humble beginnings, the son of a poor salt-and-tobacco-shop owner, to become a highly successful trial lawyer and Italy's greatest forensic orator. He was a member of parliament most of his life as well as the editor of *Avanti*, the well-known socialist newspaper. A tireless reformer, he was both a republican and a socialist and at the end of his life a fascist sympathizer who believed in coaxing the political institutions to produce the penal codes he thought would improve the well-being of all.[2]

After a year of arduous study and considerable financial hardship, Gaitán presented a proficient but narrowly drawn thesis on criminal premeditation. He graduated magna cum laude from the University of Rome and read the thesis before King Immanuel, Mussolini and his entire cabinet, and his professors and fellow students. In an emotional scene Ferri awarded the Colombian the coveted Ferri Prize. Gaitán became the first Latin American to be named to the Italian section of the International Society of Penal Law. Early in 1929, when he had already returned to Colombia, Gaitán was informed that Ferri had incorporated his thesis into his course on legal positivism.[3]

Following his graduation, Gaitán traveled through Europe and spent a few months in Paris. There he became acquainted with other Colombians, including Alejandro Vallejo, a Liberal, who later commented that Gaitán's dark skin and debonair behavior made him stand out among the other Latin Americans there.[4] Gaitán visited the museums and cathedrals of Europe and cultivated an interest in art and literature. He returned from his international trip in 1928 laden with books in various languages and with paintings of Italian Renaissance statues. With a renewed sense of nationalism, he deplored the "subservience of the country to foreigners."[5] Although he was not opposed to foreign investment, he felt that Colombians should be treated as well as visitors.

Gaitán quickly became a pole of attraction and one of the main architects of the Liberal victory two years later. His rise to fame was meteoric. After an intense campaign in Bogotá's barrios and the surrounding towns of Cundinamarca, he was elected to the House of Representatives on a dissident Liberal list.[6] From the center of politics he initiated his attack on the social and political institutions that surrounded him and began his climb to power. With the *leopardo* Silvio Villegas, he led Bogotá crowds during the June 8, 1929, riot against the corrupt municipal administration. Three months later he launched his celebrated two-week attack against the Conservative regime of Abadía Méndez and against the army that had massacred the banana workers in the northern coastal town of Ciénaga, on strike against the American-owned United Fruit Company. The ill-organized strikers wanted a moderate wage increase, job security, and the elimination of company stores, to which

many were hopelessly in debt. At first the strikers had the support of Ciénega's shopkeepers, who expected their interests to be advanced by a more
competitive market.

Gaitán caught the attention of the entire nation with the *"bananeras"*
debate in the halls of Congress in September.[7] It was in fact not a debate at all,
for there was only one speaker anyone listened to. All who did knew that the
voices of the government and the military were muted because they had no
rebuttal. From Ciénega, where he had gone to investigate the massacre,
Gaitán traveled slowly back to Bogotá, stopping whenever he could to tell the
growing crowds about what had happened to their fellow countryfolk who
worked in a small northern town for a banana company owned by foreigners.
He promised to represent the massacred and their widows and children and
to speak for all Colombians who lived in remote corners without the respect
of the powerful in Bogotá. Once in the city, Gaitán began his orations at five
every afternoon, when the legislative session had recessed for the day. Exhausted, he would end late each night to the acclaim of the crowds that
surrounded the Capitol and carried him through the streets and to his home
or office.

Gaitán's long, meandering speeches in Congress were a model of his
embryonic political style. Claiming to be interested in defending the widows
of the massacred banana workers, he attacked the entire government as the
worst the long Conservative reign had produced; protesting that he was not
interested in politics, he called on the new generations of Colombia to bring
the Conservative rule to an end; stating that he was only concerned with cold
facts, he offered gory details of maimed bodies; asserting that he was the voice
of reason, he spoke softly about historical laws and sociological theories, only
to fly into a rage at the injustices he was uncovering; lauding the military as
a bipartisan pillar of social order, he lambasted the officers who had ordered
the massacre; defending the character of the American people, he argued
that large U.S. corporations brought only death and destruction. Finally, he
used the home of the politicians to threaten them with the *pueblo:* "and I
have confidence in the multitude," he declaimed. "Today, tomorrow, or the
day after, that multitude which suffers injustice in silence will know how to
become desperate. On that day, oh scoundrels, there will be grinding of
teeth."[8] Gaitán's use of teeth as a symbol of animal aggression would become
a continual motif in his oratory.

Gaitán demonstrated a knack for inverting his contemporaries' conception
of what was normal. He called on his followers in the galleries, who hung on
his every word, to wear small black-and-white skulls on their lapels. Thereby
Gaitán established a direct, personal link with his followers at the same time
that he made them active participants in the debate and in the plight of the
banana workers. Luis Eduardo Ricaurte, popularly known in Bogotá as *"el*

coronel" and later to become Gaitán's personal bodyguard, proudly recalled how he walked the streets of the capital city as a young man—"me and my skull!"—shocking the contented citizens of the city.[9] Gaitán brought the specter of death and repression into the streets of Bogotá and into the lives of the nation's remote upper classes.

Gaitán wasted no time once the Liberals won the election on February 9, 1930. He became the spokesman for the "advanced forces" of the leftist Liberal youth. He traveled throughout the country, continually warning the politicians of the fury of the *pueblo* should they dare to back down from their electoral promises. Calling constantly for reforms, he became the nagging conscience of the *convivialistas*.

Gaitán was elected president of the House of Representatives for the 1931 legislative session. His Liberal colleagues honored him with the presidency of the Liberal National Directorate, making him the leader of the still weak and disorganized party. In an effort no doubt to temper the young *caudillo's* reformist zeal, President Olaya Herrera made him second vice-president and third in line for the presidency.[10] In 1932 the faculty of the Universidad Libre unanimously voted him its new rector, charging him with bringing the university into line with the modernizing forces he represented. When in November 1932 Gaitán was getting ready to visit Mexico, Chile, Argentina, and Uruguay, Olaya asked him during his trip to explain to foreign officials Colombia's position in the border dispute with Peru over the Amazonian town of Leticia.[11] This, however, would be the only time in his career that the *convivialistas* would name Gaitán to represent them abroad, and even here he did not travel as an official emissary of the Colombian government.

In 1932 Gaitán fitted as comfortably as he ever would, both personally and ideologically, within the left wing of the party. Hailed as its unquestioned leader, he was given a huge popular demonstration in Tunja by Plinio Mendoza Neira and Darío Samper, editors of *Acción Liberal,* the ideological mouthpiece of the more progressive Liberals, who were struggling to ease the Conservatives' historic grip on Boyacá. In his speech Gaitán warned that the dentures of the rich would tremble at the sight of the coming democracy.[12]

The first issue of *Acción Liberal* (May 1932) was devoted to Gaitán. Samper described him revealingly as a solitary proletarian rebel who inspired fear in the rich by his struggle against a humble background and in favor of social justice, a socialist who believed in peaceful, evolutionary change.[13] In a letter to the journal, Gaitán explained the ideas of the young leftists. "Politics," he wrote in words reminiscent of his debates against the classicists, "is not a metaphysical, immutable, and transcendent conception that exists above both time and space."[14] According to the moderate Liberal newspapers *El Tiempo* and *El Espectador,* Gaitán had defined the spirit of the young nonconformists in the party.[15] In the second issue of *Acción Liberal,* Alejandro

López, the Liberal's most eminent economic theorist, threw his support behind Gaitán. He brought him into the mainstream of the party by stating that both he and Gaitán believed in the middle classes against the "notables" and in the redistribution of private property rather than its elimination.[16]

At the same time, these commentators also perceived a difference between the politicians and Gaitán. Alejandro López, himself a man of humble origin, noted that Gaitán defended the rights of the poor without first asking the permission of the rich.[17] And Samper remarked that "he speaks against the politicians before the *pueblo*, and presents them as the enemies of social justice."[18] Both López and Samper felt that Gaitán represented what they believed in, but they also saw that his political practice and his oratory were somehow different from those of the other politicians.

As a young congressman Gaitán offered the nation the ideas he had first espoused in *Las ideas socialistas*. In a speech entitled "The Social Function of Property," delivered September 15, 1930, Gaitán continued his argument that a social problem existed in Colombia and that it could best be solved through the redistribution and control of private property.[19] The bills he presented during the first two legislative sessions were opposed by the president and faced stiff bipartisan opposition in the still Conservative-dominated Congress. They languished in committee for the rest of Olaya Herrera's administration. Gaitán's legislative debacle may have dispelled from his mind any illusion that the revolution the *convivialistas* had in mind was the same as his.

Gaitán easily resolved the inherent tensions of his ideology by favoring small property owners over the propertyless and leaving room for the capitalist. In "The Social Problem" he asserted that "the social problem . . . develops not from the volume of capital, but from the equity or inequity that presides over the relationship between the worker and the patron." Thus, he concluded, "If the larger capitalist inspires norms of equity in his relationship with the worker, for that worker there is no social problem."[20] Gaitán argued that private property was not at the root of the social problem: "That is why I have said that what is to be attacked is not property, because in all juridical systems, under all historical climates, it exists and will always exist."[21]

Gaitán directed his efforts in Congress to the salaried middle class and to the rural *colonos*. Both worked on others' property but were closer to obtaining some of their own than was the urban proletariat. Gaitán felt that these two groups would lead the socialist forces of Colombia.[22] Instead of attempting to eliminate the exploitative relationship between capital and labor, he sought to pass laws ensuring a decent level of reciprocity and protection for workers. He suggested that they be given a say in running private enterprises, even helping to make decisions on wages, working conditions, and the mediation of labor disputes. He also called for an eight-hour day, accident and health insurance, paid holidays, and the protection of women and children in the labor force, all social initiatives that became law under Olaya Herrera.[23]

Gaitán disclosed what he meant by socialism. Using the organic model, he argued that it was only through the relationship among the cells of the organism that life was ensured. A cell could die, but the organism would remain alive. A capitalist mentality, according to Gaitán, was based on the individualistic criterion of the isolated cell: "socialist criteria," on the other hand, "reside in the relationship among men."[24] Thus "social function," "socialist criteria," and "socialism" were all vaguely the same. During the rest of his career he was more comfortable speaking about a "socialist sensibility" than about socialism.

At the same time Gaitán argued against unregulated market competition. It encouraged the concentration of resources and the growth of monopolies. "The problem with bourgeois society," he told his fellow congressmen, "is that the law of competition does not actually exist to its full extent . . . for the great majority of citizens cannot compete with those who own the means of production."[25] The uncontrolled distribution of products permitted middlemen and speculators who were "deaf to piety, deaf to science and justice,"[26] to manipulate the market in order to raise consumer prices. It benefited large producers and was biased against small consumers.

Once Gaitán had openly defended the role of private property but argued against the market as the regulator of a society of private interests, his view of the state as the cohesive force in society came to the foreground. "We cannot conceive of law where there is no harmony, and it does not exist where there is no equilibrium. From this we deduce that it is the function of the state . . . to harmonize individual wills."[27] For the social theorist who believed history had overstepped its bounds, leaving the individual alone and unprotected, the protection of the individual became the duty of the state.[28]

In his most far-reaching proposal, Gaitán suggested amending the constitutional provision granting the individual an absolute right to property. He argued that property ownership was a duty that carried with it social responsibilities and urged Congress to pass a bill expropriating without indemnification all lands not under cultivation by their owners and distributing these among the peasantry.[29] The Conservative opposition argued that property should remain an individual right with certain social functions. Thus, Gaitán's initiative was absorbed into a compromise known as the "social function of property."[30]

Nevertheless, in 1932, the year in which he seemed destined to reach ever more influential positions, he was also assailed by Liberals and Conservatives. He earned the enmity of Enrique Santos Montejo, the Liberal journalist, whose family's newspaper, *El Tiempo*, accused him of betraying the party to socialism.[31] Santos, who wrote under the nom de plume "Calibán," was the era's most celebrated editorialist. He was an old-style Manchesterian liberal with a fervent belief in Catholicism and the value of private property. He had an uncanny ability to orchestrate compromises between Liberals and Conservatives and among the rival leaders of his own party. Calibán was constantly on the alert against dictatorial tendencies from the left and the right, and worried that any organization or social planning might lead to the demise of public life. In June he attacked Gaitán for blaming all the *pueblo's* ills on the Liberals and, more significantly, for attempting to invert the social pyramid.[32] In the years to come Calibán would perceive Gaitán as the greatest threat to his ideals.

The tenuous alliance between the president and Gaitán came to an end when the latter failed to support the juridical separation of Bogotá from the department of Cundinamarca, which was Olaya's pet project. In the background, López, next in line for the presidency, operated to hamper Gaitán's career. And Gómez, recently returned from his post as ambassador to Germany, also perceived Gaitán's popularity as a major obstacle to his own ambitions. Throughout that year Gaitán was increasingly chastized for being naive and romantic, and his vigor was regarded as a sign of immaturity. Slowly, the epithet *"el negro* Gaitán," "black Gaitán," gained currency in the cafés and salons of Bogotá.[33]

After reaching the heights of power in such a short time, only to find that both he and his reform proposals were unacceptable, the harsh realities of class and race must have dawned on him forcefully. By the end of 1932, he knew that no matter how hard he tried, or how successful he was, he would never be a part of the elite. He would always be looked down on, maybe all the more for his success: his actions would be interpreted as the result of *malicia indigena,* Indian malice, the nebulous trait that whites believed determined the actions of Indians, mestizos, and blacks; ambition would be seen as vanity; the quest for justice as demagoguery; political passion as social discomfort; and the drive for power as personal opportunism. Instinctively, Gaitán understood that the elite would always regard his rise more as result of their willingness to make room at the top for individuals of lower birth than as a result of his own merit. Spurned, he defiantly demanded to be accepted on his own terms.

Joining Ranks on the Outside

Gaitán was far from being the only one unhappy with the Olaya Herrera government. Most of the Liberals agreed that the few labor laws and land entitlement and housing projects the regime initiated were an insufficient social program. Yet Gaitán's criticism was different. He continued to speak of the goals of their generation and wondered whether the *nuevos* now in power were not acting much like the older leaders they wished to supplant. Gaitán worried about what the government was doing. He was more preoccupied, however, with *how* his generation was behaving. His attack was directed mainly against the style of *convivencia*.

Gaitán officially left the Liberal party in October 1933. Along with Carlos Arango Vélez, who had also studied under Ferri, he organized the Unión Nacional Izquierdista Revolucionaria (UNIR). The decision to separate himself from the party must have been a wrenching one, a measure of his despair. It contradicted his belief that he was a Liberal and that the party was the central vehicle for change. More important, Gaitán's withdrawal ran against his inclination to integrate society into a harmonious whole around existing institutions.

For Gaitán the *convivialistas* had already failed to take advantage of their unique opportunity to stop the growth of capitalism. With every passing moment the capitalist grew stronger and the propertyless mass larger, and it became more difficult to alter the seemingly inexorable path of history. Disillusioned, he exclaimed in August 1934 that "nothing has changed in the republic. . . . Our phrases to the multitude were nothing more than an electoral hoax. . . . A barricade of conventionality . . . and . . . silence pervades politics."[34] He now believed that his generation had the same "homeopathic temperament as the previous generation."[35] Cold and distant, they passed laws as before and held private conversations on public issues without delving into the real social and economic issues that the *pueblo* faced. Rather than closing the breach between themselves and their followers, the *convivialistas* seemed bent on expanding it. "That moderation, that serenity, and that calmness that has graced our inspired politics is a strategy in defense of our laziness and our conformity."[36]

With the UNIR Gaitán sought to produce outside traditional politics what the politicians had been unwilling to produce within it: a closer, more organic relationship between leaders and followers.[37] The acronym UNIR, signifying in Spanish "join" or "come together," was no accident. At the moment of his separation, it cogently revealed Gaitán's positivist ideal of a cohesive society where the closely functioning parts prevented conflict from arising.

The UNIR showed the imprint of Gaitán's personality and ideas. It revealed the practical day-to-day political activity he felt was needed to transform society. It gave him the first outlet since the University Center for Cultural Propaganda back in 1920 for his indomitable energy and organizational abilities. He dedicated himself to it fulltime and financed it with his own limited funds.[38] He looked immediately to the countryside for the problems to be solved and for his constituency. Gaitán turned to the *colonos* and the *minifundistas* in the coffee-growing areas of Cundinamarca and Tolima and crisscrossed the land, leaving an Unirista committee of well-known provincial leaders to compete with the Liberals and Conservatives.

The UNIR's organizational style was markedly different from that of the traditional parties. It reflected its leader's belief that politics should be the guiding principle in the private life of the *pueblo* and the glue of society. The rank and file of the independent movement were active members who were given identity cards. They participated in permanent local organizing committees that were vertically linked through personal contacts and through the newspaper, *Unirismo*, to leaders at the regional and national levels. Rather than concentrating on electoral politics, Gaitán's aim was to change the behavior of his followers. He encouraged the use of hymns, uniforms, insignias, and decorations to elicit a sense of discipline and participation and affect the members' conceptions of themselves.[39] In contrast to the abstract rhetoric of the *convivialistas*, Gaitán implored the peasants to take daily baths and brush their teeth regularly and filled the back seat of his car with bars of soap to distribute among them. Thus, the movement became known by foes and friends as the "revolution of soap" and the "campaign of the toothbrush."[40] Enrico Ferri's teachings were alive in the UNIR.

After three years and with little to show for his efforts, Gaitán's underlying premises and beliefs remained unchanged. He continued his concern with personal hygiene as a means of raising self-esteem. He was still struggling for a "progressive abolition of the exploitation of man by man" through the establishment of an "equilibrium between production and consumption." He wanted to "stabilize the worker against the contingencies of salary."[41]

The Unirista program included rigid controls on consumer prices, rents, and market speculation. It called for a progressive tax, the nationalization of credit to ensure better terms for small urban and rural property owners, and a limitation of land ownership to a thousand hectares. It provided for a social security system organized by the state and funded equally by workers and employers, the participation of delegations of workers on the boards of directors of private companies, and collective labor contracts agreed to by both sides. To strengthen the family in a society where illegitimate children and fatherless homes were widespread, it stipulated the abolition of legal differences between legitimate and natural children, legalized civil divorce, and called for the juridical equality of the sexes.

Gaitán was the only politician of the period to be actively concerned with the place of women in society.[42] Since female suffrage was not granted until 1957, his interest is a vivid indication of the sincerity of his reformist initiatives and his egalitarian faith. Critical of male supremacy, his solutions were similar to those he proposed for other forms of inequality and exploitation. He called on men, who had all the advantages, to face their social and human responsibilities and revise the hierarchy in favor of the disadvantaged female.

He felt that men were obliged "to create an environment in which [the woman] might become educated, channeling her toward activities that are profoundly necessary for her liberation."[43] Just as he felt that he had little to gain from the reforms he pushed and that the duty of the politician was to work against many of his privileges by "raising" the *pueblo*, so too did he feel that men should balance their relationship with women.

Gaitán's insight that moderation, serenity, and reason lay behind *convivialista* politics was the basis of his critique. He objected to the excessive use of reason and to the "verbalist criteria of politics. . . . I cannot accept the postulate," he said in his defense of the UNIR against Liberal and Conservative critics in 1934, "that has invaded the minds even of the new generations, according to which deep passions, the fervent love of ideals, convert a man into an insubstantial and romantic being."[44]

Gaitán called for a balance between reason and passion. The role of passion in social life was rooted in his vision of individuals proudly defending their property and their place in society. Having nothing to hide, for they owned nothing that could not be seen, they could openly and confidently express themselves both in private and in public. This vision contrasted sharply with that of a bourgeois world where profit and property were obtained through intangible, hidden investments that the capitalist strove not to disclose and that forced him to be cautious and circumspect in social life. Seeing a similar imbalance between reason and passion in the personalities of the *convivialistas*, he came to the conclusion that their partisanship was false. They could say one thing in public yet believe quite another.[45] It was possible for Liberals and Conservatives to agree ideologically but disagree emotionally, thereby maintaining a farcical partisanship. "Maybe that is the way," Gaitán told them, "to explain the fact that the leading Liberals and Conservatives have the same ideas, practice the same systems, even though their denominations are different and so are the hatreds that lead them into conflict."[46]

How could it be, he asked, that politics had become simply a matter of temperament? For him the answer lay in a changing economy that was altering the relationship between politics and social classes. Capitalism had changed it all. Although the parties were multiclass in their structure, both now served the "invasion of new capitalist elements." Politics, Gaitán concluded from the vantage point of the UNIR, had become "a matter of class."[47] "Now Liberal and Conservative leaders are in agreement."[48] In a revealing statement, Gaitán accused the *convivialistas* of knowing that they had no disagreements: "I know that in public you do not admit this . . . that this statement will never leave your lips. But I have heard it from the majority of you in private. You make that confession at every moment, and you cannot deny it."[49]

Gaitán turned the *convivialistas'* belief in reason on its head. He maintained that passion was far-sighted and the basis of historical change: "the idea is always relatively fleeting; it corresponds to a reflex of the reality of the moment. Sentiment, on the other hand, tends always to perpetuate itself by influencing future generations."[50]

Distant, insincere, and unproductive, the *convivialistas* contradicted Gaitán's most treasured goal of a society based on merit. By 1934 he had concluded that the "notables," as he sarcastically called them, "were pitiful subjects of unknown merits" who had been falsely "elevated to the category of men of state."[51] Thus, in his Manifesto of the UNIR, Gaitán argued that the state should represent "the productive organs of the economy" rather than be the domain of *politiqueros* who lived off politics and performed no useful function. He suggested that members of Congress be elected by the vote of both workers and employers[52] and that the powers of the presidency be curtailed. To fill appointed state positions he proposed a hierarchically organized civil service based on merit and experience and made possible by a radical reorientation of the nation's educational system from formal, academic learning to technical and vocational training. He called for a "rigorous limitation of the so-called liberal careers in order to put an end to the abundance and mediocrity of professionals" who spent their lives in "bureaucratic occupations unrelated to their studies."[53] In his view a complex and modern society needed competent managers. Students had varying interests and abilities, and education should encourage them to contribute to society according to their abilities and expertise.

Gaitán's defection from *convivencia* was a source of great concern for the Liberals. The Conservatives at first welcomed the division in the Liberal ranks but soon began to worry when it appeared that Gaitán's appeal might cross party lines.[54] The Liberals, suddenly in power after forty years of opposition, found themselves opposed by their own most outspoken and popular leader. Uncertain about the effect of Gaitán's opposition, the Liberals mocked and belittled him.

Juan Lozano y Lozano led the reevaluation. He scolded the *caudillo* in 1934 for preferring to "deviate through harsh paths."[55] He added that Gaitán's vanity was unbecoming, for emotion had no place in Bogotá. The city, he wrote, "had forgiven Gaitán his talent, his ambition, and his victories. But it will be a long time before it forgives him his autographs, the italicism of his language, his deep-marine-blue shirts.[56] And Lozano ridiculed the organization of the UNIR, charging that soon the Uniristas would come out into the street with pennants and secret greetings. "All this seems a little comical . . . in a city with as accentuated a critical spirit as Bogotá."[57] According to Lozano, the public men had gotten used to Gaitán's constant rhetoric about "the exploiting classes, constricting capitalism, and the mother with child in arms who has not the bread to calm her crying child. We intellectuals of the urban clique," he went on, "smile casually at the more lively and emotional of the oratorical and parliamentary insults of the disheveled orator."[58]

Nevertheless, Lozano did not disguise his fear. Although the *convivialistas* might not take the *caudillo* very seriously, he admitted that workers and peasants did. "Gaitán is today the only politician who enjoys his own electorate."[59] If Gaitán should be successful in the UNIR, Lozano concluded, "then Liberals and Conservatives, Masons and Jesuits, tyrians and trojans will find ourselves in anguish, organizing coalition upon coalition to oppose the advance of the armies of Gaitán."[60]

The pages of *Acción Liberal* were closed to Gaitán. Lozano was invited to present the official party statement excommunicating the rebel. For Lozano, Gaitán was a socialist with no place in the party. He represented the inevitable growth of socialist forces that Liberals would have to oppose in the future. At the same time, Lozano followed the official line of *Acción Liberal*, which sought to keep Gaitán from preempting the left by charging that Unirismo was a narrowly nationalistic, rightist movement.[61]

In the same issue, Germán Arciniegas, the intellectual founder of *Universidad*, the organ the *convivialistas* used before they came to power, launched a revealing attack on the UNIR as a rightist movement. He claimed that it represented private ownership and a class of small landowners. Arciniegas contrasted it with a group he called "the Liberal left in parliament," which favored the state takeover of productive lands not cultivated by the owners and the establishment of state-run cooperatives. Whether for partisan reasons or not, Arciniegas came closer to understanding the UNIR and its leader than did most other *convivialistas*.[62] Gaitán represented a class rather than the state.

Posts of Responsibility

Gaitán's return to the Liberal party was inevitable. In open opposition, he became easily classifiable, isolated from the rank and file, and increasingly powerless. In 1934 he lost his seat in Congress, and with it a national forum. Everywhere he went large and emotional crowds acclaimed him, but he was told by peasants and workers that they could not easily vote for him now that he was no longer a Liberal.[63] The power and patronage of local leaders was too strong, and support for them was a safer bet. When a divided UNIR ran a slate of candidates for various departmental assemblies in May 1935 over Gaitán's objection, the movement received only 3,800 of the more than 475,000 votes cast.[64] The UNIR was already in its death throes when Gaitán found peasants exchanging their bars of soap for alcoholic beverages at local stores.[65]

Outside *convivencia* Gaitán enjoyed little of the security he had had as a

Liberal. The UNIR was violently repressed by Liberals and Conservatives. Unirista headquarters all over the country were attacked, as were peasants who acted in the name of the movement. On February 4, 1934, early in the Unirista movement, Gaitán was nearly assassinated when police and groups of Liberals attacked a crowd of 2,000 gathered in the central square of Fusagasugá to listen to the *caudillo*. Four Uniristas were killed.[66] Finally, Gaitán found that the newly elected President Alfonso López had incorporated many of his demands into his platform. It seemed that change would come at last. Thus, when López offered him a seat in Congress by placing him high on the electoral list, Gaitán's decision to return was far easier than his decision to leave had been two years earlier. But more than any of his actions it earned him his reputation as a self-seeking opportunist.[67]

The *convivialistas* were relieved when Gaitán returned to the Liberal party. Conservatives no longer had to worry that he would take the peasant vote away from them, and Liberals could expect him to cease his attack on them. Traditional politicians used the failure of the UNIR as evidence of their own legitimacy and the futility of third party movements. They took Gaitán's turnaround as a sign of his acceptance of their politics and an indication that he would behave responsibly. They now felt that Gaitán was controllable and maybe even co-optable. His popularity would again bring votes to the Liberal party, and his legitimacy would bolster their credibility.

Gaitán easily gravitated to the middle ground he had left. Suddenly a national figure again, he toured the nation in loyal defense of the López administration.[68] As before, he attracted large crowds that afforded him a distance from the Liberals. López perceived the *caudillo* as a threat to his own popularity but was now unable to attack him. He instead appointed him mayor of Bogotá in June 1936.

Gaitán did not graciously accept the high responsibility being placed on his shoulders. Instead of being sworn in by the governor of Cundinamarca, he postponed taking office until June 8, the seventh anniversary of the 1929 riot, and orchestrated a "spontaneous" triumphal march to "occupy" the mayoralty in the name of the *pueblo*. Carried on the shoulders of the crowd down the Calle Real to the Plaza de Bolívar, he accepted the municipal government from an unknown orator.[69] The next day *El Tiempo* failed to mention the demonstration but gave front-page coverage to the banquet for the mayor hosted that evening by Juan Lozano y Lozano, to which 120 of the city's elite had been invited. Now powerful, Gaitán moved with ease from the street and the *pueblo* to the salons of the *convivialistas*. Once there, Gaitán listened to Lozano warn him that his juvenile illusions and outbursts had come to an end now that the young Liberal had the responsibility for the capital city in his hands.[70] The reasons he had been named mayor appeared obvious. The mayoralty was the first of three high-level posts offered him between 1936 and 1943 by three Liberal presidents. Yet none of the positions succeeded in curtailing Gaitán's impetuous style.

Gaitán's ideology was clearly revealed during his eight months as the city's chief administrator. At no time during his life was he more comfortable. The city had been the scene of most of his struggles. He had been an elected member of the municipal council since 1930 and had always taken a deep personal interest in the city's development.[71] For him, as for most of the *convivialistas*, Bogotá was the center of the nation and the home of civilized life. Whatever López's ulterior motives were in offering the *caudillo* this powerful position, Gaitán was ideally suited for the job. As both the center of public life and increasingly the home of the *pueblo*, Bogotá was the ideal place for his politics. Being mayor allowed him to become intimately involved in the day-to-day life of its inhabitants and carry out concrete improvements. He worked with such unbounded zeal that the ever-cautious Calibán exclaimed after just three days that "Bogotá has at last found its mayor!"[72]

Gaitán enjoyed the position. Although he felt estranged from the politics of *convivencia*, he wanted to feel at home in that world. He understood the codes of behavior that underlay the life of public men and was aware that personal comportment, reason, and the social graces were a necessary, albeit insufficient, part of gaining entry to and succeeding in politics. With his belief in private property and in honesty and propriety in public life, the formal behavior of the politicians came easily to him. As mayor he was able to perform the refined and formal political rituals expected of the nation's leaders with a grace and naturalness that belied his humble origins. He used the time-honored methods of politics in his daily life: education, oratory, the sense of service and sacrifice for the *pueblo*, and, above all else, the strength of his personality. In both his public and his private behavior, Gaitán could exemplify the practice of reason and morality for which his generation claimed to stand.

Gaitán adopted the habits of the *convivialistas* as his own. He wore well-tailored suits and drove the latest model American automobiles. Shortly before he became mayor, he married a strikingly attractive upper-class woman from Medellín. He bought property in a new residential area to which other *convivialistas* were also moving. He owned stock in major corporations and had a reputable law office, even though he attended to the poor while the rich were left to wait their turn. He bought a small farm in a temperate area close to Bogotá, as did most other prominent leaders. He collected a large library with books in many languages and adorned his office with the paintings of Italian statues he had brought from Rome. He sought membership in the city's exclusive private clubs. When he was twice denied entry into the prestigious Jockey Club, where leaders of both parties gathered to comment on their exploits—the only mayor of Bogotá ever to be denied admission—he said little but, privately hurt, refused ever to return there for formal functions.[73]

The new mayor's initiatives immediately polarized public opinion. He named three technocrats with few political connections to top posts and asked fifteen Conservatives to join his administration. They did not. Although he considered the whole city his audience, he concentrated on the over five thousand municipal employees over whom he had direct control rather than the city's poor and unemployed. While many of the poor supported his measures through weekly demonstrations in front of the mayor's office facing the Plaza de Bolívar, the city's more affluent citizens and many of the politicians ridiculed him for his penchant for details and for becoming embroiled in trivial tasks unbecoming to a mayor. After only two months Calibán had second thoughts about his original enthusiasm: "But on occasions he exaggerates and lets himself be carried away by his excessively impetuous temperament. A figure as important as the mayor of Bogotá would do well to remain calmer."[74]

Gaitán continually toured barrios that had never before seen a mayor. He went into the homes of the poor carrying small gifts, "explaining to them," as his biographer Osorio Lizarazo recounts, "the advantages of a decorous and dignified life."[75] He set up a weekly radio program to explain his policies and mounted a loudspeaker on the Plaza de Bolívar. On August 21 he drew overflowing crowds to a conference at the Teatro Municipal. It was the start of a tradition that came to be known as *viernes cultural*, "cultural Friday." During the conferences he defended his mayoralty as part of a campaign to "raise the social level of the popular classes" and to bring "health to a sick, vice-ridden, and carefree race."[76]

As mayor Gaitán liked to walk the streets in the predawn hours to see whether municipal employees were properly dressed and arriving for work on time. Many employees feared to leave their posts for longer than the allotted fifteen-minute coffee break lest the mayor be walking about. Gaitán insisted that streetsweepers show up at work bathed and wearing the boots that the municipality provided for them.[77] He launched a public health campaign to inform lower-class residents about the hazards of walking barefoot. By October he had distributed over nine thousand pairs of low-cost, durable shoes to public employees, who were to pay for them in installments. He ordered sanitary facilities and public baths built downtown. He opened lunchrooms throughout the city for construction workers. Their wives were instructed to bring lunches in especially designed containers and were obliged to sit at tables provided for them rather than lounging about in public parks, as was the custom. He insisted that women vendors in the open-air markets wear white aprons and be clean at all times. He called on all Bogotanos to care for their yards and made them responsible for the condition of the sidewalk in front of their homes. He insisted that a front porch light be installed in every home, especially in the more dangerous sections of the city.[78]

Gaitán also beautified Bogotá. He had trees planted along major streets and made sure that the parks were well maintained. He limited the size of commercial advertising signs and ordered that they be written in Spanish, rather than the foreign languages then in vogue, and that they not protrude onto the street. He had cement statues whose contours had been reshaped by the rain removed as public eyesores. In one of his most controversial actions, he removed trolley cars from the congested Calle Real and had the street paved in an effort to create a street mall where citizens could stroll and look at shop windows. When the pavement mixture turned out to be mainly tar, causing pedestrians to stick to it, the city's affluent and the press heaped ridicule on the mayor. Merchants found their clientele rapidly diminishing, and Gaitán was forced to allow the urban congestion to return to Bogotá's main thoroughfare.[79]

The mayor organized school restaurants where charitable organizations and the city provided free, well-balanced breakfasts. He ordered that all students be given notebooks so that they would not have to carry heavy chalkboards to and from school each day. He closed the worst schools, upgraded some, and constructed others. School bus service was expanded. Just as in his youthful days at the University Center for Cultural Progapanda, he attempted to bring high culture to the *pueblo*. He required all visiting artists to give one free performance on Sunday morning at the Media Torta, an amphitheater he had built expressly for that purpose.[80] And he instituted a street book fair. By October over 47,000 books had been sold in a city of some 400,000 inhabitants.[81]

Gaitán did much to incorporate working-class neighborhoods into city life. He eradicated the worst slums, which were located just above the abandoned Paseo Bolívar that circled the city on the edge of the mountain. No doubt recalling the fate that befell la Ñapa there in 1923, he transferred the area's inhabitants to two new neighborhoods, completed and paved the road, and had the Paseo Bolívar patrolled by the police. He extended electric and sewerage lines to lower-class barrios, paved many of their dirt roads, and extended public transport to them. He also started public housing projects for municipal employees[82] and offered them low-cost medical treatment at the municipally owned Hospital de San José. He organized an employment agency to circumvent the pervasive clientelism of politics. He set up a central warehouse in order to control speculation and regulated the distribution of goods to and from city markets. In addition, he established fixed prices for staples according to their quality.[83]

The mayor's health and clothing initiatives did not meet with unanimous approval among the poor. While most must have been pleasantly surprised that the mayor paid so much attention to their lives, the changes he proposed made many feel awkward and uncomfortable. The women of the markets felt sheepish at first in their white aprons, although many did come to feel proud of their new status. Workers who had never worn shoes found them constraining and Gaitán's insistence on "soap and razor" became onerous for those who had no bathing facilities.[84]

The greatest controversy was stirred by Gaitán's objection to the *ruana*. In his mind the simple wool poncho with the slit at the top was a filthy garment that concealed even more dirt underneath. The reaction of Escipión Fernández, a blacksmith, was typical: "It seems to me that public officials have no right to get mixed up in one's form of dress. I would not change my *ruana* for the most expensive overcoat. My *ruana* protects me from the cold and rain. It serves as a blanket at night . . . My *ruana*, a good *ruana*, costs six pesos. A bad overcoat costs thirty pesos. Would the mayor's office pay the difference?"[85]

From the mayoralty Gaitán extended his attack against the *convivialistas*. In a highly political speech delivered in the Teatro Municipal on December 2, 1936, entitled "A Political Subject That Does Not Belong in Politics," Gaitán inverted the politicians' conception of themselves: they were proud of their rationality—he claimed they had none; they rejected passion—he claimed they had little else. The emotional basis of their politics, however, was a superficial "leftover of the subconscious" from past struggles. Liberals and Conservatives reacted reflexively, rather than ideologically. Agreeing with the public men that reason served the long-term transformation of society, and passion led to immediate victories, Gaitán wondered why his colleagues could only think of the immediate present. Calling for "harmony and equilibrium between the volitional and passionate forces and the uniform and homogenous principles and programs"[86] of politics, he concluded that it was "necessary to have an orientation to the multitudes that will permit us to know where we are marching, what our purpose is. . . . [We need] something much more dense than reflexive action that can reach the multitude and orient it."[87]

Gaitán used the speech to keep himself between the politicians and the *pueblo*. He chastized the *convivialistas* for being distant and not understanding the psychological, often irrational, motivations behind crowd behavior that he as a positivist did understand. The multitude, he informed them, had to be directed, implying that only someone like himself who was close to the *pueblo* could do so. Gaitán took the opportunity to criticize Darío Echandía, then minister of interior, who in a moment of oratorical excess had declared that the masses were never wrong: Gaitán asserted that it is "men of selection who can orient, illuminate, and direct the undeniable forces of the multitude. The multitude needs a compass that will orient it."[88]

A month after his speech, Gaitán signed a decree that precipitated the end of his tenure. The decree required taxi and bus drivers to wear uniforms, for, in Gaitán's view, the driver of a public vehicle was a "disseminator of disease." The uniform, moreover, would serve to raise the "condition" of drivers to the level of dignity they deserved.[89] Gaitán declared that his goal as mayor was the "total civilization of the *pueblo*," and that hygiene was the "backbone of the modern state."[90] His purpose was to integrate the *pueblo* into a homogeneous city life, making it look and act less like rural folk and more like the urban, Europeanized middle and upper classes. Many of the drivers favored the uniforms, and one of their unions, the Sindicato Nacional de Choferes, supported the measure.

Nevertheless, Gaitán's efforts as mayor came to an end because of the opposition of the larger Asociación Nacional de Choferes (ANDEC), quite possibly urged on by leaders with ties to both parties.[91] Gaitán made it clear that he was serious in his intention to impose the measure. At the first sign of the ANDEC strike, Gaitán called in the police and warned that he would welcome a dictatorship to make the city run efficiently.[92] But the day after he thought he had obtained the support of López, he was informed by the governor of Cundinamarca that the city had a new mayor.[93] Thus, Gaitán learned that he would not preside over the ceremonies, just six months away, marking the four hundredth anniversary of the city's founding.

Ejected suddenly from the highest position he had ever held, Gaitán went, almost plaintively, to defend himself in Congress. He did not rally the *pueblo* around him; instead, he defended himself as a leader who had the right to be above his followers. Although Gaitán undoubtedly felt that López was behind his fall, he did not attack the president. Instead, he blamed obscure Conservatives masquerading as Liberals as well as the weak governor who had given in to the pressures of the masses. Gaitán defended himself as a man of the left, neither a communist nor a Marxist, who believed in order. A public official, he argued, should never be deposed simply "because there exists in the street a real pressure that demands his dismissal." To accept that principle would be to "negate the very basis of the state [and it] would come tumbling down"[94] Suddenly back in private life, Gaitán defended himself as a man of order representing the "principle of authority."[95]

The Class Limits of Cleanliness

After losing the mayoralty Gaitán did not return to national prominence until he was named minister of education by Santos in 1940. He was forced to withdraw as the nation's chief educator after eight months when his secularizing ideas incurred the wrath of the church and the opposing party. In 1943 acting president Darío Echandía made him minister of labor, a position Gaitán used as a stepping stone for his presidential drive.

His actions and words during those years demonstrated that Gaitán was increasingly drawn to a social order in which one class predominated over another. As he practiced politics, his vision of a society of two extensive, productive social classes—one of small property owners and another of propertyless workers—held together in equilibrium from above by the state, came sharply into focus. As he moved from one public post to another, Gaitán came to rely more heavily on the regulatory action of the state. When he was a law student he saw the state abstractly as the juridical embodiment of the nation through which laws to transform society could be enacted. In the early 1930s he perceived the state as the regulator of the unequal relationship between the capitalist and the worker. When he was mayor of Bogotá he felt that it was the responsibility of the municipal government to provide shoes for employees and workers. When he became minister of education he wanted the state to have more of a say in the school system than the church. As labor minister he attempted again to induce higher levels of reciprocity in the capital-labor nexus through health legislation and state arbitration of labor conflicts.[96]

Although the embryonic character of capitalism in Colombia made Gaitán's idealization of small property holders reasonable, it also dictated an increased role for the state in society. Gaitán admitted that the overarching role he advocated was a response to the underdevelopment of society. Lacking capital and productive capacity, Colombia needed a push from the state. The more Gaitán relied on the state, the more moderate he became. As he emphasized the regulatory power of an agency outside the capital-labor nexus, whether that nexus was dominated by large capital or small, he lifted the responsibility for the exploitation he saw within it away from the individuals participating in it. By attempting to bring a measure of equality and reciprocity to the relations of production, the state legitimized a social order in which capitalists, large or small, dominated workers and employees. As the state regularized the functioning of society, it moved to socialize the results of production rather than the human relationships existing within production itself.

Gaitán may have had no choice but to turn to the state. Quite possibly the division of labor and the involvement of the government within the bourgeois order were already too far advanced for anyone to turn back the clock. The more he focused on the productive needs of society, rather than directly on the needs of consumers, the more he was forced to rely on the state. Even so, by turning to it he reproduced a hierarchical social order. Insofar as it was to be dominated by "small capital," Gaitán was directly representing the interests of a petit bourgeoisie needing to distinguish itself from the haute bourgeoisie at the top and from the growing proletariat at the bottom.

It was perhaps inevitable that the moderate strain in Gaitán's thought would push his egalitarianism to one side. Since his thought was neither inspired by a collectivist spirit nor designed to produce a sense of class consciousness among workers and peasants, he did not readily perceive the tension between his egalitarianism and his political practice. Nor did he have, therefore, a theoretical basis for keeping the inequality produced by capitalism at the forefront of his thought, and the positivist ideal of equilibrium, now enforced by the state, in the background.

At a banquet given in his honor when he became minister of education, Gaitán argued against an educational system founded on the theory of equal individual abilities. Not everybody, Gaitán now believed, could become a lawyer or a doctor. He argued besides, returning to his belief in work, that "a mechanic, a carpenter, an industrial chemist, signify more than a mediocre medical doctor or a suspicious small-time lawyer."[97]

In 1942, between jobs as minister of education and minister of labor, he delivered a speech entitled "Russia and Democracy." Here he expressed uncharacteristic discomfort with the idea of a democracy as a system of elected officials.[98] As Gaitán had turned Marx's conception of history on its head in *Las ideas socialistas*, he now did much the same with the ideology of the Russian Revolution. Gaitán praised the Soviet constitution for its hierarchical character. Soviet society, in his view, was organized according to the principle of "from each according to his ability, to each according to his work," which he found not to be "an egalitarian principle."[99] He contrasted it with the true, but theoretical, equality of the French Revolution. "Where is justice more closely realized," he asked rhetorically, "in this [Soviet] inequality based on ability and work, or in a false theoretical equality that actually keeps the individual from the opportunity to develop his real capabilities?"[100] By "disciplining" inequality and providing work for all, the Russian Revolution had solved the underlying conflict of society. "Without men educated to legislate in industry, in education, and in the economy, there cannot be democratic representation, for democracy is not a matter of quantity but of quality."[101]

Gaitán obviously felt that he was an important part of that democratic quality. He was a one-man show. From his solo defenses as a criminal lawyer to his campaigns as the mayor of Bogotá, he overwhelmed friends and followers. He always put a distance between himself and others. No other figure of significance and popular appeal emerged from the ranks of the UNIR. Gaitán encouraged neither a sense of camaraderie among his followers nor a system of collective decision making. He does not seem to have questioned the personalistic style that was to become the essence of his magnetic appeal to the urban masses. Perhaps he never felt the need to. His superior oratorical skills enhanced his lone image. His role as a politician with a sense of service to an entire nation, to the *pueblo*, rather than one with specific ties to distinct groups, must have legitimated for him his singular place.

After his success as a lawyer and his prominence as a member of the Liberal party, the presidency symbolized for Gaitán the culmination of all his goals. He felt that every Colombian should have similar aspirations.[102] But he believed he was better suited to the position than any of his contemporaries and that he would serve the nation as others could not. Just as his conception of the role of merit conformed with his small capitalist ideal, his growing conviction of the unequal ability of individuals and the harmonizing function of the state coincided with his drive for power.

When the *convivialistas* systematically opposed him, Gaitán's ideas of a hierarchical meritocracy received daily confirmation. The *convivialistas* demonstrated, to Gaitán at least, that they had to be replaced with individuals who were meritorious and capable. Once Gaitán felt comfortable with a hierarchy, his style of politics was no longer at odds with his ideology. For the practical politician the powers of hygiene were not as miraculous as they seemed. Some individuals were cleaner than others no matter how many baths they took.

4

The Expansion of Public Space

In Colombia there are two countries: the country of politics [*país político*] that thinks
. . . of its power, and the country of nationhood [*país nacional*] that thinks of its work,
its health, its culture, all of which are ignored by the country of politics. Dreadful
drama in the history of a *pueblo*.

Jorge Eliécer Gaitán (1946)

Rushing into the Middle Ground

Early in March 1944 on a small farm outside of Bogotá, surrounded by his
closest friends and associates, Gaitán decided finally to take the plunge and
run for president.[1] The decision came in the middle of López's crisis-torn
term of office, two full years before the election. The president himself was
being widely accused by *El Siglo* of having approved the July 15, 1943,
assassination of Mamatoco, a popular thirty-five-year-old black boxer who
had turned to politics to denounce Liberal party irregularities within Bogotá's
police forces, where he had been a coach. In addition, Silvio Villegas charged
that López and his son, Alfonso López Michelsen, had profited illegally from
the World War II-induced nationalization of the Handel, a threshing company owned by Germans. Four months after Gaitán's decision to run, a group
of military colonels took the president prisoner in Pasto while he was touring
the southern part of the country. They backed down rapidly when they failed
to gain popular and military support.[2]

Gaitán knew that he was bucking all the odds and that his campaign would
provoke the wrath of the *convivialistas*. He knew that he would need that
opposition to be at all successful, for much of his prestige among the *pueblo*
depended on it. He would have to run against the leaders and the machinery
of his own party. Gaitán was again setting out on his own, but this time he kept

77

the comforting Liberal mantle wrapped closely around him. He was to be the true Liberal.

Gaitán campaigned as though there was never a doubt in his mind that he could win the election.[3] Rarely had he been denied, and he had always overcome the stumbling blocks placed in his way. The fact that the decision to run came two years before the election is an indication of his seriousness. It also demonstrates his awareness that his campaign would have to be different from all previous ones. The behind-the-scenes deals that had crowned previous presidents would have to be replaced by a mass movement that would cancel those decisions at the election booths. In Gaitán's mind a two-year campaign did not seem so long.

Several factors led Gaitán to embark on this lonely trail. By 1944, with two decades of unprecedented victories behind him, he had established an enviable position within public life. He also knew that he would always be seen as an outsider in *convivencia*. More important than these personal considerations was his conclusion that there was little honor left in the world of traditional politics. All around him Gaitán saw the center of the social order giving way: in the Santos "pause" and the conformity López displayed in his second administration, in the inability of the *convivialistas* to develop new forms of leadership, and in the corruption and immorality all could see in the highest public offices.

Gaitán's hope that *convivencia* could cut capitalism down to size had ended. Far from being solved in the thirteen years since the Liberals and Conservatives of his generation had come to power, the backwardness and injustice in Colombian society that they had exposed so daringly in the 1920s had intensified. At the beginning of *convivencia* Gaitán's critique was tempered by optimism. Now he saw society farther along the road to domination by an uncontrollable and impersonal market.

Gaitán was convinced that something had to take the place of *convivencia*. The historical mission of his generation was no more. He feared that the decline in authority that the Liberals were producing through their behavior in office was inviting social turmoil and unrest. He saw that the reforms they had all hoped to bring about had not been realized because of the fear that gnawed at the private and public lives of his colleagues. By 1943 he had concluded that the leaders displayed a "dread of autonomous struggle," and that they were in "a panic" at the idea of "walking without parameters." They seemed to him to have given up. "They are scattered men," he said in an interview, "lacking in potential, in the unity of perspective that is characteristic of all generations."[4] Gaitán's own worst fears had come to pass. "The most incapable, the most inept, the most ignorant, the most corrupt have dislodged men of high ideals from politics. . . . there is a tremendous confusion of values, and now nobody knows who is who and what each pursues.

There must be a revolution hatching in this society."[5] Recognizing the fear of the *convivialistas* and the confusion of the times, he set out to restore order.

Gaitán was in the middle again.[6] His position established, he began his disconcerting actions. It seemed that his time had finally arrived. It was no longer necessary to leave the Liberal party and form his own movement, for the Liberals had abdicated the middle ground by turning their backs on their own ideals. Gaitán was not the dissident but the true Liberal campaigning against the party hierarchy for failing in its Liberal mission. He could now attack *convivencia* from within, condemning the new extremists who were creating social chaos and economic disorder. By 1944 Gaitán was able to further his own personal and political ambitions by campaigning for his most cherished beliefs: morality, order, and responsible leadership. He now held the central ground in politics, much as the corner shopkeeper was the linchpin of a harmonious social order in his vision of society. He was in the middle of history, too, for in seeking the presidency in the name of the failed ideals of *convivencia* he became the fulcrum between a future he wished to produce and a past he wished to see return. It was Gaitán's turn to restore order to Colombia.

The significance of Gaitán during these two years resides not so much in his ideas as in his experimental performance. He created confusion in the norms and mores of society: it was his trump card. Gaitán had always been at his best in opposition, when he could point to the shortcomings of those in power and accuse them of responsibility for the plight of the *pueblo*. Never before had he had so much to blame on the *convivialistas*. Gaitán transformed politics by thrusting himself body and soul at them with a continuous vengeful fury that they had previously witnessed only in spurts. He claimed to represent order and public life, yet he caused havoc wherever he went; he claimed to represent reason, yet he elicited potentially uncontrollable passions among the *pueblo;* he claimed to represent morality, yet he acted vulgarly in front of the *pueblo;* he claimed to represent *convivencia,* yet he spent most of his time with the *pueblo.*

Gaitán's decision to remain a Liberal was in part an expression of his deeply ingrained love for the party and its ideals. He was now demonstrating confidence in his ability to juggle the roles of "responsible" *civilista* and "irresponsible" *caudillo* while keeping the attention of the *pueblo* riveted on him. The decision also reflected an equally deep-seated need to join together the disparate groups of society and to bring equilibrium to the extremes. His goal was to rebuild the central institutions of society and return virtue to public life. This could be more easily established through the existing Liberal party than through the creation of another. It was only in that middle ground that Gaitán felt comfortable. Yet at the same time he had a personal need to stand out. Thus, 1944 was Gaitán's moment, for the success of his campaign depended on his keeping the middle ground and remaining independent.

Had Gaitán claimed the mantle of Liberalism but not etched out an independent position, he would have been like any leader of *convivencia*; had he maintained his independence by leaving the Liberal party, the *convivialistas* would have excluded him, both physically and ideologically. He would have created none of the confusion that was the basis of his success. Gaitán's campaign was based on the unexpected and the bizarre. He went about shocking the traditional leaders, keeping them constantly on the defensive, and thereby creating the links with the *pueblo* that were ultimately the source of his strength. Gaitán obviously enjoyed the fright he inspired in the politicians and the social elite of Bogotá. All eyes focused on him.

There was never much doubt that Gaitán would refuse to subject himself to the wishes of the party leadership. The solitary figure rejected all alliances and made no compromises. He remained unclassifiable by making himself look larger than life, the embodiment, not of petty interests and ideologies, but of an inevitable historical process. In a widely publicized interview with Juan Lozano y Lozano shortly after he announced his presidential intentions, Gaitán responded caustically to Lozano's half-playful, half-serious effort to classify him for his numerous readers. What Gaitán had in mind was quite simple: "a socialist platform of the Liberal program" that would offer everyone a place to live and a plot of land to cultivate.[7] He countered the insistent rumors that he was a fascist by stating that that ideology "leads all human activity to sustain a monstrous idea, the state."[8] Nor was he a communist, as so many of the rich feared, "for that system requires a great human conditioning as yet impossible to achieve in Colombia." Gaitán offered, in addition, a revealing criticism of communism. He was opposed to it "because it suppresses controversy, [and] is totalitarian." "Social life," he added, "is founded on the equilibrium of opposed forces."[9] Sounding much like his opponents within the parties, Gaitán told Lozano that the difference between those parties was inevitable: "they are two antagonistic conceptions of society; and the difference between the parties will only disappear when the human spirit is no more."[10]

Gaitán was sufficiently imbued with traditional partisanship to take seriously the idea that the parties embodied the forces of progress and reaction in history. More important, however, he needed the differences between the two, for they offered him the opportunity to slip between the parties and oppose both for their underlying identity. By transcending traditional partisanship, Gaitán could point to his own independence and appeal for Liberal and Conservative votes. He felt little doubt about his motivations. The two parties, he told Lozano were "working on a plane of simple mechanical politics, and not of intellectual transcendence."[11]

Gaitán effectively maneuvered between the parties. Although he attacked the Conservative leaders in the same breath in which he chastized the Liberals, he was able to keep the doors open to the opposition party. In a sense, Gaitán was ideologically and politically close to the Conservatives. His critique of capitalism in the name of a higher moral order struck a sympathetic chord among them. Both looked to the restoration of an age gone by. Gaitán's long struggle reminded them of their own utopian vision of a society free of racial and class prejudice where the individual with merit and ambition could rise to the top.[12] Although many of Gaitán's beliefs and actions pointed to the collectivism they dreaded, he also contradicted that massification of life through his own example. His aggressive behavior, moreover, made many Conservatives, and especially the old *leopardos,* yearn for the *mística* and the party heroism that, they felt, had been lost through the Liberal victories. Finally, they too opposed the Liberals who were in power for growing lax in office and forgetting the statesmanship and morality they had once upheld.

The Conservatives made various attempts to reach an understanding with Gaitán, some more serious than others. In an obvious attempt to deepen the divisions in the Liberal party, Gaitán's attack on López's regime was given a great deal of attention in the Conservative press. Laureano Gómez backed the "candidate of the *pueblo,*" and until a month before the election, *El Siglo* was Gaitán's unofficial mouthpiece. The relationship between the two was sufficiently close to fuel later rumors that the Conservatives had underwritten the *caudillo*'s campaign.[13]

The most serious attempt to bring Gaitán into the Conservative fold came late in 1942, before his campaign had even begun. Rafael Azula Barrera, a leading Conservative thinker, along with the Conservative poet Eduardo Carranza, the Liberal Eduardo Caballero Calderón, and some apolitical technocrats, asked Gaitán to lead a bipartisan national crusade. They proposed a "moral parliament" composed of individuals of known technical expertise to oppose the "parliament of the politicians."[14] Gaitán's enthusiastic response left them with the impression that something might come of the suggestion. But nothing did. Azula Barrera harbored the expectation that Gaitán might join them as late as September 1945, when he discovered that neither he nor his fellow Conservatives had been invited to the huge open-air convention during which Gaitán was nominated for the presidency.[15] He concluded that Gaitán had remembered his failure in the UNIR and had opted to remain within the cloak of Liberalism.[16]

The traditional animosities between the leaders of the two parties greatly helped Gaitán. Had they formed a common front against him, he would have been deprived of the opportunity to assail them for the emptiness of their differences. He could more easily have been branded as an outsider to the traditions they both upheld, and his ability to maneuver would have been substantially narrowed. The greater the confusion within the public domain, the easier it was for Gaitán to be ambiguous.

Corporeal Gaitán

Gaitán soon became the issue of the campaign. His figure and his voice, his gestures, language, and oratory became the principal subject of conversation in the cafés, homes, and clubs of Bogotá. The nation's elite became obsessed, not only with his crude language and dark skin, but with his teeth, his orifices, and even the perspiration that formed freely on his forehead and upper lip as he delivered his orations.

The *convivialistas* had always shown a preoccupation with their teeth. When he was a young man Gaitán's own large teeth had been a source of embarrassment.[17] The young Alfonso López was subjected to surgery because of his large front teeth. Alberto Lleras Camargo was known throughout his life as *"el muélon"* because his teeth jutted out of his mouth.[18] But Lleras Camargo was a mild-mannered man whose teeth were not threatening. Gaitán's teeth, however, had always been a symbol of aggression and anger. Germán Arciniegas admitted that Gaitán's mouth was for him a source of constant fascination, for his teeth were symbols of his personality: "all the teeth were acute, sharp, canine, and the architecture of the upper jaw finishes off in gothic, with teeth that form a pointed arch."[19]

Everything that was physical about Gaitán became deeply symbolic. The paternalistic diffidence with which he had been treated in the past turned into fear and loathing. As a politician with undue ambitions he was one thing; as a presidential candidate he was quite another. At the same time, the campaign finally unleashed Gaitán. The moments of conciliation and weakness were gone. While the political leaders were repelled by Gaitán's behavior, his followers rejoiced at the earthy exploits that made him look like one of them.

Gaitán knew what he was about. Soon all of Bogotá was draped with his picture. His eager lieutenants reached walls that had never before seen a poster, and often Gaitán himself followed them to make sure that no block had been missed and that the posters had not been sloppily plastered to the walls.[20] Early in the campaign Gaitán instructed Daniel Rodríguez, a Bogotá photographer, to make him look as ugly as possible for the official photograph.[21] Most of his pictures show a dark-complected Gaitán, his eyes half closed in the culturally recognized sign of suspicion and distrust held to be characteristic of *malicia indígena*, the "malice of the Indians." Invariably Gaitán showed himself sneering, his mouth open, his teeth bared in a menacing grimace. The best-known picture was the most unusual. It showed not only Gaitán's face and shoulders, as was customary, but his entire body, standing erect, with his clenched fist raised defiantly into the air. In order to demonstrate his closeness to the *pueblo*, he had picture upon picture taken of himself surrounded by the poor. After having been vilified for so many years as "*el negro* Gaitán," the presidential candidate was now forcing his image on every Bogotano. Once the bane of his existence, Gaitán's body suddenly became a source of liberation.

It is hardly surprising that Gaitán was acutely aware of his body. After all, he had been reminded of it almost daily. As a child he was weak and sickly, and the material deprivations of his youth could only have made him more conscious of his physical needs. His continuing self-reliance must also have led him to concentrate not only on his mental abilities, but on his physique as well. He took good care of himself. As a young man he had worked to expand his lungs, trained his voice to withstand the strain of his aggressive oratory, and stood for hours declaiming before a mirror. His habit of jogging through the Parque Nacional in the early morning[22] earned him much ridicule from his political opponents, who saw the activity as unbecoming for a man of learning. He smoked sparingly and rarely drank alcohol. Often he was among the first to return home from the ceremonial gatherings or demonstrations that he staged.[23]

Gaitán proudly admitted that public speaking came naturally to him. At the height of the campaign, he easily gave between eight and ten speeches in one day.[24] He did not have to think about his next oration the way he had to conceive an editorial. In his entire oratorical career he wrote out in advance only five speeches.[25] For all the other occasions, he was confident that he could express himself extemporaneously. Nor did he think about his gestures beforehand. Quite the contary. "When I am in front of the *pueblo*, I am fundamentally transformed. I feel an irrepressible emotion, an intoxication without limits."[26] Emotion was what his oratory was all about. Lest the transformation fail to appear, Gaitán's trusted lieutenant, *el coronel* Ricaurte, was ready to put a bit more brandy into the cup of water on the podium.[27] Without a prepared text, Gaitán was free to change his words and indulge his passion to match the mood of the crowd and enter into a spontaneous dialogue with it. It was more than confidence that allowed Gaitán to address his audience without a text. He felt that he represented the *pueblo* and that his personality and ideology responded to and harmonized with those who came to listen.[28] As he himself expressed it, he was a "deep interpreter" of the *pueblo*.[29] Little could go wrong.

The *convivialistas* were shocked and enthralled by Gaitán's oratorical style. As early as 1933, when Gaitán was just beginning to perfect his delivery, his podium style was captured by Germán Arciniegas, the Liberal who had also grasped the class character of the UNIR. This is how he must have been seen by many a *convivialista:* "The moment Gaitán begins his speech, he initiates a constant gymnastic performance; he gathers himself and stretches out, . . . wields his hands as though they were attached by nerves, wrinkles his brow, sharpens his nose, all with so much vigor that the veins in his neck expand, and thirty minutes after starting he is bathed in sweat, his hair is soaked, his shirt collar resembles a rag, and one can say that he actually splashes. . . . In a Wagnerian crescendo he speaks for two, even three, hours. Toward the end, in a fury, he turns his head swiftly, making his hair, caked to his forehead, fly out; his throat becomes inflamed, he opens his shirt and loosens his tie. . . . It may be said that this is an exaggeration, but I have seen spit emanate from his mouth, spit that forms two small clots at both ends of his lips."[30]

According to his biographer Richard Sharpless, Gaitán began his speeches in a slow and measured voice. "But gradually he accelerated the flow of words. His voice became hoarse and emotional, his body tensed, his arms slashed the air. As his listeners responded with shouts and applause, his voice grew louder and his charged phrases came faster and faster. At the climax of a speech he spouted one phrase after another, building the emotions of the audience and himself to a peak of intensity. . . . Customarily, when he finished speaking, he disappeared rapidly from the scene."[31]

When Gaitán rose to the podium he knew that the crowd saw in him more than a public personality, more than a superior man of reason. Gaitán, the orator, inevitably projected both a public and a private persona. Between the anonymous crowd and the man who rose from poverty to chastize the rich and the powerful there existed an affinity the *convivialistas* could never have elicited. Gaitán's need to express publicly the trials of his private voyage from poverty to power coincided with the crowd's need to be told of its leader's successes and to project its own future on his example. So Gaitán talked naturally about his humble background and the hardships of his youth, his family, especially his mother, his accomplishments, and his suffering. Whenever he was in front of a large and sympathetic crowd, he would laud himself and his listeners for having produced this splendid collective experience, invariably referring to it as the first in the nation's history.

As Gaitán listened to his opponents declaim, he could not help but notice that although the crowds admired their rhetorical skills and the lyrical quality of their words, they had difficulty identifying with the abstract philosophical concepts they expressed.[32] Those orations had had their day. For Gaitán the development of capitalism had forced economic and social issues upon the consciousness of the *pueblo*. By the 1940s such abstractions as liberty and justice had a hollow sound. Gaitán believed that the *pueblo* was no longer interested in what he called the"dead reality of form." Instead of "simply seeking refuge in harmonious rhetoric," he called for a dialogue of "facts and reality" that satisfied the new sensibility of the crowd.[33] Gaitán laced his oratory with references to the crowd's preoccupations—food, housing, and employment. The time was ripe for Gaitán to use oratory as a vehicle to express his own social and economic concerns.

Not surprisingly, then, Gaitán relied on oratory at the expense of written manifestoes. He spoke almost constantly. During the campaign, his *viernes culturales* at the Teatro Municipal became an institution. The *pueblo* with awesome regularity, filled the Teatro and the nearby streets that surrounded the Presidential Palace. According to the psychohistorian Mauro Torres, Gaitán's oratory was a "permanent dialogue . . . a live and permanent lesson for a *pueblo* that has no books and no teachers."[34] Gaitán's critics were not far off the mark when they accused the *caudillo* of believing that he would solve everything with his next oration.

The explicit dramatization of Gaitán's body was disconcerting. Through it Gaitán pointed to the open behavior of individuals who stood forthrightly behind their beliefs and actions. It contradicted the circumspect actions in defense of the status quo that the *convivialistas* hid behind the private-public distinction. Forms of bodily control were an integral part of the *convivialistas'* highly structured formality and the key to their separation from the *pueblo;* Gaitán's break was a conscious rebellion against the social boundaries that the elite maintained.[35] By sweating profusely, brashly baring his armpit, extending his arm into the air, and showing his teeth, Gaitán reminded his opponents of their own animality. He contradicted their belief in themselves as the expression of reason and spirit rising above physicality. Moreover, he heightened their sense of isolation as civilized, superior whites surrounded by primitive, animallike mestizos and Indians.

Gaitán's conscious informality encouraged an intimacy with the *pueblo* that the *convivialistas* sought by all means to avoid. His ability to be refined and calm during conversations held within the culture of *convivencia* confused them even more. Gaitán took them, at least conceptually, away from their ritualized roles. If Gaitán could behave responsibly at their level of discourse, only to return irresponsibly to the *pueblo* out on the street, then their own distance from the *pueblo* was not as safe as they might have hoped. Gaitán's body bridged the social worlds of the politicians and the *pueblo*.

Gaitán's physical presence was felt in other ways as well. The Gaitanistas introduced an unaccustomed violence into politics in the cities. When *El Tiempo* failed to mention Gaitán for weeks at a time, his followers would stone its windows in a late-night ritual that even the newspaper's writers and workers came to understand.[36] Front-page news of the incident was proof for the *convivialistas* that they faced uncontrollable mobs, but Gaitán's followers understood that their leader was determined not to be a traditional Liberal. Gaitán's followers drove Lleras Restrepo out of the campaign when they drowned out his speech one evening in the Teatro Municipal and followed him all the way home.[37] When Lleras quit, the Liberals attempted to oppose Gaitán with the always reluctant Darío Echandía, but he too dropped out of the race after strategically placed Gaitanistas at his rallies continually asked him aggressive questions.[38]

Only Gabriel Turbay persevered. As ambitious as Gaitán and as much of an outsider, Turbay began his own campaign when Gaitán had been on the hustings for almost a year. He too was met everywhere by hostile crowds of Gaitanistas that had to be disbanded by the police.[39] Without Lleras Restrepo or Echandía to fall back on, the Liberal leaders had little choice but to place their hopes on Turbay. Two outsiders divided the party: Gaitán, bent on changing it from the outside, and Turbay, bent on reforming it from within. The Liberals were hopelessly divided.

On July 23, 1945, three days after López resigned the presidency, the Liberal *jefes* met, according to custom, behind closed doors to make Turbay the official standard-bearer of the party. Not a single Gaitanista participated or was consulted in the deliberations, and a Gaitánista crowd intimidated the delegates as they made their way into the posh Teatro Colón.[40] After deciding on Turbay, the Liberals quickly settled on Lleras Camargo, López's loyal lieutenant, to fill the remaining fifteen months of López's term.

Entering the Household

Gaitán campaigned as a Liberal in defense of the central institutions of society. He could not count, however, on the machinery of the party and knew that he did not want to run the narrow and clientelist campaign that the party would impose on him. His success depended on his ability to mobilize the *pueblo* into new organizations and to make its presence continuously felt in the streets. He and his lieutenants painstakingly built a political infrastructure outside the traditional parties. It was rudimentary at best and depended entirely on the figure of Gaitán. Far removed from a modern institutionalized political party, the Gaitanistas constructed something that was nevertheless revolutionary. For the first time the *pueblo* was being brought into institutions that were not at the beck and call of the traditional leaders. Although tied to one man, the Gaitanista organizations could not be easily disbanded by politicians. The presidential campaign implied a mobilization that contradicted the traditional manner in which leaders brought their followers in and out of politics. This mobilization was filled with noise, music, parades, battle cries, and emotional slogans.

Gaitán's first act was to found his own weekly newspaper, for the established papers were hardly mentioning him, and he knew that he would have to build his own channels of communication with his followers. Gaitán called it *Jornada,* a term that could refer to a journal or a daily paper but, more important, meant a day's labor. Gaitán was expressing his dual role in society as well as his beliefs by tying the intellectual effort of producing a newspaper and leading a political movement to the daily labor that, he felt, lay at the heart of social order. He meant *Jornada* to be different from *El Tiempo* and *El Siglo*. He understood that the traditional Liberal and Conservative press was primarily designed to be a vehicle of cultural expression by which the *convivialistas* demonstrated their place in public life. He did not want to address the *convivialistas* so much as the *pueblo*. "We must call things by their name," he told Luis David Peña, the paper's first editor; "we cannot speak in euphemisms, nor deviate with useless words from the intention of our thought. The *pueblo* must be spoken to in direct language."[41] Gaitán did not enjoy writing, and did so rather poorly. Nonetheless, he supervised each issue carefully and ordered words and sometimes entire editorials changed.[42]

Other differences between *Jornada* and the *convivialistas'* papers lay in their ownership and distribution. Whereas *El Tiempo* belonged to Eduardo Santos, *El Espectador* to the Cano family, and *El Siglo* to Laureano Gómez, Gaitán did not have the capital to own his paper. *Jornada* was underwritten by voluntary contributions, small and large, from poor and middle-class followers. Thus, the success of the paper was tied to thousands of contributors who were the proud holders of bonds that established their credentials as bona fide members of the movement. With some legitimacy *Jornada* could bill itself as the "paper of the *pueblo*." Hundreds of Gaitanistas sold the paper aggressively on the streets and in the cafés and trolleys of Bogotá. They fanned out through the city loudly hawking the paper and walked into stores and offices, often disrupting business. They thought nothing of demanding that a passerby acquire a copy or, better still, make a substantial contribution. They walked in groups and rode the trolleys loudly commenting on the day's editorial. In cafés they read entire sections out loud, disturbing conversations at other tables.[43]

Ultimas Noticias, a radio program in Bogotá featuring Rómulo Guzmán, one of the most fervent Gaitanistas, tied the movement together throughout the country and spawned similar programs elsewhere. At midday thousands of Gaitán's followers would put down what they were doing to rejoice at Guzmán's deliberately vulgar and earthy tones. Guzmán became an extremely popular figure and a key member of the presidential campaign. His program was broadcast from loudspeakers blaring out from Gaitanista headquarters and roving trucks. Each midday the *convivialistas* cringed as they heard themselves lambasted with words they never imagined could be broadcast. There was no respite. When Guzmán fell silent, the loudspeakers around town would play a tape of one of Gaitán's latest speeches.[44] And when these fell silent, anonymous Gaitanistas sprang up on street corners to deliver impromptu orations much like those they had just heard.[45]

The Gaitanista campaign was set to popular music. This was perhaps its

most significant innovation, for it sidestepped the traditional discourse
between leaders and followers. Popular songs composed for López during the
Revolution on the March had not caught on. The Gaitanista songs were set to
the *porro*, a popular dance rhythm hardly known by the elite. *Porros* like "A
la carga," which was taken from one of Gaitán's battle cries, and "Jorge
Eliécer Gaitán" produced among followers a sense of solidarity that words
could not achieve.

These innovations in Colombian politics seem simple and commonplace.
Yet their implications cannot be overemphasized. Gaitán was reaching the
pueblo as no one had ever thought of doing. He did not have to call his
followers to a public plaza but could speak to them at work and during their
leisure moments. He entered their homes and became a part of their daily
lives. They gathered around the radio to listen to his programs and speeches
and danced to the music of the campaign. Guzmán's emotional news, Gaitán's
passionate oratory, and the romantic ideals that laced the *porros* engendered
ties between the leader and his followers that no other politician could match.
The *convivialistas* could feel the rules of the game shift beneath them.
Gaitanismo was everywhere, in places where public life had never been
before.

The campaign grew out of a small, loyal, largely clandestine band of men.
Known as the JEGA, after Gaitán's initials, its public life was the reverse of
Gaitán's: whenever he was safely placed in high office, the group virtually
disbanded; but whenever he fell from grace, the group rose up to keep him,
at least to some extent, in the limelight. Its members vividly recall their
exploits during the first months of the UNIR and the period just after Gaitán
was fired as mayor of Bogotá.[46] Their most heroic exploits and longest hours
of work, however, came as the presidential campaign was getting off the
ground.

The internal structure of the JEGA is revealing, for it mirrored Gaitán's
ideas on social organization and may even have been a microcosm of the type
of society he might have tried to bring about. According to Jorge Villaveces,
one of the first *jegos*, the organization's ideology sprang from Gaitán's statement in *Las ideas socialistas* that he was the enemy of poverty but not of
affluence. Thus, it comfortably included members of many social classes. As
Villaveces graphically expressed it, its members looked to a society in which
"as the matron wore jewels, the worker wore shoes; as the banker enjoyed his
country estate and automobile, the peasant had a clean home in the country
and a tractor to drive; as the industrialist educated his sons abroad, the sons of
artisans could attend the national universities."[47] In the JEGA men of learning
counted for more than workers, but each had his own valued role. It was
divided into six groups: intellectuals, businessmen, professionals and university students, workers (usually independent artisans), "popular captains," and

"heroic combatants."[48] Luis Eduardo Ricaurte, one of the first members, proudly remembered it as a brotherhood of selfless and passionately committed men led by "middle-class but well-bred" individuals who had not been accepted into the "high elite."[49] Workers like himself accepted a subordinate role. This inequality was openly recognized. Members went through different rites of initiation: intellectuals proved themselves through consistent advice to Gaitán and workers through long hours of postering, protecting their leader, and leading demonstrations. Each "won the position he deserved according to his value, culture, intelligence, and personal effort."[50] For Ricaurte this meant that each had to *cotizarse*, or make himself accountable to Gaitán as best he could.[51] The members of JEGA divided themselves according to longevity and intensity of effort into three groups, known as class A, B, and C, that transcended class background and occupation.[52]

In a surprisingly short time the campaign became a movement. In June 1945 José María Córdoba, a meticulous organizer who took great pleasure in knowing that Gaitán carefully reviewed most of the endless letters Córdoba sent to Gaitanistas all over the country,[53] reported that committees were in place in all departments except Nariño.[54] In just over a year the Gaitanistas had produced an infrastructure of national, regional, and local committees that rivaled those of the traditional parties, and were certainly much more active.

Gaitán had little to offer local politicians who volunteered to set up a Gaitanista cell in their community, thus going against the wishes of the Liberal party hierarchy. Even if some believed that Gaitán would accomplish what no other politician ever had and win, they were taking a significant risk. The fact that they could establish "Liberal Gaitanista" committees undoubtedly lent them some comfort, especially in those towns where no Liberal organization was in place. So too did the prestige they gained in their community by associating themselves with the maverick politician. Narrow and clientelistic political ambitions, however, played a smaller part in the Gaitanista movement than they did in the traditional parties. *Mística*, a belief in Gaitán, and pressure from below were more significant. A movement led by one man at the top developed from below.

Córdoba did what he could from Bogotá to encourage local leaders, writing to everyone, Liberal or Conservative, who offered support. Since the campaign was perennially short of money,[55] he continuously exhorted committees to raise their own funds, for they could expect little help from Bogotá.[56] He and Gaitán prompted local leaders to set up their own elections, insisting that only honest and reputable members of the community stand for them and that headquarters in Bogotá be informed of the results so that a roster could be kept and credentials sent to the victors. "This is a true democratic organization," Córdoba wrote to provincial leaders on March 22, 1945, "since the oligarchy does it the other way around, naming directors without consulting popular opinion."[57]

Gaitán understood that he was the glue holding the local committees together. He encouraged the *pueblo* to write directly to him, or to *Jornada*. The Gaitán Papers consist largely of letters and telegrams sent to him from all over Colombia. Gaitán conscientiously answered as many as possible. Although this was time-consuming and expensive, it was critical in promoting his bond with thousands of Colombians who had never met him. The impact as Gaitán's responses arrived at local postal or telegraph offices in small outlying communities can only be guessed at. Followers who suddenly enjoyed new prestige among friends and neighbors were not likely to change affiliation.

Gaitán traveled extensively. He was the first Colombian politician to make continuous use of the airplane, and his trips to communities both large and small were carefully staged. An advance party of five prominent leaders, usually headed by the labor expert Hernando Restrepo Botero, worked with local committees to produce the largest possible mass spectacle.[58] Days before, extra copies of *Jornada* were distributed along with recordings of Gaitán's speeches, and contacts were made with radio stations and photographers. The *caudillo's* visits were publicized through loudspeakers mounted on trucks. A festive atmosphere was created with flags, pictures of Gaitán, and the movement's songs.

The leader would characteristically stop on the outskirts of town to await the delegation of local notables who would escort him into town either by car or on horseback. Once there, Gaitán was greeted with fireworks, music, and large confetti-throwing crowds. Before meeting with leaders to discuss the issues facing the region and the state of the campaign, Gaitán addressed the crowd that invariably filled the central plaza. His speech varied little, but he did attempt to discuss the main problems affecting the local population.

Córdoba used the promise of a Gaitán visit as an incentive for local leaders to organize their community and solidify support. He informed them that the leader's presence could only be worthwhile if a well-defined organization added to his national prestige.[59] He exhorted followers to create committees in barrios, workplaces, and schools, or simply among friends and within women's groups. Córdoba chastized Gaitanistas in Girardot, where Gaitán had first been elected in 1923, for failing to build cells among newspaper and lottery vendors, shoeshine boys, and baggage carriers.[60] He regularly sent form letters to the communities Gaitán was to visit imploring them "not to waste the enthusiasm . . . but to keep the *pueblo* in a state of constant agitation after the *caudillo* has departed."[61] Finally, he requested committees to send accounts and photographs of the visit to *Jornada* and to use the occasion to have citizens send their endorsements to the newspaper.

Despite these efforts, however, the major emphasis was on Bogotá. Instead of looking to the countryside as he had during the UNIR period, Gaitán concentrated on the capital and other large cities. The change was more than a response to growing levels of urbanization and to the influence of the Liberal party among urban voters. It was only logical that, as a Liberal, he would organize his movement from the central stage in Bogotá, as did the *convivialistas*. Moreover, Gaitán had begun to realize, at least since his eight months as mayor of Bogotá, that much of his power resided in the city multitude and that his opponents could best be challenged with crowds that were close to where they performed the rituals of public life.

By early 1945 each working-class and middle-class barrio of the city had a local committee offering social services never before considered by the few Liberal and even fewer Conservative committees that sprang up around election time there. Gaitanista headquarters in the barrios became centers of political information and gathering places where bazaars, weddings, and first communion parties were held. They served as cultural centers and even, on occasion, temporary clinics.[62]

By September the city was ready to receive the largest influx of crowds in its history. The major efforts of the Gaitanistas in 1945 were aimed at staging a huge spectacle, a "week of passion" to be held in Bogotá from September 16 to 23.[63] It was designed to alter the face of politics and the character of public life. During the week over a thousand little-known provincial Gaitanista delegates gathered in Bogotá to nominate Gaitán for president in the first public, open-air convention in the nation's history. According to Córdoba, it was to "be the *pueblo* in all its classes that will come together . . . to tell the nation that the candidate for the presidency will not be the delegate and the prisoner of small cliques . . . but the direct representative [*personero*] of the popular will."[64]

Preparations started months in advance. The first letters were sent to committees on August 20, but in Bogotá the organization was by then already in full swing. Organizers were divided into two groups. The first met every day at noon in the Casa Gaitanista in downtown Bogotá to prepare for the convention itself. The other group saw to the activities that were to surround the convention.[65] Under Córdoba's direction local committees were instructed to elect delegates and to relay their names to Bogotá so that organizers in the city could prepare for their arrival. Delegations had to pay their own way but were received by neighborhood commissions that found them lodgings and made sure that they were comfortable in the big city. Córdoba made a point of asking committees to send along bands from their regions to demonstrate the national character of the movement and offer regional delegates a taste of their home areas. Although he encouraged the participation of bands from as far away as the northern and western coasts, most came from nearby Boyacá and Tolima.[66] The *cumbia* and other African-inspired rhythms did not reach the highlands of Bogotá.

The week of passion began on Sunday, September 16. Gaitán was acclaimed by 70,000 Bogotanos as he toured many of the lower-class barrios.[67] In each he made a short but impassioned appeal. His itinerary was carefully planned so that each barrio knew when the *caudillo* would appear and could organize its activities accordingly. At each stop Gaitán ate the food offered him, rejected the alcohol, and watched with barrio leaders and delegates as the *pueblo* enjoyed itself before him. He was invariably implored to stay longer than intended and eventually arrived at his childhood barrio of Egipto four hours behind schedule. It was nine o'clock, three hours after sunset, but the *pueblo*, 15,000 strong, was still waiting for him in the cold night wind.[68]

By September 21 *El Tiempo* was worrying about all this activity. In an editorial entitled "A Specter of Anarchy," it commented on the "commotion in both the Congress and the barrios," and the "multitudinous pressure" that could be felt everywhere. The editorialist wrote that Gaitanismo was an "antidemocratic attitude" in the spirit of Mussolini and Hitler and contradicted the open, Liberal "criteria of life." In the face of the crowd, the Liberal writer concluded that the nation stood to lose everything: "the direction [of the nation] cannot be subjected to the impetuous uncertainty of the impassioned multitude."[69]

The day before, Thursday, September 20, representatives from over a hundred barrios of Bogotá had participated in a two-hour motorcade through the central streets during the afternoon rush hour. Taxi, truck, and municipal and departmental bus drivers painted their vehicles with campaign slogans and the names of the participating barrios.[70] On Friday the labor unions of Bogotá, led by the workers of the municipal electrical company, demonstrated in honor of Gaitán in the Plaza de Bolívar. On Saturday night five thousand Gaitanistas, including the delegates to the convention, paralyzed traffic with a torchlight parade that wound its way around the Presidential Palace and the *capitolio* and down the Carrera 7.[71] The city was covered with over twenty thousand flags. Paraders were divided into groups of six hundred, each marcher carrying a torch that had been collected weeks before from railroad workers, who threw them from the moving trains to waiting Gaitanistas. Organizers used the tops and bottoms of garbage cans that they got from the Gaitanistas in the public works department to fashion the collars that protected their hands from the dripping kerosene.[72] On that night the *pueblo* took over the streets surrounding the public buildings, and the *convivialistas* stayed home behind the familiar walls of their lighted homes.[73]

On Sunday the convention began and ended on the streets of the city. From four strategic barrios four separate crowds moved upon the city at previously

Foto Lunga

The Gaitanista torchlight parade on the Calle Real, September 22, 1945.

determined times. One crowd gathered before the tombs of the popular Liberal *caudillos* Rafael Uribe Uribe and Benjamín Herrera to cloak the new movement with Liberal legitimacy.[74] Together, the crowds arrived at noon at the Circo de Santamaría, the bullring just north of the city center, chanting and singing the slogans and songs of the movement.

The Oration

As Gaitán walked through the central arches of the bullring, the historic schism between private and public life was being bridged in Colombia. The crowd of 40,000 had been waiting for him almost a full three hours.[75] They saw more than an august public figure walking to the center stage. They saw a man of the *pueblo* who had once been like themselves, but who had made good in society. Before them stood Gaitán, living proof that their hopes for a better life might someday become a reality. He entered the public arena not as a representative of abstract notions of reason, but as a man upon whom the *pueblo* could project its aspirations. Gaitán was impeccably dressed in a black double-breasted suit, with a coat draped over his arm and a hat in one hand. He was accompanied by his father, by Doña Amparo, his aristocratic-looking wife, and his wide-eyed young daughter, Gloria. Gaitán had brought his family to the crowning event of his life. No *convivialista* had ever done so before.

Gaitán's oration was the most innovative and meaningful of his public life.[76] Its power resided in his ability to establish a strong reciprocal bond between himself and the crowd.[77] It was couched in timeless philosophical concepts and sweeping historical generalizations. He spoke of morality, honesty, and decency in government, of the accountablility of leaders and the value of individuals. He was addressing the aspirations that people have felt throughout history and turning them into an acute and sensitive critique of the inner workings of *convivencia*. The words, images, and even the sentence structure he employed graphically exposed the formal style of politics that was the secret behind *convivencia* and, for Gaitán, the cause of its failure. Gaitán turned everything around and symbolically transformed his spectators into the actors of history.

The oration contrasted sharply with the surrounding euphoria. It was surprisingly sedate. Instead of the short, choppy declarative statements that Gaitán ordinarily used to heighten the emotions of the crowd, here he spoke in long, lyrical phrases. He did not employ aggressive slogans to involve himself in an emotional exchange with the *pueblo*, as he did in most of his campaign speeches. He ended, instead, on an unusual note. In place of his accustomed call to action, Gaitán appealed abstractly to God and the nation: "God knows," he exclaimed dramatically, "that Colombia deserves good luck. And He will not ignore the fact that all we ask for is the good luck of Colombia" (p. 406). When he finished he was not sweating and he was not hoarse.

The speech also lacked the biting criticism of the Liberals in power that was the major thrust of his barrio speeches. Not once did he mention traditional partisanship. Nor did he mention his opponents. By referring to them only impersonally as leaders, chiefs, functionaries, bureaucrats, and, at worst, oligarchs, he denied them a place on his stage and made their petty wrangling seem already a thing of the past. There was only one public figure on that stage: Gaitán.

Gaitán displayed a remarkable sensitivity to the feelings of the crowd. His somber tone fitted the historic moment that both he and his spectators were experiencing. He must have realized that the first popular convention to nominate its own presidential candidate was not the occasion for vulgarity or earthy language. For the crowd it was a momentous event that called for respect for the nation and the expression of high ideals.

Foto Lunga

Gaitán delivering the oration in the Plaza de Santamaría, September 23, 1945.

Gaitán touched on many familiar themes: society as an organism seeking equilibrium; the moral basis of society; the need to recover the ideals of the past; the positive role of private property; the ideal of meritocracy; and the corruption of traditional politics. These, of course, were Gaitán's most cherished themes. At that moment he must have believed that his own hopes were shared by those before him. He spoke a language that expressed those ideals and that his audience could easily understand. He did not use the idiom of class struggle before a crowd that did not see itself as a class. He talked to the *pueblo* about its struggle against an oligarchy. He discussed working people and how their human potential was being destroyed by professional politicians. His critique came from within the norms of the period and was based on the belief that they could and should be fulfilled. Gaitán and the crowd were both on the same historical level: the ideals of *convivencia* were still those that sparked the imagination.

Gaitán spoke directly to his audience, leaving no question about whom he was addressing. And he addressed them as never before. He used the formal second person plural, *vosotros*, that the *convivialistas* employed to address one another. Gaitán rarely used the formal construction in his barrio speeches. This time he offered the crowd the respect that leaders usually reserved for one another. An often repeated formula made his intentions clear: first he referred to the crowd, then to himself, and finally to both together, to "us" *nosotros*. "To *vosotros* . . . is denied . . . the right to be Liberals. We feel only contempt for that abusive pretense of the lords of decadence" (p. 403). At the end he identified outright with the crowd: "*Vosotros y yo . . .*" (p. 406).

Gaitán placed the crowd at the center of a world historical process that transcended the traditional parties in Colombia. "It just so happens that our *pueblo* has the ability to think and to criticize; it is a nucleus of great sensitivity to the notions of ethics and law" (p. 402). They had gathered that afternoon, he told his listeners, to protest against the corruption and immorality that arose inevitably all over the world when leaders removed themselves from their followers and became "drunk with power." This, he exclaimed, "constitutes an explanation of your [*vuestra*] presence, however fleeting, in this place to express your support for a movement that at the moment I lead, in the most vast and imposing political demonstration in the annals of the citizens of Colombia" (pp. 392–93).

The gathering, Gaitán proclaimed, was a response to the world-wide decline in morality that was spearheaded by European fascism, "the most deafening system of moral decomposition of our time." That decline was embodied in Colombia in the corruption of politicians with a sensuous desire for power, who treated the "state as booty in war," and in the "inadmissible marriage of politics and business" (p. 397). The decline in morality, which Gaitán saw as the "specific force of society . . . the most evident, real and concrete of all social realities," signaled the confusion that heralded the decline of civilization. For with the breakdown in the "norms of conduct" that taught the individual to respect the rights of others, harmony among men was lost. Inevitably, as the controllers of the state became rich and powerful, "the meritorious man of work . . . shunning the immorality of public life" allowed "those without merit to reach the top" (p. 396). In this chaos everything appeared to be as it was not. Leading politicians, whom Gaitán characterized as "satisfied possessors of the public purse," appeared as "captains of revolution"; "agents of reaction" came across as "men of action" (p. 397). Thus, he and his followers declared their responsibility to do "exactly the opposite" of what was taking place. Gaitán proposed a struggle for decency, a politics of sincerity, truth, and virtue, all attributes more personal than they are political (p. 398).

Gaitán developed an imaginative critique of *convivencia*. The confusion of the times made possible, he said, the most salient feature of politics in Colombia: the "mountain of abstract concepts" that masked reality (p. 402). Instead of producing real accomplishments, politics had turned into a "simple description of projects" (p. 401); rather than actual results, there was much "verbal effort" (p. 400); the reality of daily life was transformed into a "verbal simulation" (p. 401); and, finally, the defense of the family was "much spoken about at the same time that public offices create the most scandalous propaganda stimulating alcoholism and gambling" (p. 397). Gaitán was talking about the very essence of *convivencia* and teaching his audience to be skeptical and to look for the hidden personal motivation behind public statements, for the real flesh-and-blood person behind the public image. He was undermining the safe distinction between public roles and private selves. "We cannot accept," he concluded, "the solidarity of our party with the . . . leading groups" (p. 402). If Gaitán had learned to distrust the *convivialistas*, so could the crowd.

A striking metaphor established the relationship between Gaitán and the crowd. "I do not believe in the messianic or providential destiny of men," he declared. "I believe that no matter how great an individual's qualities, he cannot make his passions, his thoughts, his determinations the passions, thoughts, and determinations of the collective soul. I believe that there does not exist, in either the past or the present, an individual capable of acting over the masses like the chisel of an artist. . . . The leader of great popular movements is he who possesses a great sensitivity, a plastic ability to capture . . . in a given moment the impulse that labors in the agitated depths of the collective soul, he who becomes converted into the antenna to which rise the demands for the moral, the just, and the beautiful in order there to find expression, later to return systematized to the bosom from which they emerged" (p. 393).

To the crowd it must have seemed that the *caudillo* was giving himself a secondary role. Yet Gaitán was asserting his leadership, no doubt because he deeply felt it, but also because he believed his followers needed him. If Gaitán had previously seen himself as the master of the "primitive" instincts of the crowd, the historic proportions of the spectacle he had organized may well have caused him to pause and feel that he was indeed sharing the stage with the crowd whose impulse he was receiving. The metaphor thus captured the intimate reciprocity of the leader and his followers.

It is difficult to gauge the effect of the oration on the crowd. Although none of the Gaitanistas I interviewed could have admitted absence from the bullring, it is dangerous to base conclusions about the deeper mood of the crowd on their proud individual statements. However, as the crowd took Gaitán into itself and carried him through the streets of Bogotá, it chanted an apparently spontaneous slogan that openly contradicted the formal and distant relationship between leaders and followers in *convivencia* and showed, at the very least, that Gaitán had established a firm bond with his listeners: *"Guste o no le guste, cuadre o no le cuadre, Gaitán será su padre"*—"Like it or not, agree or not, Gaitán shall be your father."[78] The slogan, moreover, demonstrated the crowd's willingness to impose that quasi-paternal relationship on others. Finally, it symbolized a conviction that the members of the crowd were young and immature in matters of history, but that they would learn and one day displace their aging father. The crowd felt a historic change taking place. As it left it chanted, *"En el Circo de Santamaría, murió la oligarquía"*—"In the Circo de Santamaría, the oligarchy has died."[79]

The Conservatives of *El Siglo* publicly savored the growing division within Liberal ranks and gave top billing to the Gaitianista convention throughout the second half of September. Most Liberals, on the other hand, hoped it would go away. According to the Conservative politician Azula Barrera, after the convention the Liberal press imposed a "dictatorship of silence" on the rebel.[80] *El Liberal* did not mention the convention at all, and *El Espectador* acknowledged it with only one picture. The nominally nonpartisan society paper, *Cromos*, also published only one picture. *El Tiempo*, as part of its ongoing attempt not to be baldly partisan, ran a front-page but deadpan story. The Liberal response appeared in editorials, which were more often read by party leaders than by the rank and file. The moderate *La Razón* captured the feelings of many Liberals and Conservatives when it wrote, "The Circo de Santamaría has always been used for barbaric spectacles like bullfighting and boxing. No place is more appropriate to launch the candidacy of Dr. Gaitán."[81]

El Tiempo officially sounded the alarm in its editorial the day after the convention. Calling it a "bizarre combination of the dramatic and the grotesque," the leading Liberal voice asserted that Gaitán represented a greater menace than the feared Conservative *caudillo* Laureano Gómez, for Gaitán attacked the Liberal regime while still claiming to be a Liberal, thus proving himself untrustworthy and unpredictable. According to the editorialist, the Liberal party faced a very serious problem: Gaitán's "doctrinaire *caudillismo*" would lead them down the path of personalistic arbitrariness, antidemocracy, and totalitarianism, all threats presumably not seen in Gómez. Gaitanismo had been taken over, *El Tiempo* concluded, by an avalanche of multitudes, by "instinct more than reason."[82]

In his first response to the convention, Calibán, taking a typically paternalistic tone, nostalgically remembered that "at first we treated Dr. Gaitán and his actions with little seriousness. His gray automobile and color-coordinated tie, his suit, shoes and hat, as well as his pretense—in addition to being a future presidential candidate—of being the best driver in Bogotá and surrounding towns, made us laugh." That casualness, Calibán concluded, was no longer possible. Nevertheless, he comforted himself by refusing to recognize the changes Gaitán was producing in politics: "Gaitán is practically alone. The small group of influential citizens that surround him lack prestige. Below him is only the popular and undisciplined mass."[83]

By the following day Calibán's fears had grown considerably. He recognized that Gaitán's politics was beyond the pale of *convivencia*, for the *caudillo's* popularity derived from his use of words: "Gaitán speaks to them [the *pueblo*] in a language that is easier to understand, and he addresses their passions and not their reason." Colombia's most respected journalist began to despair. "With the Gaitanistas in the Palace of the Presidents," he wrote, "none of the political and social foundations that have made this an amiable land, and have earned it the respect of our sister republics, would remain standing. . . . I could not live with the catastrophe."[84] On September 26 Calibán decided that the "victory of Gaitanismo would be the defeat of everything our forefathers fought for."[85] The *convivialistas* criticized Gaitán's convention as a mere spectacle of demagoguery that catered to the lowest impulses of the *pueblo* and made their own civilizing statesmanship of reason more difficult. It could be nothing but a fleeting, vulgar, and emotional spasm.

But for Gaitán the spectacle was everything, not so much because he was a demagogue as because he was a positivist with a notion of historical change. He believed that political and social life conditioned individual behavior and that a spectacle like the one he had fashioned could alter the *pueblo's* conception of itself. He also understood, of course, that the *convivialistas* feared the crowd, the reviled *chusma*, even more than they feared him, and that his own power was a measure of his ability to act in concert with the crowd. The convention was important precisely because Gaitán believed that the *pueblo* could learn from it and act accordingly.[86] Osorio Lizarazo aptly refers to Gaitán's stress on "theatricality" and his sense that it was "indispensable to also mobilize the fantasy" of the pueblo.[87] In an interview during the week of passion, Gaitán asserted that he wanted to provoke "a total change, creating a climate, an ambience, a totally different spiritual situation.[88] For Gaitán, playing to the public was the essence of politics.

Words as Weapons

After that memorable September afternoon, Gaitán's oratorical power was firmly established. His performance in nominating himself for the presidency gave him the confidence he needed in the arduous campaign that lay ahead. He became an orator who never doubted his rhetorical abilities and knew that his power resided in his words. Gaitán was not responsible for the prominent place of oratory in Colombian politics. He adopted a traditional practice to create a symbiotic relationship between himself and the crowd.

Gaitán understood that linguistic shock had a subversive quality in Colombia's highly verbal and formalistic culture. He was aware that the baroque and aristocratic texture of the *convivialistas'* orations intimidated barely literate audiences,[89] and he could sense the liberating effect of direct and popular forms of expression on those audiences. Yet his vulgarity was carefully measured. Gaitán was known as the "orator of the *mamola.*" The term, a rather mild expletive with a meaning similar to the verb "to chuck" in English, was personally insulting and physically aggressive. It was also a play on words and conjured up images of human and animal sucking. Gaitán used it, to the obvious delight of the crowd, every time the *convivialistas* intimated that he ought to lay his presidential aspirations to rest. The *convivialistas* were outraged and claimed that they would not permit their children to listen to him.

Tonality and intonation were important ingredients of Gaitán's oratory. Prolonging the vowels and crisply sounding the consonants of key expressions, he made the words fly out of the side of his mouth. "*Pueeeblooo,*" he intoned at the end of his speeches, "*¡aaa laa caargaa!*" ("Charge!"). Gaitán's heavy and growling delivery was in a marked contrast to the melodic, calm, and lyrical rhetoric of the *convivialistas.* He appealed to the emotional, subjective sensibilities of his audience. Although he was capable of delivering reasoned and logical arguments on technical subjects before select groups,[90] more often he spoke to fantasies that sparked the imagination of the crowd. To search for a clear line of argumentation in Gaitán's more political speeches is to misunderstand them. The orations were designed for dramatic effect, not intellectual consistency. He often returned to the same point, taking his listeners back and forth from one theme to another, reaching rapid conclusions, and supporting them much later or not at all.

Gaitán's speeches were filled with social and political content. His emotionalism and spontaneity and the simplicity of his words did not mean that he had thrust aside his ideology in order to transfix the crowd. Quite the contrary. His easily understandable phrases were a remarkably complete expression of his world view and a condensation of the ideas he had consistently held since writing *Las ideas socialistas* twenty years earlier. They also tellingly reflected his middle place in society. Few of Gaitán's slogans were his own, as his opponents quickly pointed out, but when they came from his mouth they held new meanings.

Gaitán's words require close attention. He played astutely on the contrasting worlds of the *convivialistas* and the *pueblo.* He was best known for popularizing the distinction between the *país político* and the *país nacional* and using it to demonstrate the distance that separated leaders from followers: the *convivialistas* inhabited the former, the *pueblo* the latter. But Gaitán reversed the places these two "countries" had for the *convivialistas*. The metaphor was also a synoptic expression of his class ideology, which pitted a small, unproductive and meritless elite against a large majority defined by its need and ability to work. Gaitán returned to his favorite organic image. He likened the *país político* to a putrefied organism whose head, voice, and tentacles were strangling the productive impulses of the *pueblo*. Politics, Gaitán said, was simply "mechanics, a game, a winning of elections, knowing who will be the minister, and not what the minister is going to do. It is plutocracy, contracts, bureaucracy, paperwork, the slow, tranquil usufruct of public office, while the public *pueblo* is conceived of as grazing land and not a place of work that contributes to the grandeur of the nation."[91]

Gaitán referred to the leaders of the *país político* as oligarchs, a term they used to accuse one another of the use of public office for private gain. Gaitán thereby added an economic dimension to his political critique of the *convivialistas*. As a result of the public corruption and nepotism that characterized the López regime, the term gained a particular bite during the war years. Coming from Gaitán, the accusation had an added sting. For Gaitán was an outsider, and he was using public office, if not for financial gain, for something much worse: to move from the bottom to the top of society. The crowds understood, on the other hand, that the leader used the term to refer to the system of decision making represented by the closed conversations of the *convivialistas* as well as the boardroom meetings of corporations, or, as Gaitán referred to them, "monopolies."[92]

Gaitán's slogan "*El pueblo es superior a sus dirigentes*" ("The *pueblo* is superior to its leaders") took the reversal to its logical conclusions.[93] It was the most far-reaching of all his slogans, for it pointed to an overturning of the social order. Gaitán threatened the leaders with what they most feared, an ochlocracy, and he offered his followers a democracy. This slogan seemed to take Gaitán back to the egalitarian spirit that was at the heart of *Las ideas socialistas* but did not fit comfortably with his more recent emphasis on the meritocratic ideal. Its significance should not be exaggerated. Gaitán did not repeat it often, and today it is hardly remembered by his followers.[94] He first developed the idea before a select group of medical doctors, whom he was careful to include in the *pueblo*. The slogan, reflecting his conviction that the leaders of Colombia were mediocre men, was a call for doctors, professionals, and technocrats to take an interest in politics.

The slogan is, nevertheless, consistent with Gaitán's habit of speaking highly of the *pueblo*. In an impromptu speech in Caracas, he went so far as to say that "we have learned to laugh at those decadent generations that see the multitudes of our tropics as beings of an inferior race."[95] And shortly after his speech to the physicians, he claimed that Gaitanismo was a "great movement of the Colombian race," and that the crowds on the streets "were exactly the opposite of anarchy," a "normal part of a true democracy."[96] In his oratory the feared *chusma* became the *"chusma heroica"* (the "heroic mob"), and the despised *"gleba"* became the *"gleba gloriosa"* (the "glorious glebe"). But Gaitán was not a demagogue who promised his followers the impossible. He was harsh and demanding of them, urging them to be honest, moral, and hardworking. He never promised them a reversal of the social order that would place them suddenly at the top, living a life of luxury at the expense of toiling politicians. He was too committed to social order, and too conscious of the dangers of such promises.

Gaitán did not believe, moreover, that followers were naturally superior or equal to their leaders. In the speech to the doctors, he explained what he meant by the superiority of the *pueblo*. He admitted that some individuals were able to excell on their own. But "with the multitude the phenomenon is different. . . . Separate, they are insignificant; together, they are the strong basis without which the apex does not exist. . . . If collective processes mediocratize the mind and reduce it, those same processes raise the minimal men and place them at the level of mindfulness."[97] Thus, Gaitán believed that participation in a cohesive and purposeful crowd could make individuals more social. The crowd could civilize the *pueblo*. He shared the *convivialistas'* hierarchical vision of society, but his vision of the social pyramid was broader.

Yet another masterfully crafted slogan—*"Yo no soy un hombre, soy un pueblo"* ("I am not a man, I am a *pueblo*")—reunited the two worlds that Gaitán had separated and reversed. He represented a new order with himself as head of the *país nacional*. The slogan contradicted the traditional distinction between private and public life. Gaitán was claiming to be an entirely public figure for reasons that were precisely the opposite of those of the *convivialistas*: they separated themselves from the *pueblo;* he was giving himself over to it. For his followers the slogan meant that their leader, a distinguished man with the character to challenge the *convivialistas*, was returning to the *pueblo* from which he had come.[98]

Gaitán's other major slogan, *"Por la restauración moral y democrática de la república"* ("Toward the moral and democratic restoration of the nation"), succinctly captured the elusive ideal of a return to a social order that the *convivialistas* had betrayed. It must have produced an intense feeling of racial isolation in the white elite, which saw any restoration, any return to the past, that was not led by them, as a return to the indigenous, pre-Hispanic origins of the nation.[99]

Even Gaitán's simple call to arms—*"A la carga"*—contained a meaning that is not readily apparent. The word *carga* also signifies a physical burden, a heavy weight to be carried. Every time Gaitán called the *pueblo* to action at the end of his orations, he was eliciting images of the daily world of labor. Gaitán ended most of his speeches by repeating these slogans. As the crowds grew accustomed to the ritual, he would call out, *"Pueblo,"* and the crowds responded: *"¡A la carga!" "¡Pueblo!" "¡Por la restauración moral y democrática de la república!" "¡Pueblo!" "¡A la victoria!" "¡Pueblo!" "¡Contra la oligarquía!"*

The power of Gaitán's oratory was not lost on the *convivialistas*. Azula Barrera wrote that he "was the first to speak to the national proletariat in direct language, creating an aggressive class consciousness without the obscure Marxist phraseology, and a more elevated concept of its own worth." Through Gaitán's oratory, the Conservative historian concluded, the poor realized "that behind politics there existed the zone of their rights, the real range of their economic aspirations, the concrete world of misery, and of their collective victory."[100] The Liberal politician Abelardo Forero Benavides could only agree. "He spoke [to the multitude] in a language that could be its own. . . . The boundary of the theater was transposed through the microphones into all the homes, shops, and attics."[101] According to the Conservative Mario Fernández de Soto, Gaitán's oratory did not win him a place in the Academy or the Atheneum. But his "power resided primarily in his extraordinary ability to create between himself and the masses who followed him a community of spirit and emotions and aspirations so intimate that [the crowd] delivered itself completely to him."[102] After the May 5, 1946, election, Calibán wrote that Gaitán was a "born *caudillo* of the multitudes. The cities consecrate him."[103]

Gaitán's oratory was a complete representation of the man. He stood above the crowd, demonstrating his prowess. He forged a unity with the *pueblo* to lead the nation to a new compromise, a balance between leaders and followers. He spoke proudly and passionately, for he believed that the warmth of emotion was as much the basis of society as was the cold reason of the *convivialistas*. And he revealed both his public and private selves, for he had nothing to hide. The new order would be built around individuals who stood up openly for their beliefs. Gaitán was like the corner grocer who stood proudly in front of his windows displaying the staples of daily life.

5

The Pressures of Power

Cursed are those in government who conceal behind kind words their irreverence for
. . . the *pueblo*, for they shall be marked with the finger of infamy in the pages of
history.

Jorge Eliécer Gaitán (1948)

Crisis Conversations

Success spelled trouble for Gaitán. Once they arrived, difficulties followed
him with disconcerting persistence. The more powerful he became within the
país político, the less room he had to maneuver and the harder it became to
maintain his ties to his followers.

By the end of 1945 the Liberals were in hopeless disarray. The *jefes* had
little choice but to rely on Gabriel Turbay to stop Gaitán. But Turbay was a
turco, as Colombians of Middle Eastern background were pejoratively
known. The son of poor Syrian-Lebanese immigrants, who had settled in
Bucaramanga just months before he was born in 1901, Turbay was the only
man left who was willing to endure the campaign. He had long coveted the
presidency.[1] When Olaya Herrera was selected as the Liberal presidential
candidate in 1930, Turbay quickly joined his campaign. Although Turbay
had been something of a radical in the late 1920s, during the election he
sought to represent the legitimacy of *convivencia*. He was rewarded first with
the Ministry of Foreign Relations and then with the Ministry of Interior. At
thirty, he was one of the youngest members of the government. He quickly
gained a reputation as one of the most capable of his generation. By the
mid-1940s he was a master of compromise. In 1943 he became the Colombian
ambassador to Washington, a position widely understood to be a prerequisite

for the presidency. Turbay did his utmost, in other words, to overcome his poor background and ethnic origin and to gain acceptance among the elite. One political commentator marveled at how well "this Arab" had adapted to Colombia's high society. He had friends in the highest circles and frequented the most exclusive clubs; he even enjoyed being photographed wearing knickers on the golf course.[2]

Turbay's chief lieutenant, Abelardo Forero Benavides, captured the differences between the two Liberal contenders: "Turbay was refined, subtle, imaginative, voluble. Gaitán was persistent, stubborn, tenacious, diligent. Turbay understood politics as an art of attraction, of the diplomatic handling of men, of parliamentary combinations and ingenious strategies. Gaitán always understood politics as a way of acting on the multitudes."[3]

Most of Turbay's Liberal colleagues could not bring themselves to campaign for him. Although Santos grudgingly backed him, he could only bemoan the Liberal standard-bearer's foreign name, Turbay Abounadar. "If only his name were Juan Ramírez," he exclaimed time and again.[4] López was not on speaking terms with Turbay, and the Conservatives were even more appalled by the prospect of a "foreigner" in the presidency. Guillermo León Valencia swore that they would wage a crusade "against the *turco* in a new battle of Lepant."[5] Juan Roca Lemus, an intransigent Conservative who wrote for *El Siglo*, remembered the 1946 election as a "battle between the Indian and the foreigner, the *antipatria*," and concluded that "the Indian [was] preferable, one hundred percent."[6]

Despite their deep apathy to both Turbay and Gaitán, Liberal leaders were convinced at the outset that their party could not lose the election. Although they were more seriously divided than at any time since 1930, the Conservatives had made no move to oppose them. The leaders were also confident that their official candidate would defeat the dissident. After all, no one had ever reached the presidency without an official party endorsement and the help of the party machine. The party stood to change little with Turbay as president, and the leaders could still exercise control and hope to recapture the highest office in 1950. Better still, the Liberal leaders could afford to remain on the margins of the contest as the two outsiders battled one another. The leaders only occasionally reminded Liberal voters that Turbay was the official candidate.

On March 23, 1946, just six weeks before the election, everything changed. Laureano Gómez adroitly manipulated the Conservative convention, which had had no intention of proclaiming a candidate, into nominating a moderate who, unlike himself, could be seen as a candidate of national conciliation. Mariano Ospina Pérez was a smiling, silver-haired patriarch from an affluent coffee-growing family that had already produced two presidents. The contrast between the Conservative candidate and the two Liberals could hardly have been greater. Ospina Pérez had first been nominated for the presidency in 1930 in an attempt to break the deadlock between Valencia and Vázquez Cobo. Now the roles were reversed, and Ospina Pérez appeared to be the ideal candidate to unite his party and defeat the divided Liberals. He was the closest that *convivencia* had come to producing an efficient technocrat. He held an engineering degree from Louisiana State University and was an expert in the production and distribution of coffee.[7] He also had many links to the leaders of the opposing party. Despite the acrimonious conflicts that had undermined *convivencia*, Ospina Pérez was on friendly terms with almost everyone. He had always taken nonpartisan positions and as director of the Federación Nacional de Cafeteros had earned the admiration of the leading Liberals. The Conservative candidate had more in common with López and Santos than either Turbay or Gaitán did. Ospina Pérez was the unofficial candidate of *convivencia* itself.

After sixteen years in power, the Liberals were suddenly staring defeat in the face. Gómez's coup sent the Liberals searching frantically for a quick solution to their problem. Since they had little or no influence with either candidate, their only hope was that the two ambitious men might resolve the issue on their own. Santos therefore set the stage for a conversation between them. *Convivencia* was resorting to its traditional and time-honored means of bargaining. Neither candidate could easily refuse the call for Liberal conciliation, even though they were placed in an awkward position. Turbay was implicitly acknowledging the legitimacy of Gaitán's claim to be running a Liberal campaign. Gaitán was participating in the conversations of which he was so critical. Moreover, Turbay was the official candidate, and it could hardly be presumed that a deal would lead to the victory of the dissident.

The conversations began on April 3. From the beginning it was obvious that Turbay had the advantage. Thus, he took a more active role, talking at length about their predicament, the traditions of the Liberal party, and his official endorsement. He compared himself with Gaitán, frankly stating that he felt he had more domestic and international experience. It was Turbay who had to draw up the arrangement that would unite the party around him, yet keep Gaitán satisfied and his followers placated.

Gaitán remained silent, leaving most of the talking to Julio Ortiz Márquez and Luis Eduardo Gacharná, who accompanied him on each of the three days. Gaitán lost his bargaining power as soon as he began to act within the norms of *convivencia*. Yet if it was Gaitán who had to resign, the mass movement he had created would now make it easier for Turbay to lay down his ambitions. On the first evening Gaitán addressed an unruly crowd that demanded to know what its leader was doing. Gaitán acknowledged that conversations were going on, but distinguished them from the "normal" conversations: "I have to tell you that it is true that we have initiated with Dr.

Turbay a series of conversations, but, as I have already said, our procedure has to be different and distinct, so that we are loyal to our followers."[8] Gaitán hoped to make these conversations different by talking about them in public.

The first day's talks ended on a hopeful note. The two men reached a tentative agreement, an antioligarchy pact, that they discussed further on the following afternoon: Turbay would become the sole candidate of the Liberal party, thereby defeating Ospina Pérez, and Gaitán would head the party and be first designate (vice-president) and the official, and equally unbeatable, presidential candidate in 1950.[9]

The conversations had all the outward appearances of calm rationality. Turbay informed the press that Gaitán was showing "sincere, patriotic concern";[10] Gaitán insisted that they "never ceased being cordial and honorable."[11] Ortiz Márquez asserted that the conversations were characterized "by the highest patriotism, within a climate of complete harmony, for it is logical to think that between individuals as eminent as Drs. Gaitán and Turbay, frictions or clashes could not develop."[12]

Both men produced the appropriate public acknowledgements. Turbay told *El Tiempo*, for example, that Gaitán had expressed his willingness to resign if his action "would be sufficient to produce a vigorous national campaign capable of ensuring a victory."[13] Gaitán agreed. He publicly acknowledged his willingness to withdraw "on the condition that I am shown that the political outcome of my resignation would produce . . . a definitive battle against the candidate of the Conservative party."[14]

The pressures from the crowd and from the politicians, however, were too much for the conversations. Gaitán's followers made his position next to impossible, while the Liberal leaders undercut Turbay. The crowd that confronted Gaitán convinced him that his resignation might cost him dearly. Ortiz Márquez admitted as much. "I must confess that the unease we found . . . at the remote possibility that unity might be produced around someone other than Gaitán took from us much of the justified optimism that had comforted us after the first day."[15] Gacharná expressed his fear of the followers' reaction should Gaitán withdraw. On the third and last day of the talks, Ortiz Márquez drove the point home. "We are facing a social revolution, and the leader of that revolution is Gaitán. And revolutions are not susceptible to pacts. Gaitán is a political fact . . . and even he may not be able to control the movement he leads."[16]

The Liberal bosses reacted angrily, for they were facing a coup. What else they could possibly have expected from these conversations is unclear. Santos informed Turbay that he would no longer be able to support him if he agreed to the deal, and López asserted that he would not back either man for the presidency.[17] López was convinced that unless the party settled on Santos as a compromise, "the decision [of the voters] will be adverse."[18] But the Santos candidacy was clearly impossible, for neither Turbay nor Gaitán would bow to him, and a three-man race would only compound the problem. López, not modifying his opposition to both outsiders, lent his unspoken support to the candidate of the opposition.[19] The Liberals were in worse shape than before.

Gaitán's reaction was predictable. He felt that he had been manipulated. He had entered the conversations in good faith, expressed his willingness to compromise, and been undercut by López and Santos. He had nothing to show for his efforts. On April 8, two days after the conversations ended, he went to the Teatro Municipal to rebuild his ties with the *pueblo*. "Here there can no longer be any conversations," he screamed. In a breathless, confused, and directionless speech, the *caudillo* lambasted "all those cold people, all those who lack the tremendous rush of life, of history, and of the life of passion, the calculating chessplayers" of politics. "Why is my sincerity being played with in this manner?" he pleaded. "Why is my tolerance shrewdly exploited one day to seduce me into a compromise only to provoke me into intransigence thereafter . . . ?" Gaitán claimed that he had never been a party to the antioligarchy pact, because he knew that it would have irreparably divided the Liberal party.[20]

Smitten by the politicians, he turned to his followers. "I do not believe you are inferior," he told them. "We feel proud of this old, indigenous race and hate the oligarchs who ignore us." He invited them to join his crusade to change the "political customs" of the land. "I swear to you," he concluded, "that in the moment of danger, when the call to battle has been proclaimed, I shall not remain in my library. Know that at the signal of the battle I will be present in the streets leading you [*vosotros*]."[21]

Victory in Defeat

The Liberals muddled through. There was little they could do except rally around their official candidate and hope that few Liberals would vote for the dissident. Turbay remained confident of victory until the very end. He ran a lackluster, formal campaign, spent much of his time with the party bosses, and did not attempt to match Gaitán's gigantic spectacles. Despite their deep pessimism, the Liberal leaders did what they were accustomed to doing in the best of times. They relied on the traditional legitimacy of Liberalism and on the ability of the party to get out the vote.

All the Liberal leaders except López, who remained conspicuously silent, spoke of Turbay's victory. But their words revealed their discomfort. "Genuine Liberalism," Calibán wrote on April 10, "has no other choice but to firmly support Dr. Gabriel Turbay" in the face of the "dangerous fascist who

A Gaitanista campaign rally in the Plaza de Bolívar, April 1946.

is followed by a heterogeneous mass."[22] On April 16 Juan Lozano called on all Liberals to back Turbay.[23] *El Tiempo* reported that the CTC, the largest labor federation, also favored him.[24] So too did the Communist party, alleging that Gaitán was a "dangerous personalistic adventurer with fascist overtones."[25] Just before the election, Santos reiterated his position in stronger, but still reserved, terms. "I am a Liberal," he wrote, "and as a Liberal I see that Dr. Turbay defends and holds Liberal doctrines. . . . the Turbay candidacy is the only one capable at this time of defeating the Conservative reaction."[26] The Liberal press told its readers that a vote for Gaitán was a vote for the Conservatives, and *El Tiempo* played up the few alliances there were between Gaitanistas and provincial Conservatives.[27]

For the Liberal leaders as well as the Conservatives, the Gaitanista threat to *convivencia* must have dimmed considerably. Nevertheless, the dissident's noisy campaign caused both to coalesce around their old ideas and point to

Gaitán as the outsider. The Liberals initiated a series of traditional conferences on the state of the nation. They were held in the Teatro Municipal, with
Gaitán pointedly excluded. In addition, the *convivialistas* demonstrated to
themselves and their followers, that they stood on common ground. On April
13 Turbay and Ospina Pérez met for a highly publicized interview in the
Jockey Club, the one building in Bogotá to which Gaitán did not have free
access.[28] On May 3 the leaders of both parties met there again. *El Tiempo*
published a large photograph of the occasion, with Turbay flanked by his
most trusted assistants, Abelardo Forero Benavides and Germán Zea
Hernández, and accompanied by Ospina Pérez as well as Laureano Gómez,
his son Alvaro Gómez Hurtado, Juan Uribe Cualla, and Luis Ignacio Andrade.
As though the point were not obvious, *El Tiempo* published another picture
of the *convivialistas* at the Jockey Club above one of Gaitán walking through
the streets of Bogotá.[29]

The end of the campaign came four days before the election. On April 30
Calibán sat back and wrote, "Thank God the speeches of electoral propaganda that were raising the political temperature are over. With an emotional
and sentimental *pueblo* like ours, it is great mistake to hurl sparks upon an
inflammable multitude."[30] On election eve the three candidates delivered
calm and measured radio speeches, calling on their followers to respect the
law and the traditions of the parties. When election day came and went
without major commotion, the *convivialistas* exulted at the *pueblo's* demonstration of civic culture.[31] A respite from the most intense political campaigning the *convivialistas* had ever witnessed was now possible.

Most were surprised at some aspect of the electoral results. Ospina Pérez
won with 565,260 votes. Turbay came in second with 440,591. Gaitán trailed
with 358,957. Turbay, deeply depressed, went into voluntary exile in Paris,
where he died in his hotel room scarcely a year and a half later. The Gaitanistas were also shocked. Ortiz Márquez recalled that they "knew beforehand
that Ospina would defeat us. But it never crossed our minds that Turbay, the
candidate who addressed empty plazas, would beat Gaitán by more than a
hundred thousand votes."[32] For the Gaitanistas the results were a sobering
reminder of the power of the Liberal party to get out the vote. Liberal leaders
acknowledged that their optimism had been a sham. One day after the election, Calibán admitted that "we went into the disaster with our eyes open."[33]
But he was surprised that Gaitán had done so well. He had won in every major urban center except Medellín, Ospina Pérez's traditionally Conservative
hometown.[34] "Gaitán," Calibán wrote, "showed incredibly surprising
strength," and he recognized the predicament of the Liberal party, for the
dissident was "the master of the urban masses," without which "Liberalism
cannot return to power."[35]

Most surprised of all, possibly, were Gaitán's followers. What they had experienced was so new and different, so apparently inevitable and historic, that the defeat seemed impossible. They could not understand how the power they had felt had produced such meager results.[36] Dumbfounded and confused, they took to the streets to demand that the election of a Conservative with fewer votes than both Liberals be set aside. Believing that the Liberal division had been orchestrated by the leaders to stop Gaitán, they stoned party headquarters. They demanded that their leader reject the election results, and Gaitán's lieutenants even considered a coup.[37] The crowd paralyzed the city. The Calle Real was full, while the government offices were empty.[38] There was little government in Bogotá as the Liberal leaders realized that their sixteen years in power had come to an end. Many remembered the day as one in which a coup would have been easy.[39]

Gaitán did not appear to be either angry or upset. Nor did he seem overly surprised, or even disappointed. Instead, he acted relieved. The Conservative victory allowed him to remain in the middle between a minority government he could easily oppose and the *pueblo* he could still represent. With the Conservatives in power, he could take over the Liberal party in opposition. In the Liberal defeat, he saw his own victory. It is not surprising that he interpreted the election results as a mandate to take over the Liberal party. Immediately after the election, Córdoba and his new assistant, Alvaro Ayala, acting in the name of the National Liberal Directorate, telegraphed local Gaitanista committees to acknowledge the Conservative victory. Córdoba ordered the post office to reroute all mail for the Liberal Party to the Gaitanista offices.[40]

Those who awaited Gaitán did not hear from him. He was nowhere to be found. He remained silent, legitimizing the results and remaining within *convivencia*. The difference between his reaction to the election and that of the crowd foretold the difficulties he would encounter reconciling his dual roles as *caudillo* and *civilista*. He was moving too close to traditional power to easily retain his ties to the *pueblo*. After the election the conversations of *convivencia* would be a constant part of his life.

Gaitán waited still another day to make his first major address. More explicitly than ever, his words revealed the conflicting roles he was playing. He called for order, recognizing the Conservative victory and reiterating his commitment to the nation's institutions; he threatened to create anarchy and mob rule if his followers were not granted due respect and if the Conservatives used their victory to replace Liberals in the state bureaucracy. He kept his followers at bay, arguing that the defeat had been a victory, for the battle could now begin. Finally, he let both sides know that he alone held society together, that he represented public order, and that he could have unleashed civil war right after the election.[41] Later Gaitán would recall that "I could have made a revolution on May 6, 1946, when I had a Liberalism embittered by defeat in the palm of my hand. I did not do it because we would have handed the nation over to anarchy."[42] The fact that Gaitán could threaten the *convivialistas* with an unarmed and largely unorganized crowd is in itself an indication of their fear.

It was also tenuous ground on which to build an independent position. Gaitán faced increased pressures to become a responsible member of the political elite. The demands were many. He had to seek Liberal unity without being engulfed by the traditional leaders; please the crowd by attacking the politicians, yet work closely with the Liberals in Congress and elsewhere who sought his leadership; continue to announce the bankruptcy of *convivencia* while working with congressional leaders on an alternative to Ospina Pérez's program; and criticize the Conservatives and still collaborate with them in their proposed government of National Union. There were too many conflicting roles to play. A successful Liberal legislative progam might mean that *convivencia* actually worked; no program at all would undermine his leadership in Congress. Cooperation with members of the opposing party might make the *pueblo* suspect his motives, but too strong an attack might reduce his ability to challenge them within the established rules.

The *convivalistas* now understood that they had to deal with Gaitán as one of the party leaders. At first his old opponents tried to curb their criticism. They urged him to modify his stridency and spoke highly of his sudden serenity and respect for law. He was encouraged to accept their belief that no oligarchy existed, "that to attack the Colombian elite . . . is to attack democracy." They sought to convince him that decisions of state had to be made at the top, not in the public plaza, for the *pueblo* could not reach decisions on its own. The future, they said, coming close to Gaitán's own meritocratic ideal, lay in educating the *pueblo* and "choosing the best and most able."[43] In bringing Gaitán into the fold, the Liberals appeared ready to open *convivencia* a little to accommodate Gaitán's aspirations and followers.

The Liberals worked to reunite the party along the old lines. "Simple unity is enough," Calibán wrote on May 9. All that was necessary, he intimated, was for Gaitán to accept Liberalism without all the hoopla that had surrounded his campaign. He decried Gaitán's "*mística*, discipline, organization," and told him that it was not necessary "to wake up at the crack of dawn, abandon one's profession," and travel all over the country.[44] Although he liked Gaitán very much, he concluded, the *caudillo* would do himself and the Liberals a lot of good if he would just recover his sense of humor.[45] The message was clear: abandon the politics of the public plaza, return to the conference halls, leave the followers behind.

Gaitán tried to stay outside those conference halls, yet keep their doors ajar.

During the following months he met many times with Liberal leaders, including López and Santos, in attempts to build a common platform and electoral strategy for the March 1947 elections. In December his name was mentioned as a possible first designate,[46] but he rejected the idea, no doubt feeling that the relatively powerless post would unduly compromise him, as had happened before in the Olaya Herrera government. Instead, he invited the Liberals to join him in preparing an open convention like the one that had nominated him for the presidency in 1945. Understandably, the party leaders rejected the idea, and Lleras Restrepo proposed a closed convention that would guarantee the old leaders a majority.

For Gaitán the convention was a critical issue that transcended his own immediate survival. A closed convention ensured that the political customs of the elite would not change. It signified the continuing chasm between the *país político* and the *país nacional,* with the *pueblo* as a passive spectator in national life. Without the participation of the *pueblo,* meritorious individuals could not be tapped for leadership positions and pride could not be instilled among the followers. Having expanded political space so dramatically during his campaign, Gaitán was not about to allow a return to the private rule of the few. For the Liberal leaders the issue was no less important. Not only would Gaitán undoubtedly put them to shame in an open spectacle, but such a convention violated the norms of public life as they understood them. It would have a vulgarizing, demeaning effect and would offer the *pueblo* at least a nominal role in deciding who belonged in public life.

The Liberals thus remained as divided after the election as before. Gaitán pursued his plans for a popular convention in January 1947 to nominate the Liberal candidates for the March congressional elections, and the Liberal leaders appointed their most respected figure, Eduardo Santos, as their official candidate.[47] This time the Liberals were determined to win. They regained some of the drive that they had lost with Turbay. Santos invited Luis López de Mesa, from the right wing of the party, and Darío Echandía and Adán Arriaga Andrade, two leaders with ties to labor, to join him in a vigorous campaign.[48] The Liberals were confident that they would finally deal Gaitán a well-deserved defeat.

Gaitán's relationship with the Conservatives after the election was no less conflict-ridden, and it revolved around equally essential issues of public life. Ospina Pérez began his presidency by promising to avoid the violent Conservative reconquest that most Liberals feared. "I shall be a president of Colombia," he declared in his inaugural address on August 7. "I did not come to power to serve the interests of one party, but those of the entire nation. In my government," he went on, "will participate the most respectable and capable men of the diverse tendencies that divide public opinion."[49] He promised a government of National Union. Since the Liberals still had a majority in

Congress, controlled most departmental assemblies, and held local power in many municipalities, to promise otherwise would have been folly.

Ospina Pérez and Gaitán met prior to the inauguration. Gaitán was impressed by the president's knowledge and apparent good will and surprised by how little they disagreed. Gaitán informed Azula Barrera, Ospina Pérez's private secretary, that their conversation should have been made public so that the "nation would be informed about how two political adversaries . . . talk about what ought to be done for the benefit of the nation." It is curious, he added, "what happens in our country. Many of the men of both parties profess the same ideas, but on the street we destroy one another struggling for the same proposals."[50] Afterwards he went to the Teatro Municipal to make public his conversation with the president-elect.

Despite this promising start, however, the two men could not reach agreement. Both believed that "party governments" led to the clientelism and corruption that had characterized the latter years of Liberal rule. For Ospina Pérez the solution lay in inviting the most capable leaders of both parties to join the government, and he asked Gaitán for a list of such individuals from the Liberal party. What he was proposing however, was a government of Liberals and Conservatives rather than a coalition of the parties. Serving at his behest, the Liberals would be responsible to him. It was an idea that fitted well within the norms of public life. The cabinet would be composed of politicians who were responsible to neither their party, their ideological positions, nor their constituencies. They would be free to pursue public life.

Gaitán did not like the idea at all. He demanded a coalition in which Liberals would be accountable to the party and a politics based on programs and ideology, party discipline, and the accountability of the leaders to the *pueblo*.[51] Ospina Pérez's suggestion came from within the *país político*. Gaitán insisted that ties be promoted with the *país nacional*. The president prevailed.

The pressures on Gaitán made themselves acutely felt during a wave of strikes and riots in October and November in Bogotá, Cali, and Barrancabermeja, the nation's petroleum center.[52] Partly because of his customary remoteness from the workers and the CTC, Gaitán had not been involved in the planning of the strikes, which were a response to Ospina Pérez's monetarist economic policies aimed at curtailing inflation through reduced government spending and a decrease in real wages. On October 31 Ospina Pérez ordered the military to repress the riots in Bogotá and placed Cali under military control. In the ensuing conflict one worker was killed.

Gaitán remained aloof. He had just undergone an appendectomy and was convalescing in the hospital. From there he issued no statements to the strikers, although he likened the government's action to the brutal repression of the banana workers' strike of 1929. During the crisis the president called leading Liberals and Conservatives to the Presidential Palace. Gaitán reported that he would try to go to the *palacio* or would send someone in his place. He did neither.[53]

The working class was not at the forefront of Gaitán's struggle. Perhaps it was too small to warrant more of his attention, or too closely tied to López's reforms of ten years before. It may well have been that he considered the workers' demands too narrowly economic, whereas his concerns were more broadly social and cultural. He seemed more comfortable speaking to the individuals of the *pueblo* than to workers in organized unions. His discourse remained primarily moral.

The strikes produced the first of many cabinet crises. The Liberals who had joined the government feared that they would be blamed for the clampdown on workers and asked for the opinion of their congressional colleagues. Parmenio Cárdenas, speaking for Gaitán, responded that there was little the Liberal party could say, for they had joined the cabinet, over Gaitán's objections, as public figures and not as official representatives of the party.[54] They had little choice but to resign.

The Gaitanista movement was changing as the leader drew closer to power. Politicians who had previously opposed it sought to join the bandwagon. Established Liberals like Darío Samper, who had organized Turbay's campaign, along with Francisco José Chaux, Francisco de Paula Vargas, Parmenio Cárdenas, and Armando Solano swelled the ranks. Some joined out of conviction; others, out of expediency. Gaitán welcomed them. Older Gaitanistas complained bitterly, but to little avail. These new Gaitanistas were more like Gaitán than many of the workers and artisans he had previously gathered around him. They also more nearly represented the independent middle-sector groups around which Gaitán proposed to build a harmonious society.

Samper became the new editor of *Jornada*. Once he joined such writers as Jorge Padilla, Alejandro Vallejo, and Eduardo Caballero Calderón and the newspaper became a daily in January 1947, it began to resemble the traditional political press. Luis David Peña, the former editor, and Germán Arango Escobar, the manager, both quit.[55] The new editor attempted to turn *Jornada* into an intellectual voice to rival *El Tiempo*. Its pages were filled with accounts of art, philosophy, and the latest currents in Western thought, with reviews of ballets and theatrical pieces that few in the *pueblo* ever thought of attending and of books few would read. *Jornada* became an outlet for the more intellectual of the Gaitanistas.

Gaitán toned down his speeches. He continued to attack the *país político* and its oligarchs, but he also stressed the differences between the Liberal and Conservative parties. In one of his first speeches after the election, he explained that democracy could flourish only in a two-party system. 'Where there is not a party in government and a party in opposition, there cannot exist a true democracy." The two parties had to restrain one another, produce an equilibrium, and prevent the growth of totalitarianism.[56] But, he added, he did not believe in opposition for the sake of opposition, as did the old leaders, such as Santos and López. Party competiton had to be built on public platforms that would benefit the entire nation.[57]

Jorge Franklin, the famous caricaturist, captured Gaitán's duality on the cover of *Semana* on November 4, when the conflict in Cali had just begun to heat up. The *caudillo* was defined as "demagoguery, distrust, and prudence." On a background divided into light and dark sections, Franklin depicted a dark-skinned Gaitán, smiling maliciously, his eyes completely shut, his hair straightened with brilliantine but still standing on end. His wide-open mouth circled his entire face, which was supported by solid white pillars in place of teeth. The mouth was painted red. Finally, to symbolize Gaitán's ambivalence toward *convivencia*, he wore a stiff white collar and a large white bow tie, the formal attire of the political elite.[58]

Gaitán's popular convention in January 1947 was a repeat performance of its 1945 predecessor. Preparations had begun in April of the year before.[59] Delegates came from across the nation. It had all the pomp and ceremony, the music and the noise of the first. Gaitán's image was everywhere. The convention was again preceded by a torchlight parade through central streets. Gaitán toured the city's barrios. The week of the convention was named the "week of the reconquest of power." Gaitán spoke in the Circo de Santamaría and was carried through the streets of the city after his stirring speech, this time to the plush Teatro Colón, where Turbay had been nominated for the presidency two years before. There he met for three long days with the delegates to hammer out an election platform, the Plataforma del Colón.[60]

The convention offered the crowds little they had not experienced before. Gaitán's speech was little remembered. Rather than auguring a new dimension in politics, the convention was a confirmation of Gaitán's continuing popularity. It was his signal to the *pueblo* that he was still with them, that he was indeed different from the other politicians. It was an effort to keep the public world from shrinking back into the conference rooms.

The 1947 convention was, nevertheless, more formal than the first. *Semana* tried to make it appear that the delegates were no different from those of the *país político*.[61] It was organized into six commissions. The deliberations were elaborately staged. They began with salutes to Gaitán and to the Liberal *pueblo*. Next, a greeting was sent to the president of Venezuela. Gaitán's mother was honored, and a greeting was extended to his wife. Rómulo Guzmán, the popular Gaitanista radio broadcaster and now also a Gaitanista congressman, was lauded. The convention discussed at length and approved

GAITAN

Demagogia, desconfianza y prudencia.

Caricature of Gaitán. *Semana,* November 4, 1946.

a proposal condemning the traditional press for impugning the honor of the Gaitanistas.[62]

Gaitán's electoral program demonstrated that his ideas had changed little since he wrote *Las ideas socialistas* in 1924 and that the tensions that had characterized his ideology had been resolved in favor of its more moderate strains. Gaitán no longer spoke of the inherent contradictions between labor and capital, or about the need to harmonize the two by restructuring the workplace. He called for blending political and economic democracy.[63] He proposed a stronger state role in economic, social, educational, and cultural affairs to enhance an "egalitarian social harmony."[64] The platform appealed directly to the salaried middle classes by promising job security, a minimum wage tied to the cost of living, and the defense of the family as a basic moral institution of society.

The Liberals thus faced the *pueblo* in the March congressional elections as divided as ever. Both sides were confident of victory. Gaitán exulted at the continuing divisions, for he felt that they made easier his task of getting out the vote and maintaining discipline over his followers. "Divided," he exclaimed, "we will win."[65] He was right. The results left Santos's followers in shock. Gaitán soundly defeated the regular Liberals by 448,848 votes to 352,959. The Conservatives also increased their vote to 653,987. Gaitán had reversed the figures of the past election and now held a solid claim to being the *jefe único* of Liberalism. Heading the list for the Senate from the department of Cundinamarca, Gaitán defeated his archrival Lleras Restrepo by 32,780 votes to 9,671.[66]

Gaitán's victory was the breaking point of *convivencia*. The regular Liberals were stunned. They left public life behind, obviously convinced that Gaitán was unstoppable and determined not to share it with him. Of the major leaders only Echandía remained, reluctantly joining the Gaitanista ranks. With him came Plinio Mendoza Neira, who established a close relationship with Gaitán and kept open the channels of communication to the *convivialistas*. Eduardo Santos left for Paris, stating at the airport that he was "definitely" retiring from public life. Yet he challenged Gaitán to survive without the bosses, and gave him nine months to hang himself. In nine months he would be back.[67] López was living in New York, where he was Colombia's chief delegate to the United Nations. Lleras Camargo stayed on in Washington, where he was the director of the Pan American Union. Lleras Restrepo retired to private life and to a career as delegate to international conferences. Calibán's reaction was carefully understated. He acknowledged that "we can like Dr. Gaitán or not. . . . But we have to recognize that against everything we believed, he improved his position considerably."[68] Calibán stayed in Colombia but admitted that much had changed in his daily life and that he was forced to travel abroad more often than he wished.

Defeat in Victory

Gaitán's most impressive electoral victory further complicated his politics. Between the presidential election of 1946 and the congressional contest of 1947, his role as mediator had made it difficult for him to plan; now he hardly had time to think. By June he was the *jefe único*. He was responsible for the party's legislative program and its relationship with the Conservatives. Yet he did not have effective control over the party machinery. He had created a parallel structure but the old party remained largely intact. The old leaders, whether in Congress, private life, or abroad, continued to oppose him. The leader of Liberalism was still a dissident.

Most difficult of all, Gaitán was now responsible for the lives of Liberals in the countryside, who were increasingly forced to defend themselves against the onslaught of Conservatives encouraged by their leaders at both the national and the local levels. Ospina Pérez appeared unable to control the rank and file of his party. As reports of killings and persecutions reached the capital, nobody could doubt that the levels of *la Violencia* had increased dramatically since the Conservative electoral victory. By the end of the year partisan conflict had claimed almost 14,000 lives.[69] But there was little Gaitán could do. The more his party participated in government, the more it too was responsible for the partisanship that was proving so destructive.

The result was legislative paralysis. The Plan Gaitán, which called for an easing of credit to small producers and the increasing influence of the government in the Banco de la República in order to implement this policy, got nowhere in Congress.[70] Neither did most of the Conservative initiatives, for these were opposed by the Gaitanistas. A second result was an uncertain policy toward the president. Gaitán was caught in the crosswinds of his own party. Many of its leaders, old and new, obviously wanted to participate in the Ospina Pérez government. If he did not cooperate with the opposing party, Gaitán would have to offer an alternative. There was none within the legal parameters of *convivencia*. Yet Gaitán was fundamentally opposed to the personal collaboration upon which the president insisted. Thus, at times Gaitán authorized the presence of Liberals in the cabinet and at others he refused it, causing endless cabinet crises. Shortly after the March victory, he reversed his longstanding policy and allowed Liberals to be named by the president without being held accountable to the party. While he reiterated his belief in open, public participation, he also admitted that "if the Liberal ministers are called to the government because of their abilities and virtues, far from any political compromise, I have believed, and continue to do so, that any veto by the party would be out of place."[71]

Gaitán's new-found power also complicated his relationship with the new bipartisan cabinet. Ospina Pérez wisely acknowledged Gaitán's victory and named as ministers four Gaitanistas, Moisés Prieto, Delio Jaramillo Arbeláez, Francisco de Paula Vargas, and Pedro Eliseo Cruz. With his own men in the cabinet, Gaitán's ability to criticize the Conservatives was undermined. Even though Ospina Pérez had appointed the Gaitanistas, it was obvious that they were accountable to their leader as other Liberals were not and that Gaitán was therefore partly responsible for government policy.

Gaitán's relationship with organized labor also became more difficult. He again remained silent during the unsuccessful general strike called on May 13 by the CTC and its leader, Victor Julio Silva, a Gaitanista sympathizer. Journalists clamored to hear his views. On the evening of the strike, Gaitán promised a "sociological examination" of the situation in three days. What he produced was in fact a rambling and emotional three-hour speech in which he claimed that oligarchs would try to make him look irresponsible and subversive if he supported a strike against a government with Liberal ministers.[72] The strike, he concluded a week later, was "legal" and "just."[73]

Gaitán's effort to maintain his independent, middle position ended in September when he clearly overstepped the bounds of *convivencia* by launching a passionate and personal attack on the president for "illegally" importing tear gas from Panama on U.S. Air Force planes. This action, he charged, demonstrated Ospina Pérez's and the Conservative party's total disrespect for the poor and for the law. The president, he asserted, had betrayed the nation and should resign. Gaitán must have felt that public sentiment would back him up, and also that the tear gas threatened his power by discouraging crowds. The issue heated up rapidly because the president took the accusation as a personal affront and became convinced that Gaitán was an unscrupulous demagogue who would stop at nothing to ingratiate himself with the *pueblo.*[74]

The Liberal-dominated Congress quickly started an investigation, and it looked, momentarily, as if the government might fall. The investigation found, however, that the tear gas had been originally requested by Lleras Camargo during the preceding Liberal administration and that Ospina Pérez had only reactivated the request after the October riots.[75] The president, moreover, eloquently defended the use of tear gas as a humane way of handling Bogotá's unruly mobs. It had been transported in U.S. planes because the Colombian military lacked suitable facilities. His words reflected his sense that he had been deeply insulted by Gaitán. "I have been and will continue to be the president of Colombia for all Colombians. I shall bequeath to my sons the clean and honest name of my forebears and my burning love for Colombia."[76] Gaitán's reputation among politicians of both parties suffered. Moreover, Ospina Pérez and Gaitán did not speak to one another again. Gaitán's ties to the Conservative party had been cut.

After the October municipal election, the *convivialistas* were close to despair, for Gaitán's unequivocal victory in March was reconfirmed. With Gaitán at their head, the Liberals had again outpolled the Conservatives and captured every major city except Pasto. Gaitán's seemingly erratic leadership and wavering policies toward the Conservatives appeared to have no effect on his popularity. On December 19 Calibán wrote, "The way things are going, Dr. Gaitán will kill Liberalism, but without Dr. Gaitán, Liberalism dies. Why? For the simple reason that Gaitán has the masses. . . . We are therefore facing a tremendous dilemma."[77] Echandía came to the same realization. "Every time Gaitán sticks his foot into his mouth," he remarked graphically, "he has another 100,000 votes."[78] The old rules of *convivencia* no longer applied. By January 6 *El Siglo*, which had long acknowledged Gaitán's power in the city, had begun to fret over the *caudillo*'s drive to "disrupt the tranquility of our countryside," where the Conservatives' traditional power lay.[79] Finally, at the end of January, the idea of a Conservative-Liberal coalition against Gaitán made its way into print for the first time. *Semana* reported that worried Conservatives "were expressing in the intimacy of their own circles the need to oppose him with a coalition, with either a Conservative or a Liberal."[80]

That same month *Eco Nacional* called for a return to the principle of authority in the face of Gaitán's disobedient mob. "When authority loosens the reins, the anarchic instincts overflow, and chaos inexorably triumphs."[81] Far-right Conservatives called for a direct attack on Gaitán, who, they thought, represented either a "fascism of the left or a shameless socialism that does not dare confess its true name." While the traditional parties encompassed all classes, Gaitán preached class conflict and the hatred of the rich. Dialogue with such a movement was impossible, for reason could not deal with emotion. "A thesis can be refuted," the newspaper concluded, "but not a passion."[82]

Aspects of public and social life that the *convivialistas* had once taken for granted were now threatened. Their gathering places were no longer their own. The streets of Bogotá seemed strangely alien. The noise of the city bothered them. Even the radio and music sounded discordant. In August *Semana* was still describing the Jockey Club as a "moving example of *convivencia*. Citizens of all political parties arrive there . . . and comment on politics. . . . Education and good manners prevent outbursts of sectarian passion there . . . and gentlemen don't show their teeth."[83] By December the same weekly was reporting that the club was beginning to lose its character as a "somber conclave of the rich" thanks to the presence of "revolutionary" Gaitanistas.[84]

The *convivialistas*' nervousness could be seen elsewhere. On December 7 *El Tiempo* complained about the vulgarity of the *porro*, which the Gaitanistas had popularized and politicized. The presitigious daily objected to the obsession with food, particularly pork, in its lyrics. Some themes were not fit for respectable citizens.[85] Three weeks later *El Tiempo* urged its readers to turn to the simple, romantic, and joyful cadences of Christmas carols, the *villancicos*.[86] In March 1948 the governor of Cundinamarca ordered the police to stop the sale of *Jornada* on the streets of Bogotá because the shouts of its vendors distracted government employees from their duties.[87]

Gaitán's political use of the radio was also irritating.[88] On April 1, 1948, *El*

Liberal divided Colombia into two nations, much like the *país político* and the *país nacional*. Members of the former read the newspapers, while workers, peasants, and the middle classes listened to the radio.[89] *El Siglo* recognized that "in the most advanced systems of modernity . . . the radio waves are made for the malicious Indian."[90] They feared that the illiterate mass would not be able to judge the true meaning of Gaitán's words. Rómulo Guzmán's "outbursts of savagery" came under particular attack.[91] According to the Conservative politician Juan Uribe Cualla, Guzmán was "judged by those who do not know how to write, and listened to by those who do not know how to read."[92] *El Siglo* produced a long string of cartoons dramatizing the vulgarity and emotionalism of Gaitán's programs. In one a man wants to listen to Gaitán's radio speech, but wonders how to keep his children from hearing it. In another an aroused hospital patient accosts a nurse, who warns him that he should not listen to Gaitán's program (February 5, 1948).

The Conservatives attempted to counter Gaitán's "verbal barbarity" with their own program of "Colombian voices . . . a new house of spiritual, patriotic emotion" over Radio Nacional.[93] They played classical music and featured programs on the life and times of Goethe and Mozart as well as their own political commentary. The latter, delivered in a calm voice, usually emphasized the complex character of the economic and legislative policies of the Ospina Pérez government. In addition, the Conservatives often turned the airwaves over to the church.[94] At one point *Jornada* was led to comment that a "smell of the sacristy" emanated from the radio.[95]

At the end of 1947 *El Tiempo* dedicated an editorial to the subject. Radio, it said, represented the decadence of both the written and the spoken word, and thus of culture itself. Editorialists were used to measuring every word, and orators carefully considered their language. In the past, politicians were responsible because they could be held accountable. Radio broadcasters, on the other hand, were irresponsible. Hitler and Mussolini had used the radio to demagogic advantage. Unable to see their audience, broadcasters could say whatever they pleased. They worked in anonymity, whereas orators were like teachers before their pupils, or a doctor with his patients. Since "the mass of the *pueblo*, the man on the street, is but an atom lost in the multitude, radio changes democracy into ochlocracy, the rule of the mass."[96]

The *convivialistas* became acutely aware of Gaitán's many roles and of the confusion he was spreading in public life. *El Siglo* showed a Gaitán with two faces: that of an almost respectable politician, and that of a bear promoting subversion and *caudillismo* (November 15, 1947). In another cartoon Gaitán held up two books, entitled "Collaboration" and "Opposition" (October 24, 1947). In a third he donned masks of Hitler, Mussolini, and Stalin (see page 123). Rafael Azula Barrera saw Gaitán's ambiguity as a contradiction. "Gaitán's tremendous and fatal contradiction consisted in trying to utilize an

The many faces of Gaitán. *El Siglo*, February 29, 1948.

explosive rhetoric for simple electoral aims, because his caustic language, by affecting sick sensibilities, [pushed] the multitude toward direct action, and not to a civil solution at the polls."[97] In January 1948 Silvio Villegas called Gaitán's politics a "double game": on the one hand, responsible collaboration; on the other hand, personal attacks, civil resistance, and revolt. The time had come, said the one-time agitator, for Gaitán to choose between the cabinet and the street.[98]

The Decline of Public Life

Sensing that their public life was imperiled, the *convivialistas* shed their calm demeanor. They now openly displayed their racial ideas and belief in a society divided into social classes. There was nothing subtle about the new attack on Gaitán. The Conservatives, freer to express their minds about the opposition *caudillo*, led the way. *El Siglo* printed photographs of naked Indians armed for battle and labeled them Gaitanistas (January 22, 1948). Another cartoon depicted a black "Gaitanista tribe" knifing a white man to death (see page 125). In yet another, a fortune teller informs Gaitán that his future is black, the same as his skin color (August 4, 1947). The ridicule that had always been heaped on Gaitán for trying to join the elite private clubs intensified dramatically. The Gaitanistas' lack of culture, and therefore of class position, was represented by a domestic servant's refusal to wear the type of clothes that her Gaitanista employers owned (see page 126).

El Siglo lashed out against the "restorer" for having taken the Conservatives' own slogan from them. The Conservatives felt that he was in no position to restore anything, let alone the moral and democratic principles of the nation. They saw themselves as the true restorers of a moral and spiritual nationhood undermined by the freewheeling Liberals over the past sixteen years. *El Siglo's* attacks reflected their fear that a Gaitanista return to the past would lead back to the nation's indigenous and African roots and that this ideal motivated Gaitán's defense of the Colombian race. In their fear, the Conservatives did not bother to distinguish between blacks and mestizos.

Interior Minister José Antonio Montalvo also saw the choice as "*caudillismo* or political parties."[99] Gilberto Alzate Avendaño, writing in *Eco Nacional*, saw Gaitan's problem as racial: "This is a politics of *malicia indigena* confronting a politics of patriotic honesty."[100] Many of the elite attributed Gaitán's predicament to his inability to grasp the art of high politics. Liberals felt that Gaitán "knew how to speak in public. . . . But in private he did not know how to converse. He has no nuance and no delivery."[101] The Conservative politician Mario Fernández de Soto thought that Gaitán suffered from a "darkness of judgment characteristic of those who find in the problems of economic life the most important cause, the principal driving force, behind the development and organization of human societies."[102]

LA TRIBU GAITANISTA

The Gaitanista "tribe." *El Siglo*, January 17, 1948.

EL USO DE CIERTAS PRENDAS

"Don't worry, *señora*, those that you leave here and those that your husband left when he was elected with Dr. Gaitán are [clothing] we the decent people of Bogotá do not use."

Gaitanista clothing. *El Siglo*, January 4, 1948.

Gaitán never responded to these attacks. It may well be that, liberated by the presidential campaign, he was no longer bothered by criticism. He must also have sensed that the arrogance that the elite had previously shown toward him had been replaced by fear. The attacks therefore were proof of his power over them. Gaitán's close followers, however, were very much aware of the racial and class overtones of the criticism. Gaitán's biographer Osorio Lizarazo wrote that the press published "photographs of robbers and drunks, of petty delinquents and prostitutes" and described them as Gaitanistas.[103] José

María Córdoba wrote that the *convivialistas* were afraid that "the old Bogotá gentlemen would be replaced by the mob. . . . They saw the *ruana* invading the public plaza and the theaters," and traveled abroad as much as possible to escape the atmosphere of social revolution that Gaitán had produced.[104] Gaitán must also have realized that these personal attacks would only help him, for an attack on him was now also an attack on his followers. This was the main advantage that Gaitán derived from his middle position during this period. Nevertheless, his difficulties within the Liberal party were sufficient to make him consider sharing the leadership with Darío Echandía. He quickly changed his mind, however, when the Gaitanistas protested.

On February 7 Gaitán staged the most dramatic spectacle of his life, the Manifestación del Silencio. He needed to attack the regime, reassert his ties to the crowds, and at the same time do something to end the growing levels of *la Violencia* in the countryside. He could do little to stop the rural strife, which was fed largely by Conservatives using their power in Bogotá to run Liberals out of municipal offices in outlying areas. *La Violencia* quickly exceeded Bogotá's control. If anyone could have ordered a stop, it would have been the Conservative leaders. While the *convivialistas* blamed one another for *la Violencia* and sent out countless investigative commissions, Gaitán called his urban followers into the Plaza de Bolívar at dusk. At least one hundred thousand Bogotanos heeded his call. The crowd was ordered to wear black and to bring large black banners. It was to gather in complete silence as a sign of mourning for the dead of *la Violencia*. There were to be no cheers, and no songs. Gaitán wanted a "sacred silence" to produce unity within the crowd.[105]

Gaitán's lieutenants warned him that political passions were running too high for him to control the crowd.[106] But he insisted, citing the sociologist Gustav Le Bon's statement that the masses were "not an unconscious and irresponsible mass, difficult to control."[107] "I am the social order," he proudly asserted. It was his most disconcerting claim, pointing to his ability to keep the *país político* and the *país nacional* at peace while in the same breath warning of war.

Gaitán carefully inverted the liturgy of the public plaza. The words were few and somber. He spoke for scarcely five minutes, selecting each word with the utmost care. The multitude became an active participant in the demonstration, expressing its collective voice in its silence. Gaitán's speech was filled with religious language. He did not speak to the *convivialistas* through the crowd. Instead, the crowd spoke through him to the politicians: "Señor Presidente Ospina Pérez. Under the weight of a profound emotion I address Your Excellency, interpreting the wishes and the will of this immense multitude that hides its burning heart, lacerated by so much injustice, under a clamorous silence, to ask that there be peace and mercy for the nation."[108]

Foto Lunga

Gaitán addressing the Manifestación del Silencio in the Plaza de Bolívar, February 7, 1948.

Gaitán held immense power at that moment. He could have ordered the crowd to surround every public building in the city, or even attack the *palacio*, scarcely three blocks away. Or he could have ordered it to stay in the plaza until the Conservative regime responded to the call for peace. There was not much the police or the military could have done. Instead, Gaitán demonstrated yet again his respect for law and did the most powerful and disconcerting thing of all: he ordered the crowd home.

Gaitán's ability to bring his followers to life and make them disappear again inspired more fear in the *convivialistas* than any violence or mob action could have. Gaitán had again performed unpredictably. With the display of collective discipline, he had proven that at that moment, at least, the *pueblo* was conscious and responsible, and thus a direct challenge to their public life. It was Gaitán who had made the *pueblo* what it now was, and he alone could control it. It is hardly surprising that many recall that evening as a revolutionary moment.[109] The response from the Liberal press was hushed. Only *El Siglo* retained its customary brashness. For the Conservative daily the

Bogotanos dressed in black and wielding black flags represented the "restoration of negritude in opposition to the whiteness of national peace."[110]

The convening of the Ninth Pan American Conference in Bogotá in early April brought the promise of relief to the beleaguered politicians. It would bring the U.S. Secretary of State, George Marshall, as well as the foreign ministers of all the American republics. The conference was an occasion of deep significance for the *convivialistas*. More than ever before, public life was the be-all and the end-all for those who had not emigrated from Colombia. Ospina Pérez named twelve politicians from both parties to represent Colombia as plenipotentiary ambassadors.

After Gaitán's public call for peace and Conservative accountability, the Liberals could hardly stay in the cabinet. Late in February they resigned under heavy pressure from their congressional colleagues. Could they still participate in the Pan American Conference if the Conservatives held power alone? The Liberals sent an official commission to the president to seek a resolution to this impasse. The commission, headed by Echandía, excluded Gaitán because his personal relations with Ospina Pérez were so strained.[111] The talks were unsuccessful, but none of the Liberal protagonists could adequately explain why or say whether they would resume the talks at a later date.[112] Ospina Pérez had put the Liberals off by insisting that their conversations had no official bearing and that the solution to the cabinet crisis lay with the congressional leaders of both parties, and not with a commission of Liberals and the Conservative president. For one reason or another, Ospina Pérez was delaying any possibility of an accord.

The Liberals had all resigned by sending the president courteous notes in which they lauded his work and informed him of the decision of their party; none of them resigned irrevocably. Thus, the final decision was left to the president. For a month they did not hear from him and remained at least nominally in their posts. Since they had all joined the cabinet of their own accord, rather than as the result of a party decision, it was unclear whether their resignations were effective if the president did not act on them. Domingo Esguerra, the minister of foreign relations, who had the most to gain from the coming meeting of international leaders, announced that he wanted to stay.[113] On March 17 Samuel Arango Reyes decided to formally return to his post.[114] It became obvious that the Liberals did not want to take "the trip into the desert," as *Semana* graphically termed their resignation.[115]

When *El Siglo* asked why the Liberals were still in the cabinet, *Jornada* responded, almost a month after the crisis began, that the president had not answered the letters of resignation, which, it stated, was "a matter of elemental courtesy."[116] On March 18 Gaitán finally declared that enough was enough. "It seems to me that the matter of [personal] loyalty to the president has been decorously met. The five Liberal ministers are gentlemen . . . to whom, at the very least, the president should have acknowledged receipt of their letters, which they wrote in courteous and respectful terms."[117] Gaitán called on them to leave their posts.

With the exception of Domingo Esguerra, who claimed that his decision to join the government had been a personal one, the Liberals resigned, this time irrevocably. On the next day the Liberal leader Julio César Turbay Ayala indignantly ordered Esguerra's letter to the party returned to him unanswered.[118] Gaitán's response was more graphic. He ordered his lieutenants to pelt Esguerra with rotten eggs in the streets of Bogotá. When the Gaitanistas got to him, he was with the Ecuadorian ambassador, making final preparations for the conference. The incident received much attention in the press. *El Tiempo* stated that the "attack destroyed Bogotá's tradition of culture."[119] *Jornada* reported it as a massive protest against government policies.[120] *El Tiempo* called on Gaitán to control his crowd: "It could be said that the public order in Bogotá depends on Dr. Gaitán, since he has more than 50,000 followers here."[121] Rebuffed by his party and publicly humiliated, Esquerra resigned.

Now the issue of participation in the conference became pressing. Echandía and Gaitán finally carried the day with their argument that domestic politics and international diplomacy were distinct realms of public life. When the Conservatives had been in power before 1930, they asserted, Liberals had taken up diplomatic posts, and the Liberals had named Conservatives to ambassadorial posts during their sixteen years in power. The two leaders argued that the nation's international reputation was at stake, and the Liberals could only help uphold it.[122]

It is difficult to overestimate the importance of the conference for the *convivialistas*. It was especially significant for the Conservatives. Through it they intended to recover the city from Gaitán and his followers. Thus, they began to prepare for the conference as soon as they came to power. The issues that would be discussed during the meeting of foreign dignitaries were important, but they paled into insignificance beside the need to bolster the public stage in Bogotá. The upcoming event had a special significance for Azula Barrera. In his mind it symbolized the return of Colombia to the center stage of continental diplomacy, a position that had been lost since the death of the Liberator Simón Bolívar.[123] But for no one was this more important than Laureano Gómez. He conceived an intense, personal interest in the preparations for the conference as soon as Ospina Pérez won the May 5, 1946, election. The Pan American Conference represented the superimposition of a new public life over a domestic one that was being vulgarized.

The Conservatives spared no expense in refurbishing the public stage and making themselves and their nation respectable in the eyes of the foreign dignitaries. New buildings were constructed and old ones refurbished and whitewashed. Hotels were remodeled. New streets were built. The *capitolio* was reconstructed the year before the conference so that it could serve as its headquarters. Meanwhile, congressmen met in cramped quarters in the national library. Boatloads of sleek German-built Mercedes Benz automobiles were imported. Four thousand white porcelain cups with the Colombian emblem were ordered from the House of Demevildre-Coche of Brussels, and three thousand pieces of crystal were acquired from the Parisian firm of Val. St. Lambert.[124] One of Gómez's pet projects was the construction of an opulent restaurant and dancing hall, the Venado de Oro, on the foothills overlooking the city. Billed as Bogotá's most modern construction, it stood in stark contrast to the slum dwellings that marked the slope along the Paseo Bolívar, which was finally paved to facilitate access to the restaurant. Outside stood a gold-plated figure of a deer. The restaurant, far removed from the center of the city, was seen by the Gaitanistas as a typical example of Conservative excess and disregard for the poor, and Gómez was soundly attacked. He, however, argued that the restaurant would serve as a sort of Jockey Club for common folks, *gente común*, who needed a decent place to go. Another of Gómez's pet projects met with less success. The huge, gaudy concrete balls that he had ordered constructed around the Plaza de Bolívar to hold the flags of the American nations were removed a few days before the conference began as a public eyesore.[125]

The government also strove to rid the city's streets of beggars and vagabonds. The acting commander of the police, Virgilio Barco, was ordered to direct the effort. By the time the conference began, more than three hundred older vagabonds and drifters had been picked up. The mayor, Fernando Mazuera Villegas, tried to get the street vendors off the streets. Stray dogs were ordered poisoned. In addition, the citizens of the city were urged to keep the front of their homes clean and tidy, to cut the grass, and to fix the sidewalks.[126]

The *jefe único* of Liberalism was the only political leader not named to any of the delegations to the conference. Many explanations were offered by both Liberals and Conservatives for Gaitán's exclusion. It was claimed that he had limited international experience. Nevertheless, everybody in Bogotá knew why Gaitán had been left out. As early as November of the preceding year, Gómez had complained that "Gaitán was the only Colombian who wanted to smear the conference" and to exhibit the Colombian people before the world as an "African horde."[127] Gaitán had argued for Liberal participation in the conference when he knew he would not participate. He remained completely silent about his exclusion. He was too proud a man to complain, and possibly too powerful to care. For his followers, however, it was a deep, personal insult. On April 9, one week into the conference, both Gaitán and his crowd were quiet as the world watched what was going on in Bogotá.

6

The Middle Ground Disappears

If I am killed, avenge me!

Jorge Eliécer Gaitán (1948)

¡Mataron a Gaitán!

Gaitán liked the streets of Bogotá. He found safety in public. When he walked out of his office, the shoeshine boys stood at attention. He knew many of them by name, and talked easily with the lottery vendors. Women waited to give him flowers. In his favorite café the waitress rushed to serve him. His 1947 dark-green Buick was easily recognized, and small crowds gathered around it. When Gaitán drove away, bystanders stopped to watch.

Gaitán enjoyed letting the *convivialistas* know that the streets were a natural place for him. "Many of my friends," he told his Conservative friend Rafael Azula Barrera, "tell me that this can, at times, be dangerous, given the political situation. But don't you think that I am the one Colombian who has a true life insurance policy? . . . I feel more secure in the streets," he added with obvious delight, "than anywhere else."[1]

Gaitán's safety, however, was always on his lieutenants' minds. People all over Bogotá talked openly about what a threat to the social order he was and how his behavior would get him into trouble. The possibility that he might be assassinated was common gossip. On December 21, 1947, *El Deber*, a Conservative Montería newspaper, called for the *caudillo's* elimination.[2] His lieutenants never stopped warning him, and the JEGA made elaborate plans to keep him surrounded. The Gaitanistas were especially concerned about the

Bogotá police and about Coronel Virgilio Barco, a shady character of Conservative leanings who was interim police chief in Bogotá.[3] The Liberal press objected to the *chulavitas*, the rural recruits from staunchly Conservative regions in Santander that the Conservative regime had brought to Bogotá to replace Liberal policemen.

Early in 1948 *Jornada* denounced the persecution of leading Gaitanistas by the police, who were increasingly referred to as the *popol*, the political police.[4] Barco later admitted that he had ordered plainclothes policemen to provoke Gaitanistas so that the police could disrupt their activities.[5] Even Judge Pedro P. Pérez Sotomayor of the Fifth Circuit Court in Bogotá warned the *caudillo* that anyone who wished to harm him could walk unchecked into his office.[6] Gaitán scoffed at the warnings and reproached his lieutenants when he discovered them following him.[7]

Protection would define Gaitán as a regular politician, not a man of the *pueblo*. Bodyguards would prevent easy and spontaneous contact with shoeshine boys, lottery vendors, and the matrons at the market. Gaitán felt that if he could not walk the streets of Bogotá, he did not represent the public order. So, ramrod stiff, carefully dressed and groomed, he walked proudly through the city. "I will not be killed," he told his most assiduous protector, *el coronel* Ricaurte. "If I am killed, not one stone will be left unturned."[8]

Bogotá was quiet at 1:00 p.m. on Friday, April 9.[9] A few cars and taxis and an occasional trolley car moved up the mile-long Calle Real from the Avenida Jiménez, the city's main intersection, past the new Ministry of Communications, the cathedral, and the *capitolio*, where both the Senate and the House met, to the Presidential Palace. Lottery vendors awaited the afternoon crowds. Outside Gaitán's office on the Calle Real, a few feet from the Avenida Jiménez, shoeshine boys discussed the leader's successful court defense of an army lieutenant who had killed a journalist.[10] The shops and banks were closed for the midday break, and the municipal employees were lunching and napping at home. The Pan American Conference held no plenary session that day. The city's main restaurants, the Temel and the Continental, were filled with local politicians and foreign dignitaries. The lower-priced Monte Blanco, a restaurant overlooking the Calle Real and Gaitán's office, was just as full. The dark cafés that lined the Calle Real, less frequented by foreign visitors, were doing their normal midday business. Dark clouds hovered over the *centro*, as the downtown area was known. It looked like rain; it usually did on April afternoons.

When in Bogotá, Gaitán kept to a strict daily schedule. He arrived at his office by 8:30 and divided the following hours between his law practice and politics. From 11:00 to 12:00 he received Liberal and Gaitanista politicians. At midday he moved from his office to the reception room to receive anyone who wanted to talk to him. The politicians knew that Gaitán was unavailable to them during the first hour of each afternoon. Between 1:00 and 1:30 Gaitán left his office to lunch, either at home or in one of the city restaurants. He was usually back before 3:00. The afternoon hours were spent on his law practice, and Gaitán often went to court. After 6:00 he met again with his lieutenants to map out the next day's political strategy.[11]

Gaitán was keeping to his schedule on April 9, even though he had arrived home at 4:00 that morning after winning his case for Lieutenant Cortés Poveda. He was in his office before 9:00 and had finished attending to the problems and complaints of Bogotá's poor before 1:00. Lunch was ready at home, but Plinio Mendoza Neira had arrived earlier to invite him to lunch at the Continental.[12] Mendoza Neira had not always been a Gaitanista. He had come aboard after the March 1947 congressional elections, but was never far from the *caudillo's* side thereafter.[13] The two were accompanied by three of Gaitán's most loyal lieutenants, Alejandro Vallejo, co-editor of *Jornada*, Jorge Padilla, the treasurer of Bogotá and a frequent contributor to the newspaper, and Pedro Eliseo Cruz, an eminent Bogotá physician and a Gaitanista senator from Cundinamarca. Gaitán had a 3:00 p.m. appointment with Fidel Castro, a young Cuban who was in Bogotá as a delegate to a congress of Latin American university students that had been scheduled to coincide with the Pan American Conference. The two men had met a few days earlier.[14]

Gaitán was in unusually good spirits as they left the office. His surprising court victory had convinced him that he should publish his legal cases. Mendoza Neira and Gaitán walked ahead through the short and narrow passageway from the elevator to the street. The other three followed close behind. Mendoza Neira, on Gaitán's right had taken the leader's arm and was talking as they approached the street. It was 1:05 p.m. They had reached the street and had taken no more than a few steps when Mendoza Neira felt the *caudillo* wheel, as if to turn back. Three shots rang out, then a fourth. Mendoza Neira saw a man holding a gun in front of them.[15] Vallejo saw him too: "He was perfectly in control of himself . . . in his eyes there was a look of hatred."[16]

Gaitán fell heavily to the ground. His friends were momentarily paralyzed. Cruz was the first to kneel beside the fallen leader. He lay on his back. Blood trickled from a hole in the side of his head. He was breathing with difficulty, and Cruz could not find a pulse. As the doctor raised his leader's head, gastric juices flowed from his mouth. Cruz felt a cold hand. "All is lost," he muttered.[17] Gaitán had been hit in the back by two other bullets, which tore through his lungs, always the source of his power. A third lodged in the back of his head.

Gaitán's assailant was immediately caught, grabbed from behind by a police officer, Carlos Alberto Jiménez Díaz, who happened to be walking past.[18] The man turned on his heels, raised his hands, and dropped the gun.

Another police officer, Ciro Efraín Silva González, helped Jiménez rush the man through the sparse crowd to the Droguería Granada across the street, where an employee was frantically trying to close the grating.[19]

Mortally wounded, Gaitán lay on the ground for at least ten minutes. Mendoza Neira had rushed off to find transport to a clinic. Shocked passers-by shouted for a taxi. As though from nowhere, a black one appeared. Gaitán was carefully lifted onto the back seat. Mendoza Neira and Cruz followed in another taxi. The procession raced through the nearly empty streets to the Clínica Central, five blocks away. Gaitán was carried into the clinic at about 1:30.[20]

Few had witnessed the attack. Those who did were too bewildered to react. No one tried to stop the two policemen from taking the assailant. Instead, they strained to get a look at Gaitán on the ground. Their faces were ashen. Most trembled. Some pushed forward and tried to touch Gaitán. Screams could be heard. Others sobbed uncontrollably. As they looked at one another in silent recognition, the tragedy slowly dawned on them. Shocked and afraid, they whispered the news. *"Mataron a Gaitán ... Mataron a Gaitán"* — "(They) killed Gaitán... (They) killed Gaitán." As the black taxi sped away, the news grew louder. *"¡MATARON A GAITÁN!"*

There was an inexorable finality about what had happened. The leader was gone for all those who witnessed the shooting. It mattered little that he had been rushed to a clinic, where doctors would try to save his life. The assassination had been on everyone's mind. It was too predictable. His death was inevitable. He was too dangerous and too feared by the leaders of both parties. They saw a dead man lying on the street. He looked so different, lying helplessly on the ground, from the way they remembered him, walking proudly down the street, standing arrogantly behind the podium, his face flushed, and his arms flailing.

The first thoughts were of revenge. "They" had killed Gaitán, those higherups who opposed him, who feared him, who attacked him, who referred to him as *"el negro* Gaitán." Who else could possibly want Gaitán dead? Angry men and women turned around and faced the drugstore that sheltered the assassin, the man who had been "ordered" to kill.

Inside the drugstore, the frightened assailant had been thrown into a corner behind the counter, far from the front windows. Officer Silva González had called his headquarters but, to his surprise, received no answer.[21] Jiménez pleaded with his captive. "Tell me who ordered you to kill, for you are going to be lynched by the *pueblo.*" "Oh, Señor," the man answered . . . "powerful things that I can't tell you, oh, Virgin of Carmen, save me!"[22]

Outside they heaved against the grating. It held for only a few minutes. Felipe González Toledo, a well-known journalist from the Liberal daily *El Espectador*, arrived just as it gave way.[23] He had little trouble reaching the gate. The crowd was still small. José Jaramillo Gaviria, a tall, well-dressed man who fought a few years earlier with the Liberal guerrillas in *la Violencia* in Sumapáz,[24] was one of the first to reach the cowering figure. Grabbing him by the hair, he dragged him into the street, where he was thrown violently to the ground.[25] A shoeshine boy hit him over the head with his box. Somebody else heaved a heavy anvil at him.[26] Blood spurted from his head. The first dense though small crowd of the afternoon surrounded the assassin, making it impossible for others to reach him. As everyone tried to kick the limp body, a police badge hit the pavement.[27]

Not everyone rushed to attack the assailant. Across the street men and women cried openly as they stared at the spot where Gaitán had lain. Josué Gómez Eslava, a twenty-nine-year-old small businessman, soaked his blue handkerchief in Gaitán's blood.[28] Marino López Lúcas, a lawyer and refugee from the Spanish Civil War, broke into tears as he dipped his handkerchief into the leader's blood.[29] The national tricolor and the red flag of the Liberal party appeared out of nowhere.[30] Stripes of black cloth were tied to them, while the national flag was draped over the death site.[31]

Two men were dying in Bogotá at the same time. On a metal bed in the emergency room of the Clínica Central, Bogotá's best-known figure was surrounded by frantic doctors and nurses. On the street a few blocks away, a furious crowd bore down on a man nobody knew. Gaitán never regained consciousness. He imparted no orders. He died at 1:55.[32] His assassin probably died moments earlier, being dragged down the Calle Real to the Presidential Palace.

¡A Palacio! ¡A Palacio!

The most dramatic moments in modern Colombian history occurred after 1:05 p.m. on April 9. Every urban Colombian heard about the bullets fired at Gaitán in Bogotá. The news instantly enveloped the capital city. Trolley drivers yelled through their open windows, ringing their bells. Men, women, and children ran up and down the streets wailing the news. Taxi drivers honked their horns. Buses stopped at checkpoints, and drivers relayed the message by phone. Church bells rang out. The railroad carried the news to outlying areas. Hands turned instinctively to the radio dial.[33] Rómulo Guzmán had just finished his daily program of Gaitanista news and commentary. Distraught and bewildered, he wailed hysterically into the microphone. The radio carried the news to every corner of the nation.

Radio announcers were in a void, with no hard news and only their anguished thoughts and feelings to air. Was Gaitán dead or alive? Who shot him? Was there more than one assassin? Who was behind it? For Rómulo Guzmán, the answers were obvious: Gaitán has been killed by the Conservative government of Mariano Ospina Pérez. His thoughts matched those of thousands who dashed into the street.[34] The Conservatives must be punished. The *pueblo* of Bogotá was in the streets. Something had to be done to right this wrong.

Many broadcasters immediately sensed the danger in Gaitán's sudden disappearance and warned their listeners to stay in their homes or places of work.[35] The minister of interior was heard over the airwaves denying that Gaitán had been shot.[36] Radio Nacional, the official organ of the government, played funeral marches. Everywhere Bogotanos stopped what they were doing. Some stayed home and sobbed to themselves, worrying about their loved ones on the streets.[37] Others went to the closet for black mourning clothes.[38] Many knelt to pray for Gaitán's soul and for the future. Others quickly left their work hoping to arrive home in time. Many of those who feared Gaitán alive were little relieved at the news of his death. Uppermost on their minds was the *pueblo*. Everyone knew that more blood would be spilled.

One Liberal commentator, Isaac Gutiérrez Navarro, was traveling home for lunch on a bus when the news reached him. "If this turns out to be true," he said to his seatmate, "it will be terrible for the nation." The man responded that maybe it was a personal vendetta, not a political crime. Gutiérrez acknowledged the distinction. "You're right," he responded, "if it's not political, maybe it won't be so serious."[39] On that day Gutiérrez thought that the traditional distinction between the private and the public would continue. From the moment Gaitán was shot, however, the distinction disappeared.

Thousands of Bogotanos never thought of returning to their family and friends. They rushed into the streets. Leading *convivialistas* of both parties thought instinctively of the consequences of Gaitán's death, their actions that day, and the inevitable reaction of the angry mob. They rushed to two scenes of power that remained in all the confusion. Leading Liberals went to the Clínica Central, to speak for Gaitán should he recover, or take his place should he die. Leading Conservatives rushed to the Presidential Palace to surround their president. It was no accident that the clinic and the *palacio* were among the few buildings in Bogotá that survived.

Many of Gaitán's closest followers, friends, and colleagues, the lawyers and professionals who directed his campaigns, became senators and representatives, and wrote for *Jornada,* rushed to his bedside. Pain drove them to be close to him. They went to touch him, and to confirm the horrible news. They were numb, and many fell into a trance that they could not shake off. José María Córdoba, the efficient secretary general of the movement, walked the streets for hours, sometimes running with others, sometimes walking about by himself.[40] Some "class A" working-class members of the JEGA who had been with Gaitán since the 1930s stayed on the streets, trying to bring order to the confusion. Rage drove them to think of avenging their leader's death, what-ever the consequences. Gaitán's lieutenants were caught between the leading Liberals, who sought to inherit his power, and the growing number of people on the streets, who wanted to express their anguish and act out their revenge. Their dilemma was the one endured by Gaitán when he was alive.

Gabriel Muñoz Uribe, a long-time Gaitanista organizer, arrived at the scene while the assassin still lay on the ground. Muñoz Uribe gave the order that was immediately on everyone's lips: "*¡A palacio! ¡A palacio!*" ("To the palace! To the palace!").[41] Two lottery vendors, Jesús Delgadillo Morales and Lázaro Amaya, were there to follow him.[42] Gaitán's bodyguard, *el coronel* Ricaurte, now without a body to guard, arrived when the procession was beginning. Through his tears he saw two men whom he had often seen before, but whose names he did not know, each grab a leg and begin to drag a body at the head of the crowd. Somebody shouted, "That's Gaitán's assassin!" Ricaurte saw arms dragging limply behind a head. He did not know if life remained in that body; nor did he care.[43]

Few saw familiar faces. The only Gaitanista intellectual present was Jorge Uribe Márquez. The Liberal politician Julio César Turbay Ayala later won-dered: "Maybe I was one of the first politicians to be on the street, in the middle of the *pueblo*, raising my indignant protest against the vile assassina-tion of Dr. Gaitán."[44] An eyewitness remembered seeing him try to deliver an oration.[45] It mattered little who was there. The marchers were united by their reaction to the attack on Gaitán and their feeling that something had to be done. The political prestige, social class, and party affiliation of the individual became irrelevant. Men in suits and ties, men and women in work uniforms and in *ruanas* and *alpargates*, individuals from the social classes Gaitán believed he represented, joined the cohesive group as they marched up the Calle Real. There were perhaps fifty in all. Empty spaces divided them. From safe vantage points along the sidewalk and the balconies, spectators watched them stretch along the Calle Real. Some joined the march while others watched it pass. Some may have stepped to the side.[46] As the procession reached the Ministry of Communications betweeen the Calle 12 and the Calle 13, a third of the way to the *palacio*, Ricaurte caught sight of a large Gaitanista of Italian descent named Marcucci. Ricaurte, also popularly known as "el chiquito" because of his small size, remembered grabbing Marcucci by his lapels and lifting him off the ground. "Marcucci, Marcucci, come join the revolution!" he screamed at the startled man.[47]

The march to the *palacio* took twenty or twenty-five minutes. The marchers moved rapidly, taking long steps. Occasionally they stopped, as if to reassure themselves. They grew tired of dragging the assassin's body, which now seemed heavier than when he was alive, and must have taken turns.[48] They shouted to bystanders to join them, to increase their confidence in their ill-defined mission. When they reached the Plaza de Bolívar, where the Calle

Foto Lunga

An early Liberal-Gaitanista protester on the Calle Real.

Real circled the cathedral, they hesitated. "*¡A capitolio!*" went out the cry.[49] The building was to the marchers' right. Some remembered that the *capitolio* was filled with foreign dignitaries attending an international conference. But the marchers' original destination had been the home of the Conservative president, and it again became a goal. Justice could not be found in the *capitolio*. The marchers continued toward the *palacio*, arriving at the corner of Calle 8 before 1:55. Gaitán had not yet been declared dead.

As the marchers made their way down the Calle Real, they stripped the assassin's body of clothing, as if they had agreed that this man did not deserve an identity. The shirt came off first. When the pants made dragging the cadaver difficult, they came off too, and someone hoisted them up on a stick, waving them from side to side.[50] Next to the pants waved various Colombian flags. "*¡Viva Colombia!*" they screamed,[51] "*¡Abajo los conservadores!*" feeling, perhaps, that they represented the nation Gaitán had defended against the Conservative traitors.

They marched to the *palacio*, rather than on it, with no intention of attacking or seizing it. The idea of taking power came fleetingly into the minds only of Gaitán's most fervent followers. The marchers were not prepared to contest the power of the Conservative regime. They went to the *palacio* to protest against a transgression of the moral order, dragging the assassin's body along as visible proof of that transgression, and as a sign that they had taken justice into their own hands. Awaiting an explanation of the crime, they threw the assassin's nude body against the door of the *palacio*. "*¡A palacio!*" "*¡A que expliquen!*" They shouted, "Let (them) explain."[52]

The protesters did not besiege the *palacio*. They were too few to surround the block, and they were still seeking contact with the Conservative leadership. Their feelings toward the regime were still ambiguous. No attempt was made to cut the telephone wires and isolate the *palacio* from the rest of the city and the nation. Nor did anyone think of entering the *palacio* through the sewer pipes.[53] It was the protesters' uncertainty that allowed the Conservative leaders to enter the building during the afternoon.

The protesters wanted to know why their leader had been killed. Yearning for a response, they looked up to the presidential balcony in the traditional ritual of the public plaza. But the president never appeared. The thought never crossed Ospina Pérez's mind. There was to be no presidential response. Ospina Pérez saw a mob. As the protesters stood expectantly before the closed *palacio* doors, the traditional link between leaders and followers was breaking apart. The social order was beginning to crumble around the walls of the *palacio*.

Gatherings of *Convivialistas*

Ospina Pérez had inaugurated the agricultural fair in the presence of the members of his cabinet, Secretary of State Marshall, and many other dignitaries; he left earlier than expected. As his limousine maneuvered the narrow corner into the *palacio*, the president saw a small crowd gathering outside. A red taxi raced past with its passengers shouting something out the windows. Ospina Pérez worried about the image of Colombia the foreign delegates would take home with them.[54] The president was met by General Rafael Sánchez Amaya, the head of the army. "Your Excellency, (they) have just killed Gaitán." The president was incredulous. "That's impossible," he answered. The general assured him that it was true and said that Foreign Minister Gómez was on the telephone.[55] Gómez, returning from the fair, had learned the fateful news when his limousine was diverted from the *palacio* by the rapidly forming crowds. The president summoned his cabinet, declared a state of siege in Bogotá, and immediately clamped heavy censorship on international news.[56]

The president's wife, Doña Bertha, immediately thought about what

Foto Lunga

President Ospina Pérez at the agricultural fair moments before the assassination. *Left to right:* President Ospina Pérez, his wife, a presidential aide, Rómulo Betancourt, Ambassador Pietri, and Laureano Gómez and his wife.

Gaitán's death would unleash. In her eyes Gaitán was the leader of a *"chusma* without God or law that he had incited in his orations."[57] On hearing the news, she went to her private chambers, took off her gloves, placed her purse on a chair, and took two revolvers from her closet, strapping one to her waist. She then called the Jesuit school and instructed the priests to take her youngest son, eleven-year-old Gonzalo, to the American Embassy. There, she felt, he would be safe, and he could quickly leave the country if need be. She joined her husband downstairs and suggested that they go to his offices, safely located on the second floor. When he answered impatiently that he was not going to hide, she shrewdly convinced him that the president belonged at his desk.[58]

Slowly the president's advisors arrived at the *palacio*. Rafael Azula Barrera, the president's private secretary, came from his home in a taxi so that he would not be recognized by the protesters. He sat away from the windows.[59] José Vicente Dávila Tello, the minister of communications, came in a friend's car rather than in his official limousine, and entered undetected through a side door.[60] On hearing the news the minister of education, Joaquín Estrada Monsalve, rushed first to his office, then home to order his family moved to a friend's house, before arriving at the *palacio* before 2:00 p.m.[61] Minister of Interior Eduardo Zuleta Angel went to confession, donned a *ruana*, and disguised as a man of the *pueblo*, sneaked into the *palacio*.[62] The secretary of the presidency, Camilo de Brigard Silva, also arrived. Others did not. The most intransigent and hated Conservatives were kept away from the *palacio*. Luis Ignacio Andrade, the minister of public works, went from the hospital, where his wife had just been operated on by Hernando Anzola Cubides, the minister of health, and to the Ministry of Defense.[63] Try as he would to reach the *palacio*, Gómez was continually rebuffed by the president. Ospina Pérez told José Antonio Montalvo that he was not needed.[64] Also absent were the former intransigent Guillermo León Valencia and the old *leopardos* Silvio Villegas and Augusto Ramírez Moreno, all Colombian delegates to the Pan American Conference. The fiery orators of the right were silent on April 9.

Former president Alberto Lleras Camargo, widely regarded by the Liberal rank and file as a traitor for having presided over the 1946 election, was in Bogotá for the conference. Quick-thinking detectives drove him to the home of a friend who lived on a secluded street in a new northern barrio.[65] Darío Echandía, the second most influential Liberal leader and the *convivialista* closest to Gaitán, arrived at the Clínica Central when Gaitán was still alive. He soon concluded that the *jefe único* would not survive and summoned the Liberals.[66]

Lleras Restrepo, although retired from politics, heeded Echandía's call. "As soon as I found out about Gaitán's assassination," he later recalled, "I realized that a very grave situation would be created in the country, and especially in Bogotá, and not wanting to remain isolated in my home in Chapinero, I went to my office."[67] From there he continued to the clinic. Also there were a number of Liberal leaders: Alfonso Araújo, who had many personal contacts with the Conservatives; Julio Roberto Salazar Ferro, who had accompanied the Liberal delegation to Santander in February to investigate the outbreak of *la Violencia* there; Alonso Aragón Quintero, a member of the Liberal delegation that visited the president in March on the eve of the break between the parties; and Alberto Arango Tavera.

The scene inside the small, understaffed, and ill-equipped clinic was chaotic. Seven doctors and many nurses hovered over the unconscious body. Gaitán was given oxygen, a tranfusion of plasma, and morphine to ease the pain he could no longer feel. The doctors tried to set up a portable X-ray unit to track the passage of the bullets.[68] Gaitán's wife, Doña Amparo, sat desolately in a corner, flanked by Don Eliécer, Gaitán's father, and Manuel Antonio, his brother.[69] Pedro Eliseo Cruz came out of the emergency room and, noting the scene, walked back inside.[70] When he came out the next time, his face told all. "There is nothing to do. The *jefe* is dead."[71] A brief silence filled the room. Then the doors to the emergency room opened, and Doña Amparo entered, followed by as many as could squeeze through. They filed past Gaitán's body. Children climbed on the outside window sills for a glimpse of the dead *caudillo*. Someone walked up to the second-floor balcony to announce the death.

Those who waited outside the clinic had remained subdued, hopeful that Gaitán might appear on the balcony. Now, they felt betrayed. The doctors were loudly insulted for failing to save Gaitán's life. When Echandía walked onto the balcony, he saw a mob unlike any he had ever seen. He remembered it as a "multitude that screamed, people who did not allow anyone to talk or anything to be said."[72] No one silently awaited his words. Instead, his name was cried out again and again. "*Viva* Echandía! *Viva* Echandía! *Viva el partido liberal!*" Although attention was focused on him, Echandía could not gain authority over the multitude. His quiet personality and soft voice were no help. A photograph shows him on one side of the balcony, hands resting passively on the balustrade. He is surrounded by men with arms stretched out, obviously attempting to create silence. One man holds a Colombian flag; another, a glass of water for Echandía. The pleas for calm went unheeded. The ritual of the public plaza had been turned around. The crowds formed spontaneously and screamed up at the balcony. Whereas Ospina Pérez never appeared, Echandía was unable to respond to the demands that came from below. The social order was crumbling around the walls of the Clínica Central.

The Liberals had nothing resembling a coherent plan.[73] They could hear the crowd calling for Echandía's return. As they talked, news came that the Ministry of Justice and the Gobernación de Cundinamarca, across from Gaitán's office, were in flames. After an hour of deliberations, fire billowed from the windows of the Ministry of Interior across the street. The Liberals' worst fears were being confirmed: the *pueblo*, Gaitán's *chusma*, was destroying the city.

A minority of the Liberals argued that they should join the *pueblo*, create a revolutionary junta headed by Echandía, and demand an immediate change in government. Most, however, supported Carlos Lleras Restrepo's suggested constitutional alternative:[74] an agreement whereby the president would resign to placate the crowd and restore order to the city and the nation.[75] Lleras Restrepo's option would divide the Liberal leaders from their followers while still seeking to fulfill their wishes. For none of the Liberals felt that they could lead the crowd. Their choice was no choice at all.

But how to contact the Conservatives? The Liberals had withdrawn from the government just over a week earlier. An overture to the president might easily be interpreted as a sign of weakness. Their problem was suddenly solved. Araújo informed them that they had been summoned to the *palacio*.[76] They were immensely relieved and perhaps not even surprised at this fortunate turn of events. After all, the Conservatives were a minority government, and the party's leaders had even less hold over the multitude than the Liberals did. In their momentary relief, the Liberals did not seek to confirm the invitation. Perhaps they had heard only a rumor, or simply what they most wanted to hear. Or the summons had been mentioned as a possibility, and they heard it as a fact. In any case, the Liberals named a delegation from among themselves to call on the president.

The Gaitanista leader Darío Samper was left out and stayed at the clinic for the moment. Pedro Eliseo Cruz remained by Doña Amparo's side. Rumors spread that Gaitán's body was to be carried at the head of a march on the *palacio* to demand Ospina Pérez's resignation.[77] Everyone in the clinic knew that the sight of the cadaver would have infuriated the multitude even more, goading it to more direct action. Doña Amparo, Pedro Eliseo Cruz, and a few friends along with Gaitán's body, were hostage to the crowd.

The seven members of the self-appointed Liberal delegation entered a street black with people and smoke from the burning Ministry of Interior. The Liberals set out at about three.[78] Their progress was painfully slow.[79] They had no police escort, and none of them tried to address the multitude in order to bring some order to it. The Liberals were almost swallowed up. They were surrounded by pressing throngs that wanted to look at them, for they had been inside the clinic, close to Gaitán. Others were waiting for a word from the leaders, and for a sign of the leadership that they had so suddenly lost. They learned little more than that the leaders were headed toward the *palacio*.

Everyone clamored for Echandía, who walked quietly in the middle of the delegation. The Liberal leaders could now hear the rallying cries of the *pueblo* at first hand. "¡A *palacio!*" "Down with the Conservative government!" "¡*Viva el partido liberal!*" ¡*Viva* Echandía!" They walked through a sea of faces, through the threateningly anonymous world of the *pueblo*. The contrast between the mood of the leaders and that of the followers could hardly have been starker.

Echandía and Lleras Restrepo tried to reason with the strangers closest to them. Lleras remembered trying to "avoid having the *pueblo* follow us and clash with the troops."[80] News of the *convivialistas'* imminent arrival at the intersection of the Calle 12 and the Calle Real preceded them. The noise of the multitude gave notice of their approach. The news rippled down the street to those who were gathered at the corner. As it swelled, the leaders found it increasingly difficult to move. They must have lost any hope of shaking those that swarmed about them. Unable to walk, they stumbled over their own feet. They were now virtual prisoners of their followers.

Gerardo Molina, Antonio García, and the Gaitanista leader Carlos H. Pareja were attempting to address a throng at the corner of Calle Real, which the *convivialistas* were slowly approaching. Molina was trying to impress his listeners with the significance of the moment and the need to replace the Conservative government. He wanted to go beyond partisan demands: they must replace the oligarchies Gaitán had attacked and achieve social and economic change. But Molina sensed that few were paying attention. He felt "totally confused," unsure of what orders the multitude would accept.[81]

As the *convivialistas* approached the corner, they must have begun to realize that they were not so much answering the president's call as turning into the leaders of a popular insurrection. Once close to the Calle Real, which led directly to the *palacio,* they had to make a rapid decision. If they moved toward the *palacio* with the *pueblo* behind them, the Conservatives could hardly regard them as politicians coming to discuss the reestablishment of order. They would never get to the president's office; they might even die at the hands of the Presidential Guard and the army. Just before they arrived at the corner, the *convivialistas* ducked into the narrow doorway of the Teatro Nuevo[82] and disappeared for almost two hours. The crowd at the corner of the Calle 12 waited for leaders who never appeared.

Foto Tito

The crowd searches for order in the Plaza de Bolívar.

Molina had considered joining the Liberals but thought better of it. He concluded that his presence at the *palacio* would not help the conversation, since he had staunchly opposed the regime and any collaboration with the Conservatives. The "born" leaders, on the other hand, had collaborated with Ospina Pérez, and many were his personal friends. They could get from the Conservatives what Molina, an enemy of the regime, could not. No less important, he knew that his presence could not advance his social and economic goals. But he never saw the leaders. He did not have a decision to make. Slowly, the old political hierarchies of public life were reemerging in the uncertain and confused behavior of the *convivialistas*.[83] With Gaitán gone, his closest lieutenants felt that it was not their place to join the Liberals in their conference rooms. The traditional leaders returned to the foreground. The moderates of both parties were moving toward one another.

The *País Nacional* and the *País Político*

The first crowd on the afternoon of April 9 had a clearly defined direction. Marching down the Calle Real offered a sense of purpose that receded quickly once they were outside the doors of the Presidential Palace. Now they waited for a response. Some began to feel uncertain. The longer they stood there, the less cohesive they became. Gabriel Muñoz Uribe and Jorge Uribe Márquez, the Gaitanistas who had led the way to the *palacio*, took stock of the situation. They had been joined by no more than fifty men. Muñoz Uribe counted five guns, which he presumed had been obtained from sympathetic policemen who had joined the march either because they were Gaitanistas or Liberals whose jobs were being imperiled by the new Conservative government, or because they were afraid that the protesters would turn against them, for the rumor had quickly spread that Gaitán's assassin was a policeman.

Muñoz Uribe was wondering how many soldiers were protecting the *palacio* when he saw a man grab a rifle that a guard was carelessly poking through the railing. The man retreated a few steps with the rifle before he was shot from within the *palacio*. For Muñoz Uribe that rifle was the first weapon won by the revolution. The man killed just a few feet away from him was the day's third victim.[84] Agustín Utrera, standing farther back, remembered that the first shots came from inside the *palacio* walls. He saw a man fall. Another man standing next to him was wounded. Utrera helped him into a nearby hotel and then ran toward the Plaza de Bolívar.[85]

Muñoz Uribe and Uribe Márquez left in search of arms, passing the Second Police Precinct, located between the Calles 8 and 9. They returned to where Gaitán had been shot, then walked two blocks west to the Carrera 9, where they led others into two nearby hardware stores, took guns, machetes, picks, and shovels, and distributed them. They returned to the *palacio* with some two hundred men.[86]

Frightened by the shooting, the crowd in front of the building had moved back from the gates. Eighty soldiers of the Presidential Guard, led by Lieutenant Silvio Carvajal, left their headquarters on the corner of San Agustín, at the intersection of the Calle Real and the Calle 7. Carvajal left forty men protecting the southern corner of the *palacio* under the command of his brother Jaime and led the remaining half of the contingent up the half-block to the entrance. The crowd seemed uncertain about the guard, and made room for the advancing soldiers. They may not have realized that the guard would have to either protect the *palacio* or join the attack.[87] Many saw it as a neutral force, somehow above the conflict it was unhesitatingly entering. The military, after all, was not supposed to become involved in politics. Some cheered the guard, perhaps even believing that it might join them. This instinctive reaction expressed a yearning for the order and discipline symbolized by the smartly uniformed soldiers. The guard was the only definable institution in the growing void. Some, however, knew better. On seeing the Presidential Guard, José Jaramillo Gaviria ran south, down the Calle Real, toward two police stations located between the Calles 2 and 3. For him the attack was over.[88]

When the Presidential Guard arrived at the main entrance to the *palacio*, Carvajal ordered the crowd to disperse. He left twenty men to protect the gates. The protesters offered little resistance, and the block in front of the building was cleared in a matter of minutes. Only the body of Gaitán's assassin remained. With the remaining twenty men, Carvajal pushed the crowd back in the direction of the Plaza de Bolívar. The next block—between the Calles 8 and 9, in front of the Second Police Precinct—was also quickly cleared. Guzmán Aldana, the commander of the station, stood with the government, but his men ignored his orders. Carvajal ordered the station closed and pushed on to the Calle 10, the last block leading into the plaza.[89] On one side of the street stood the Capitol; on the other, the Jesuit Colegio de San Bartolomé. At this point the crowd began to resist, as though aware that once forced into the open plaza, the members would cease to be part of a unit. Carvajal ordered his men to retreat to the middle of the block, lie down on the street, and aim at the crowd, which suddenly moved forward into the open space. Feeling threatened, the soldiers opened fire. The dead and wounded fell on top of one another.

By two-thirty, scarcely forty-five minutes after the marchers had arrived, and fifteen minutes after the guard had appeared, the *palacio* had been successfully defended. Nearby streets had been cleared, and the soldiers controlled all the intersections leading to it. The officers of the Presidential Guard, many of whom were home eating lunch when Gaitán was assassinated, returned to their stations. With the exception of the momentary fright of Carvajal's troops, the defense was carried out steadily, with the guard encountering only minimal resistance. The attack by Carvajal's troops was the first official violence against the *pueblo* in Bogotá in living memory. It sent shock waves through the multitudes. Their spontaneous protest had been met, not only with presidential silence, but with the deadly action of the guard. Protesters and bystanders heard the shots, and the news spread rapidly throughout the city.

It began to rain after the street in front of the *palacio* had been cleared. It was a light, intermittent drizzle at first, and did not last long. But the drizzle returned and persisted. After four o'clock it turned into a downpour, persuading many to head for home. Later the rains would douse some of the flames that enveloped the city that night. Many believed that the rains saved it from total destruction.[90]

Muñoz Uribe and his followers arrived at the Plaza de Bolívar at about three, forty-five minutes after he and Uribe Márquez had left the *palacio*. Uribe Márquez had disappeared, but Muñoz Uribe was joined by a police captain, dressed in civilian clothes, whom he knew only as Villamil. On the other side of the plaza he saw the soldiers of the guard who had secured the entrance to the Calle Real a half-hour earlier. The plaza was almost empty except for the bodies strewn about. He saw men running into the *capitolio* while small groups stood anxiously on the edges of the plaza, seeking the protection of the cathedral walls on the eastern side and the colonnades of the municipal building on the west. The Botella de Oro, a well-known café on the northern edge, was overflowing with people. The eager Gaitanista saw the "proletarian masses" gathering behind him. Muñoz Uribe led his men up the Calle 10 toward the Carrera 4 in an attempt to reach the *palacio* from the east. But behind him others advanced straight into the Presidential Guard. Muñoz Uribe remembered hearing shots ring out and being told that some of those who had failed to follow him had been killed. It was the second confrontation between the crowd and the guard.

The side streets Muñoz Uribe walked were filled with disoriented and confused people. As he ran up the Calle 10, he saw many standing around the recently refurbished Palacio de San Carlos, which housed the Ministry of Foreign Relations, and around the Teatro Colón across the street. He pushed on until he reached the Carrera 4, leading his men south along it until they reached the Calle 8, which would lead straight down into the *palacio*. But as they turned down that street, they were attacked from behind by roving members of the Presidential Guard. Muñoz Uribe managed to duck into a church, but as many as eleven of his men lost their lives. For Muñoz Uribe, any hope of a coordinated, armed attack on the *palacio* was gone. He stayed in the church a long time, while the growing crowd pressed on the troops who controlled the intersections leading to the *palacio*.[91]

On the southern side of the *palacio*, José Jaramillo Gaviria tried to coordinate an assault of his own. After rushing from the *palacio* when he saw the guard, he ran south along the Carrera 8 to the Calle 2, where a police station was located. He demanded that Commander Hernando Albornóz Plata open the arsenal to the *pueblo*. He then led his armed band of followers, firing their rifles into the air, to the Calle 4, just three blocks from the *palacio*, where there was another police station. A policeman pushed a small white flag through the open door. They forced their way in, took the arms, and proceeded north toward the *palacio*. Jaramillo Gaviria divided his followers into three groups: one advanced through the Carrera 9 to surround the building from the west; another went straight up the Calle Real; and he took his own group up to the Carrera 6 to attack from the east. Some men entered the buildings that encircled the *palacio*.[92]

From inside the walls of the Presidential Palace, the attack looked very different. President Ospina Pérez thought that he was facing an all-out offensive. In his mind the *palacio* was "the final goal, the principal objective, the maximum preoccupation of the rioters, since once they had taken the *palacio* and killed the president, the republic was in the hands of the revolutionaries." The president saw the burning of public buildings and other actions as diversionary tactics in a general revolt against the *palacio*.[93]

For other Conservatives the threat was equally ominous. Most of the Presidential Guard had gone home for lunch, and the military garrisons to the north and west of the city were seriously understaffed. The Conservatives felt unprotected by the forces of order and besieged by the entire city.[94] The president's desk was moved away from the windows, and preparations were made to smuggle Ospina Pérez and Doña Bertha to their native city of Medellín and, if the need arose, from there to the United States or a nearby country. The president adamantly rejected all escape plans, even though he felt that he and his wife might well be facing death. Yet, just to be safe, he sent his friend Jorge Plata to the American Embassy with instructions for the handling of his personal belongings should he have to travel to the United States after all.[95] He told his advisors and cabinet that they were free to leave. They all stayed by his side.[96]

Doña Bertha worried that a single Molotov coctail might set the old and largely wooden frame ablaze. She prepared to put on men's clothes so that her honor would not be violated by the mob.[97] Major Iván Berrio informed Estrada Monsalve that they had sufficient ammunition to hold off the rioters for five days. The minister of education must have felt greatly relieved, for he perceived a drunken mob of ten thousand men, armed with guns, machetes, swords, pickaxes, sticks, stones, and whisky bottles, joined by the entire police force, marching toward the presidential residence. In his mind the attack was coordinated from all eight intersections that led to the *palacio*.[98]

Azula Barrera saw a crowd equally large and full of suicidal fanatics prepared to throw themselves at the Presidential Guard, which had little choice but to mow them down. For him the attack was "the beginning of the end": the demise of a civilized community led by men of reason and based on the deference of the poor to the rich. The rioters were a "real human hurricane that emerged suddenly from the earth, moving almost electrically to fall upon the city from the mountains."[99]

Azula Berrera called on his friend José María Villarreal, the Conservative governor of the department of Boyacá, to send as many troops as he could spare. Ospina Pérez ordered General Rafael Sánchez Amaya, the general director of the army, who happened to be at the *palacio*, to have his troops retake the studios of Radio Nacional and protect the banks and the city's financial district, as well as the Catholic schools for girls and the many convents and cloisters downtown.[100]

The siege mentality that rapidly enveloped the Conservative leaders is easily understandable. They felt threatened by their weakness at the polls, acutely aware that they had been outvoted by the Liberals in the May 1946 election that brought them to power and in the subsequent congressional elections. They were weakest in the urban areas, especially in Bogotá, where Gaitán had been strongest. They more easily identified with the stable hierarchies of rural life, which for them nostalgically symbolized the basis of the nation. They were out of touch with the anonymous urban multitudes that had threatened them throughout the Liberal Republic. Now they were responsible for maintaining order in those urban areas, including a city of around a half-million people who had launched themselves against society.

During their two years in power, Bogotá's *chusma* had, under Gaitán's direction, grown larger and more threatening. In the streets the Conservatives could feel the decline of the accustomed deference. Few ventured out at night, less for fear of being robbed than for fear of being accosted by a roving band of Gaitanistas.[101] Just two months earlier they had witnessed the awesome discipline of the urban crowd during Gaitan's Manifestación del Silencio. Not only were they accused of instigating *la Violencia* in the countryside, but the accusation came from a multitude more orderly and peaceful than they had imagined possible. When that crowd took to the streets to protest against their leader's assassination, the Conservatives expected the worst. Although they were outraged that radio announcers were placing responsibility for the assassination on them, they could hardly have been surprised at the accusation. The antagonism they felt coming from the crowd was too intense and their sense of impotence too strong for them not to imagine the most violent outcome. Their anxiety was heightened by the presence of the international delegations and the world press in Bogotá.

The Conservatives' fear made them see the crowd as more purposeful and coherent than it was. Their initial response was prompted by images of conspiracy, for they were unable to conceive of individuals who were strangers to one another acting coherently. Fear led them to envisage many revolutionary leaders—Gaitanistas, Liberals, and communists alike—manipulating the rioters to overthrow the government. A few hours after the *palacio* seemed secure, the government leaders concluded that the onslaught was part of an international communist conspiracy.

When President Ospina Pérez reasoned that the burning of public buildings was but a diversionary tactic, he was following the same logic. His conclusion showed the primacy he gave to politics. In his mind the struggle between the parties defined his own existence and that of the entire nation. Since independence his family had dedicated itself to the Conservative party. The idea that some Liberals might use the moment to take power, and destroy the city in the process, did not seem farfetched to him.

The Conservatives did little once the building had been secured and Ospina Pérez had issued his original instructions. The banks and the schools were protected, and the Radio Nacional building retaken, but little else was done to protect the city from the crowd. The only concerted military action came at Radio Nacional. Soon after news of Gaitán's death reached the army barracks in Usaquén, seven miles north of the city, a cavalry squadron just returning from the agricultural fairgrounds was ordered to Bogotá. The squadron, with the officers on horseback, jogged all the way to the city and headed directly to the radio station, located on the northwestern edge of the downtown area. Benito Rojas, a soldier in the squadron, did not know where the cavalry was headed until he was ordered to take the building from the students who controlled it. The unarmed students were rapidly overwhelmed. The squadron kept the building until relieved by the infantry, whereupon it was ordered to the Plaza de Bolívar to defend three tanks headed there.[102]

By four o'clock the radio station was again under government control.[103] A calm voice came on to declare that only a few disturbances were upsetting the general order throughout the land. The announcer even implied that Gaitán had not died; he was at the "edge of his grave."[104] The Conservative government offered no encouraging information, no news of the situation in Bogotá and the rest of the country, and no instructions on how to reestablish order.

Once the *palacio* was secure, the Conservatives waited for the demonstration to subside after the crowd had vented its anger. In the midst of the tumult, Ospina Pérez told his advisors that "time is our best ally."[105] By seven o'clock Estrada Monsalve had concluded that "the last revolutionary attempt had been defeated. The revolution was a riot. There will only be booty for those who have pillaged."[106] Ospina Pérez and the military probably did not deliberately leave the city unprotected in order to entice the crowd away from its original political aims, as many were to charge later. Yet they did believe that after the first attacks had been repelled, the crowd no longer threatened the political order. Their best strategy was to do as little as possible. As long as a semblance of political authority was maintained, as long as the banks were protected by a few soldiers and the major industries were left untouched, social order would survive. Most of the public buildings had gone up in smoke before they could have reached them in any case. Moreover, the ties between the government and urban commerce were weak. The merchants' association, CONFENALCO, formed in 1942, had little influence in politics. The Conservatives saw the merchants merely as the distributors of goods produced in the factories and on the land, not as a foundation of national wealth. Finally, they knew that there was little they could do with an urban crowd run amok. Indeed, that crowd confirmed the barbarity of the Colombian nation outside the public realm of *convivencia*.

The government's impact on the riot was therefore minimal. The president's instructions to cut the city's electrical supply went unheeded until nightfall.[107] That order was aimed at the radio stations, but many broadcast until approximately ten-thirty that evening.[108] Here again Ospina Pérez demonstrated his preoccupation with stopping a political revolt without regard for the hardships of ordinary Bogotanos in the darkness. Hospitals, for example, could not function without electricity.

The Presidential Guard made little attempt to extend its control to the nearby streets where stores were being looted. Virgilio Barco, the acting commander of the police, claimed to have remained in his office issuing instructions to subordinates in the precincts, unaware that they had either joined the revolt or been prevented from doing so only because their commanders had locked the doors.[109] Daniel Ramos Ramos, commander of the fire department, was ordered back into his station in the early afternoon by the Presidential Guard lest the fire trucks be destroyed by the rioters.[110] There was no stopping the flames that enveloped the city center. The city was left unprotected. That afternoon and again in the early evening, the American Embassy cabled Washington that the city was in the hands of a mob and no public forces were in sight. The next morning an embassy cable reported that the police, the army, and the fire department had never appeared that night except around the *capitolio* and the Presidential Palace.[111]

Throughout the afternoon the army generals remained loyal to the government and kept most of the soldiers in the barracks. Only a cavalry squadron, some infantry, a few truckloads of soldiers, and three tanks left Usaquén and the Ministry of War. Members of Ospina Pérez's inner circle, and especially his wife, later described the generals as paralyzed by fear and confusion.[112] Yet the generals and the government were in constant contact, and General Rafael Sánchez Amaya remained in the *palacio* until the surrounding streets had been cleared. He had been the first to tell the president of the attack on

Foto Tito

The *bogotazo.*

Gaitán. Before he left for the Ministry of War, he reassured the president of
the military's loyalty, despite reports to the contrary.

The passivity of the military had many causes. They faced a completely
unprecedented situation. Most of their activity had been restricted to rural
areas. Their role within Bogotá had been limited to maintaining order in
isolated demonstrations and strikes. Soldiers had never faced an urban crowd
before, let alone one that appeared to be out of control. Bogotá's garrison had
been almost halved by the normal yearly turnover of recruits, and the new

soldiers had not yet received proper training.[113] Although the generals had nearly eight hundred men at their disposal, they wondered about their soldiers' reactions in front of such a crowd. They knew that Gaitán had sympathizers in the ranks who might refuse to fire on the *pueblo* or even join the rebellion. Even if the soldiers did as ordered, the new recruits inspired little confidence. If they refused, the last bulwark of order would be gone.

The generals must also have wondered about how repressing crowds on behalf of an unpopular, minority government would affect the military as an institution. The soldiers would be responsible for killing innocent civilians. Worse still, if the Conservatives handed power over to the Liberals, the military would be seen as a reactionary force that had come to the defense of the old regime. In such an eventuality, the generals would certainly lose their posts. Finally, the Presidential Guard seemed to be in control of the situation around the *palacio*. The generals may have concluded that the *palacio* was safe from the crowd. Bogotá was not.

7

The Crowd

We have come to destroy, to end everything, not to steal!

A rioter (April 9, 1948)

The Crowd and the Social Order

Although violent, the first actions of the crowd followed traditional lines. The first protesters had partisan aims. They marched on the *palacio* to seek justice from a Conservative government for the death of a Liberal. Others followed Liberal leaders who walked to the presidential residence in search of a political solution to an infraction of the moral order. The first targets were the symbols of Conservative power: the *palacio*, *El Siglo*, and the detective headquarters across the street.

By two-thirty a dense group of men and women stood outside the *El Siglo* building demanding Gómez's head and the end of Conservative rule. One man cried hysterically as he tried to pry the bricks loose with his fingernails.[1] The protesters threw rocks at the building, and someone suggested that they burn it to the ground. No one knew quite how to go about it until a driver brought a can of gasoline from his nearby cab. Soon the building was in flames.[2] Heliodoro Africano, an off-duty police sergeant, looked up to see Bogotá's crime files flying out the windows of detective headquarters.[3] The *El Tiempo* building, on the other hand, was left intact, and a rioter who accosted Roberto García-Peña was subdued when he was shown a picture of the editor chatting amicably with Gaitán.[4] Later that afternoon the building that housed *El Espectador* was saved when someone remembered that *Jornada* was published there.[5]

155

The crowd destroys the Gobernación de Cundinamarca on the Avenida Jiménez, a half block from the site of the assassination.

During the two and a half hours after Gaitán's assassination, the crowd's activities broadened and gained strength. Across from where Gaitán had been shot, the Gobernación de Cundinamarca, where Liberals and Gaitanistas held a majority, was seized. By two o'clock the scene resembled a ticker-tape parade as those who were inside the building ransacked archives and desks. Paper, office machinery, and furniture were thrown into the street. Rioters took over trolley cars and private automobiles, stuffed them with the property of the Gobernación, and set them afire.

Across from the Clínica Central rioters set fire to the Ministry of Interior, housed in what once had been a private residence. A half-block up the street the Third Police Precinct was the first to fall to the crowds, whose members worried that the police would disband them in order to protect the officers many held responsible for Gaitán's death. Shortly after Lieutenant Carvajal's men opened fire on the crowd on the Calle Real, a small crowd rushed the *capitolio*, breaking doors, chairs, and desks and ripping down the ornate curtains. More than a hundred foreign diplomats were caught inside.

By the time *El Siglo's* offices were beginning to go up in flames, those who had gone to the *palacio* had been violently pushed back and the building secured. The subsequent attacks on the *palacio* were uncoordinated and easily repelled. Armed men in the blocks surrounding it tried individually to get closer, and some went up to the roofs of nearby buildings to shoot down at the *palacio*. But the building was not seriously threatened again. It was no longer a target. Less than an hour later, before three-thirty, the multitude surrounding the Liberal leaders on their way to see the president lost momentum and direction when the leaders ducked into the theater, not to be seen again for several hours.

Throughout the two and a half hours after Gaitán's assassination, people streamed into the city center from the outlying neighborhoods and even nearby towns. Some arrived in time to participate in or at least witness the first partisan actions. Many more made it into downtown Bogotá after the attack on the *palacio* was over. They saw dead bodies in the Plaza de Bolívar. When the stonesmason Pío Nono Barbosa Barbosa, an early member of the JEGA and one of Gaitán's most loyal followers, arrived outside the *palacio*, the Calle Real had been cleared, and only one body, which he assumed to be that of Gaitán's assassin, lay in front of the building. He continued down the Calle Real, unopposed by the soldiers who lined the street, searching the crowd for familiar faces that might offer him friendship and some idea of what to do.[6] The time for partisan actions appeared to be over.

The people streaming into the city after two-thirty did not differ from those downtown when Gaitán was shot, but the actions open to them were not the same. They could no longer attack the *palacio* or follow the Liberal leaders there. They could no longer burn *El Siglo*. They entered an area where many had already been killed. Hardware stores had been looted, trolleys and cars overturned, police stations taken, and prisoners released. Three or four public buildings were in flames. Both life and private property, once thought inviolable in Bogotá, had been destroyed.

The streets, except those surrounding the *palacio*, belonged to the crowd. Its anonymity was total. Acquaintances failed to recognize one another, pain

The body of the assassin lies before the doors of the Presidential Palace.

and anger having transformed their faces.[7] Leaders, Liberal and Conservative, were nowhere to be seen. Gaitán, who had restrained the crowd, was
gone. In that void, the crowd found courage and strength, but also fear, for its
leader was dead, the future uncertain, the present unknown.

The inability of the protesters to focus on specific political goals opened the
way for deeper waves of anger against the hierarchical social order. No longer
guided by party lines, the crowd turned against the symbols of public power.
Soon they were bent on turning society upside down, on destroying everything that had once been reputable: what had once been legitimate ceased to
be so; what had once been the buildings of the *convivialistas* were taken over
by the *pueblo;* what the poor lacked, or had to pay for, they took; what had
once been the domain of the politicians was overrun. Leaders ceased to be
leaders. The crowd took over, systematically destroying the symbols of
power, inequality, and exclusion that had once been so easily accepted.[8]

Walking through the streets of Bogotá that afternoon, the Gaitanista José
Vicente García felt that the crowd raging around him wanted "to level
everything, to burn everything in order to reconstruct anew."[9] The Gaitanista
labor leader Hernando Restrepo Botero thought that the crowd wanted to

destroy for the sake of destroying.[10] Luis Cano Jacobo, a Gaitanista lawyer, looking back at what he witnessed, wondered how anything was left standing.[11]

It seemed that Gaitán's followers were bent on bringing individual and collective life to an end so that the social order would not survive their leader's death. One leading Gaitanista seriously proposed poisoning the city's water supply so that the whole population would go the way of the leader.[12] A lone figure sobbed on a street corner, crying out to no one in particular: "Come on, you cowards, kill me! I defy you. I'm a Liberal. Here. Kill me!" Another bared his breast and yelled, "Come on you cowards, and get me if you dare!"[13]

The rioters rapidly became drunk. Some of Gaitán's followers may have had a drink with lunch, then gulped down a few quick shots when they heard the news. But most of the drinking occurred after the hardware stores had been looted and the political action of the crowd had run its course. Rioters broke into liquor stores filled with expensive foreign alcohol. They downed the bottles right away, not saving them to take home. The idea of thinking ahead to another day was unbearable. They destroyed what they could not drink, wrecking the stores, throwing their wares into the street.

The crowd drank in a mass wake to commemorate a leader whose body it had been denied. Many drank to extinguish their pain. They drank to console themselves. They drank to make their tears flow more freely. They drank to drown the fear of the consequences of their actions and their fear of what was yet to come. They drank for the courage to continue destroying the city.[14] They drank to forget, to fall unconscious and see the darkness they willed for the entire social order. They drank to communicate, to lessen their anonymity. The sharing of bottles became a ritual. All who refused were branded as traitors and representatives of the old order.[15] They drank because those fancy bottles had been denied them. Unable to afford such luxuries, Bogotá's poor had always wondered about the taste of whiskey, bourbon, cognac, and gin. Could one get drunk faster? Were the hangovers lighter? Now it was their turn to drink the alcohol of the rich.

Later that night the journalist Felipe González Toledo had trouble avoiding the piles of human excrement on the street. In the darkness he missed the vomit. He concluded that the rebellion had suffered from indigestion.[16] That indigestion showed the power of individual life in the face of a collective death wish.

After Muñoz Uribe's second attack on the *palacio*, the rioters stormed the elegant Palacio de San Carlos, which the government had refurbished at great expense for the Pan American Conference. They heaved tables, desks, chairs, shelves, files, typewriters, and adding machines through the windows. Smashed chandeliers and lamps were thrown into the street. Ezequiel Benavides entered the luxurious building out of curiosity. "I wanted to see what

it looked like inside," he recalled.[17] Below, the rioters were making two piles
of debris, one on the Calle 10 in front of the Teatro Colón and the other on the
Carrera 6 in front of the Museo Colonial. José V. Espinosa, a curator at the
museum, hurriedly brought the director's car inside the patio, locked the
museum's doors, and peered through the gates. He watched in astonishment
as "fine and luxurious" things flew out the windows. Before his eyes they were
set on fire.[18] At about that time a young man came rushing past and swiped
a cushion. An older woman, almost certainly a vendor from a nearby market,
ran after him and wrenched the cushion away. "We have come here to
destroy," she screamed at him, "to end everything, not to steal!" She walked
back and threw the cushion into the flames.[19] But across the street the equally
luxurious and more accessible Teatro Colón was left untouched.

Armed with gasoline from cars and nearby gasoline stations, and with oil
and cooking gas from their home stoves, the rioters attacked virtually every
public building in downtown Bogotá. Some carried gasoline-filled bottles to
make Molotov cocktails but had no rags to use as wicks. Yet they worked with
astounding efficiency and speed. As some stormed buildings to destroy their

Foto Tito

Rioters overturn an automobile on the steps of the Capitol.

contents and force everyone out, others prepared the Molotov cocktails.[20] The idea was to destroy buildings, not take lives.

Both the Palace of Justice, where many prisoners were held, and the Ministry of Justice were attacked. Cells were broken into, and prisoners given their freedom. It seemed only logical. Across the street from the Gobernación, the rioters sacked the Ministry of Education, the Ministry of Public Health, and the Procuraduría, the offices of the public prosecutor. They also went after the Ministry of Communications, which the first marchers had ignored as they dragged the body of Gaitán's assassin up the Calle Real.

The rioters attacked public buildings previously open to them only for bureaucratic transactions in which the *pueblo* had to show respect for officials who seemed to belong there. Buildings where leaders of both parties had decided the fate of the excluded were now suddenly prey to the ravaging crowd.

The churches of the city maintained a silence that contrasted starkly with the tumult outside. They stood for awhile like serene islands, immune to the devastation, but soon they too were engulfed. Rioters forced open the archbishop's palace, the offices of the archdiocese, the palace of the apostolic nuncio, the pope's ambassador, and the Universidad Javeriana for women. They searched for the various cloisters, convents and girls' boarding schools that were located downtown. The cathedral of Bogotá, on the Plaza de Bolívar, was the last to feel the rage of the multitude. The church of Egipto was encircled by women of the barrio, who prevented men from ransacking it.[21]

Various motives led the rioters into the churches. They were being shot at from the steeples, and many thought that priests were doing the shooting.[22] The church had long been associated with the Conservatives. More significantly, it was a pillar of the social order that the mob wanted to destroy. Long submerged antipathies toward Spanish Catholicism may also have surfaced. The crowd sought to silence another voice that had distinguished good from evil, right from wrong, in a society that that day had itself turned immoral.[23]

Those who ran into the churches broke the stained glass windows and turned the pews into firewood. They wrecked the gilded altars, pulled down the statue of the Virgin Mary, and wrenched the holy cross from the altar. Some defecated there.[24] Father Arturo Franco Arango tried to defend the archbishop's palace. When he saw that the multitude was prevailing, he swallowed the hosts to keep them from being desecrated, and urged his fellow priests to don disguises and prepare their escape. Father Franco carefully hid the statue of Mary under his clothes and left the palace with Monseigneur Emilio de Brigard, whom he left safely at a friend's nearby home. He then continued to the Seminario Mayor, almost one hundred blocks north, where the archbishop of Bogotá, Ismael Perdomo, was convalescing.[25] Once Father Franco had left, the mob took over the building. More than six thousand books were burned. They wrecked famous paintings, broke crystal and porcelain, took jewels, ripped apart the priests' robes, and destroyed the ecclesiastical archive.[26]

Throughout the afternoon and early evening men assaulted convents and cloisters, no doubt seeking to fulfill deeply hidden sexual fantasies on defenseless nuns and young virgins. Some cloisters were defended by soldiers, Ospina Pérez having delivered prescient instructions to this effect hours earlier. But most were difficult to find, for they had no identifying signs and were located in the middle of large downtown blocks and behind churches. Thirty-two Franciscan sisters of the Convent of Our Lady of the Conception realized that they were under attack at about five o'clock. Since they had made a vow never to return to the outside world, they could not escape. Instead, they prepared to burn themselves inside the convent. Hours later, however, they were saved from the flames by a neighbor, Jorge E. Rodríguez, who guided them over the walls into his own home.[27]

The destruction of Bogotá's public buildings was interrupted around four o'clock by three army trucks rumbling down the Calle Real toward the *palacio*. By then most of the buildings had already been sacked. The multitude welcomed the tanks, climbing on them and gleefully following behind. In the midst of the chaos the tanks were seen as a sign of the return to order. Soldiers sat atop the tanks as if fraternizing with the rioters. As once before that afternoon, they thought that the military was on their side and draped the tanks with red flags and the national tricolor. They may have been encouraged by soldiers who sympathized with the Liberal cause and shared their reaction to Gaitán's assassination. The possibility of a political revolt was suddenly reemerging. Inside the *palacio* the Conservatives feared that the tanks had joined the rioters.[28]

As the tanks arrived at the Plaza de Bolívar, the first two continued down the Calle Real past Carvajal's troops. Before the first tank could reach the *palacio*, however, Captain Mario Serpa, the commander, was shot as he stood on his tank. The bullet may have come from the protesters, or from the Presidential Guard, which was still uncertain about the military's loyalty. Perhaps one of his own men shot Serpa. Lieutenant Manuel Jota Sánchez took command, while Serpa was rushed to the *palacio*, where he died shortly thereafter. Lieutenant Alvaro Ruíz Holguín of the Presidential Guard also soon lost his life close to the *palacio*.[29]

Meanwhile the last tank had turned around to face the Plaza de Bolívar from the southeastern corner, close to where Carvajal's men had first opened fire on the crowd. The soldiers aimed at the crowd and opened fire. Few had time to get out of the way.[30] A partisan Liberal rebellion against the Conservatives was now definitely over, only moments after it had been reawakened in the minds of the multitudes.

The Sack

The looting of Bogotá's shops had begun before the tanks appeared, but at that time it was still isolated. The looting spread after the rioters were mowed down in the Plaza de Bolívar, almost as though in those deaths the survivors saw their own lives returning. Slowly, merchandise previously strewn about was picked up by looters thinking of another day. The open doors of the hardware stores and of food and liquor stores proved inviting. The plunderers' lingering respect for private property had been undermined by the previous looting. Their fear was reduced by the lawlessness around them, and by the absence of the police and military. Moreover, most of the merchants had left for the safety of their homes.

The sack of Bogotá's downtown commercial area was spearheaded by individuals who were no longer so determined to destroy. Many of the looters had arrived after Gaitán had been shot and after many of the public buildings were in flames. The pillaging spread quickly, attracting everyone except a few of the most committed Gaitanistas.[31] Men, women, and children participated. Bogotá's poor were joined, somewhat more timorously, by middle-class people for whom the goods in the store windows symbolized a way of life they envied. Pictures show well-dressed middle-class women weighed down by lamps and other household furniture. About two hours after the full-scale pillaging began, darkness fell. The pillagers worked until just before dawn, when soldiers sent to Bogotá by Governor Villarreal arrived. After the massive destruction of the city, the pillaging was a sign that the social order would survive. Looters were thinking of the reproduction of their daily lives.

The sacking was concentrated in the downtown commercial sector, an area twelve blocks long and seven blocks wide.[32] It stretched from the Calle 21 to the north to the Calle 10 to the south, and from the Carrera 3 to the east to the Carrera 10 to the west. The area was bisected from north to south by the Calle Real, and from east to west by the Avenida Jiménez (Calles 13 and 14). Gaitán's office lay squarely in the middle. To the south the sacking stopped at the Plaza de Bolívar, where the Presidential Guard controlled the streets surrounding the *palacio* and beyond which few well-known commercial establishments were located. Only a few stores outside this downtown area were sacked. Some market stands of the Plaza de los Laches, to the west, and the Plaza de las Cruces, to the south, were raided. These were easily defensible, but their owners may have been downtown helping loot the more luxurious establishments.[33] In outlying neighborhoods a few food stores were attacked, but generally the looting was contained in the area of the destroyed government buildings.

The plundering mob worked with astonishing speed and thoroughness. Few stores were left untouched, but not everything was taken. Cans of peaches and peas, unknown to the looters, as well as caviar and pickled herring, rapidly disappeared from the shelves. Perfumes and cosmetics were taken from drugstores and medicines left behind. Looters hoisted clothing, furniture, and appliances onto their backs to make the trek back to their barrios. Often they sold their loot at ludicrously low prices to middle- and upper-middle-class people waiting on their doorsteps. Some stores were deliberately spared, such as Gaitán's father's bookstore on the Calle Real. Only a block away, on the other hand, the bookstore of the Gaitanista Carlos H. Pareja was raided while he was on the radio trying to calm the crowds. Gaitán's famous dark-green Buick, parked just two blocks from the Plaza de Santander, where hotels were burned, was left untouched.[34]

Hardest hit were the Calle Real, with its many small clothing stores owned by Syrians, Lebanese, Jews, and Turks, collectively referred to as *polacos* and known for their high markups and unsympathetic credit policies; the Calle 12 between the Clínica Central and the Calle Real, filled with jewelry stores primarily owned by western Europeans; and the Carrera 8, known as the English Street for its exclusive stores featuring fine British clothes for men and women.

That afternoon, 157 buildings in downtown Bogotá suffered serious damage;[35] 103 were a total loss. These figures do not include government buildings and many of the churches. For the former there is no reliable information, and the latter are included in the government records only if they filed claims. (Many did not, but the zealous government officials who headed the Junta de Daños y Perjuicios made their own evaluations and disbursed the appropriate funds to them.) Thus, these 157 buildings do not include many that were the prime targets of the crowd.

The largest claim for real estate damage came from the Congregación de Hermanos de las Escuelas Cristianas, the order that owned the Universidad de la Salle, which was burned to the ground on April 10. The religious order claimed that the building was worth 1,243,485.00 Colombian pesos ($706,525.56). The Junta de Daños y Perjuicios paid half that amount, 778,228.00 ($442,175.00). The archdiocese of Bogotá notified the junta that its two buildings were completely destroyed but made no claim. The Junta reimbursed it 221,978.50 ($126,124.14). The archbishop likewise made no claim, but received 208,944 pesos ($118,718.18). The Universidad Javeriana received 102,048 pesos. Gómez made two real estate claims to the junta—140,939 pesos ($80,078.97) for *El Siglo*, and 47,136.20 pesos

Foto Lunga

The Calle Real leading into the Plaza de Bolívar, two weeks after the *bogotazo*.

($26,781.93) for his home, which was in the name of his wife, María Hurtado de Gómez. He was paid in full.

The Junta de Daños y Perjuicios received real estate claims totaling 18,761,692.00 pesos ($10,660,052.00). According to its own appraisal, the damages actually came to only 8,600,134.86 pesos ($4,886,440.20). Both in absolute terms and in view of the large claims made by the church and by Gómez, this is a modest sum. One reason it was not greater is that many of the destroyed buildings were old one- and two-story structures housing cafés or small stores and interspersed between government buildings and other more modern structures. The Calle Real from Gaitán's office to the Plaza de Bolívar was lined with these small, inexpensive buildings.

Most of the losses are attributable to stolen and destroyed merchandise. The government received a total of 1,818 claims for losses in commerce and industry, which included private property in general, with a total value of 63,163,122.99 pesos ($35,888,138.00). The largest claim—for 2 million pesos ($1,136,363.60)—again came from the Congregación de Hermanos de las

Escuelas Cristianas. Other church organizations that lost property did not present claims to the government. Of these 1,818 claims, 34 were for more than 200,000 pesos ($113,636.36). Gómez made another claim for 301,837.00 pesos ($171,498.29) for unspecified losses in commerce and industry. All told, Gómez claimed that he lost almost $400,000.00 to the rioters. He was the only politician to make a substantial claim.

Some merchants successfully protected their stores. Daniel Valdiri, owner of one of the city's most exclusive clothing and appliance stores, put large photographs of Gaitán in his windows and distributed ties to the throngs outside. His store was passed by. Another merchant quickly painted over his windows and posted a "for-rent" sign. In other cases minimal resistance was enough, not because the looters were cowardly, as merchants and the press later claimed, but because they knew that there were unprotected stores around the corner. One merchant antagonized the looters by challenging them to take his store. They did.[36]

The pillaging turned out to be a feat beyond anything the looters had ever imagined. They filled their stomachs, dressed in finery, and furnished their homes. For many these goods were a consolation for Gaitán's death. For others their actions were retribution, a momentary equalization of society. It was their moment to get what the rich had always had. Thus, the looting had a redemptive quality that helped reestablish social order. One man stood before the windows of a harberdashery, carefully trying on one hat after another. Finally, satisfied with one, he nodded and walked off.[37] He was thinking about tomorrow, when he would proudly walk through the clean streets of Bogotá and into a government office, there to gain the respect of public officials.

The Crowd from Within

The crowd found it difficult to act according to patterns of conflict and cooperation that in normal times had been dictated by the rules of political partisanship and social class. Now Liberals became indistinguishable from Conservatives. Distinctions between rich and poor disappeared. Individual differences in comportment, manners, family background and occupational status, and language and learning found no easy expression. Everyone appeared to be roughly alike. Only dress styles remained to distinguish social class and occupation. But even here the homogenizing urban environment had rendered the old distinctions between European clothing and the *ruana* of the *pueblo*, between shoes and *alpargates*, less stark than during Gaitán's mayoralty a decade before.[38] The difference between a finely tailored suit of English cloth and its coarser, baggier national counterpart faded. Individuals reacted more according to the circumstances of the moment and their feelings than according to social rank.

Old social, political, and personal animosities surfaced, and many must have taken advantage of the chaos to act on them. In addition, hostility and despair over the assassination led to aggressively violent behavior. The end of the brief period of partisan actions and clashes with the military deprived the crowd of a clear opponent threatening its existence. Without an outside focal point, group solidarity proved difficult, and individuals turned on each other. Many written eyewitness accounts emphasize such conflicts. Machete duels broke out, one wayward rock led to a wave of others in response, people who accidentally brushed against one another reacted with rage. Some vented their frustrations on the first person they saw. They stole belongings and looted goods from one another.[39]

Less noticeable was the cooperation that took place. Individuals attempted to create a new sense of community, not only through their slogans, and their targets, but by helping and sharing. Alcohol became a base of that solidarity. One man walked around forcing others to accept his cigars.[40] Some took more loot than they could carry and left it on the street, where they knew that another deserving person would pick it up. Strangers went out of their way to save each other's lives. Sergio Céspedes, a Gaitanista, was shot in the leg shortly after the tanks secured the *palacio*. He was running across the Plaza de Bolívar to assist an injured man when he was hit from behind. He fell, but managed to hobble to the Calle 10, where he lost consciousness. He awoke to find that a man in his mid-twenties was dragging him up the street. The stranger tied Céspedes's tie and shirt around his leg to stop the bleeding. Céspedes remembered others coming to their assistance before he fainted again. He woke up many hours later on the operating table of the Clínica Central.[41]

Another Gaitanista, Ezequiel Benavides, was shot in the shoulder late in the afternoon as he was trying to approach the *palacio*. Two others died next to him. He did not know whether he had been shot by the Presidential Guard, by rioters, or by one of the prisoners who had been released. He remembered being taken into a nearby home by a man in civilian clothes. Afterwards he was told that the man had been a prisoner and had carried him on his back to the Clinica de Santa Lucía.[42] Still another Gaitanista, Adelmo Toro, was shot at the Plaza de Bolívar as he walked behind those who marched toward the *palacio*. He remembered seeing the soldiers machine-gunning the crowd. He was taken to the Red Cross by a uniformed traffic policeman.[43]

The well-known Liberal photographer Parmenio Rodríguez was shot at that same corner. The bullet went through his hand, camera, and leg. Daniel Rodríguez Rodríguez, the dean of Bogotá's photographers, rushed to the scene when strangers told him that his cousin had been shot. With the help of other strangers, he carried the wounded man to the Clínica Central, where he died a few hours later.[44] Leo Matíz, a Colombian photographer who was working abroad, had returned to Bogotá to cover the Pan American Conference. He was also shot from behind. As he lay defenseless on the street, someone took his overcoat, a ring, and his camera. Others took him to the Clínica Central, where they left him on the ground with the other wounded. When he awoke the next morning, he recognized Dr. Luis E. Botero Jaramillo, an old acquaintance, who made sure that he was properly attended.[45]

The rioters destroyed the Ministry of Finance, but left the banks alone; the latter did not symbolize the social order in the same way. They attacked the public home of the Minister of Foreign Relations, the Palacio de San Carlos, but ignored the Jockey Club and the Gun Club, where the political and economic elites met to deliberate the fate of the *pueblo*. Nor did they attack the Teatro Colón, symbol of the cultural tastes of Bogotá's high society, although it was just across the street from the Palacio de San Carlos and had also been remodeled for the Pan American Conference. They took all the private property they could carry but did not touch the records of real estate and property transactions housed in the offices of the notaries public.[46]

The rioters responded to the direct impact of politics on their lives. The part of the social order they attacked was the one in which they could easily see decisions being made about their lives. The symbols of economic control receded into the background. On the evening of April 9, they set the torch to Gómez's home, far to the west in the town of Fontibón. They also burned the Venado de Oro, the luxurious restaurant overlooking the city, which Gómez had built. The homes of Bogotá's largely unknown upper class of landholders, industrialists, and financiers in the northern suburbs were left untouched.

The passions of the day also remained rather abstract. No public figure lost his life in the riot, despite the radio reports that Gómez and Guillermo León Valencia were swinging from the lampposts in the Plaza de Bolívar. Only Alfonso Araújo was attacked, and that may have been by accident. The only other politician of note who was injured was Felipe Lleras Camargo, brother of former president Alberto Lleras Camargo. Felipe Lleras, known as *"el chiverudo"* because of the goatee he sported, was a well-known and popular figure in Bogotá who openly sympathized with Gaitán and was seen urging the crowds on during the riot.[47] The mob went after the symbols of political power, not the individuals atop the political hierarchy. Even the foreign delegates, prominently featured in the press only days before, were left alone.

At 10:56 p.m. the U.S. Department of State received a priority telegram from U.S. Ambassador Willard L. Beaulac stating that the entire U.S. delegation, including George Marshall and Secretary of Commerce Averell Harriman, was safe, as was the embassy, located just two blocks from the Plaza de Bolívar.[48] In an editorial two days later, the *New York Times* wrote that "all the members of the foreign delegations seem to have escaped hurt. The rioters were discriminatory in their attacks to that extent at least."[49] In the passions of that afternoon, the foreign visitors were quickly forgotten. Whatever notions of imperial power and foreign exploitation may have been in the *pueblo's* mind, they quickly vanished as soon as Gaitán was shot. The *bogotazo* was a local affair.

The crowd represented a reversal of the society not only because its internal structure contradicted the hierarchical order, but because its members suddenly appeared to be behaving like political *jefes*. Now the crowd had a public existence above the individual lives of its members, allowing each to join with others as equals and work together. The crowd turned on its head a social order where only the leaders had a public life, ruling over a *pueblo* buried in its private concerns. The public life of the *convivialistas* was a life of reason. The public life of the crowd was a life of passion. For a few brief moments, the public existence Gaitán had envisioned for the entire society, based on individuals acting out of passionate conviction, had come to pass.

How many were killed that afternoon on the streets of Bogotá? "We shall never know. We shall never know" is the answer, regardless of who is asked. Gaitanistas, Liberals, and Conservatives, rich and poor, intellectuals and physicians, all agree that a true count of the dead has never been made. Estimates vary wildly. Today, as time and the lack of evidence magnify the massacre, the guesses run into the thousands.

The hospitals and clinics of the city filled rapidly with the wounded and the dead. From the moment Gaitán was shot, doctors, interns, residents, and nurses knew that a crisis was upon them. In the city's largest hospital, the San José, Fernando Tamayo, a young doctor, took control as the incoming wounded created a panic among the staff. The directors of the hospital had gone home for lunch and now could not return to their posts. Tamayo quickly established his new-found authority and stifled the demand that the hospital attend only to Liberals. He proclaimed it neutral ground and prepared the staff to attend to all those who needed assistance.[50]

Tamayo stayed in the hospital for the next four days. He estimated that over a thousand wounded were cared for. Only twenty-nine died. Most did not have lethal wounds. Many were simply drunk. Some had machete wounds, probably incurred as they struggled among themselves. Many had been wounded by revolvers, and the worst, those who had been shot with Mausers, came later in the afternoon. Most lived, for the majority of them had been shot below the knees.

Before darkness fell, the military high command had ordered Dr. Alberto Vejarano Laverde and the marines to clear the streets of the dead. An epidemic was feared. With four dump trucks, Dr. Vejarano combed the downtown area picking up the cadavers strewn about. He also went from hospital to hospital to pick up those who had died there. He and the marines worked all evening and late into the night, starting again the following morn-

ing. The trucks made periodic trips to the Cementerio Central, where they
deposited the bodies. Dr. Vejarano made only a rough estimate of the number
killed, for he could not keep track of all the trips that were made. He came to
be known as *"el enterrador del régimen,"*—"the regime's gravedigger."[51]

The cadavers lay for days in the Cementerio Central while thousands of
Bogotanos filed past in search of lost friends and family members.[52] At the
urgent behest of the U.S. secretary of state, the American Red Cross sent
$50,000 as well as medical supplies and food, to the Colombian Red Cross, the
only organization in the country that attempted to coordinate a relief effort.
Maurice R. Reddy, a Red Cross disaster relief expert with considerable experience in the Caribbean, arrived in Bogotá on April 14 to head up the relief
effort.[53] On April 17 he wrote that the number of dead exceeded 500 and
might reach twice that figure, while those known to be in hospitals were about
1,500.[54] Another 1,000 were thought to be in need of nursing care and first aid.
When Reddy left Bogotá on April 27, he wrote to his superiors in Washington
that the number of deaths "may have exceeded 1,000 and injuries were

Foto Lunga

The dead of the *bogotazo* in the Cementerio Central.

suffered by 2,500." While the city's hospitals and doctors were overtaxed and overworked, he added, the injured were receiving excellent care.[55]

Despite the arduous efforts of hundreds of doctors and their assistants, the crisis was overwhelming. Dr. Fred Soper, the director of the Pan American Sanitary Bureau, was in Bogotá for the Pan American Conference. His impressions of the riot mirrored those of countless Colombians and foreigners: Bogotá looked like one of the European cities bombed during World War II. He reported to the American Red Cross that the position of the government was so precarious that no steps were being taken to coordinate an emergency medical care program, and that the hospitals were taxed beyond their capacity. Dr. Soper heard of one Colombian news photographer, shot while taking pictures, who bled to death in a nearby hospital because of the large number of casualties ahead of him.[56]

Published estimates of the number of dead run from has high as 2,585 in a recently published work on *la Violencia*[57] to as low as 549 in *El Tiempo* and *El Espectador* a month after the riot.[58] The official figures of the city of Bogotá show only a slight rise in the number of dead in April over other months that year.[59] The city apparently did not think to include the dead of the *bogotazo* in its statistics.

The figures presented in *El Espectador* on May 10 and in *El Tiempo* on May 11 are the best available.[60] According to the former, 65 of the cadavers were never identified. *El Tiempo* stated that 30 of the deaths were attributable to natural causes, and that 164 of the dead were women. There can be little doubt, however, that these figures understate the reality. There was not much concern with keeping accurate records. Many of the cadavers identified in the Cementerio Central were taken away by family members and friends without official permission.[61] In the barrios of Bogotá, many clandestinely buried their own, fearing government persecution of the relatives of *los muertos del nueve de abril*, the dead of the *bogotazo*.[62]

Who were they? Who composed the crowd? Who were the rioters and the looters? There is not enough evidence to answer these questions. The moment was too fleeting and spontaneous, and the government showed little interest in finding an answer. The long lists of dead and injured that appeared in the press in the following month give us no indication of their political affiliations, class backgrounds, occupations, or residences. The 1,208 individuals who went to the Red Cross to get food, housing, medical assistance, and employment or to search for their loved ones came from all over the city and included the unemployed, artisans, municipal workers, and intellectuals.[63] We cannot tell from all these lists whether they participated in the riot or were bystanders, whether those who were injured were attacking the *palacio*, looting stores, or hit by stray bullets. The crowd of the *bogotazo* remains largely anonymous.

Foto Tito

The armed *pueblo* holds the Colombian national flag.

Nevertheless, some evidence can be obtained from written and oral testimony. The crowd was urban but lacked a strong working-class base. Many workers, such as those of the Bavaria brewery, stayed away from the city center and may even have protected their factories.[64] The crowd cut across class lines, including workers in small establishments, employees, and the self-employed, middle-class professionals, state and municipal employees, workers in the electrical company, the telephone company, and the water department, trolley and taxi drivers, railroad workers, artisans, independent carpenters and construction workers, stonemasons and builders, janitors and building guards, policemen, street vendors and lottery vendors, barbers, café employees, shoeshine boys, streetsweepers, prostitutes, and criminals. Women who owned stands in the city markets, young and old alike, joined in groups, waving flags and leading the attack on various buildings.[65]

Those who became part of the crowd were those that Gaitán sought to address and represent. They were part of that large urban coalition that he felt had been excluded from economic and political decision making. In this broad sense it was a Gaitanista crowd. Yet conspicuously absent were the shop owners whose proud stance had offered Gaitán the image of a smoothly functioning social order.

8

The Demise of *Convivencia*

It was a cyclone. The cyclone of the beast, the shame of humanity, that hurled itself against Bogotá—oh poor, beloved Bogotá!—and razed the best that she had.

Calibán (April 16, 1948)

Reemerging Hierarchies

On the afternoon of April 9 the traditional hierarchies of public life were turned upside down. The crowd took center stage. The traditional leaders, with hardly enough time to respond to events, became spectators. The Conservatives in government were relegated to the gallery. The Liberals turned their backs on the crowd, squinting for a glimpse of their Conservative colleagues above them in the darkness. The *convivialistas* never quite knew what they were doing. Liberal and leftist critics of *convivencia*, normally on the margin of politics, worked frantically to direct the crowd toward their own political aims.

Liberals who were critical of *convivencia* or played no prominent role within it, socialists who saw the Ospina Pérez regime as a counterrevolution against the moderate gains of the Liberal Republic, and Gaitanistas who had little decision making power within the movement remained closest to the crowd. Some remained on the streets, while most regrouped to find some way to keep politics uppermost in the minds of the multitudes.

Minutes after Gaitán's assassination university students seized the Radio Nacional building.[1] From there army captain José Phillips attempted to organize the revolt. Phillips admired Gaitán and had served as his assistant in the trial of Lieutenant Cortés Poveda the evening before. Students declared

173

the victory of the revolution against the Conservative regime and announced that the offices of *El Siglo* were in flames, that the police and military had joined the multitude, and that the *palacio* would soon fall.[2] Phillips lent military prestige to the revolt and asked the army not to fire on the *pueblo*. The assassination, he informed his listeners, was an official crime that would be solved only if the government was overthrown. He urged everyone to remain vigilant.[3]

Other radio stations were also seized. Eugenio Cañavera, an announcer at Radio Nueva Granada, occupied the station with the help of well-known journalists from *El Liberal, La Razón,* and *El Tiempo.* They hooked up with Rómulo Guzmán at Ultimas Noticias. So did La Voz de Bogotá. Cristóbal Páez took the microphones and speakers of Radio Cristal out to the Calle Real to broadcast the revolutionary slogans and to enable his audience to hear the multitude.[4]

Gerardo Molina met with Jorge Uribe Márquez, who had joined in the first march to the Presidential Palace, and other critics of *convivencia.* He remembers the Gaitanistas as too grief-stricken to organize political actions.[5] Jorge Zalamea Borda, a well-known Liberal author and journalist just returned from his post as ambassador to Mexico, suggested that a fiction of authority was needed to organize the *pueblo.*[6] The group formed in response to this suggestion named itself the Executive Committee of the Central Revolutionary Junta of Government and decided to go to Ultimas Noticias, to silence Guzmán as much as to deliver their own orders. Molina believed that their "place was there, for we could not communicate with the masses, who heard nothing." They aimed to instruct their listeners on how to overthrow the Conservative regime.[7]

Molina took the microphone as the provisional president of the executive committee. "You are listening to Dr. Gerardo Molina in person . . . who is addressing all of Liberalism throughout the country to communicate the imperative decrees that have been determined by the Central Revolutionary Junta of Government. . . . The revolutionary movement controls all communications, the streets of Bogotá, and the other principal cities of the country. . . . The popular reconquest of power has begun. . . . I inform you also that our movement is looked upon with sympathy by progressive governments throughout the world. We have the support of countries inspired by the ideals of democratic reconstruction that are the basis of our organization and of our movement and struggle."[8]

The rebels issued orders to Liberals throughout the country. They called on Bogotá labor leaders to create civic police groups; they ordered the police, whom they claimed to control, to stand by for further orders; they demanded that the *pueblo* remain on the streets and assured them that the military and police had joined the revolution; they ordered all airports closed.[9] Zalamea

Borda exclaimed that Santos was flying home from New York to take over the government. Carlos H. Pareja, a Marxist lawyer with close ties with Gaitanismo declared that the Conservative government had fallen. "The life of Gaitán is worth many Conservative lives," he declared. Joaquín Tiberio Galvis, a well-known independent Liberal, boasted that international public opinion would recognize the Liberals as an insurgent movement if the constitutional head of government and his "triad of assassins and businessmen" were not handed over to the *pueblo* within the next six hours. Both Molina and Galvis were looking beyond Colombia for support. Another voice repeated Gaitán's call to action: "*¡A la carga!*"[10]

Exhausted and convinced that he had done all he could, Molina slowly returned home through streets lit only by the fires raging in nearby buildings.[11] After nightfall most of the rebels went to the Fifth Police Precinct on the city's northern outskirts, close to the working-class barrio of La Perseverancia and the Ministry of War in San Diego, to join police captain Tito Orozco Castro and the Liberal Politican Jorge Nassar Quiñones, who had taken control of the station. Zalamea Borda and Adán Arriaga Andrade, a provincial Turbayista leader who had just been named the first governor of the largely black western department of Chocó, now became the new leaders. Arriaga Andrade thought that the riot offered a unique opportunity to overthrow the Conservatives, and saw the crowds as the main obstacle to that goal. Frightened and worried that drunken rioters interested only in immediate spoils would destroy the Liberal revolution, he called on the police to jail the looters. As an intellectual, he felt that he was responsible for filling the void left by the silence of the Liberal leaders and immediately established a telephone line to the Liberals at *El Tiempo*.[12] Arriaga Andrade spoke with *El Tiempo* at least every half-hour to confirm his hold on the station and to ask about the Liberal delegation that was heading toward the *palacio*.[13]

Antonio García, the prominent socialist economist and occasional Gaitán advisor, did not follow his friend Molina to the radio station after they lost contact with the Liberals. He was convinced that radio broadcasts would fall on deaf ears and wanted to stay on the streets. He remembers an afternoon of "complete anarchy" in which he did what he could to bring about some order on the streets.[14] He roamed about for hours imploring the crowd not to loot, drink, and destroy as he searched for familiar faces and helped the injured.[15]

Lower-ranking Gaitanistas also remained on the streets. Many were members of the JEGA who had been with the first crowd. After he left his hiding place in the church and defied the tanks that defended the regime, Muñoz Uribe continued his efforts to avenge his leader's death. He went to Liberal headquarters, where the Gaitanista leaders Jorge Villaveces and Alvaro Ayala were talking with sympathetic military men about forming a "war committee." Muñoz Uribe was quickly named president, but the group could not remain together once it reached the crowded streets.[16] Agustín Utrera, the barber who had joined the first march on the *palacio,* also went to Liberal headquarters. There he convinced the Gaitanista leaders that he could gather two hundred "men of confidence. . . . men who did not wear ties," who could save the revolution. When he returned with some men, the Gaitanistas were gone.[17]

Gaitán's middle- and working-class lieutenants, long the organizational backbone of the movement, felt as alienated from the crowd as did those trying to control it from afar. Although they stayed on the streets longer, they too were shocked at the *pueblo's* wanton destruction and looting. Hernando Restrepo Botero, one of Gaitán's labor leaders, vainly tried to stop the looting.[18] Octavio López, Gaitán's secretary while he was mayor of Bogotá, thought that the multitudes had gone mad and implored them to stop drinking and looting. He nearly fainted in the confusion and was dragged home by his sons.[19] According to José Vicente García, another dedicated follower of Gaitán's, the herd instinct had taken over.[20] Clímaco Aldana, one of Gaitán's secretaries, spent the afternoon rushing from the Liberal headquarters to his home with Gaitán's private papers and correspondence.[21]

Ricaurte could recognize no one after the three tanks turned on the crowd at the Plaza de Bolívar. He returned to La Perseverancia, the barrio he had helped organize for Gaitán, where he was well-known. On the way he saw thousands of people rushing downtown. When he arrived he found that most of his friends were gone. He gathered a few men and led them back, but they all lost contact with each other on the crowded streets. It was an impossible situation, he recalled: "Everyone did what he wanted . . . nobody was thinking."[22] Carlos J. Sánchez also returned to his barrio in Chapinero, where he tried to assemble a committee. With a few others he went downtown, but they too were separated. He returned home a few hours later to learn that two of his men had been killed. For hours he remained shut up in his room.[23] Valerio and Bernardo Valverde, Gaitanista organizers of the barrio El Vergel, rushed downtown, walked around, listened to speeches, and were given two machetes that they did not know what to do with. After the tanks turned on the crowd, they grew desperate. They remembered that they had unthinkingly walked past their mother's small café, located on the Calle Real next to the Ministry of Communications. They rushed to protect it, and then returned to organize civic committees to protect El Vergel from looters and criminals.[24]

The Gaitanistas' inability to influence the crowd cannot be explained only by the spontaneous anger of Gaitán's followers. Gaitán had ensured that only he would have power within his movement. Everyone's attention was to be focused on him alone. An organizational infrastructure might have curtailed his power and his direct relationship with the *pueblo*. Once he was gone, no lieutenant could step into his shoes. The JEGA, semi-secret and devoted to protecting the leader, could do little in public. The barrio committees that Gaitán used to structure his tours and bring out the vote lacked any internal organization or chain of command and never got off the ground. A few Gaitanistas like Ricaurte thought of mobilizing their barrios, but scattered geographic sections of the city could not be the basis of the revolt.

The politicians most out of touch with the crowd and the least active and effective were the leaders of the Communist party. It was a small party organized on closed and strictly hierarchical principles, and it had traditionally opposed Gaitán. Its secretary general, Gilberto Vieira, found his party headquarters sacked. With nowhere to meet his comrades, he walked the streets, trying to find Molina and the executive committee but ending up at the offices of *El Tiempo*, the center of traditional Liberal power. From there he contacted Arriaga Andrade and called for a general strike to bring down the government. Vieira later acknowledged that the general strike, observed by large sectors of labor after April 9, had only served to demobilize the *pueblo* in the days following the riot.[25]

The many foreigners in Bogotá had little to do with what was going on in the streets. Most of the Pan American Conference delegates remained holed up where they were being lodged, in private homes, hotels, the Congress building, or the headquarters of the Presidential Guard. There was one notable exception. Fidel Castro never went back to Gaitán's office for the second interview.

In the streets where Gaitán was shot, he saw "crazed people running . . . with an indescribable fear in their eyes. . . . a state of indescribable rage was created." The popular insurrection Castro saw reminded him of accounts of the fall of the Bastille.[26] He feared, however, that nothing would come of those spontaneous and leaderless actions. He quickly joined a small group of men that was attacking a police station. Inside, he took a tear-gas gun, donned military boots, shirt, and cap, grabbed a rifle and sixteen bullets, and ventured out again.

Castro joined a group of protesters armed with rifles, guns, machetes, and iron beams who were preparing to move on the Presidential Palace. A few blocks down the street they were fired upon by soldiers (probably Lieutenant Carvajal's men) and by others who he was told were priests connected with a Catholic school (probably the Colegio de San Bartolomé). From there Castro went to a radio station that had been taken over by university students and was under attack from the military (probably Radio Nacional). Passing the Ministry of War, he tried to persuade soldiers to join the crowds. Everywhere he attempted to organize those around him, but could not tell friend from foe.

Castro spent a "disagreeable evening, filled with uncertainty" in a police station on the western edge of the city. He had time to think about what he had been doing that afternoon. "I thought about Cuba, my family, and many other things, and I asked myself if I should stay there in that useless situation. And I really had doubts. I was completely . . . alone at that moment, without a Cuban friend. I had few ties with the Colombian *pueblo,* and with the students I had only conceptual ties, ties of ideas." But, he said to himself, "The *pueblo* here is the same as in Cuba, as everywhere else."[27] The next morning he was whisked out of the country by the Cuban ambassador to the Pan American Conference.

The actions of Liberals, Gaitanistas, Conservatives, and the military were all circumscribed by the Liberal delegation heading for the presidential residence. The putative government at Ultimas Noticias named itself the executive committee of that delegation. The Liberals at the Fifth Police Precinct immediately contacted *El Tiempo* to find out where the delegation was. The Liberals at *El Tiempo* in turn became the delegation's official representatives outside the *palacio.* The Gaitanistas who conferred at Liberal party headquarters accepted Echandía's leadership over the Liberal revolt. Vieira went to the offices of *El Tiempo* in search of the delegation, and even Castro learned that the Liberal bosses were on their way to the *palacio.* At no time was the authority of the delegation challenged.

Echandía and his colleagues took a circuitous route to the *palacio.* Their progress through streets lined with burning buildings was often interrupted. They left the Teatro Nuevo through the back door and retraced their steps eastward toward the Clínica Central along the Calle 11 in order to avoid the throng-filled Calle Real. Once they reached the Carrera 6, which ran parallel to the Calle Real and would have taken them just one block east of the *palacio* had they gone south, they decided that the trip was too dangerous. They again retraced their steps, this time toward *El Tiempo,* located on the Calle 14. They met Don Luis Cano. The elderly, white-haired, and widely respected owner and publisher of *El Espectador* had been an architect of *convivencia.* He naturally joined the delegation.[28]

Once they reached the offices of *El Tiempo,* the delegation resumed the deliberations begun at the Clínica Central and continued at the Teatro Nuevo. They chose Araújo to walk to the *palacio* alone, thinking he had a better chance of reaching it undetected. Araújo was more than half-way there when he was caught in a crossfire on the northern edge of the Plaza de Bolívar. A woman supporting herself on his arm was shot, and Araújo fell to the ground. He turned back to *El Tiempo.*[29]

With night rapidly falling, the Liberals ventured out again. They edged along the remaining buildings in single file, with broad spaces between them. Carlos Padilla fell far behind and would have been shot by a policeman had the Liberals not protected him. Once close to the *palacio* they faced its well-guarded doors. From a nearby café Araújo telephoned to announce their arrival. During those long hours they had not attempted to contact their Conservative colleagues. Were the Liberals unsure of their mission? Had they in fact been summoned by the president? Perhaps they thought that the Conservatives would change their minds and decide to keep them out on the streets. Whether or not the late call was received, the doors of the *palacio* were ajar when they arrived moments later. They slipped through. Once inside they were about to be taken prisoner when a soldier called out to let them through because the president expected them.[30]

It had taken the Liberals all afternoon to join the Conservatives. Although they hesitated and repeatedly detoured, they never wavered in their intention to speak with them. Roberto García-Peña remembers that when he saw the Liberals at *El Tiempo*, they were convinced that they had to reach the *palacio*.[31] The chaos that surrounded them only underscored that feeling. Their trip had spanned much of the riot, from the burning of the first buildings to the looting of the stores. The multitudes that the Liberals saw as they walked out of the Clínica Central at three o'clock were far different from those they saw as they reached the *palacio* at seven. The *bogotazo* had occured in between.

The Conversation

When the Liberals joined the Conservatives, they had lived through the most frightening moments of their lives. In a few hours they had experienced death and destruction on a scale they could never have imagined. They saw public buildings go up in smoke. Possibly for the first time, they felt that their lives were in danger. *La Violencia* in the countryside suddenly seemed very close. Their public personalities no longer protected them. In fact, the reverse was true: they felt endangered precisely because they were public figures. The Conservatives knew that the Liberals had survived an ordeal and were relieved to be with them behind the protective walls and the Presidential Guard.

The conversation should have ground to a halt moments after it started. There was nothing to discuss. There was little if any room for bargaining. Yet there was little the *convivialistas* could do but talk, and talk they did. Once they were together again, the traditional leaders of the Liberal and Conservative parties staged the most celebrated conversation in Colombian history. As the city burned around them, they talked slowly, calmly, with all the respect and deference that the codes of public life imposed upon them. Each was given his turn, and each summed up the situation as best as he could. Liberals told about what they had experienced outside the *palacio*, and Conservatives about what they had experienced inside the walls. They groped for a solution all could accept.[32]

How to address the issue of power? Some of the Liberals grew impatient, openly complaining that they were losing precious minutes. Lleras Restrepo interrupted several times to say that the conversation was not progressing as they had hoped. Echandía sat quietly in the background, seemingly unconcerned. Ospina Pérez helped the Liberals along: "Then what you want is for the president to resign, is that not so?" Lleras Restrepo pounced on this unexpectedly favorable turn in the conversation. "This point seems to me to be very interesting, and we should begin to consider it immediately," he said.

The president's response revealed the weakness of the Liberals' position as well as his own understanding of how the collective interests of both traditional parties might best be represented. The president agreed with Lleras Restrepo that the point was interesting. He told them that he did not covet power and that the presidency was a sacrifice for him and his family. If he resigned, however, he would be betraying the nation that had elected him. Moreover, he and his party would inevitably be regarded as accomplices in Gaitán's assassination, and his honor, his family's, and his party's would all be tarnished.

The president was implying what should also have been obvious to the Liberals. The legitimacy of traditional partisanship would be undermined and further collaboration between them might prove impossible if a street crime and the crowd forced a change in government. He left the most telling point for last. "We must consider what would happen in the departments; at least six would march toward the reconquest of power. . . We would face then an inevitable civil war."

Whether the Liberals still believed that they had a chance of capturing power, or felt the pressures of the crowd, or were trying to test whether the president was as sure of himself as his poise seemed to indicate, they tried once more to convince him. Some time elapsed before they played their last card. Don Luis reiterated his admiration for the president, but asked him to resign as a service to the nation for which "future generations of Colombian democracy will be eternally grateful to you." The president must have felt some irritation at the Liberal's narrow perspective. In a calm voice he uttered what would become the most celebrated statement of the conversation. "Don Luis, . . . for Colombian democracy and for the future generations of which you speak, a dead president counts for more than a fugitive president." The Liberals capitulated. "What then do you propose to do?" they asked, almost plaintively.

Throughout the evening Ospina Pérez walked in and out of his office to keep informed of the situation in the other cities. Here also the Liberals were at a disadvantage. All that afternoon they had received only sparse news about the actions of Liberals and protesters elsewhere. The Conservatives were certain that their survival depended on what happened in Bogotá and in the *palacio*, and that the other cities would follow the capital's example. Estrada Monsalve said as much: "The victory of Bogotá is that of the entire nation."[33] Once the Liberals had joined them and the political onslaught on the streets had subsided, calm was also returning to most of the rest of the nation. The petroleum center of Barrancabermeja remained in the workers' control. But the rebels of Barranquilla, Cúcuta, and Cali had been subdued by the military, and the municipal buildings that the crowds had seized were again in the hands of the authorities. Late into the night Ospina Pérez worried about a radio station in Ibagué, capital of Tolima, that continued to issue revolutionary slogans.[34]

Twice the conversation broke down, but the Liberals could not bear to go back out into the cold, dark night. The longer they talked, the more they must have realized that the man who had been an outsider to so many of those previous conversations was dead.

The Liberals' immobility in the *palacio* was an extension of their earlier condition in the street. In the afternoon their followers at the radio stations and the police stations waited for them to arrive at the *palacio*. Throughout the night they waited for them to get out of the *palacio*. Adán Arriaga Andrade called *El Tiempo* incessantly to find out what was going on, worrying that he could not keep the policemen under his control much longer.[35] The radio stations fell silent. The Liberals at *El Tiempo* knew as little as anyone else. The rest of the nation also waited. The languid pace of the conversation was putting an already exhausted political revolution to sleep. The Liberals, voluntarily trapped within the *palacio*, disarmed the lingering revolt. The triumphant Conservatives did what they had done anxiously all afternoon: wait. Together in the *palacio*, the *convivialistas* controlled events outside by doing very little, simply because they continued to be regarded as leaders, first by the crowd and then by other politicians.

At eight in the morning the entire army high command arrived at the *palacio* at the instigation of Gómez, who had managed to reach the War Ministry at midnight. He had told the generals that the president would be receptive to a military government. Every time the Conservatives spoke with him during the night, the hysterical Gómez repeated the same phrase: "military junta, military junta, military junta!"[36] The man who had most distrusted the crowds and had lost his newspaper and his home to rioters felt that social order could be rebuilt only by the military.

The generals who came to see the president were hesitant. None of them had any political experience. Throughout *convivencia* the politicians ruled without them. They too had just been through a harrowing experience. Aware of the minor role they had played in the defense of the city, they were uncertain about their reception in the *palacio*. Nevertheless, they felt the responsibility of establishing order, especially since it was widely rumored that Gaitán's widow and daughter would lead the crowd carrying Gaitán's body to the *palacio*.

Following Gómez's suggestion, the generals offered to relieve the president of his official duties and replace the civilian government with a military junta. Ospina Pérez refused but offered to include some of them in a civilian-military cabinet that he would lead. Realizing their mistake, the generals declined, saying that they would be lost in the separate ministeries and the armed forces would be left without a unified command. They pledged their support for the president instead.[37]

The generals' intervention was important in bringing the *convivialistas* closer together after an evening of fruitless talk. The Liberals also opposed a military government, and, like the Conservatives, perceived a threat to their public lives should the military take over. Ospina Pérez had offered to reshuffle his cabinet to accommodate the military. The old idea of a new cabinet had been introduced. The *convivialistas* rapidly coalesced behind it.

Ospina Pérez took the initiative. He offered the Liberals a bipartisan cabinet and a government of National Union. He would name Echandía minister of interior.[38] The choice seemed perfect. Not only had the crowd acclaimed Echandía and the Liberals proposed him for the presidency hours earlier, but he alone among the Liberals had not asked the president to resign. Echandía seemed, furthermore, to be a man without political ambitions. Serene and responsible, he was much like the president himself. The Liberals jumped at the opportunities that opened before them. "The minister of war should also be a Liberal," one of them exclaimed. But Ospina Pérez was ready: "The minister of war will be Lieutenant General Ocampo." Germán Ocampo was the nation's highest-ranking general. Undaunted, another Liberal insisted that the director of the police had to be a Liberal. "I have just named Colonel Régulo Gaitán as chief of the police," the president responded. He added that the minister of justice would be a close friend of Gaitán's so that a thorough and impartial investigation of the crime could be ensured.[39] The positions that Ospina Pérez had filled were those the Liberals most coveted. Echandía informed the president that he would not be able to accept his post until he knew the composition of the cabinet.[40] But Ospina Pérez was not about to pick names, then and there, that the Liberals could oppose. He told them that the cabinet list would be ready within three hours.[41] Everyone understood that it would exclude Gómez and Lleras Restrepo. It was not the time for extremists.

The Liberals emerged from the presidential residence almost fourteen hours after they had arrived. They left in daylight and walked through streets lined with soldiers. Knowing that in just a few hours they would again be talking to the president, they headed for the offices of *El Tiempo* to sell their followers on the coalition. Over the din Echandía called the meeting to order, and Lleras Restrepo presented the ultimate argument for the coalition: should the president be forced to resign, they would face a civil war that no party leader would be able to control.[42] The Liberals hardly needed to be persuaded, and the Gaitanistas Uribe Márquez and Villaveces concurred with the *convivialista* logic.[43]

The leaders moved to an inner chamber and sat in a small circle to wait for the presidential verdict. Echandía answered the president's call and jotted down the names of the new cabinet members as his colleagues hovered nervously around him, each straining for a look at the list.[44] Ospina Pérez had reshuffled the cabinet with a minimum of change. He had to make room for six Liberals in the entirely Conservative thirteen-member cabinet that had been in office since March. With General Ocampo as minister of war, the president could now name six Liberals and six Conservatives, the first time that the odd-numbered body would be evenly divided between the two parties.

The president's solution was entirely logical. He had already removed the two members of his own party, Gómez and Montalvo, whom the Liberals would not be able to approve. He had kept Andrade, thereby offering Gómez some guarantees and facilitating his exit. He replaced him with Zuleta Angel, who was his interior minister, thus keeping the one man whom the Liberals could unquestionably trust while at the same time opening up Zuleta Angel's post for Echandía. Zuleta Angel, moreover, had wide experience in foreign affairs and diplomacy and would be able to handle the delicate matter of the Pan American Conference.

The president still had to remove four incumbent Conservative ministers. Eliseo Arango, the leader of the intransigent *leopardos*, and Joaquín Estrada Monsalve, the controversial minister of education and, since March 21, the minister of mines and petroleum, were two logical choices. The others were the moderate but little-known minister of agriculture, Alfredo García Cadena, and the equally little-known minister of health, Hernando Anzola Cubides. Both men had been in their first cabinet positions for less than two weeks. He kept the other four Conservatives, José María Bernal, José Vicente Dávila Tello, Guillermo Salamanca, and Evaristo Sourdis. They were loyal to him, had little political experience, and had all spent the night in the *palacio*. Of the six Conservatives who lost their jobs, only Estrada Monsalve had been with the president the evening before.

Ospina Pérez brought into the cabinet two Liberals who had served on it prior to the March crisis. Minister of Education Fabio Lozano y Lozano had served the evening before as liaison with the military. Samuel Arango Reyes was returned as minister of justice. While he was not one of Gaitán's friends as the president had promised, he had earned the fallen leader's confidence.[45] Pedro Castro Monsalvo, an agricultural engineer with a long career in politics, was named minister of agriculture. Jorge Bejarano, a founder and director of the Colombian Red Cross, became minister of health. He had already held the position in 1946 and 1947. Finally, Alonso Aragón Quintero was given the key position of minister of mines and petroleum. He was president of the Senate and had been a relatively quiet member of the delegation that had spent the night in the *palacio*. He would have to reestablish order in Barrancabermeja.

The new cabinet was composed of old faces. The only innovation was the inclusion of General Ocampo, the first military man to become part of a *convivialista* cabinet. Ospina Pérez did not bring any members of his own party into the executive branch of government. The six Conservatives who remained had been in office when the crisis erupted. Eight of the Liberals and Conservatives had held positions in a previous bipartisan cabinet, and only three—Echandía, Castro Monsalvo, and Aragón Quintero—had never held a cabinet post in the Ospina Pérez government. The Liberal chiefs were greatly relieved, for the Gaitanistas had been shut out. The president had gone along with the unwritten rules.

After having been buffeted about in a crisis they could not control, the Liberals had an understanding that allowed them to walk honorably into a coalition. They were no longer being rushed into one response after another with little time to think. The deliberate pace of politics could return, and with it the public life they so cherished.

The Body of Gaitán

In the pre-dawn hours of April 10, Bogotá's streets were empty but for the soldiers from Boyacá. After waiting all night in the Clínica Central, Doña Amparo could at last take her husband's body home. She had help from Pedro Eliseo Cruz, who obtained a simple coffin from a nearby funeral home. Unable to find a hearse or truck, he placed the coffin on a mule-driven flat bed normally used to transport goods to market. Slowly they made their way out of the city center to the Gaitán home, forty blocks to the northwest.[46] But this was not to be the end of the story.

The *convivialistas* had little choice but to stage a public funeral. If they buried Gaitán clandestinely in an unmarked grave, they would have promoted his inevitable martyrdom and been unable to claim him as their own. By burying him in public, they could turn him into a *civilista;* not to do so would make him a subversive *caudillo*. But where to bury him? At first it was reported that Gaitán would be laid to rest either next to the statue of the Liberator in the Plaza de Bolívar or on the Calle Real, where the Liberal leader Rafael Uribe Uribe had been killed in 1914.[47] But those were public places, and either would inevitably serve as a rallying point for the *pueblo*. Moreover, all were within the "forbidden blocks," the central area that had witnessed the crowd's greatest destruction and had been cordoned off by the military. The *convivialistas* feared a return of the crowd to the city center for the funeral. To bury Gaitán within sight of the Presidential Palace was to invite a riot more awesome than the first. They considered the Cementerio Central, fifteen blocks northwest of the center, but that also seemed too threatening.

The *convivialistas'* most immediate problem was Gaitán's widow. They did not have Gaitán's body. During their long conversation the evening before, they had forgotten about the fallen leader, and now a small group of Gaitán's most loyal followers kept a constant armed vigil around the body to prevent it from being abducted.[48] Acting largely on her own, Doña Amparo steadfastly refused to authorize her husband's burial unless Ospina Pérez was first overthrown. In addition, she stipulated that neither Santos nor Lleras Restrepo should become president.[49] She insisted that her husband's assassination was a political crime planned within the highest reaches of the Conservative regime with the possible connivance of some Liberal leaders. Her implication, of course, was that Santos and Lleras Restrepo had a hand in his death. Moreover, the labor leaders insisted that they would not call off the general strike until Ospina Pérez resigned and Gaitán was buried.[50]

By the morning of April 10, few of the expectations held by Gaitán's followers had come to pass. The change in government they expected in the night was nowhere to be seen. The empty streets were patrolled by soldiers they did not know. The radio stations they usually listened to were silent, and only a few copies of *El Liberal* could be found. *El Tiempo, El Espectador,* and *El Siglo* did not appear. From sparsely worded and intermittent broadcasts on Radio Nacional came the news that the Conservative regime was still in power. *El Liberal* confirmed the shock. Nobody knew for sure what had happened but the rumors spread that the Liberal leaders, in time-honored fashion, were joining a coalition government with the Conservatives. Some hope remained, however, for *El Liberal* reported that Liberals elsewhere were still in control of towns and municipalities.[51]

According to the official news, order had been reestablished in Bogotá and most of the nation. But it was not the crowd's order. Martial law had been imposed and a 6:00 p.m. curfew clamped on the city.[52] Nobody knew where Gaitán's body was. Few dared venture into the street. Soldiers ordered those who did to walk with hands raised above their heads, making them look as vulnerable as they felt. They could not wear their new clothes for fear of being apprehended by the military and maybe even chastized by neighbors. Guilt compounded sorrow and confusion.

It was Saturday, normally a half-day of work, but Radio Nacional instructed everyone to remain at home. The general strike held. Employees of banks and government agencies knew that neither would function. Garbage collectors and streetsweepers understood that their awesome tasks would not start that day. There was no public transport, and many trolley drivers knew that their vehicles had been destroyed. Policemen, whether they had joined the crowds or not, worried that they would be dismissed.[53] Few Bogotanos had enough food at home to last more than a couple of days.

This alien order was not as complete as the government made it seem. The Liberals at the Fifth Police Precinct did not give up until April 12, when the new coalition government prepared to bomb the building from the air and attack it with heavy artillery.[54] As his first act as minister of interior, Echandía unsuccessfully attempted to extract from Ospina Pérez a promise of political amnesty for the rebels, and he tried to coax them out of the building, imploring them not to commit imprudent acts. Echandía believed that the rebels were heavily armed. In fact, Arriaga Andrade never distributed the guns and rifles that were under lock and key in the police station. The rebels were defenseless and finally surrendered to the army.[55]

In the morning the Universidad de La Salle, one of the few large religious institutions in the city not targeted the day before, was burned to the ground. Small bands of men also looted the municipal warehouse and some of the food markets, which were left largely unprotected by the military.[56]

For Gaitán's followers the most shocking news was the rumor that their leader had been assassinated not by the Conservatives, but by a man nobody knew, a common drifter who had apparently acted out of private motives of revenge.[57] Whether they believed this or not, they were robbed of a comprehensible, political explanation for their leader's death. For Gaitán to have been killed by the government was one thing, for it confirmed his power and prestige and the threat that he had come to symbolize; for him to have been killed from a purely private impulse was quite another. It made his death senseless and impossible to accept.

On the evening of April 11 the president spoke to the nation. Addressing his audience as *"colombianos,"* he spoke to Conservatives as well as Liberals, workers and peasants, all citizens of the Colombian nation.[58] "Never had a city been subjected . . . to a greater sacrifice" than Bogotá, he declared. "Its buildings, its monuments, and its rich mansions were the object of a vandalistic destruction that reduced to rubble works of art and beauty, the pride of Colombian culture. Everything we had built with tremendous effort in order to present ourselves in a dignified way before friendly nations was barbaricly annihilated. Our national history does not know a more shameful page of desecration and cowardice. As the capital of the republic, this generous metropolis, which has always opened its hospitable doors to all the sons of the Nation, did not deserve such humiliation and disrespect. In the name of culture I condemn these assaults that degrade us before the civilized world."

The president was able to speak in the moralistic language of public life to all the "sons of the Nation" because his sights were raised beyond the nation's borders. Not only was he worried about Colombia's image abroad and the impression that the foreign ministers and their delegations would take home with them, but he also felt that the "outburst of barbarism" was not home-grown. "Alien, yes, alien were those hands," he proclaimed, "that were criminally raised. . . . It was not the *pueblo* of Colombia, it was not Colombian souls, it was not the hearts of Colombia, it was not the arms of patriots, that started the fires in the historic buildings, the stores, the schools, the temples, the homes, the modest factories. It was a spirit alien to us. . . . We face a movement of communist inspiration and practices."[59] Ospina Pérez had been convinced since the evening of April 9 that communists were responsible for the riot. Only this could explain what had taken place. The *pueblo* alone could never have done it.[60]

Some who listened to the president's calm appeal felt comforted and reassured. Many more were perplexed. Those who had besieged the *palacio*, robbed stores, and destroyed the Palacio de San Carlos and the other historic buildings did not know that foreign communists had told them to do so. Few could have felt proud of their actions, especially when they did not result in a change in government, and they may have even felt a measure of shame.[61] But they also knew their actions were the result of their outrage and an expression of their fury. Could they have been manipulated? Had their anger been used by others whom they did not know? Was the destruction of Bogotá's buildings the result not of their hatred, but of a plan concocted beyond the borders of Colombia? Had they been led to loot?

These questions inevitably found their way into the minds of the rioters.[62] They had no evidence to refute the president's claims. The moments after Gaitán's assassination were sufficiently confusing that they must have pondered the possibility that they had been manipulated. So many of them could hardly believe what they had done. The idea of communist conspirators made a certain amount of sense. For some of the rioters the idea was comforting. The president's charges meant that they had not been responsible for their actions.

Ospina Pérez's explanation equally absolved the *convivialistas* of complicity in Gaitán's assassination and responsibility for the riot. If the entire affair had been hatched abroad, they could not be held responsible for the social conditions that might have led to such an outburst. Their place in society as public figures would not be in question. If the *bogotazo* had been produced by communists, public life in Colombia might still be possible.

The government attempted to back up these charges. The homes of foreigners were searched for implicating evidence. The entire leadership of the Communist party was imprisoned, and newspapers printed detailed information about their meetings in the months prior to April 9. Their criticism of the Pan American Conference was sufficient, in government eyes, to implicate them in Gaitán's assassination and the riot. On the evening of April 9, the government had already stated that the assassin was a communist.[63] The leftist Venezuelan leader Rómulo Betancourt, who headed his country's delegation to the conference, was singled out, and his connections with Colombian leftists were investigated.[64] On April 12 the *New York Times* correspondent Milton Bracker filed the first uncensored account of the riot from Balboa, Panama. He reported that the Colombian government was encouraging correspondents to play up the "Communist angle" of their stories. Dispatches that emphasized "normalcy" and the efficiency of military control, and soft-pedaled politics were sure to pass the censors.[65]

The conspiracy theory did not at first gain wide adherence. Even though Ambassador Beaulac's telegrams to the State Department during the afternoon of April 9 asserted that communist-led mobs had taken over the city under the direction of communist radio broadcasters,[66] Washington remained doubtful, and Secretary of State Marshall kept silent on the issue in Bogotá until April 12. On April 11 a *New York Times* editorial concluded that the *bogotazo* "was not a true political revolution. The small Communist Party apparently did not instigate the rioting, but only jumped in to take advantage of it."[67] Many of the foreign delegates remained unconvinced as well. Thomas Dewey, however, the Republican presidential candidate, charged on April 10 that the *bogotazo* followed a "classic Communist pattern."[68]

On April 12 Secretary Marshall, referring to recent events in Europe, stated that the riot followed "the same definite pattern as the occurrences which provoked the strikes in France and Italy." He placed the blame on Moscow.[69] That day Colombia broke diplomatic relations with the Soviet Union.[70] On April 19 a U.S. House of Representatives subcommittee on intelligence opened hearings on the entire affair.[71] The *pueblo* of Bogotá was exploited by U.S. politicians who knew next to nothing about it to promote their own political careers and the Cold War mentality then beginning to be fostered.

On April 14 the Pan American Conference resumed its deliberations in a Liberal schoolhouse on the northern outskirts of the city. Although Secretary Marshall left early and many delegations were evacuated from the city along with many American citizens, the conference continued to work until the end of the month. Marshall did not leave until it had passed a declaration stating that communism was a foreign agent "incompatible with American liberty and the dignity of the individual."[72] The resolution had been on the original agenda. After the riot there could be no doubt that it would pass.

Gaitán's burial, originally scheduled for April 12, was postponed three times.[73] On April 15 the Liberals persuaded Victor Julio Silva of the CTC to call off the general strike. On April 17 they reached an agreement with Doña Amparo. They offered to buy the Gaitán home and turn it into a national monument and eventually a large popular museum for the *pueblo* if she allowed Gaitán to be buried there. Doña Amparo remembered that Franklin Roosevelt had been buried in his garden and thought that their own would be an appropriate resting place for her husband.[74] She also agreed to go to the funeral but not take part in it, and to withdraw her demand that Ospina Pérez resign.

This solution exceeded the *convivialistas'* greatest expectations. Gaitán would not have to be moved at all; he would be buried on the outskirts of the city, and in a private building rather than one of historic national sites in downtown Bogotá. The *pueblo* would undoubtedly feel pride and satisfaction at seeing its leader's home turned into a public monument but would find little room to congregate in the narrow residential streets outside the house. Gaitán, the outsider to *convivencia*, would remain outside the physical boundaries of the public arena.

Once this decision had been made, the Liberals, who were responsible for burying the fallen leader, since he would not be accorded the national honors of a state burial, decided to turn the funeral into a mass demonstration to reestablish their hold over the crowd. They self-consciously attempted to repeat the discipline and somber tone of Gaitán's Manifestación del Silencio. The occasion, of course, ideally lent itself to that effort. The Gaitanistas at *Jornada* went so far as to implore Gaitán's followers to act as they had on that historic date.[75] The *pueblo's* silence was to mean that the Liberals controlled the crowd and that it accepted their leadership. Through the *pueblo's* mournful conduct, the Liberal leaders sought to reconfirm its passive role in national life. On the *pueblo's* silence they attempted to impose their oratorical art.

The meaning of Gaitán's ritual escaped the Liberals. The silence that he had created in the Plaza de Bolívar was a symbol of the *pueblo's* demand for life, not its recognition of death. Gaitán's silent demonstration had been directed at the government to protest against *la Violencia* that it inflicted from above. The funeral was aimed from above at Gaitán's followers to quell the violence that they had inflicted from below. On February 7 Gaitán had implored the president to bring order to the lives of the *pueblo*. By speaking in its name, he had challenged the traditional hierarchies of public life. The *convivialistas* wanted to restore that hierarchy through a public spectacle in which the *pueblo* would again be the passive spectator.

In life Gaitán had stood between the politicians and the *pueblo*. Now the politicians stood before the *pueblo* without him. The ceremony was short. It took place in the large Parque Nacional on the northern outskirts of the city, only a few blocks from the Gaitán home. There was no balcony, so a makeshift stage was built and loudspeakers were hung from trees. Three orators spoke to more than one hundred thousand mourners.[76] Two were Gaitanistas. Darío Samper and Jorge Uribe Márquez delivered eloquent, heart-wrenching eulogies. But the man who gave the major address was Lleras Restrepo, the new leader of the Liberal party and Gaitán's most insistent enemy. As he got up to speak, some in the multitude turned their backs to him.[77]

He spoke in his quiet, barely audible voice. "*Señores liberales:* here begins the procession of the masses of the *pueblo,* who are going to offer *their* last respects to the man whom just days ago *they* saw leading *them,* indomitable and strong, symbol of all popular aspirations . . ."[78]

Lleras Restrepo spoke in the only way he knew how. Standing in front of the *pueblo,* he talked not to it, but about it. He talked through the *pueblo* to the other political leaders, to the *señores liberales,* those who had the power to influence history. Lleras Restrepo was returning oratory to its place as an expression of public life. He stated that he too felt "the sorrow of the *pueblo."* He spoke about the *pueblo's* relationship to Gaitán as though the *pueblo* were an entity beyond his own realm of existence. He told the other leaders what they had all learned so well. "For weeks, for months, for years, he [Gaitán] maintained with the *pueblo* an uninterrupted dialogue the mere memory of which causes amazement, and there came a moment in which it was not possible to distinguish between the two voices: that of Gaitán and that of the *pueblo."*

Lleras Restrepo's words showed that he too had understood what Gaitán had been about. The orator encouraged his fellow Liberals to build on Gaitán's example, for the *caudillo* had succeeded where they had all failed. Gaitán had had the sensitivity "to gather the vague clamor of the agitated multitudes." After Gaitán the *pueblo* could no longer be excluded from public life. "Behind us is the vain gesture of those who believe they can find all their political programs in their own heads. . . . Behind us lies the aristocratic isolation of the ruling groups. . . . Behind us lie the policies conceived within narrow circles and never explained publicly in the open air of the agora." He called for a closer link between leaders and followers. "It is no longer possible to do politics in Colombia . . . without the *pueblo.* . . . We will solve nothing by distancing ourselves from the masses, and by making them feel different from us."[79]

In his funeral oration Lleras Restrepo revealed the deep schism that existed between the politicians and the *pueblo.* It was as though the leaders and the followers of Colombia lived in two different countries. Gaitán's mourners could hardly feel that they had participated in his funeral.

After the three short orations, the procession, headed by Doña Amparo and her eleven-year-old daughter, made its way rapidly to the encounter with Gaitán's body. Doña Amparo and Gloria were left behind as they neared their home. The Liberal leaders walked through the narrow doorway of the house before them. *El Tiempo* had explained that Gaitán could not be buried in the garden because of "technical difficulties."[80] Apparently even the garden was too accessible a shrine. An unknown army chaplain and two parish priests officiated as the casket was lowered into a deep hole in the living room.[81] A minute of silence was observed. Quickly the Liberal leaders departed.[82] All afternoon the *pueblo* lined up outside to walk into the house and pay its last respects. Moments after the six o'clock curfew, the doors of the house were closed. For the *convivialistas* a measure of civility had returned to Bogotá. The *pueblo* was left outside.

The End

The politicians went back to practice the politics of parlor conversations and personal deals. No matter how hard they tried, however, they could not turn back the clock to the period before Gaitán changed politics. Neither could they move forward without him. Gaitán had mobilized the *pueblo* and raised its expectations. The traditional conversations seemed strangely out of date, yet none could follow Gaitán's example in the public plaza. Few wanted to.

Leading Liberals and Conservatives knew that none had the personality or the temperament to duplicate Gaitán's symbiotic relationship with the *pueblo*. They understood also that the *pueblo* would never follow them as it had followed Gaitán. Nor could they raise any of the Gaitanistas in their place, for the leader had always kept them out of the limelight. Gaitán's political style, in fact, now made it even more difficult for them to lead the *pueblo*. Perhaps without Gaitán's vivid experience before them, some might have developed into popular *caudillos* in their own right. But the fallen leader had set an example that they could not replicate and had raised expectations that they did not know how to fulfill. Worse still, Gaitán's style and power came from his belief in the inherent worth of the *pueblo*. Not only had they never shared Gaitán's optimism, but after the riot they could only recoil from the *pueblo*.

The actions of the *pueblo* on April 9 led the *convivialistas* into an anguished reappraisal of the very nature of their society and their place within it. Their thoughts were filled with doom. The destruction that the *pueblo* had wreaked on Bogotá confirmed the worst fears of both Conservatives and Liberals. Despite their collective efforts since the 1920s, and despite the urban peace over which they had presided, it seemed that the *pueblo* retained primitive and barbaric traits too strong to overcome. The Conservatives were now convinced of what they had always suspected: Bogotá could not be the civilizing and unifying center of Colombia. The Liberals lost their remaining hope: that the civility of peaceful urban life would alter the mentality of the *pueblo* and bring Colombia the progress that disorder had long prevented. The *convivialistas* now questioned the very viability of the Colombian nation.

After the violent destruction they had witnessed, Gaitán seemed more like a friend than an enemy. In the pages of *Sábado* Abelardo Forero Benavides cogently analyzed the riot, the meaning of Gaitán's politics, and the need for a coalition between the parties. In his mind the riot amply demonstrated the fragility of social order. "That very fine organization," he wrote, using words with which everyone who had experienced the riot could identify, "in which each citizen had a place, a right, an orbit, and, above all else, a superstructure of government . . . disappears easily. In an hour of collective madness social categories are overturned. . . . there is an instant in which nobody can feel privileged, or defended, or supported by fortune or guns, or by authority, . . . or by a last name." He concluded that Gaitán had held that order in place by masterfully disciplining the *pueblo*. Although he understood that the rich would find it hard to believe, since they thought that Gaitán had preached class struggle, it was his death that now enabled class conflict to threaten the entire social order.[83] He worried that conflict would be encouraged from above by Liberal and Conservative leaders who "come together with much fanfare to tell the majority that there is a group different from the *pueblo*, a group that thinks in a different way."[84] Once Gaitán was dead, the *convivialistas* came to admire him, but when they spoke well of him in public, the *pueblo* derisively referred to their discourse as *el gaitaneo*.

History seemed suddenly split in half. Liberals and Conservatives began to see an idealized past where social and political hierarchies were respected and the *pueblo* kept its subordinate place in society, and a chaotic present in which social mores and civil customs were lost in the *pueblo*'s passionate outbreak.[85] Liberals and Conservatives searched desperately for something to salvage from the ruins. Perhaps such destruction as they had witnessed happened only once in a nation's history. Maybe it was unique, possible only because of the murder of a man like Gaitán, the likes of whom none of them would probably ever see again. They wanted to believe that the outbreak had been planned and that the *pueblo* had been manipulated into acting against its nature. Thus, they turned to communist infiltrators. Not surprisingly, the Liberals continued to hope, against their own convictions, that the Conservatives had orchestrated the entire affair. Conversely, Conservatives could not shake the idea, indeed the wish, that the riot had been hatched among naive and rebellious Liberals.

These stubborn rationalizations, as well as the *convivialistas'* more immediate partisan needs, fueled the distrust between them. The Conservatives remained suspicious of the Liberals' motivations during the *bogotazo* and doubted that the Liberals' commitment to authority was strong enough to control the urban crowd, especially now that Gaitán was dead. They also feared that the Liberals, in their drive for power, might manipulate the crowd aganst the constitutional order. In addition, they used the Liberals' allegedly rebellious behavior on the evening of April 9 to build their own legitimacy as the true representatives of the constitutional order.

El Siglo continued to insist on the Liberal's traitorous intentions, despite Ospina Pérez's assurances to the contrary, and to demand that they be tried for treason as the intellectual authors of the riot.[86] In late June the Conservative newspaper published a telegram that Echandía had sent to Santos in New York in the very midst of the riot. In it Echandía asked Santos to return to Colombia in order to take over the presidency. In the uproar that ensued, the Conservatives accused the new minister of interior of the coalition government of mutinous behavior.[87] Moreover, Conservatives insisted during the months following the riot that a true understanding between the parties was impossible unless the Liberals expelled "communists and cryptocommunists" from the party.[88] In fact, the Conservatives were divided on these issues, opposite stands being taken by the now moderate Guillermo León Valencia (the future president) and the intransigent Gilberto Alzate Avendaño. The dissension only served to undercut the president's commitment to the coalition.

The Liberals, on the other hand, were caught between the pressures of cooperating with the opposition and the partisan expectations of their followers. They could not openly claim that the communists had caused the *bogotazo*, since this would only enrage many in the Liberal rank and file who believed that their outburst had been a legitimate and spontaneous expression of protest. The more they defended themselves against the Conservative charges, the more they appeared to have betrayed their followers' expectations. To expel Uribe Márquez, Darío Samper, and Victor Julio Silva, the "cryptocommunists" named by the Conservatives, might have caused an irreparable break between the Liberal leadership and the labor movement. Instead, the Liberals reiterated their commitment to the labor unions. The coalition got off to a shaky start.

Bogotá newspapers were filled with unsubstantiated stories of conspiracy. The *convivialistas* were obviously unable to believe the conspiratorial tales they themselves wove. While they gained a measure of solace from repeating the old ideas, they could nevertheless not shake the idea that the *pueblo* was in fact responsible for the destruction of the city.

In the weeks after the riot, Liberals, Conservatives, and even Gaitanistas condemned the *pueblo* as a subhuman force that hurled itself against the traditional institutions of the nation.[89] Whether from longstanding fear of the mobilized *pueblo* or a more recent need to distinguish themselves from it, the *convivialistas* created a black legend. They portrayed the *pueblo* as the antithesis of the nation. Animal metaphors filled the air. Luis López de Mesa, widely regarded as Colombia's premier sociologist, quickly replaced Gerardo Molina as rector of the Universidad Nacional. From the nation's first institution of higher learning, he launched a systematic attack on the *pueblo*. He divided the crowds of the *bogotazo* into six malevolent types: the reckless, the fanatics, the resentful, the professional delinquents, the curious, and the innocent criminals. He concluded that Colombia could never become a great nation.[90]

The black legend did not go unopposed. Those who defended the *pueblo* used a Marxist-inspired distinction between the good and the bad *pueblo*. Years afterward Molina claimed that only certain sectors of the *pueblo*, "the *déclassé*, the resentful, the ruffians that mill around urban centers," were responsible for the destruction of the city. He noted that "the best of the *pueblo*, the nuclei linked to production, maintained their political morality."[91] According to Gilberto Vieira, the riot had degenerated into mob action because of inadequate leadership, the Liberals' betrayal, and the inevitable spontaneity and disorganization of the lumpenproletariat.[92]

This interpretation was preceded by a more far-reaching defense of the crowd of April 9. In a legal treatise designed to protect both politicians and rioters from criminal prosecution, Luis Carlos Pérez argued that the actions of the *pueblo* represented a political and social rebellion against the established order: the *palacio* was attacked as a symbol of crime and corruption; government offices were destroyed in protest against the stifling hold of the bureaucracy; stores were looted to protest against the rising cost of living. Thus, he concluded, the *pueblo* had acted politically rather than instinctively within the chaos produced by the willful retreat of the military and the passivity of the Liberals. The government and the political leaders, not the *pueblo*, were responsible for the death and destruction that took place in Bogotá and the rest of the nation.[93]

The black legend, nonetheless, became history. The *pueblo* heard itself condemned in the leaders' oratory and read the denunciations of its actions in the *convivialistas'* newspapers. The effect of this attack on the collective consciousness of Gaitán's followers can only be guessed.[94] Few read the legal and sociological treatises in which their actions were more sympathetically recorded. Suggestions and offers were made to build monuments to the dead, but in the end the tributes to the fallen were limited to a poem by the Venezuelan Miguel Otero Silva and an essay by Darío Samper.[95]

The church legitimated and compounded the politicians' rejection of the *pueblo* by excommunicating those who had desecrated the church and taken its property.[96] Priests accompanied soldiers into the humble homes of their parishioners in search of hidden loot.[97] The military went so far as to rip the black ties from the Gaitanistas who wore them as a sign of mourning.[98] Those daring enough to wear new clothing on the streets of the city were hauled in for interrogation. Known Gaitanistas lost their jobs, and the entire municipal police force was dismissed.[99] The poor of the city were derisively referred to as "*nueveabrileños*" ("these people of the ninth of April"), and the only drink that many could afford, the popular and inexpensive corn alcohol, *chicha*, was prohibited on the grounds that it led to the demoralization and the mental and physical degeneration of the *pueblo*.[100] No statue or monument in Bogotá commemorates the dead of the *bogotazo*.[101]

April 10 brought the *convivialistas* back into a coalition like the one they had broken only weeks before. There can be little doubt that they were personally committed to it and that they saw it as the only means of keeping the society from falling apart. Ospina Pérez had long advocated a bipartisan government, albeit one that he controlled. With Laureano Gómez at least temporarily out of the picture, the moderate president had a chance of winning over the Conservative party. Among the Liberals Darío Echandía had always advocated a bipartisan understanding, and even the hardliner Lleras Restrepo was sufficiently prescient to understand that class conflict would threaten the entire social order. Echandía agreed to become minister of interior knowing that many of his policies would necessarily be unpopular with his party's rank and file.

The *convivialistas* strove to make the coalition work. They attempted to formalize their agreement throughout the bureaucracy by a novel cross-over system (*cruce*) in which ministers, governors, and mayors named deputies of the opposing party in order to assure both parties of equal access to the political spoils and to build in mutual accountability at all levels of government.[102] They attempted to dissolve the animosities that had infected public life in recent years. They believed that their rule was slipping away because of the decline in respect for authority. The "irresponsibility" of certain political figures, not least Gaitán himself, was partly to blame for the outbreak of the riot. On April 17, just hours after Doña Amparo had agreed to the burial in her home, the leaders of both parties reiterated their "common ideals" and their belief in *convivencia*. They called for a political truce and implored both parties to abstain from hostilities and to encourage instead the "tone of moderation" that civilian rule required.[103] The next day Calibán followed with his own plea. "The struggle for ideas and *mística*," he wrote, "can and should coexist with an amiable and courteous style of political activity."[104] Form was stressed above substance.

Nevertheless, the coalition was doomed to fail. After the riot the *convivialistas'* performance on the public stage made little sense. During the years of peace, Liberals and Conservatives had drawn closer together ideologically, if not always personally. Before Gaitán started his campaign for the presidency, few objective partisan differences kept them apart. Gaitán and the riot made them realize that their rule and even their society were at stake, and that they had even more in common than they had originally believed. After April 9 the distinction between the Conservatives' belief in

The *convivialistas* toast to the return of social order. *Left to right:* General Germán Ocampo, Samuel Arango Reyes, Eduardo Zuleta Angel, Darío Echandía, President Mariano Ospina Pérez, and Pedro Eliseo Cruz.

order and the Liberals' espousal of progress was lost in the apparent impossibility of achieving either.

If the Liberals had been growing more pessimistic over the years, and therefore more like the Conservatives, the *bogotazo* propelled most of them into the opposing camp. The riot eliminated the philosophical and ideological distinctions by which the *convivialistas* rationalized their rule. They were left without partisan guides to daily politics. The rational discourse through which social alternatives were supposed to arise was gone. The *convivialistas* attempted to bring order to their internal political practice by reintroducing ideology. Liberals spoke openly and defiantly of leftism and support for the labor unions. Conservatives also began to dabble in popular creeds and spoke of being the representatives of "Christian socialism."[105] But this remained largely a parlor game that most of the leaders did not take seriously.

The confusion within politics after April 9 was compounded by the leaders' radical rejection of the *pueblo*. Leading Liberals and Conservatives continued to occupy center stage, but they no longer had an audience. Their calm behavior, rational discourse, and equanimity in the face of adversity were pointless, for they no longer believed that the *pueblo* could learn from their example. At the very most, politics could lead to a semblance of order in the short run. But the deeper logic of politics, the goal of implanting customs, mores, and forms of behavior, was gone.

Nevertheless, the politicians held on to public life as tenaciously as ever. For them it was all that remained of the nation and of civility. Politics was the last barricade against barbarism, the only thing that distinguished them from the *pueblo*, the only thing that maintained a semblance of civilized life in Colombia. The *convivialistas* turned inward, forgot social reforms and political examples, and sought power as a personal and public goal of last resort. In the process the distinction between their public tasks and their personal ambitions also disappeared. In early 1949, once Ospina Pérez had temporarily lifted the state of siege, the politicians embarked on a tragedy of errors that brought the institutions of democracy to an end and opened the floodgates of *la Violencia*.[106]

Liberal and Conservative leaders spent 1949 fruitlessly debating electoral and police reforms that would enhance the power of one party or the other. In the absence of clearly definable ideological positions, personal attacks and insults took over. Alleging that they had not been offered the political posts they had been promised under the coalition agreement, the Liberals withdrew from the government in May.[107] No longer responsible for the legitimacy of the government, they began a systematic, all-out attack on the Conservative regime. The *cruce* system had backfired. Instead of ensuring harmony, it led to intense infighting and continuous turnover as the politicians of both parties maneuvered to maximize their influence at all levels of the bureaucracy. And violence encroached on public life. In September a shoot-out in Congress led to the death of a Liberal congressman, and a bullet almost certainly intended for Echandía killed his brother on the streets of Bogotá.

The presidential election scheduled for June 1950 became the be-all and end-all of public life. For the Conservatives a victory would reverse the tide of Liberal majorities that the June 1949 congressional contest had again confirmed. For the Liberals a victory would mean the recovery of the national executive that they had held from 1930 to 1946 and that they felt should never have been lost. The Liberals in Congress succeeded in moving the election up to November, when the Liberal-dominated Congress would still be in session, offering them some protection against electoral fraud, and before Conservative-inspired electoral reforms were enacted that stood to benefit the party in power.[108] With slightly less than a month left before the election, the Liberals selected Echandía as their standard-bearer. He seemed assured of victory.

On October 7, five days after Echandía's selection, Ospina Pérez proposed a constitutional amendment that would postpone the election for four years.

He suggested an interim government, equally divided between the parties, that would ensure an open and democratic election four years hence. The proposal led immediately to lengthy conversations between Gómez and Roberto Urdaneta Arbeláez for the Conservatives, and Echandía and Alfonso López for the Liberals.[109] The talks ended in failure only five days after the president's proposal. Neither side showed much interest. The Liberals were confident of victory. Gómez had his eye on the presidency.

On October 13 the intransigent wing of the Conservative party won its struggle against the moderates. Gómez won the nomination of his party for the presidency. It was a remarkable comeback for a man whose political fortunes seemed to have ended on the morning of April 10, 1948. The heightened tension between the parties undoubtedly helped the instransigents to gain the upper hand. Ospina Pérez had lost his party.

The Liberals were suddenly fearful of defeat in the face of this unexpected turn of events. In Gómez and a newly reunited Conservative party that at the same time held the reigns of government, they saw a formidable short- and long-term opponent. Although the Conservatives were the minority party, the Liberals obviously felt that Gómez stood a chance of beating Echandía, whose lackluster political style had always been a major drawback. Moreover, they knew full well that they would be excluded from all public offices in a Gómez presidency.

By October 21 the Liberals had begun to think better of their original defiance and suggested a truce much like Ospina Pérez's four-year moratorium.[110] But now the Conservatives, headed not by the president but by the candidate, were unreceptive. Desperate attempts by moderates of both parties to stave off a crisis failed. Gómez adamantly refused any conciliation. The Liberals threatened the violence of their national majority should their plea for compromise now go unheard.

Although no clear ideological or policy issues divided them, the *convivialistas* effectively undermined the institutions they had so carefully crafted since 1930. On October 28 Lleras Restrepo made his famous statement: "We will have no relationship from here on with members of the Conservative party; as long as they do not offer us a different republic, with guarantees that put an end to this infamy, the relations between Liberals and Conservatives, already broken in the public sphere, must be suspended in the private sphere as well."[111]

On November 9 Ospina Pérez declared a state of siege. It would last ten years. He closed the Congress. Law making came to an end. Unopposed, Gómez reached the presidency. The man who two decades earlier had shocked the Bogotá elite by declaring that Colombians could not be governed finally reached the abiding goal of his life. Once in the *palacio* he found confirmation for his views. His presidency encouraged the Conservatives to take advantage of the moment and seek the power, influence, and resources that were in the hands of Liberals.

La Violencia took center stage. That year almost 19,000 Colombians died as a result of it. Over 43,000 died the year Gaitán did. In Gómez's first year in office, 50,000 lost their lives to *la Violencia*.[112] In 1952, adherents of the Conservative party burned the buildings that housed *El Tiempo* and *El Espectador* and the homes of Carlos Lleras Restrepo and Alfonso López. The Liberal party ceased to function. Liberal leaders went into exile or remained in private life in the city. Members of the Liberal and Gaitanista rank and file became guerrillas.[113] Democracy headed for the hills, not to return to the city until three decades later. It was war without beginning and almost without end. It had no *caudillos*, battles, ideals, or glory.

The term used to describe the rural strife, *la Violencia*, gained wide and quick acceptance, in large measure because it made the conflict look like an objective phenomenon, something "sociological" that happened outside the intentions of human beings. Leaders of both parties could talk about *la Violencia*, "the violence," without blaming each other or themselves. Not only did the perpetrators go unnamed, but the *convivialistas*, as conscious, active, rational, and moral individuals, could not be held responsible for a phenomenon that was not intentional. Once objectified, the *convivialistas* could explain to themselves and others why they could do little to bring it under control. It was of the *país nacional*, not the *país político*. Public life was not the cause; the anarchic, private interests and passions of individuals lay at the root of the conflict. The wars of the nineteenth century had occurred first as tragedy; they returned as farce.

Conclusion

I have said the highest, the most elevated, the most unselfish mission of mankind is to participate in politics. . . . I have invited the *pueblo* to participate in politics, and I believe that the salvation of our country resides in all of us participating in politics.

Jorge Eliécer Gaitán (1947)

What is remembered? Colombians recall different pasts. Memories are so vivid that it is difficult to believe that these events occurred more than thirty years ago. It is as though Gaitán and the *bogotazo*, known in Colombia more historically and simply as "*el nueve de abril*,"[1] had taken place just yesterday, as though the long *Violencia* of which few wish to speak had not taken place between them and the past that has been recalled in these pages.

The memories of Gaitanistas are riveted on Gaitán and on the three shots that changed their lives. The leading *convivialistas* recall in minute detail their own actions on April 9, and shudder at the memory of Gaitán. Year after year the newspapers they still control commemorate their behavior. Pictures displaying the city's destruction bear captions that compare Bogotá to the European cities destroyed during World War II. The crowd is remembered for what it did, not for who was part of it. That question is not asked. The crowd remains anonymous. Colombians remember what is most important to them.[2]

Gaitán's close followers proudly recount episodes of his public life in baffling detail. While talking about him, many take on his behavioral traits, offering vivid glimpses of a man who disappeared long ago. Others have memorized long sections of his orations and replicate his voice and gestures as they loudly declaim them in Bogotá's cafés, bars, and streets. For them the future would have been entirely different had Gaitán lived. He would have

200

held the *convivialistas* accountable, Gómez would not have become president, and a minority Conservative party would never have had the opportunity to violently hang on to power. Even Gaitán's most bitter opponents concede that he would have become president on August 7, 1950.

For Liberal and Conservative leaders, as well as for Gaitán's opponents, the tragic events that followed the assassination are etched in stone: *convivencia* was doomed and the spread of *la Violencia* inevitable. Neither effect had much to do with Gaitán, but was the result of deeper historical forces. Had Gaitán lived, his ability to use social and economic hatreds to mobilize the *pueblo* might well have made the civil strife even more destructive. After the outbreak of "barbarism" on the *nueve de abril*, it was but a small step to see *la Violencia* in the countryside as the continuation of the bloody destruction wrought by the *pueblo* in Bogotá. Soon the idea developed within the elite that *la Violencia* was a cancer of the *pueblo*—or, to use another of their metaphors, a bloodletting—that had little to do with them.[3]

Smaller concerns, however, fill the minds of the politicians. Who made the fateful call at three in the afternoon on April 9? Did the Liberals ask for Conservative help, or did the Conservatives call out for the Liberals? What time did the Liberals finally arrive at the *palacio*? Who said what to whom and in what tone of voice? Did the Conservatives have dinner while the Liberals were left hungry? Was the president clean-shaven when he faced the disheveled Liberals on the morning of April 10?

These issues are of overriding importance for those who treasured the stances they took, for those who believed that their exalted public life was the embryo of the nation and of the civilizing process. The Conservatives felt that they had taken a stand on principle against the Liberals, who performed their public roles through "demogogic" appeals to the urban crowd. It was of the utmost importance that they could demonstrate that they had maintained those principles in the gravest moment of crisis the nation had ever faced. In their minds they had not produced the riot, had not killed Gaitán, and had not taken over the radio stations to urge the crowd to lay waste to the city. They were the legitimate representatives of order and the consititution, and they had defended the *palacio* from the multitude. They had to believe that they could weather the crisis on their own. They always relied heavily on their public image of pride and self-reliance, possibly because so little tied them to society. They could ill afford to show the weakness of character and the lack of confidence that an appeal for help to the Liberals would have implied. The Conservatives' public roles defined them when public life was threatened.

A gap of up to three hours separates Conservative and Liberal estimates of the hour of their reunion.[4] From the Conservative perspective, the longer the Liberals took, the more exalted their own independent roles in the *palacio* become and the more hesitant and uncertain the Liberals appear to be. For the Liberals, therefore, it is important to establish that they did not take that long and, most important of all, that they did not arrive late at night when the fires were smoldering and the rioters were returning to their homes.[5] The Liberals are not eager to speak about the events of that evening. Yet they have come closer to the truth. At seven o'clock Ambassador Beaulac cabled Washington that radio broadcasts were reporting the Liberals' arrival in the *palacio.*[6]

Who called whom? The debate has continued for decades. The Liberals insisted at the time that Camilo de Brigard Silva had invited them but concede that they were never certain whether he had the president's authorization.[7] A month after the riot, de Brigard wrote to the president assuring him that he had not done so.[8] Twenty-five years later de Brigard admitted that he had indeed placed the call, but said that he had demurred when Araújo asked if the invitation came from the president. "As soon as I knew that Gaitán had been assassinated, I realized that the only way to solve the crisis was to facilitate an understanding with Liberalism."[9]

Why has the crowd of the *nueve de abril* remained so anonymous? The answer lies deeper than its fleeting and spontaneous character. The question of who the crowd was has rarely been asked. While the riot was taking place, immediately after it was over, and ever since, almost everyone in Bogotá and the rest of the nation had a self-evident answer to the question: the crowd was the *pueblo,* the *pueblo* was the crowd. This explanation was sufficiently powerful at the time that the government did not find it necessary to launch an investigation that might offer a more empirical answer.[10] The answer has remained powerful over the years because it responds to deeply ingrained notions of the character of social life in Colombia. The fear that the *pueblo* would vent its "primitive passions" was never far from many minds. According to this idea, "everyone" participated in the riot. Only those who were not part of "everyone," only those who were not *pueblo,* did not participate. Thus, the *convivialistas,* respectable citizens, the upper classes, and parts of the middle classes, as well as workers associated with the most advanced factories, remained on the side of the law. Everyone who "could" participate did.

The crowd that took over Bogotá was generated by *convivencia,* by its strict exclusion from the public life of leading Liberals and Conservatives, and by its slow, largely symbolic, inclusion in the body politic under the leadership of Gaitán. Consistently reviled for being slovenly and ignorant by those who called themselves cultured and intelligent, the *pueblo* had been shown a more positive image of itself by Gaitán. Those who claimed to be the natural leaders of society were shown by Gaitán to be mere mortals, fearful men behind masks, who ruled in their own interests and those of the powerful and the rich, rather than for the *pueblo.*

The crowd that took over Bogotá grew out of the deeply personal relationship that thousands of Gaitán's followers had with him. The outburst of anger and revenge was expected in Bogotá as soon as the news of the *caudillo's* assassination became known. The crowd was predictable. What it did was less so.

Gaitán had taken his followers from a life in which they were excluded from the decisions that affected them to another in which they felt they participated in those decisions. His death thrust them instinctively back to the sacrosanct old hierarchies and to their lowly, deferential, and reviled place in society. As the crowd lost contact with the *convivialistas*, the old anonymous world with distant and sporadic leaders materialized again.

The actions of the crowd in Bogotá on the afternoon of April 9 were a sign of its refusal to return to the past, to retrace the distance already traversed. But the crowd could not make the rest of the trip without Gaitán. How was it suddenly to take power? The idea was never even there. Unwilling to move back and unable to more forward, the anger and frustration of the rioters had only one outlet: the destruction of a society in which they could no longer live. From the feeling of loss that enveloped Gaitán's followers at the moment of his death, from the sense of pride and cohesion that he had offered them, and from the hatred he had shown for the *convivialistas*, the crowd derived the courage, and the need, to destroy.

The crowd has remained anonymous, also, because few saw any rhyme or reason in its actions. Why bother asking about those who momentarily lost their heads in the turmoil following the assassination? If ever there was a crowd that would substantiate the idea of the disorganized and normless character of violence, riots, and collective behavior, the crowd of the *nueve de abril* would seem to be the one. There is no evidence, however, that those who were in Bogotá at the time Gaitán was killed were in any way different from those who hurled themselves against the city during the following hours. The *nueve de abril* took place in waves, but these were not determined and differentiated from each other by the innate qualities of the individuals who participated at different stages. The immediate actions of the crowd were determined by the specific situations in which individuals found themselves at various points in time. These situations were conditioned by the changing relationship between the leaders of both parties and the crowd they did not face.

The crowd was not politically uninformed. In fact, the first protesters attempted to create an order that they could understand, a relationship with the leaders of both parties that would enhance that order, and a new government that would fulfill their aspirations for a return of morality and peace. Nor did the crowd run amok. Protesters were able to pick and choose their targets. Nor did "everyone" participate. Many stayed in cafés, or watched as others marched by. Others stayed in their barrios. Many left the streets as quickly as possible. There must have been some, too, that history cannot catch: they shrugged and did not care.

The *nueve de abril* is not surprising for its destruction and looting. It is surprising because the spontaneous behavior of the crowd responded to, and can be understood in terms of, the historical relationship between the *pueblo* and the *convivialistas* and Gaitán's relationship to both. It can be understood by looking at the immediate situations in which individuals found themselves. It is surprising because it makes sense.

What about Gaitán? Were the *convivialistas* right to fear him so? Were his followers right to love him so? Only they can know, but we might venture a positive answer to both questions. The *convivialistas* had ample reason to fear Gaitán, not because he was a socialist or a revolutionary, but because he represented the fall of the *país político*. There might well have been room for *convivialistas* in a Gaitán government, but their distinct place in society would be eroded. Gaitán represented the coming together of those two countries of Colombia into a nation increasingly defined by the private needs of its citizens and governed by institutions designed to meet those needs. Once Gaitán was gone, the *convivialistas* no longer knew how to lead. They felt that they no longer had a *pueblo* to lead. History had passed them by, for they had been unable to go along. Unable to go back and unable to move history forward, they allowed *convivencia* to come to an end and *la Violencia* to take over.

Gaitán wanted to represent the *pueblo*. He was the first politician to speak directly to the majority of Colombians. He spoke their language, came from their ranks. He needed the *pueblo* to have any chance in the *país político*. In that unequal reciprocity lie the uncertain seeds of democracy. A Gaitán government would have been a government of the emerging middle-sector groups, of the petit bourgeoisie claiming to represent the *pueblo*. It was only through such a broad coalition, carried through in the long-established, multi-class parties of the nation, that Gaitán's own small class might exert its influence in society. In that class alliance, those within the *pueblo* who did not own property, workers and peasants, stood much to gain.

Convivencia was progressive. It had a future, a growing popular base on which a competitive, electoral, civilian legitimacy could be fashioned. The process of privatization that evoked the conflicts and the promise of *convivencia* contains an inevitable tension. Individuals from many walks of life are drawn into the polity, there to participate and share, through symbols and acts, in the decisions of the collectivity. Once drawn in, newly mobilized citizens face politicians who increasingly seek to control them by influencing their private lives. Gaitán can best be understood in terms of this evolving character of public life. He represented its future, its promise, and thus its threat. He is remembered.

Notes
Bibliography
Index

Notes

Preface

1 Mario Vargas Llosa, "Is Fiction the Art of Lying?" in *The New York Times Book Review*, October 7, 1984, p. 40.
2 Manuel Zapata Olivella, *La calle diez* (Bogotá: Ediciones Casa de la Cultura, 1960); José Antonio Osorio Lizarazo, *El día del odio* (Buenos Aires: Ediciones López Negri, 1952).
3 Vargas Llosa, "Is Fiction the Art of Lying?" p. 40.

Introduction

1 Elias Canetti, *Crowds and Power* (New York: Seabury Press, 1978).
2 Alexander W. Wilde, "Conversations Among Gentlemen: Oligarchical Democracy in Colombia," in Juan Linz and Alfred Stepan, eds., *The Breakdown of Democratic Regimes*, vol. 3: *Latin America* (Baltimore: Johns Hopkins University Press, 1978), pp. 28–81; Richard E. Sharpless, *Gaitán of Colombia: A Political Biography* (Pittsburgh: University of Pittsburgh Press, 1978).
3 Some of the most enlightening articles from this school of thought are conveniently gathered in Howard J. Wiarda, ed., *Politics and Social Change in Latin America: The Distinct Tradition* (Amherst: University of Massachusetts Press, 1974); Wiarda's own more developed formulations are in *Corporatism and National Development in Latin America* (Boulder: Westview Press, 1981). See also Francisco José Moreno, *Legitimacy and Stability in Latin America: A Study of Chilean Political Culture* (New York: New York University Press, 1969); Claudio Véliz, *The Centralist Tradition in Latin America* (Princeton: Princeton University Press, 1980).
4 Russell H. Fitzgibbon and Julio A. Fernández, *Latin America: Political Culture and Development*, 2d ed. (Englewood Cliffs, N.J.: Prentice-Hall, 1981), p. 9.
5 Mauricio Solaún, "Colombian Politics: Historical Characteristics and Problems," in R. Albert Berry, Ronald G. Hellman, and Mauricio Solaún, eds., *Politics of Compromise: Coalition Government in Colombia* (New Brunswick, N.J.: Transaction Books, 1980), pp. 9–20.
6 James L. Payne, *Patterns of Conflict in Colombia* (New Haven: Yale University Press, 1968). For an excellent review of the extensive literature on violence and conflict in Colombia, much of which blames these social phenomena on the collective personality of the Colombian people, see Paul Oquist, *Violencia, conflicto y política en Colombia* (Bogotá: Instituto de Estudios Colombianos, Biblioteca Banco Popular, 1978), pp. 21–35. The English version was published

in 1980 by Academic Press in New York as *Violence, Conflict, and Politics in Colombia.*

7 Glen Caudill Dealy, *The Public Man: An Interpretation of Latin American and Other Catholic Countries* (Amherst: University of Massachusetts Press, 1977).

8 William B. Taylor offers a perceptive analysis of Latin American historiography that is sensitive to the recent dialectical promise of this "dependency perspective" and points us beyond its contributions to a more holistic or, as he puts it, "connected" study of the Latin American past. See his "Between Global Process and Local Knowledge: An Inquiry into Early Latin American Social History, 1500–1900," in Olivier Zunz, ed., *Reliving the Past: The Worlds of Social History* (Chapel Hill: University of North Carolina Press, 1985) pp. 115–90.

9 Hannah Arendt, *The Human Condition* (Garden City, N.Y.: Doubleday Anchor Books, 1959), and *Totalitarianism* (New York: Harcourt, Brace and World, 1968); Richard Sennett, *The Fall of Public Man: On the Social Psychology of Capitalism* (New York: Vintage Books, 1978); Albert O. Hirschman, *Shifting Involvments: Private Interest and Public Action* (Princeton: Princeton University Press, 1982). Hirschman, of course, is one of those rare contemporary scholars who bridge time, geography, and theory and fact and are constantly searching for solutions to the problems we face. His classic *Journeys Toward Progress,* published in 1963 by the Twentieth Century Fund in New York City, continues to be a valuable source for Latin Americanists.

10 This is Gino Germani's definition of a "modern" society. The insightful comments on Latin American populism and European fascism of Latin America's premier sociologist are presented in his *Authoritarianism, Fascism, and National Populism* (New Brunswick, N.J.: Transaction Books, 1978). The passage quoted is from p. 6.

11 Steve Stein, *Populism in Peru: The Emergence of the Masses and the Politics of Social Control* (Madison: University of Wisconsin Press, 1980), pp. 15–16. For other studies of populism see Sharpless, *Gaitán of Colombia;* Torcuato S. di Tella, "Populism and Reform in Latin America," in Claudio Véliz, ed., *Obstacles to Change in Latin America* (London: Oxford University Press, 1965), pp. 47–75; Gino Germani, Torcuato S. di Tella, and Octavio Ianni, *Populismo y contradicciones de clase en Latinoamérica* (México: Ediciones Era, 1973); Michael L. Conniff, ed., *Latin American Populism in Comparative Perspective* (Albuquerque: University of New Mexico Press, 1982). Two studies of populism that are sensitive to the class dimensions of politics are Christopher Mitchell, *The Legacy of Populism in Bolivia: From the MNR to Military Rule* (New York: Praeger, 1977), and Peter F. Klarén, *Modernization, Dislocation and Aprismo: Origins of the Peruvian Aprista Party 1870–1932* (Austin: University of Texas Press, 1973). An in-depth study of a populist movement within a less hierarchical political culture can be found in Paul W. Drake, *Socialism and Populism in Chile, 1932–52* (Urbana: University of Illinois Press, 1978).

12 James MacGregor Burns, *Leadership* (New York: Harper and Row, 1978); William Reich, *The Mass Psychology of Fascism* (New York: Farrar, Straus and

Giroux, 1973); Ann Ruth Willner, *The Spellbinders: Charismatic Political Leadership* (New Haven: Yale University Press, 1984).

Chapter 1

1 Alejandro Vallejo, *Políticos en la intimidad* (Bogotá: Ediciones Antena, 1936), p. 36. López felt that there were six or seven types of Liberals: reactionary Liberals, conservatives, progovernment Liberals, antigovernment Liberals, socialists, and revolutionaries. He had no qualms about telling his Liberal colleagues that he belonged to the last category. See "El liberalismo debe prepararse para asumir el poder," in Alfonso López, *Obras selectas (primera parte, 1926–1937)* (Bogotá: Cámara de Representantes, Colección Pensadores Políticos Colombianos, 1979), p. 63.

2 Excluding the wars of independence, Colombia suffered eight major civil wars in the nineteenth century. Presidential elections were held regularly throughout the century, and only once, in 1867 was an election suspended because of the violent conflict between the parties. In the twentieth century, presidential and congressional elections were held uninterruptedly from 1904 to 1949. The Laureano Gómez–Roberto Urdaneta Arbeláez regime was overthrown in the midst of the first major outbreak of the twentieth-century conflict known as *la Violencia*, and after a four-year military interlude, elections were again held regularly after 1958, even though the strife continued into the 1960s. In the previous century only the 1857 election was popularly contested. Otherwise elections were determined by Congress or by an electoral body. In this century they have been open to the public since 1914, although both parties did not always participate. Malcolm Deas has written a nuanced and thought-provoking account of the nation-forming impact of these two parties on Colombia in the nineteenth century. See his "La presencia de la política nacional en la vida provinciana, pueblerina y rural de Colombia en el primer siglo de la república," in Marco Palacios, ed., *La unidad nacional en América Latina: Del regionalismo a la nacionalidad* (México: El Colegio de México, 1983), pp. 149–73.

3 For biographies of López, see Hugo Latorre Cabal, *Mi novela: apuntes autobiográficos de Alfonso López* (Bogotá: Ediciones Mito, 1961); and Eduardo Zuleta Angel, *El presidente López* (Medellín: Ediciones Alba, 1966).

4 J. J. García, *Política y amigos* (Bogotá: Ediciones Tercer Mundo, 1975), p. 21.

5 This aspect of López's personality is best developed by Vallejo, *Políticos*, pp. 28–29.

6 Ibid., pp. 33–36.

7 For accounts of the election from the Conservative perspective, see Aquilino Gaitán *Por qué cayó el partido conservador* (Bogotá: n.p., 1955); José Restrepo Posada, *La iglesia en dos momentos difíciles en la historia patria* (Bogotá: n.p., 1935); for the Liberal side see Luis Eduardo Nieto Caballero, "Como llegó el liberalismo al poder," in Plinio Mendoza Neira and Alberto Camacho Angarita, eds., *El liberalismo en el gobierno*, vol. 1 (Bogotá: Editorial Antena, 1946), pp. 16–30; Vallejo, *Políticos*, pp. 39–44.

8   The young politicians were proud of what they did in the streets and salons of
    Bogotá during the 1920s, and once they moved into high office, they looked
    back nostalgically to their "bohemian" days. For accounts of their lives during
    this period by others who did not become so powerful, see Gerardo Molina, *Las
    ideas liberales en Colombia, 1915–1934* (Bogotá: Ediciones Tercer Mundo,
    1974); Vallejo, *Políticos;* José Antonio Osorio Lizarazo, *Colombia: donde los
    Andes se disuelven* (Santiago: Editorial Universitaria, 1955); J. J. García, *Epocas
    y gentes* (Bogotá: Ediciones Tercer Mundo, 1977); Laureano García Ortíz, "Los
    cachacos de Bogotá," *Boletín de la Academia Colombiana de Historia* (1936):
    126–29; and Germán Arciniegas, "La academia, la taberna y la universidad,"
    Revista de las Indias 58 (October 1943): 5–15.

9   For a wonderfully nuanced account of the developing urban, *cachaco,* culture,
    and its attendant civilizing mentality, see Marco Palacios, "La clase más ruido-
    sa," *Eco,* no. 254 (December 1982): 113–56; for an overview of the period, see
    José Fernando Ocampo, *Colombia siglo XX: estudio histórico y antología
    política, 1886–1934* (Bogotá: Ediciones Tercer Mundo, 1980); also the articles
    by Jorge Orlando Melo, Alvaro Tirado Mejía, and Mario Arrubla in Mario
    Arrubla, et al., *Colombia hoy* (Bogotá: Siglo XXI, 1978).

10 Augusto Ramírez Moreno, *Los leopardos* (Bogotá: Editorial Santa Fé, 1935), pp.
    220–21.

11 José Antonio Osorio Lizarazo, *Gaitán: vida, muerte y permanente presencia*
    (Bogotá: Carlos Valencia Editores, 1979), pp. 66–67. This book was first pub-
    lished in 1952 in Buenos Aires by López Negri.

12 See Agustín Rodríguez Garavito, *Gabriel Turbay: un solitario de la grandeza*
    (Bogotá: Ediciones Prócer, 1966).

13 Ramírez Moreno offers a glorified but not entirely unrealistic fictional account
    of their exploits in *Los leopardos.*

14 Tomas Rueda Vargas, "Recuerdos de *El Tiempo* viejo," in his *Escritos,* 2 vols.
    (Bogotá: Antares, 1963), 2: 306–11. For Santos's view of himself as a young
    intellectual, see his remarks during his induction into the Academia Colombiana
    de la Lengua, July 20, 1938, in *Anuario de la Academia de la Lengua* 7 (1938):
    115–16.

15 Gaitán's caustic remarks are in *Universidad* 81, May 12, 1928, p. 412.

16 There are more biographies of Gómez than of any other member of his genera-
    tion, including Gaitán. None of them, however, come close to being dispassion-
    ate and professional. See José Francisco Socarrás, *Laureano Gómez:
    psicoanálisis de un resentido* (Bogotá: Editorial ABC, 1942); Hugo Velasco,
    Ecce homo: biografía de una tempestad (Bogotá: Ediciones ARGRA, 1950);
    Felipe Antonio Molina, *Laureano Gómez: historia de una rebeldía* (Bogotá:
    Editorial Voluntad, 1940); and Carlos H. Pareja, *El monstruo* (Buenos Aires:
    Editorial Nuestra América, 1955). James Henderson is at work on a much await-
    ed biography of this enigmatic figure.

17 The unfortunate incident is described by Molina, *Las ideas liberales,* pp.
    210–14. See also Carlos Lleras Restrepo, *Borradores para una historia de la
    república liberal* (Bogotá: Editorial Nueva Frontera, 1975).

18 Gómez's lectures were published as *Interrogantes sobre el progreso de Colom-*

bia: conferencias dictadas en el Teatro Municipal de Bogotá (Bogotá: Editorial
Revista Colombiana, 1929). The conferences were re-edited by Populibro in
1979. For Gómez's views on other matters, see his *El cuadrilátero* (Bogotá:
Editorial Centro, 1939); *Comentarios a un régimen* (Bogotá: Editorial Minerva,
1934); and *Discursos* (Bogotá: Colección Populibro, no. 1, Editorial Revista
Colombiana, 1968). Many of his writings and speeches have been recently gathered in *Obras Selectas* (Bogotá: Cámara de Representantes, Colección Pensadores Políticos Colombianos, 1981).

19 *El Tiempo,* June 9, 1928, p. 4

20 Ibid., June 10, 1928, p. 1.

21 Gómez, *Interrogantes,* p. 71.

22 The most complete account of the event is Alejandro Vallejo, *Bogotá: ocho de
    junio* (Bogotá: Publicaciones de la Revista *Universidad,* 1929); the Conserva-
    tives also covered the events in *El Debate,* June 7–9, 1929.

23 Interview 49 with Agustín Utrera, Bogotá barber and follower of Gaitán,
    December 5, 1979; interview 55 with Manuel Jiménez, follower of Gaitán,
    December 7, 1979; interview 5 with Pío Nono Barbosa Barbosa, Bogotá car-
    penter and stonemason, follower of Gaitán, April 9, 1979, and subsequent con-
    versations. This is the massacre of the banana workers made famous world-wide
    by Gabriel García Márquez in his *One Hundred Years of Solitude* (New York:
    Avon Books, 1971), pp. 280–87. Many years before García Márquez faced the
    blank page, Gaitán the practical politician proved the imaginative novelist
    wrong. For García Márquez silence surrounds the dead of that massacre. Of-
    ficial history having decreed that the dead did not die, they could not be remem-
    bered. But Gaitán had already made sure that that would not happen. Today,
    year after year, the deaths are remembered in Colombia, not as a fantasy, but as
    reality. A fuller account of Gaitán's activities in the banana workers' case is
    presented on pp. 57 and 58.

24 Mauricio Solaún, "Colombian Politics: Historical Characteristics and Prob-
    lems," in R. Albert Berry, Ronald G. Hellman, and Mauricio Solaún, eds.,
    Politics of Compromise: Coalition Government in Colombia (New Brunswick,
    N.J.: Transaction Books, 1980), p. 9-20.

25 For a thorough study of the cabinet ministers during this century, see John I.
    Laun, *El reclutamiento político en Colombia: los ministros de estado,*
    1900-1975 (Bogotá: Universidad de los Andes, 1976).

26 *El Debate,* February 14, 1930, p. 3.

27 Ibid., February 13, 1930, p. 3.

28 Although the politicians talked about *convivencia,* they never referred to them-
    selves as *convivialistas.* I find it descriptively illuminating to set them apart
    from previous generations in this way.

29 Juan Lozano y Lozano, *Ensayos críticos—Mis contemporáneos,* reprint ed.
    (Bogotá: Biblioteca Colombiana de Cultura, 1978), p. 224.

30 J. Fred Rippy, *British Investments in Latin America, 1822–1949* (Minneapolis:
    University of Minnesota Press, 1959), pp. 37, 67.

31 J. Fred Rippy, *Globe and Hemisphere* (Westport: Greenwood Press, 1972), p.
    36.

32   William Paul McGreevey, *An Economic History of Colombia, 1845–1930* (Cambridge: Cambridge University Press, 1971), p. 204.

33   Marco Palacios, *Coffee in Colombia, 1850–1970: An Economic, Social, and Political History* (Cambridge: Cambridge University Press, 1980). Palacios argues convincingly that the government was unable to promote a consistent policy with regard to the coffee interests while these were still too weak to impose their will on the government. During this period coffee remained the most important export crop, and the basis for the future boom was set (pp. 122–30).

34   McGreevey, *An Economic History*, p. 206.

35   For an in-depth study of the war and its relationship to the international economy, see Charles W. Bergquist, *Coffee and Conflict in Colombia, 1886–1910* (Durham: Duke University Press, 1978). For an analysis of nineteenth-century partisanship that stresses political and ideological factors, see Helen Delpar, *Red Against Blue: The Liberal Party in Colombian Politics, 1863–1899* (University, Ala.: University of Alabama Press, 1981).

36   Jorge E. Rodríguez R. and William P. McGreevey, "Colombia: comercio exterior, 1835–1962," in Miguel Urrutia Montoya and Mario Arrubla, eds., *Compendio de estadísticas históricas de Colombia* (Bogotá: Universidad Nacional, 1970), pp. 207 ff.

37   McGreevey, *An Economic History*, p. 198.

38   Rodríguez and McGreevey, "Colombia: comercio exterior," pp. 207 ff. For a provocative analysis of coffee growers as the working class of Colombia whose ideology and economic interests have led to alliances with the leaders of both parties that have made the twentieth-century peace possible, see chap. 5 of Charles W. Bergquist's *Workers in the Making of Modern Latin American History: Capitalist Development and Labor Formation in Chile, Argentina, Venezuela, and Colombia* (Stanford: Stanford University Press, 1985).

39   Solaún comes close to a similar perspective when he refers to the "ethos of *cultura*" and the "refined restraint" through which the politicians attempted to practice politics. Unfortunately, Solaún perceives the political culture as pathological. See his discussion on pages 9–20 of his "Colombian Politics," in Berry et al., *Politics of Compromise*.

40   Carlos Lleras Restrepo, *De la república a la dictadura* (Bogotá: Editorial ARGRA, 1955), p. 30.

41   Ramírez Moreno, *Los leopardos*, p. 227.

42   *Selected Writings of Bolívar*, comp. Vicente Lecuna, ed. Harold A. Bierck, Jr., 2 vols. (New York: Colonial Press, 1951), 1: 185–86.

43   Daniel Samper Ortega, "Elogio de Bogotá," *Anuario de la Academia Colombiana de la Lengua* 7 (1938–1939): 221. For an enlightening discussion along these lines, see Bergquist's distinction between the gentlemen's war and the guerrillas' war in the War of the Thousand Days in his *Coffee and Conflict*, pp. 133–92. For a discussion of the difficulties confronting the Liberal Santander regime after independence as it tried to promote "liberal" laws, see David Bushnell, *The Santander Regime in Gran Colombia* (Newark: University of Delaware Press, 1954), esp. pp. 166–82. I suspect that Freemasonry played an

important role in producing a separate world for the politicians. In the nineteenth century, virtually all the presidents, including Bolívar, Santander and Núñez, were Masons, as were the great Liberal leaders of the twentieth century, Benjamín Herrera and Rafael Uribe Uribe. See Américo Carnicelli, *Historia de la masonería colombiana, 1833-1940*, 2 vols., (Bogotá: Talleres de la Cooperativa Nacional de Artes Gráficas, 1975). There is less information about the relationship between the *convivialistas* and Freemasonry, although it is often speculated that many Liberals and Conservatives after 1930 were also members of the secret society. If they were not, they would certainly have been breaking with tradition. Freemasonry experienced an apparent revival during the presidency of Alfonso López. It was granted *personería jurídica*, legal standing, in 1935, and the society built a new temple in downtown Bogotá in 1939 (ibid., pp. 423, 407). Laureano Gómez always opposed them; see his attack on Freemasonry in 1942 in *Obras selectas*, pp. 677-94. Gómez considered it (along with communism and Judaism) one of the three cancers destroying Western civilization. It would be fair to assume that Freemasonry must still have had some importance in 1942 to warrant this attack.

44   Both Liberals and Conservatives expressed this lament continuously. The most systematic expression can be found in Abel Naranjo Villegas, *Generaciones colombianas* (Bogotá: Banco de la República, 1974).

45   There is no dearth of information on specific aspects of the *convivialistas'* personalities. Their backgrounds are less well known. Biographical sketches can be found in Oliverio Perry, *Quién es quién en Colombia, 1948* (Bogotá: Editorial Oliverio Perry, 1948).

46   For an analysis of the electoral system, see Robert H. Dix, *Colombia: The Political Dimensions of Change* (New Haven: Yale University Press, 1967), pp. 185-92.

47   Mario Fernández de Soto, *Una revolución en Colombia — Jorge Eliécer Gaitán y Mariano Ospina Pérez: un libro sobre Iberoamérica* (Madrid: Ediciones Cultura Hispánica, 1951), p. 61.

48   Néstor Madrid-Malo, "La política como espectáculo," in his *Ensayos y variaciones* (Bogotá: Biblioteca Colombiana de Cultura, 1978), p. 246.

49   Some of the most eloquent *convivialista* oratory can fortunately be heard in a collection of records compiled by Jorge Eduardo Girón Barrios under the collective title *Caudillos y muchedumbres* (Medellín: Discos Fuentes). The records include the rhetoric of Alfonso López, Eduardo Santos, Gabriel Turbay, Mariano Ospina Pérez, Carlos Lozano y Lozano, Gilberto Alzate Avendaño, and Jorge Eliécer Gaitán. For views on the place of oratory in public life, see Guillermo Fonnegra Sierra, *El parlamento colombiano* (Bogotá: Gráficas Centauro, 1953), p. 144. Naranjo Villegas, *Generaciones colombianas*, p. 113; Germán Arciniegas, *Memorias de un congresista* (Bogotá: Editorial Cromos, 1933), p. 19; Fernández de Soto, *Una revolución en Colombia*, p. 105; Silvio Villegas, *No hay enemigos a la derecha* (Manizales: Editorial Arturo Zapata, 1937), p. 76; for a critique see José Gutiérrez, *De la pseudo-aristocracia a la autenticidad: psicología social colombiana* (Bogotá: Ediciones Tercer Mundo, 1961), pp. 24, 29, 42.

50   In an interview with his brother in Lozano, *Ensayos críticos—Mis contemporáneos*, p. 244.
51   Ramírez Moreno made this statement in an interview with Alejandro Vallejo, *Políticos*, p. 85.
52   Lozano, *Ensayos críticos—Mis contemporáneos*, pp. 25–26.
53   Socarrás, *Laureano Gómez*, p. 91.
54   In his *Políticos*, p. 48, Vallejo draws a "psychological portrait" of a politician that they and others could use to judge those in public life. His essential characteristics are character, a passion for politics, eloquence, rhetoric, congeniality, artistic knowledge, enthusiasm, audaciousness, indifference, a sense of the present, business acumen, piety, probity, and, last, success.
55   Villegas, *No hay enemigos*, p. 27.
56   Naranjo Villegas, *Generaciones colombianas*, pp. 21–23.
57   In Lozano, *Ensayos críticos—Mis contemporáneos*, pp. 242–43.
58   James H. Billington, *Fire in the Minds of Men: Origins of the Revolutionary Faith* (New York: Basic Books, 1980), pp. 32–34, 62, 160–66; Richard Sennett, *The Fall of Public Man: On the Social Psychology of Capitalism* (New York: Vintage Books, 1978), pp. 224–39.
59   Sennett, *The Fall of Public Man*, pp. 3–44 and 337–40.
60   Hannah Arendt divides public life into the *vita activa* and the *vita contemplativa*. While stressing the value of the former in public life, she argues that both have lost ground to the new social realm of mass society. She bemoans the "rise of housekeeping from the shadowy interior of the household . . . into the light of the public sphere," the invasion of the lofty realm of the public by the quotidian. In the blurring between the private and the public, Arendt sees the origins of totalitarianism. See *The Human Condition* (Garden City, N.Y.: Doubleday Anchor Books, 1959), esp. p. 35, and *Totalitarianism* (New York: Harcourt, Brace and World, 1968).

Christopher Lasch is equally pessimistic. He too perceives an increase in the privatization that seems to come with capitalism. He sees the emergence of a self-absorbed modern culture in which the rugged individualism that characterized capitalism in its earlier, more familiar form has fallen by the wayside. He describes modern life as a clinically pathological state in which the individual depends on others to validate his self-esteem. Modern man cannot live without an admiring audience and "without attaching himself to those who radiate celebrity, power and charisma." See *The Culture of Narcissism* (New York: W.W. Norton, 1978), pp. 102–18.

Two French historians have examined this process of privatization in the histories of sex and death. Philippe Ariès summarizes the changes that have taken place in our conceptions of death from the middle ages to the present. Death, he claims, has been transformed from a socially and individually accepted occurrence in which the dying person calmly organizes a public ritual to a closed-off, private, and feared finale in which a person expresses the deepest essence of his self in his manner of dying. See *Western Attitudes Toward Death: From the Middle Ages to the Present* (Baltimore: Johns Hopkins University Press, 1979).

Michel Foucault points to a deepening of the private world under the aegis of inquisitive public knowledge-seekers who probe the deepest recesses of our minds and psyches in order to better regulate a complex, diversified social order. See *The History of Sexuality, Vol. I: An Introduction* (New York: Vintage Books, 1980).

On a less pessimistic note, Albert O. Hirschman sees a continual alternation between periods of public and private preeminence and is more sanguine about the public benefits of contemporary privatization. This may be due to his belief that the day of the public will come again. See *Shifting Involvements: Private Interest and Public Action* (Princeton: Princeton University Press, 1982).

61 For an account of early efforts to show the benefits of the private over the public as a rationale for capitalism, see Albert O. Hirschman, *The Passions and the Interests: Political Arguments for Capitalism Before Its Triumph* (Princeton: Princeton University Press, 1977), esp. pp. 7–66.

62 Mary Douglas, *Natural Symbols: Explorations in Cosmology* (New York: Vintage Books, 1973), pp. 101–2.

63 Luis Cano admitted as much as early as 1923 when he stated that "the directing classes are skeptical . . . and don't believe in the Catholic religion" (cited in Molina, *Las ideas liberales*, pp. 167–68). According to Alejandro López, "Liberalism is not an irreligious system because we place the Colombian religion at a higher plane, one that is not that of our activities and concerns, allowing each citizen to exercise absolute freedom of belief" (Quoted in Jaime Jaramillo Uribe, ed., *Antología del pensamiento político colombiano*, 2 vols. (Bogotá: Publicaciones del Banco de la República, 1970), 1:90). The church also knew at the time that López considered it the "spinal column of the nation." This was the impression of Monseigneur Carlos Vargas Umaña. Interview 20, October 31, 1979.

64 McGreevey, *An Economic History*, pp. 210–11.

65 Guillermo Torres García, *Historia de la moneda en Colombia* (Bogotá: Imprenta del Banco de la República, 1945), p. 353.

66 Comisión Económica para América Latina (CEPAL), *El desarrollo económico de Colombia: Análisis y proyecciones del desarrollo económico, Vol. III* (Bogotá: Departmento Administrativo Nacional de Estadística[DANE], n.d.), p. 22.

67 Torres García, *Historia de la moneda*, p. 360.

68 See Alejandro López's ideas in Jaramillo Uribe, *Antología del pensamiento*, 1:13–96. See also Alejandro López, *Idearium liberal* (Paris: Ediciones La Antorcha, 1931).

69 Rafael Uribe Uribe, *Obras selectas*, 2 vols. (Bogotá: Cámara de Representantes, Colección Pensadores Políticos Colombianos, 1979), 2: 415.

70 McGreevey, *An Economic History*, p. 110.

71 *El Debate*, January 11, 1930, p. 3.

72 Ibid., January 3, 1930, p. 3.

73 Villegas, *No hay enemigos*, pp. 200, 208. See also Augusto Ramírez Moreno, *La crisis del partido conservador* (Bogotá: Tipografía Granada, 1937), pp. 31–32, 40–42.

74　See Daniel Pecaut, *Política y sindicalismo en Colombia* (Bogotá: La Carreta, 1973), pp. 89-99.

75　Miguel Urrutia, *The Development of the Colombian Labor Movement* (New Haven: Yale University Press, 1969), p. 107.

76　Richard E. Sharpless, *Gaitán of Colombia: A Political Biography* (Pittsburgh: Pittsburgh University Press, 1978), p. 19.

77　Alfonso López Pumarejo, "Mensaje al congreso nacional en la instalación de sus sesiones ordinarias de 1937," in *Obras selectas*, 2:160; also cited in Palacios, *Coffee in Colombia*, p. 217.

78　For a sympathetic study of the first López administration that emphasizes these aspects, see Alvaro Tirado Mejía, *Aspectos políticos del primer gobierno de Alfonso López Pumarejo, 1934–38* (Bogotá: Instituto Colombiano de Cultura, 1981).

79　*El Tiempo*, May 3, 1936, p. 4.

80　Ibid., January 21–24, 1938.

81　Ibid., January 30, 1938, p. 1.

82　Ibid., February 3, 1938, p. 15.

83　Urrutia, *Colombian Labor Movement*, p. 154.

84　During the long period in which the Conservatives did not run a candidate for the presidency, they did of course participate in public life. Diplomatic posts abroad were among the most sought after offices. In the view of Pedronel Giraldo Londoño, *Don Fernando: juicio sobre un hombre y una época* (Medellín: Editorial Granamérica, 1963), p. 103, diplomats were "politicians in recess."

85　Lleras Restrepo, *De la república a la dictadura*, p. 212.

86　Villegas, *No hay enemigos*, pp. 152–55. The *convivialistas* attempted to maintain their differences by making them immutable. According to Alfonso Araújo, "The Liberal is progressive by nature; the Conservative is traditional" (quoted in Lozano, *Ensayos críticos—Mis contemporáneos*, p. 459). In the view of Alejandro López, "In all nations there has been, there is, and there will always be a liberal spirit and and conservative spirit" (in Jaramillo Uribe, *Antología del pensamiento*, p. 144).

87　The use of the word in this context is usually associated most closely with Silvio Villegas, who began to see *oligarcas* in politics in the early 1930s. See his retrospective comment on the period in *Sábado*, May 8, 1948, p. 31. According to the Gaitanista leader Carlos H. Pareja, oligarchy was a matter of temperament: "It is possible for the rich to have the temperament of socialists, and for the poor to become oligarchs, instruments of rich oligarchies" (*Sábado*, January 20, 1948, p. 1).

88　For a cogent analysis of the impact of the making of private fortunes on public life, see Alfonso López Michelsen, *Cuestiones colombianas* (México: Impresiones Modernas, 1955); López Michelsen also wrote a marvelously illuminating novelized account of public life during this period, *Los elegidos* (Bogotá: Editorial Tercer Mundo, 1967); see also Antonio García, *Gaitán y el problema de la revolución colombiana* (Bogotá: M.S.C., 1955), pp. 286–91.

89　Urrutia, *Colombian Labor Movement*, p. 233.

90　For studies of corruption in López's regime, see Julio Ortiz Márquez, *El hombre que fue un pueblo* (Bogotá: Carlos Valencia Editores, 1978); Carlos Galvis Gómez, *Por qué cayó López* (Bogotá: Editorial ABC, 1946).

91 Lleras Camargo's statement came in the context of an interview with Lozano, in *Ensayos críticos—Mis contemporáneos,* p. 273.

92 Few subjects in the history of Colombia have attracted as much interest as *la Violencia.* For a bibliography on the subject, see Russell W. Ramsey, "Critical Bibliography on *La Violencia* in Colombia," *Latin American Research Review* 8 (Spring 1973); 3–44. A recent scholarly work on the subject is Paul Oquist, *Violencia, conflicto y política en Colombia* (Bogotá: Instituto de Estudios Colombianos, Biblioteca Banco Popular, 1978). For a path-breaking social history of *la Violencia,* see Gonzalo Sánchez and Donny Meertens, *Bandoleros, gamonales y campesinos: el caso de la Violencia en Colombia* (Bogotá: El Áncora Editores, 1983). A regional study of *la Violencia* in Tolima is James Henderson, *Cuando Colombia se desangró: un estudio de la Violencia en metrópoli y provincia* (Bogotá: El Áncora Editores, 1984).

93 "The Colombian ruling class is given to signs of artificial supremacy." This is the conclusion reached by J. J. García, *Política y amigos,* p. 15. See also the works of José Gutiérrez, *De la pseudo-aristocracia* and *Idiosincracia colombiana y nacionalidad* (Bogotá: Editorial Colombiana, 1966).

94 Gaitán embodied the quality that anthropologists call "liminality." The concept was introduced by Arnold Van Gennep to describe the middle phase between separation and incorporation (the margin or *limen*) present in all rites of transition. See *The Rites of Passage* (Chicago: University of Chicago Press, 1960), esp. pp. 10–12 and 182–94. The concept has been used extensively by Victor Turner, *The Ritual Process: Structure and Anti-Structure* (Ithaca: Cornell University Press, 1969), esp. pp. 94–130 and 166–203. In "Variations on a Theme of Liminality," in Sally Falk Moore and Barbara G. Myerhoff, eds., *Secular Ritual* (Assen: Van Gorcum, 1977), pp. 36–52, Turner makes a distinction between "liminal" and "liminoid," claiming that the liminal of yesterday is the liminoid of today. The former term refers to collective processes most often concerned with the cycles and rhythms of the calendar, the weather, biology, or social structure, whereas the latter more often refers to an individual event produced by a liminal figure; rather than being cyclical, liminoid events are continuously generated. In this sense it may be more appropriate to think of Gaitán as liminoid. For Turner's analysis of a liminal figure, see "Hidalgo: History as Social Drama," in his *Dramas, Fields and Metaphors: Symbolic Action in Human Society* (Ithaca: Cornell University Press, 1974), pp. 98–115. Further thoughts about Gaitán's liminality are in n. 6 to chapter 4, below.

Chapter 2

1 Horacio Gómez Aristizábal, *Gaitán: enfoque histórico* (Bogotá: Editorial Cosmos, 1975), p. 28.

2 José Antonio Osorio Lizarazo, *Gaitán: vida, muerte y permanente presencia,* reprint ed. (Bogotá: Carlos Valencia Editores, 1979), p. 30. This work, by one of Gaitán's greatest admirers and a leading novelist of the period, has been a major

source for all subsequent biographies; see also Agustín Rodríguez Garavito, *Gaitán: biografía de una sombra* (Bogotá: Ediciones Tercer Mundo, 1979), p. 41.

3 Luis David Peña, *Gaitán íntimo* (Bogotá: Editorial Iqueima, 1949), pp. 88–89; José María Córdoba, *Jorge Eliécer Gaitán: tribuno popular de Colombia* (Bogotá: Litografías Cor-Val, 1952), p. 7.

4 A picture of Gaitán's home in Las Cruces is in Alberto Figueredo Salcedo, ed., *Colección Jorge Eliécer Gaitán: documentos para una biografía*, Vol. 1 (Bogotá: Imprenta Nacional, 1949), p. 18. To this day Gaitán's most devoted followers engage in heated discussions about which barrio the *caudillo* was born in.

5 Richard E. Sharpless, *Gaitán of Colombia: A Political Biography* (Pittsburgh: University of Pittsburgh Press, 1978), p. 30. This recent biography of Gaitán is the first to break new ground. Sharpless, unlike the majority of Gaitán's biographers, never met him. Much of the originality of his work stems from his use of the extensive and revealing Gaitán Papers, housed in the Casa Museo Jorge Eliécer Gaitán in Bogotá.

6 Osorio Lizarazo, *Gaitán*, p. 45. For a psychohistorical interpretation of Gaitán, see Mauro Torres, *Gaitán: grandeza y limitaciones psicológicas* (Bogotá: Ediciones Tercer Mundo, 1976). Torres argues that Gaitán's "radical failure" was rooted in his home life during infancy and adolescence, most specifically in his conflict-ridden relationship with his father. See especially pp. 22, 26–30.

7 Osorio Lizarazo, *Gaitán*, p. 9.

8 Sharpless, *Gaitán of Colombia*, p. 32; Osorio Lizarazo, *Gaitán*, pp. 35–36.

9 J. Cordell Robinson, *El movimiento gaitanista en Colombia* (Bogotá: Ediciones Tercer Mundo, 1976), p. 47. Robinson's study comes close to being an "official" biography of Gaitán. The author adds little to what was known before and repeats the subjective appreciations expressed by Gaitán's opponents as objective facts about the *caudillo's* politics and personality.

10 Osorio Lizarazo, *Gaitán*, p. 18. See, for example, his funeral orations before the tombs of Generals Uribe Uribe and Quintero Calderón, delivered in 1919 and reprinted in Figueredo Salcedo, *Colección*, pp. 27–30. Gaitán's orations throughout the years were peppered with references to past Liberal heroes: for example, his speech accepting the nomination as the presidential candidate of the *pueblo* on September 23, 1945, "Discurso-Programa," in Jorge Villaveces, ed., *Los mejores discursos de Gaitán* (Bogotá: Editorial Jorvi, 1968), pp. 401–4.

11 Osorio Lizarazo, *Gaitán*, p. 46.

12 Ibid., pp. 27–28.

13 Ibid., p. 30.

14 Córdoba, *Tribuno popular*, p. 9.

15 The platform of the coalition is in Figueredo Salcedo, *Colección*, pp. 125–27.

16 Jorge Eliécer Gaitán, "¡Valencia sí!" and "Los universitarios coalicionistas y la candidatura Lombana," in Figueredo Salcedo, *Colección*, pp. 133–35.

17 Sharpless, *Gaitán of Colombia*, p. 37; Osorio Lizarazo, *Gaitán*, p. 38.

18 Jorge Eliécer Gaitán, "El Directorio Liberal Universitario y la encuesta," a letter

written to *El Siglo*, a Liberal Bogotá newspaper, in November 1918. In Figueredo Salcedo, *Colección*, pp. 151–53.

19 Sharpless, *Gaitán of Colombia*, pp. 39–40.

20 The accusations are in letters reprinted in Figueredo Salcedo, *Colección*, pp. 140–42.

21 Gaitán's success is recounted in a letter by Juan N. Escobar Navarro to *El Derecho* of Honda, Tolima, January 14, 1918, reprinted in Figueredo Salcedo, *Colección*, pp. 142–43.

22 Gaitán defends himself in a letter to *El Tiempo* on January 8, 1918, reprinted in Figueredo Salcedo, *Colección*, p. 140.

23 Osorio Lizarazo, *Gaitán*, pp. 40–42; Daniel Pecaut, *Política y sindicalismo en Colombia* (Bogotá: La Carreta, 1973), p. 90; Miguel Urrutia, *El sindicalismo en Colombia* (Bogotá: Ediciones Universidad de los Andes, 1979), pp. 92–93.

24 Córdoba, *Tribuno popular*, p. 9; Sharpless, *Gaitán of Colombia*, p. 31, claims that Gaitán's changing schools demonstrated his early opportunism.

25 According to Osorio Lizarazo, *Gaitán*, p. 46, Gaitán was forced to live on *agua de panela*, a hot drink of brown sugar and water, and sweet bread that he obtained at reduced prices from the small corner stores in his own barrio of Egipto, and he had to study in the parks.

26 Gaitán's recollections appear in an interview with Bernardo Moreno Torralbo, "Gaitán ante sí mismo," July 1943, reprinted in Figueredo Salcedo, *Colección*, pp. 21–38; quotation on p. 32.

27 Examples of his early writings can be found in Figueredo Salcedo, *Colección*, pp. 45–77, 177–205.

28 So it was called by *El Tiempo* when Gaitán wrote to the prestigious daily to announce the existence of the center. The letter is in Figueredo Salcedo, *Colección*, p. 107.

29 Ibid., p. 106.

30 Jorge Eliécer Gaitán, "Propaganda cultural," a letter to *El Tiempo*, n.d., in Figueredo Salcedo, *Colección*, pp. 103–5.

31 President Suárez wrote to Gaitán on May 3, 1920, expressing his interest in attending. The letter is reprinted in Figueredo Salcedo, *Colección*, p. 106.

32 Gaitán's letter to *El Espectador*, on January 20, 1920, is reprinted in Figueredo Salcedo, *Colección*, pp. 119–20.

33 Press reports of the riot and Gaitán's success can be found in Figueredo Salcedo, *Colección*, pp. 154–156, 160–64.

34 Few biographers of Gaitán or students of the Gaitanista movement have studied *Las ideas socialistas* in depth. Although it created considerable controversy when it was published and the limited edition was sold out, not many of Gaitán's contemporaries ever seriously analyzed his thought as expressed in the thesis. Few of Gaitán's followers thought highly of it. Luis Carlos Pérez, *El pensamiento filosófico de Gaitán* (Bogotá: Editorial de los Andes, 1954), pp. 29–32, argues that the document is a weak, positivist tract that is antithetical to socialism. Its ideas were romantic, naive, and simple. Gerardo Molina, also a friend and follower and one of the most consistently radical members of his generation, argues in *Las ideas liberales en Colombia, 1915–1934* (Bogotá: Ediciones

Tercer Mundo, 1974), pp. 139–46, that Gaitán's ideas are in the main an expression of his need to be both a socialist and a Liberal who could work within the system. According to Molina, the main strength of the thesis lies in its demonstration that Colombia was a capitalist society and that class struggle was inevitable. In his *Gaitán y el camino de la revolución colombiana* (Bogotá: Ediciones Camilo, 1974), Antonio García argues that to look for socialism or Marxism in a doctrinal sense in the thesis is to miss the measure of the man and his time. Unfortunately, García does not look for other doctrines or ideologies. For all three, then, the thesis is not an important work, in large part because it is not socialist.

The most systematic analysis of *Las ideas socialistas* can be found in Sharpless, *Gaitán of Colombia*, pp. 44–51. Sharpless disagrees with the three authors mentioned above. "First and foremost, he [Gaitán] was a socialist. The programs he developed throughout his career can only be understood within this classification" (p. 49). This argument makes sense only if one accepts that what Gaitán did in his life was meant to pave the way for a society quite different from the one he openly advocated.

Most biographers hardly mention the thesis. Most notable is Cordell Robinson, who makes only passing references to marginal thoughts contained within it; see *El movimiento gaitanista*, pp. 116–29.

35   An abridged account of the trial is in Figueredo Salcedo, *Colección*, pp. 213–26, quotation on p. 216.

36   Osorio Lizarazo, *Gaitán*, p. 69.

37   Gómez Aristizábal, *Enfoque histórico*, pp. 56–65.

38   Ibid., pp. 66–68. Gómez mistakenly asserts that Gaitán was defending Martínez. Actually, he defended an accomplice marginally involved in the crime.

39   For an introduction to the classical school of legal thought, see Gilbert Geis, "Jeremy Bentham," in Hermann Mannheim, ed., *Pioneers of Criminology* (London: Stevens and Sons, 1960), pp. 51–67, and Elio Monachesi, "Cesare Beccaria," ibid., pp. 36–50.

40   Jorge Eliécer Gaitán, "Sociología y Antropología," in Luis Carlos Pérez, ed., *Jorge Eliécer Gaitán, su obra científica*, 4 vols. (Bogotá: Ministerio de Educación Nacional, 1952), 4:166.

41   Ibid., pp. 117–18.

42   Stephen Schafer, *Theories in Criminology* (New York: Random House, 1969), p. 123. For an account of Lambroso's ideas, see "Cesare Lambroso," by Marvin E. Wolfgang, in Mannheim, *Pioneers*, pp. 168–27. For Garófalo, see Francis A. Allen, "Raffaele Garófalo," ibid., pp. 254–76.

43   Hermann Mannheim, in his introduction to *Pioneers*, pp. 21–22; Negley K. Teeters, *Penology from Panama to Cape Horn* (Philadelphia: Temple University Press, 1946).

44   Gaitán invariably couched his defenses in terms of the principles of the positivist school and against those of the classical school. According to Gaitán, the greatest classicist was José Antonio Montalvo, a noted Conservative whose career spanned the period from the early 1920s to the 1950s. The most noted confrontation between the two came in the Zawadsky case, which Gaitán won and which

is reprinted in Luis Carlos Pérez, *Obra científica* vol. 2. Gaitán's views on Montalvo appear in Gómez Aristizábal, *Enfoque histórico*, p. 187.

45 Enrico Ferri, *The Positive School of Criminology*, ed. Stanley E. Grupp (Pittsburgh: University of Pittsburgh Press, 1968), p. 45; see also Thorsten Sellin, "Enrico Ferri," in Mannheim, *Pioneers*, pp. 283–84.

46 At the time this conception was prevalent in European sociological theories as well. The organic metaphor for society was most explicitly used by Emile Durkheim. See his *Rules of Sociological Method* (Chicago: University of Chicago Press, 1938), and *Suicide* (Glencoe, Ill.: Free Press, 1951). For a generalized critique, see Alvin Gouldner, *The Coming Crisis of Western Sociology* (New York: Free Press, 1970).

47 Ferri, *Positive School*, pp. 98–100.

48 Jorge Eliécer Gaitán, "Las ideas socialistas en Colombia," in Luis Emiro Valencia, ed., *Gaitán: antología de su pensamiento económico y social* (Bogotá: Ediciones Suramérica, 1968), pp. 49–213. Subsequent page citations for "Las ideas socialistas" appear in the text.

49 Gaitán's thought more closely resembled that of Proudhon, the moralistic defender of small property and the family, than that of Marx. Interestingly, many of the ambiguities contemporaries saw in Gaitán were those that friends and foes also perceived in Proudhon. See Alan Ritter, *The Political Thought of P. J. Proudhon* (Princeton: Princeton University Press, 1969), esp. chap. 1. An enlightening comparison between Proudhon and Marx, considerably more sympathetic to the former, is James H. Billington, *Fire in the Minds of Men: Origins of the Revolutionary Faith* (New York: Basic Books, 1980), pp. 287–305. Marx did not think highly of his archenemy: "From head to foot M. Proudhon is the philosopher and economist of the petit bourgeoisie. In an advanced society the petit bourgeois necessarily becomes from his very position a Socialist on the one side and an economist on the other; that is to say, he is dazed by the magnificence of the big bourgeoisie, and has sympathy for the suffering of the people. He is at once both bourgeois and man of the people" (in a letter to P. V. Annenkov on December 28, 1846, reprinted in Karl Marx and Frederick Engels, *Selected Works in One Volume* [New York: International Publishers, 1968], p. 678). One can easily imagine Marx coming to a similar conclusion about Gaitán.

50 For Marx's analysis of the historical development of the modes of production, see *Capital* (New York: International Publishers, 1967), vol. 1, part 4, pp. 312–35.

51 Among those who maintained an independent course but remained marginal in terms of political power are Antonio García, Gerardo Molina, and Luis Carlos Pérez. For the Communist party the most noted figures of the period are Gilberto Vieira and Diego Montaña Cuéllar. Among those who were once considered radicals—either socialists or communists—but who later joined the traditional partisan game were Gabriel Turbay, Alberto Lleras Camargo, and Carlos Arango Vélez.

52 Gaitán's views are remarkably similar in this regard to those of the Parisian sans-culottes of 1793–1794, whose mentality has been so admirably uncovered

by Albert Soboul, *The Sans-Culottes: The Popular Movement and the Revolutionary Government, 1793–1794* (New York: Anchor Books, 1972). Gaitán never advocated, as did the mobilized sans-culottes, the expropriation of everything a citizen did not need for his own survival, but he supported many of the same limitations on property.

Chapter 3

1 Alberto Figueredo Salcedo, ed., *Colección Jorge Eliécer Gaitán: documentos para una biografía*, vol. 1 (Bogotá: Imprenta Nacional, 1949), following p. 283.

2 Thorsten Sellin, "Enrico Ferri," in Hermann Mannheim, ed., *Pioneers of Criminology* (London: Stevens and Sons, 1960), pp. 227–28; Mannheim, "Introduction," ibid., p. 7.

3 Figueredo Salcedo, *Colección*, pp. 386–87; Lucas Caballero Calderón, *Figuras políticas de Colombia* (Bogotá: Editorial Kelly, 1945), p. 45; J. Cordell Robinson, *El movimiento gaitanista en Colombia* (Bogotá: Editiones Tercer Mundo, 1976), p. 52; Richard E. Sharpless, *Gaitán of Colombia: A Political Biography* (Pittsburgh: University of Pittsburgh Press, 1978), pp. 51–52.

4 Alejandro Vallejo, *Políticos en la intimidad* (Bogotá: Ediciones Antena, 1936), pp. 12–16.

5 Sharpless, *Gaitán of Colombia*, p. 55. Sharpless cites an interview with Gaitán published by *El Espectador* on February 14, 1928.

6 José Antonio Osorio Lizarazo, *Gaitán: vida, muerte y permanente presencia*, reprint ed. (Bogotá: Carlos Valencia Editores, 1979), p. 122.

7 Many of Gaitán's orations in Congress are collected in Jorge Villaveces, *Los mejores discursos de Gaitán* (Bogotá: Editorial Jorvi, 1968); an abridged version of these speeches is on pp. 30–59. A more complete edition has recently been published in *1928: la masacre en las bananeras* (Bogotá: Ediciones Los Comuneros, n.d.). The best study of the strike against United Fruit is Judith White, *Historia de una ignominia* (Bogotá: Editorial Presencia, 1978). See also Gabriel Fonnegra, *Bananeras testimonio vivo de una epopeya* (Bogotá: Ediciones Tercer Mundo, 1980); Roberto Herrera Soto and Rafael Romero Castañeda, *La zona bananera del Magdalena* (Bogotá: Imprenta Patriótica, Instituto Caro y Cuervo, 1979); Carlos Cortés Vargas, *Los sucesos de las bananeras* (Bogotá: Imprenta La Luz, 1929); Alberto Castrillón, *120 días bajo el terror militar* (Bogotá: Revista Universidad, 1929).

8 Jorge Eliécer Gaitán, "El debate de las bananeras," in Villaveces, *Mejores discursos*, pp. 58–59; also cited in Guillermo Fonnegra Sierra, *El parlamento colombiano* (Bogotá: Gráficas Centauro, 1953), pp. 196–97.

9 Interview 21 with Luis Eduardo Ricaurte, Gaitán's bodyguard, November 2, 1979.

10 Sharpless, *Gaitán of Colombia*, p. 65.

11 Ibid., p. 69.

12 *Acción Liberal*, no. 1, May 1932, p. 36.

13 Darío Samper, "Jorge Eliécer Gaitán," ibid., pp. 4–6.

14 Jorge Eliécer Gaitán, "El nuevo sentido político de las izquierdas," ibid., p. 8.
15 Cited in *Acción Liberal*, no. 2, June 1932, pp. 93–94.
16 Alejandro López, in a letter to Gaitán published in *Acción Liberal* as "Ideas del izquierdismo," no. 2, June 1932, pp. 55–63.
17 Ibid., p. 55.
18 Darío Samper, "Gaitán," pp. 5–6.
19 Jorge Eliécer Gaitán, "Función social de la propiedad," in Villaveces, *Mejores discursos*, 72-82; see also "El problema social," ibid., pp. 61–68.
20 Gaitán, "El problema social," pp. 61-62.
21 Ibid., p. 62; see also Gaitán, "Función social," pp. 78–79.
22 Sharpless, *Gaitán of Colombia*, p. 63.
23 Gaitán, "Función social," pp. 73–77; Sharpless, *Gaitán of Colombia*, pp. 62–63.
24 Gaitán, "Función social," p. 79.
25 Ibid., p. 80.
26 Ibid., p. 73.
27 Ibid., p. 79.
28 Gaitán, "El problema social," p. 62.
29 According to Sharpless, *Gaitán of Colombia*, p. 65, Gaitán's arguments in favor of property were demagogic: "he [Gaitán] used the very arguments usually spoken by his opponents."
30 Gaitán, "Función social," pp. 72–73.
31 Sharpless, *Gaitán of Colombia*, p. 68.
32 Enrique Santos Montejo (Calibán), *La danza de las horas y otros escritos* (Bogotá: Libros del Cóndor, 1969), p. 222.
33 Osorio Lizarazo, *Gaitán*, pp. 132–62, offers a detailed account of the growing prejudice against Gaitán in this period; also Sharpless, *Gaitán of Colombia*, p. 69.
34 Gaitán, "La fuerza pública al servicio del feudalismo" (August 16, 1934), in Villaveces, *Mejores discursos*, pp. 166–67.
35 Gaitán, "El manifiesto del Unirismo" (n.d.), in Luis Emiro Valencia, ed., *Gaitán: antología de su pensamiento económico y social* (Bogotá: Ediciones Suramérica, 1968), p. 256.
36 Ibid., p. 254.
37 The most detailed account of Unirismo is Fermín López Giraldo, *El apóstol desnudo, o dos años al lado de un mito* (Manizales: Editorial Arturo Zapata, 1936); the best concise account is Sharpless, *Gaitán of Colombia*, pp. 71–75 and 78–83.
38 Osorio Lizarazo, *Gaitán*, p. 174.
39 Sharpless, Gaitán of Colombia, p. 73.
40 Luis David Peña, *Gaitán íntimo* (Bogotá: Editorial Iqueima, 1949), p. 115.
41 Gaitán, "El manifiesto del Unirismo," pp. 237, 245, 252.
42 Gaitán, "Igualdad de derechos para la mujer" (December 11, 1934), in Villaveces, *Mejores discursos*, p. 173.
43 Ibid.
44 Gaitán, "Contra el mal uso de la palabra revolución," in Villaveces, *Mejores discursos*, p. 177.

45 Ibid.
46 Gaitán, "La fuerza," p. 166.
47 Ibid., p. 168.
48 Gaitán, "El manifiesto del Unirismo," p. 226.
49 Gaitán, "La fuerza," p. 167.
50 Ibid.
51 Gaitán, "Contral el mal uso," p. 179.
52 Gaitán, "El manifiesto del Unirismo," p. 249.
53 Ibid., p. 243.
54 Rafael Azula Barrera, *De la revolución al orden nuevo: proceso y drama de un pueblo* (Bogotá: Editorial Kelly, 1956), p. 63.
55 Juan Lozano y Lozano, "Jorge Eliécer Gaitán," in his *Ensayos críticos—Mis contemporáneos,* reprint ed. (Bogotá: Biblioteca Colombiana de Cultura, 1978), p. 87. *Ensayos críticos* was first published in 1934; *Mis contemporáneos* in 1944.
56 Ibid.
57 Ibid., pp. 93–94.
58 Ibid., p. 82.
59 Ibid., p. 87.
60 Ibid.
61 Juan Lozano y Lozano, "Liberalismo y Unirismo," in *Acción Liberal,* no. 8, September 1933, pp. 372–79.
62 Germán Arciniegas, "Novelín de la tierra, de los campesinos y de los patrones," ibid., pp. 344–51.
63 Interview 8 with José María Córdoba, general secretary of the Gaitanista movement, 1944–1948, July 15, 1979.
64 Sharpless, *Gaitán of Colombia,* p. 83.
65 Peña, *Gaitán íntimo,* p. 82.
66 Sharpless, *Gaitán of Colombia,* p. 80.
67 This is the argument of the Unirista Fermín López Giraldo's *El apóstol desnudo.*
68 Osorio Lizarazo, *Gaitán,* pp. 190–91.
69 Sharpless, *Gaitán of Colombia,* p. 90.
70 *El Tiempo,* June 9, 1936, pp. 1, 15.
71 Sharpless, *Gaitán of Colombia,* p. 90.
72 *El Tiempo,* June 11, 1936, p. 4.
73 According to Arturo Abella, Gaitán was twice introduced to the board of the Jockey Club by an upper-class Gaitanista sympathizer whose free-wheeling habits had earned him the enmity of his fellow club members and the Bogotá elite in general. Thus, he concluded that Gaitán was not necessarily or exclusively rejected because of his own class background, style, and criticism of the upper class. Abella obtained this information in a telephone conversation with a confidential source during our interview (interview 15, August 18, 1979).
74 *El Tiempo,* August 22, 1936, p. 4.
75 Osorio Lizarazo, *Gaitán,* p. 197.
76 *El Tiempo,* August 22, 1936, p. 4.

77 Osorio Lizarazo, *Gaitán*, p. 145.
78 *El Tiempo*, July 2, 1936, p. 3; October 5, 1936, p. 3; October 8, 1936, p. 15.
79 Interview 59 with Clímaco Aldana, mayoral assistant, December 11, 1979; interview with Ricaurte; interview 37 with Guillermo Vargas, November 28, 1979; interview 60 with Arturo Céspedes, follower of Gaitán, December 13, 1979. According to Aldana, the excessively sticky paving material was the result of a conspiracy of Liberals and Conservatives in the city's department of public works.
80 Interview 66 with Carlos J. Sánchez, follower of Gaitán, January 2, 1980.
81 *El Tiempo*, October 8, 1936, p. 15.
82 Sharpless, *Gaitán of Colombia*, pp. 92–94.
83 *El Tiempo*, July 5, 1936, p. 3; July 9, 1936, p. 1.
84 Interview with Clímaco Aldana.
85 *El Tiempo*, August 23, 1935, p. 14.
86 Jorge Eliécer Gaitán, "Un tema político que no pertenece a la política" (December 2, 1936), in Villaveces, *Mejores discursos*, p. 192.
87 Ibid., p. 194.
88 Ibid.
89 Osorio Lizarazo, *Gaitán*, p. 197.
90 *El Tiempo*, January 23, 1937, p. 1.
91 Sharpless, *Gaitán of Colombia*, p. 93.
92 *El Tiempo*, January 23, 1937, p. 1.
93 Jorge Eliécer Gaitán, "Debate sobre la destitución del alcalde de Bogotá," in Villaveces, *Mejores discursos*, p. 201.
94 Ibid., pp. 201–2.
95 Ibid., p. 211.
96 Sharpless, *Gaitán of Colombia*, p. 97.
97 Jorge Eliécer Gaitán, "Un programa educacional para Colombia" (February 17, 1940), in Villaveces, *Mejores discursos*, pp. 275–76.
98 Jorge Eliécer Gaitán, "Rusia y la democracia" (n.d.), ibid., p. 369.
99 Ibid., p. 377.
100 Ibid.
101 Ibid., p. 378.
102 Ricardo Jordán Jiménez, *Dos viernes trágicos* (Bogotá: Editorial Horizontes, 1968), pp. 25–26.

Chapter 4

1 Luis David Peña, *Gaitán íntimo* (Bogotá: Editorial Iqueima, 1949), pp. 134–35; Julio Ortiz Márquez, *El hombre que fue un pueblo* (Bogotá: Carlos Valencia Editores, 1978), pp. 23–24.
2 The charges leveled against López in the Mamatoco affair are elaborated in *El Siglo*, July 16 and 17, 1943, p. 1, and September 2, 1945, p. 1. For a general account of corruption in the López government and the Handel affair, see Ortiz Márquez, *El hombre*, pp. 14–18 and 225–27.

3   According to Richard E. Sharpless, *Gaitán of Colombia: A Political Biography*
    (Pittsburgh: University of Pittsburgh Press, 1978), p. 103, Gaitán never believed
    he would win the election. Sharpless bases his conclusion on information given
    him by Gaitán's widow, Doña Amparo Jaramillo vda. de Gaitán. Whether this
    is true or not is difficult to ascertain. In any case, Gaitán used the campaign as
    a massive educational experience for the *pueblo* through which he undoubtedly
    felt that he would some day come to power.

4   Interview with Bernardo Moreno Torralbo, "Gaitán ante sí mismo," July 1943,
    reprinted in Alberto Figueredo Salcedo, ed., *Colección Jorge Eliécer Gaitán:
    documentos para una biografía*, Vol 1 (Bogotá: Imprenta Nacional, 1949), p.
    29.

5   Gaitán's conclusions appear in an interview with Juan Lozano y Lozano, "Jorge
    Eliécer Gaitán," in his *Ensayos críticos—Mis contemporáneos*, reprint ed.
    (Bogotá: Biblioteca Colombiana de Cultura, 1978), p. 418. *Mis contempo-
    ráneos*, in which this essay appears, was first published in 1944.

6   Gaitán's quest for the presidency can be seen in terms of the four phases of
    liminality that Victor Turner distinguishes in his *Dramas, Fields and Meta-
    phors: Symbolic Action in Human Society* (Ithaca: Cornell University Press,
    1974). These are (1) the breach of formal social relations between persons or
    groups within the same system of social relations; (2) a mounting crisis that easily
    becomes coextensive with some cleavage; (3) redressive action, usually of an
    informal character, to limit the spread of the crisis; and (4) the reintegration of
    the disturbed group.

    In Gaitán's case the breach came with the September 23, 1945, convention;
    the crisis escalated when it became apparent that Gaitán did not intend to bow
    to Gabriel Turbay, the official candidate of the Liberal party; redressive action
    took place days before the May 5, 1946, presidential election in the marathon
    three-day conversation between Gaitán and Turbay. When Gaitán lost the elec-
    tion, the crisis was postponed, and the final reintegration of which Turner speaks
    was precluded by Gaitán's assassination.

7   Lozano, "Jorge Eliécer Gaitán," p. 413.

8   Ibid., p. 416.

9   Ibid., pp. 413–14.

10 Ibid., p. 411.

11 Ibid.

12 Many Conservatives saw Gaitán as the confirmation of their ideals. See Mario
    Fernández de Soto, *Una revolución en Colombia—Jorge Eliécer Gaitán y
    Mariano Ospina Pérez: un libro sobre Iberoamérica* (Madrid: Ediciones Cul-
    tura Hispánica, 1951), p. 73; Rafael Azula Barrera, *De la revolución al orden
    nuevo: proceso y drama de un pueblo* (Bogotá: Editorial Kelly, 1956), p. 377;
    even Joaquín Estrada Monsalve, a rightist Conservative who bitterly opposed
    Gaitán from 1947–1948 when he was minister of education, remembers him
    admiringly: "Gaitán was as pure as a diamond." Interview 22, November 9,
    1979.

13 The charge was reported two years later by *Semana*, October 4, 1947, pp.
    4–5.

14 Rafael Azula Barrera, in *Sábado*, June 19, 1948, p. 1

15 Interview 12 with Rafael Azula Barrera, June 31, 1979.

16 Azula Barrera, *De la revolución al orden nuevo*, pp. 159–61.

17 José Antonio Osorio Lizarazo, *Gaitán: vida, muerte y permanente presencia*, reprint ed. (Bogotá: Carlos Valencia Editores, 1979), p. 48.

18 Hugo Latorre Cabal, *Mi novela: apuntes autobiográficos de Alfonso López* (Bogotá: Ediciones Mito, 1961), pp. 179–80.

19 Germán Arciniegas, *Memorias de un congresista* (Bogotá: Editorial Cromos, 1933[?]), p. 40.

20 Interview 5 with Pío Nono Barbosa Barbosa, Bogotá carpenter and stonemason, follower of Gaitán, April 9, 1979, and subsequent conversations; interview 21 with Luis Eduardo Ricaurte, Gaitán's bodyguard, November 2, 1979, and subsequent conversations.

21 Interview 54 with the Bogotá photographer Daniel Rodríguez Rodríguez, December 6, 1979.

22 For Gaitán's bodyguard, *el coronel* Ricaurte, Gaitán's daily jaunts were a source of agony. He and his friends feared for Gaitán's safety as he ran alone in the foothills of the city. Gaitán would become furious when he found his bodyguards in the park, and in any case, Ricaurte recalls, none of them could keep up with him. Interview with Ricaurte; see also Sharpless, *Gaitán of Colombia*, pp. 117–18.

23 Interview 11 with Rafael Galán Medellín, Gaitanista legislator and mayor of Girardot, 1947–1948, July 26, 1979. Galán remembers with relish one of Gaitán's rare festive moods. While on a visit to Girardot on New Year's Eve, 1948, he outdrank all the Gaitanistas and was on his way to Ibagué, Tolima, on the next day before many could gather their wits to follow him. Gaitán's secretary, José María Córdoba, knew Gaitán's private life best. He remembers him as constantly in control of himself and always ready for the political travails that lay ahead. Interview 8, July 15, 1979.

24 Sharpless, *Gaitán of Colombia*, p. 118.

25 Ibid., p. 117.

26 Peña, *Gaitán íntimo p.* 15.

27 Interview with Ricaurte. *El coronel* admitted to "sneaking" more brandy into Gaitán's drinks, adding that "*el capitán* did not seem to mind, and he always got better" in his oration.

28 For a penetrating analysis of the importance of the harmony between the "average structures" of leaders and followers, see Wilhelm Reich, *The Mass Psychology of Fascism* (New York: Farrar, Straus and Giroux, 1973), p. 35.

29 Gaitán, speech delivered before the May 5, 1946 election, in a collection of his recorded speeches, *Jorge Eliécer Gaitán, tribuno del pueblo* (Medellín: Discos Fuentes, 1973), vol. 1.

30 Arciniegas, *Memorias*, pp. 66–68.

31 Sharpless, *Gaitán of Colombia*, p. 117.

32 This problem has been succinctly summed up by the psychologist José Gutiérrez: "the eloquence of our rhetoreticians is not easily understood by our *pueblo*, a fact that would seem absurd were it not that our *campesino* admires

the orators not because he understands them, but because of the tone of their voice, the fascinating gestures they use"; in *De la pseudo-aristocracia a la autenticidad: psicología social colombiana* (Bogotá: Ediciones Tercer Mundo, 1961), pp. 25–26.

33 Gaitán, speech accepting the position of *jefe único* of the Liberal party, October 24, 1947, in collection of recorded orations, *Jorge Eliécer Gaitán, tribuno del pueblo,* vol. 1.

34 Mauro Torres, *Gaitán: grandeza y limitaciones psicológicas* (Bogotá: Ediciones Tercer Mundo, 1976), pp. 75–76.

35 My ideas on the social meaning of the physical body come from Mary Douglas, *Natural Symbols: Explorations in Cosmology* (New York: Vintage Press, 1973), especially pp. 93–103. A more existentialist perspective is in Ernest Becker, *The Denial of Death* (New York: Free Press, 1973), pp. 25–37, 48–66.

36 Ricaurte recalls that he got to know many of the guards and writers of *El Tiempo,* who would even taunt him by asking when he would organize the next attack on the paper. Interview with Ricaurte.

37 Interview 42 with Gabriel Muñoz Uribe, Gaitanista lawyer and politician, December 1, 1979.

38 Gaitán Papers (GP), Córdoba file, May 1945; Ortiz Márquez, *El hombre,* p. 112.

39 *El Tiempo,* January 28, 1945, p. 1; March 3, 1946, p. 1.

40 Interview with Ricaurte.

41 Peña, *Gaitán íntimo,* p. 38.

42 Ibid., pp. 45–49.

43 Interview 37 with Guillermo Vargas, Gaitanista organizer of the barrio Perseverancia, November 28, 1979.

44 Arturo Abella recalls with horror the issues Guzmán raised in his program and the language he used. For Abella, one of Gaitán's most irresponsible acts was to give the airwaves to a man of so little learning and social sensitivity. Interview 15 with Arturo Abella, August 17–18, 1979. For the Gaitanistas, Guzmán was something of a folk hero.

45 *Batalla,* December 29, 1944, p. 3.

46 Interviews with Diógenes Parra (13), follower of Gaitán, August 13, 1979; Jorge Corredor (6), follower of Gaitán, April 9, 1979; Julio E. Pereira (7), April 9, 1979; with Agustín Utrera (49), Bogotá barber and follower of Gaitán, December 5, 1979; Arturo Céspedes (60), follower of Gaitán, December 13, 1979; Carlos J. Sánchez (66), January 2, 1980.

47 Jorge Villaveces's account of the JEGA is in *Jornada,* May 4, 1948, p. 2.

48 Ibid.

49 Interview with Ricaurte.

50 Villaveces, in *Jornada,* May 4, 1948, p. 2.

51 Interview with Ricaurte.

52 Most of the Gaitanistas interviewed considered themselves to be class A *jegos.* Not coincidentally, they were also the ones most willing to speak to me about their experiences and memories of Gaitán. Interestingly, José María Córdoba, the main organizer of the presidential campaign, while claiming to be a member

of the JEGA also tried to establish his distance from it, for he had not been privy to many of its actions and decisions (interview with Córdoba). Most of the *jegos* agreed that Córdoba had little to do with them.

53 Interview with Córdoba. Córdoba replaced José María Vesga Villamizar in 1944.

54 GP, Córdoba file, June 1945.

55 The movement's financial difficulties were reflected in Gaitán's inability to find a national treasurer. As late as April 27, 1945, he named Bernardo Angel, a Medellín industrialist, to the post. Angel did not accept the post until November and did so only after considerable coaxing. GP, Córdoba file, April–June 1945.

56 José María Córdoba, *Jorge Eliécer Gaitán: tribuno popular de Colombia* (Bogotá: Litografías Cor-Val, 1952), pp. 58–59.

57 GP, Córdoba file, March 22, 1945.

58 The others who often accompanied Restrepo Botero were all well-known middle-class Gaitanistas: Jorge Uribe Márquez, Hernán Isaías Ibarra, David Luna Serrano, and Germán Arango Escobar. GP, Córdoba file, May 1945.

59 GP, Córdoba file, June 1945.

60 Ibid.

61 Ibid.

62 Interview 51 with Valerio Valverde, December 6, 1979.

63 *El Tiempo*, September 24, 1945, p. 4.

64 Córdoba, *Tribuno popular*, p. 60.

65 The first group was composed of little-known Gaitanistas like Julio Macías, Manuel del Vecchio, Alvaro Rey, and Luis Carlos Perilla. The best-known was Milton Puentes, who had written a book on Gaitán in 1939. The second group was composed of Luis E. Restrepo and Rafael Pérez. GP, Córdoba file, September 1945.

66 Ibid.

67 The most complete but also the most exaggerated account of the convention is in *El Siglo*, September 16–26, 1945.

68 *El Siglo*, September 17, 1945, p. 1.

69 *El Tiempo*, September 21, 1945, p. 4.

70 *El Siglo*, September 21, 1945, p. 1.

71 The estimates of the number of participants varies. In Córdoba's own report, 5,000 marchers were involved, (GP, Córdoba file, October 1945). *El Siglo* thought the number was closer to 8,000. It is likely that the Gaitanistas were closer to the mark.

72 Interview with Ricaurte.

73 Interview with Estrada Monsalve. He felt that it was the sort of night on which respectable citizens would not want to go out.

74 Sharpless, *Gaitán of Colombia, p. 113.*

75 *El Siglo's* estimate is 50,000; September 24, 1945, p. 1.

76 Jorge Eliécer Gaitán, "Discurso-Programa," September 23, 1945, in Jorge Villaveces, *Los Mejores discursos de Jorge Eliécer Gaitán* (Bogotá: Editorial Jorvi, 1968), p. 406. Subsequent page citations for this speech are in the text.

77   For an analysis of leadership that stresses the reciprocity between leaders and followers, as I do, see James MacGregor Burns, *Leadership* (New York: Harper and Row, 1978).

78   I say "spontaneous" because I could not find any references to the slogan in the preparations for the convention and because none of the Gaitanistas interviewed, most of whom were middle-level organizers, claimed to know of any directives about it. It is cited with horror by *El Tiempo*, September 24, 1945, p. 15.

79   Ibid.

80   Azula Barrera, *De la revolución al orden nuevo*, p. 161.

81   *La Razón*, September 24, 1945, p. 6.

82   *El Tiempo*, September 24, 1945, p. 4.

83   Ibid.

84   Ibid., September 25, 1945, p. 4.

85   Ibid., September 26, 1945, p. 4.

86   For a sympathetic appreciation of this dimension of politics, often misunderstood not only by individuals like the *convivialistas*, but by academics as well, see Ferdinand Mount, *The Theater of Politics* (London: Wiedenfeld and Nicholson, 1972).

87   Osorio Lizarazo, *Gaitán*, p. 192.

88   *Sábado*, September 22, 1945, p. 1.

89   Gaitán's realization seems to have been similar to that of Nicholas Bonneville at the height of the French Revolution. He used familiar, plebian language in front of the crowd, and began to address the king in public with the familiar *tu*. James H. Billington, *Fire in the Minds of Men: Origins of the Revolutionary Faith* (New York: Basic Books, 1980), p. 35

90   Most of the speeches transcribed in the Villaveces collection, *Mejores discursos*, fall into this category. The most notable examples are "Que entienden por Unión Nacional" (July 21, 1946), pp. 455–60, "El hombre: realidad biológica y social" (n.d.), pp. 465–579, and "La reacción acelera el proceso revolucionario" (n.d.), pp. 483–91.

91   Gaitán, "El país político y el país nacional" (April 20, 1946), in Villaveces, *Mejores discursos*, p. 429.

92   In my interviews with Gaitán's followers the word *monopolios* was used by them much more often than *oligarcas* or *oligarquía*, which appear more often in Gaitán's recorded speeches.

93   Gaitán, "El pueblo es superior a sus dirigentes" (February 22, 1946) in Villaveces, *Mejores discursos*, pp. 408–17.

94   The slogan hardly ever came up in the interviews with Gaitán's followers. Many simply could not remember it, but most just discarded it as demagogic. Pío Nono Barbosa Barbosa, for example, told me, "Oh, Gaitán just said that for political reasons."

95   Gaitán, "Arenga a los venezolanos" (October 18, 1946), in Villaveces, *Mejores discursos*, p. 462.

96   Gaitán, "El hombre: realidad biológica y social," ibid., pp. 470, 465.

97   Ibid., pp. 468–69.

98 Every one of the Gaitanistas interviewed stated that Gaitán was different from all the other politicians because he was of the *pueblo*. They expressed the relationship graphically, saying that Gaitán felt comfortable around poor people, that he did not mind their food, or the way they smelled, or talked.

99 In my interview with him, Arturo Abella objected to Gaitán's claiming to be a restorer, insisting that Gaitán had no right to restore anything.

100 Azula Barrera, *De la revolución al orden nuevo*, p. 61.

101 Abelardo Forero Benavides, "El nueve de abril de 1948," in *El Espectador (Magazin Dominical)*, April 7, 1968, p. 1.

102 Fernández de Soto, *Una revolución en Colombia*, pp. 93, 71.

103 *El Tiempo*, May 6, 1946, p. 4.

Chapter 5

1 Juan Lozano y Lozano, "Gabriel Turbay," in his *Ensayos críticos—Mis contemporáneos*, reprint ed. (Bogotá: Biblioteca Colombiana de Cultura, 1978), p. 530; J. J. García, *Política y amigos* (Bogotá: Ediciones Tercer Mundo, 1975), p. 84.

2 Alejandro Vallejo, *Políticos en la intimidad* (Bogotá: Ediciones Antena, 1936), p. 63.

3 Abelardo Forero Benavides, "Viaje al fondo de la noche: lo que ví en la revolución," in *Sábado*, May 1, 1948, p. 1.

4 Pedronel Giraldo Londoño, *Don Fernando: juicio sobre un hombre y una época* (Medellín: Editorial Granamérica, 1963), p. 220.

5 Ibid., p. 231.

6 *El Siglo*, January 25, 1948, p. 2.

7 Jaime Sanín Echeverri, *Ospina supo esperar* (Bogotá: Editorial Andes, 1978), p. 58; Oliverio Perry, ed., *Quién es quién en Colombia*, 1948 (Bogotá: Editorial Oliverio Perry, 1948), pp. 324–25. On May 1, 1946, just a few days before becoming president, Ospina declared that he "aspired to the honorable title of engineer of the republic" (*El Siglo*, May 1, 1946, p. 1).

8 *El Tiempo*, April 4, 1946, p. 1.

9 Luis David Peña, *Gaitán íntimo* (Bogotá: Editorial Iqueima, 1949), p. 162; Richard E. Sharpless, *Gaitán of Colombia: A Political Biography* (Pittsburgh: University of Pittsburgh Press, 1978), p. 127.

10 *El Tiempo*, April 6, 1946, p. 1.

11 Ibid., April 7, 1946, p. 1.

12 Julio Ortiz Márquez, *El hombre que fue un pueblo* (Bogotá: Carlos Valencia Editores, 1978), p. 117.

13 *El Tiempo*, April 6, 1946, p. 1.

14 Ibid.

15 Ortiz Márquez, *El hombre*, p. 125.

16 Ibid., pp. 124–26.

17 *El Tiempo*, April 6, 1946, p. 1.

18 Ibid., April 9, 1946, p. 1.

19   A different interpretation is possible. López's silence, the nomination of a re-
     spected Conservative with many ties to the Liberals, the Liberal leaders' inter-
     vention in the conversations between Turbay and Gaitán, and their lukewarm
     campaigning for Turbay afterward can all be seen as a complex maneuver on
     the part of the *convivialistas* to defeat both Liberal outsiders. This interpreta-
     tion, widely believed by many of the Gaitanistas interviewed, is, of course,
     highly partisan. Nevertheless, one of them admitted that many of Gaitán's
     followers did not want to see the party defeated and were willing to vote against
     their leader in order to defeat Ospina Pérez. He believes that many did not vote
     for Turbay because López remained silent on the issue and did not lend the
     official candidate his support. Interview 21 with Luis Eduardo Ricaurte,
     November 2, 1979.
20   Gaitán, "Gaitán cancela las conversaciones con Turbay," in Jorge Villaveces,
     ed., *Los mejores discursos de Gaitán* (Bogotá: Editorial Jorvi, 1968), pp. 436,
     432.
21   Ibid., p. 425.
22   *El Tiempo,* April 10, 1946, p. 1.
23   Ibid., April 16, 1946, p. 1.
24   Ibid., April 18, 1946, p. 1.
25   *Diario Popular,* April 11, 1946, p. 1.
26   *El Tiempo,* May 2, 1946, p. 1.
27   Ibid., April 24, 1946, p. 1; April 30, 1946, p. 1.
28   Ibid., April 14, 1946, p. 1.
29   Ibid., May 4, 1946, p. 20.
30   Ibid., May 1, 1946, p. 4.
31   Ibid., May 6, 1946, p. 4.
32   Ortiz Márquez, *El hombre,* p. 131.
33   *El Tiempo,* May 6, 1946, p. 4.
34   Ibid., May 6, 1946, p. 1.
35   Ibid., May 6, 1946, p. 4.
36   Interview 32 with Luis Cano Jacobo, lawyer and Gaitanista politician,
     November 21, 1979; interview 37 with Guillermo Vargas, Gaitanista leader of
     the barrio Perseverancia, November 28, 1979; interview with Ricaurte.
37   José Antonio Osorio Lizarazo, *Gaitán: vida, muerte y permanente presencia,*
     reprint ed. (Bogotá: Carlos Valencia Editores, 1979), pp. 280–82.
38   *El Tiempo,* May 7, 1946, p. 1.
39   Interview 65 with Antonio García, leftist intellectual and economic advisor to
     Gaitán, December 19, 1979; interview 31 with Hernando Restrepo Botero,
     Gaitanista leader and labor organizer, November 19, 1979; interview 12 with
     Rafael Azula Barrera, Conservative historian and secretary to Mariano Ospina
     Pérez, July 31, 1979.
40   Gaitán Papers (GP), Córdoba file, May 1946.
41   *El Tiempo,* May 8, 1946, p. 1.
42   Quoted in Rafael Azula Barrera, *De la revolución al orden nuevo: proceso y
     drama de un pueblo* (Bogotá: Editorial Kelly, 1956), p. 275.
43   *El Tiempo,* May 12, 1946, p. 4.

44 Ibid., May 9, 1946, p. 4.
45 Ibid., May 26, 1946, p. 4.
46 Ibid., April 9, 1946, p. 1; *Semana*, December 13, 1946, p. 4.
47 Sharpless, *Gaitán of Colombia*, p. 144.
48 *Semana*, December 30, 1946, p. 9.
49 Mariano Ospina Pérez, *El gobierno de Unión Nacional*, 5 vols. (Bogotá: Imprenta Nacional, 1950), 1: 134.
50 Azula Barrera, *De la revolución al orden nuevo*, p. 204.
51 Gaitán, "No existe democracia . . . ", in Villaveces, *Mejores discursos*, p. 488.
52 Daniel Pecaut, *Política y sindicalismo en Colombia* (Bogotá: La Carreta, 1973), pp. 212–15.
53 *Semana*, November 18, 1946, p. 5.
54 Ibid., November 25, 1946, p. 5.
55 Proceso Gaitán (PROG), Vol. 19, folios 185–96.
56 Gaitán, "No existe democracia . . . ", in Villaveces, *Mejores discursos*, pp. 452–53; 443–44.
57 Ibid., pp. 442, 444.
58 *Semana*, November 4, 1946, front cover.
59 GP, Córdoba file, April 1946.
60 *Semana*, January 25, 1947, p. 8.
61 Ibid.
62 GP, Cundinamarca file, 1947.
63 The text of the Plataforma del Colón is in Luis Emiro Valencia, ed., *Gaitán: antología de su pensamiento económico y social* (Bogotá: Ediciones Suramérica, 1968), pp. 329–47.
64 Ibid., p. 338.
65 Peña, *Gaitán íntimo*, p. 17.
66 *El Tiempo*, March 23, 1947, p. 1.
67 Azula Barrera, *De la revolución al orden nuevo*, pp. 265, 257.
68 *El Tiempo*, March 18, 1947, p. 4.
69 Paul Oquist, *Violencia, conflicto y política en Colombia* (Bogotá: Instituto de Estudios Colombianos, Biblioteca Banco Popular, 1978), pp. 59, 232–33.
70 The text is in Valencia, *Antología*, pp. 258–328.
71 *Semana*, May 3, 1947, p. 6.
72 Ibid., May 17, 1947, p. 4.
73 Ibid., May 24, 1947, p. 7.
74 Interview 15 with Arturo Abella, Conservative historian and journalist, April 18, 1979.
75 *El Siglo*, September 19, 1947, p. 1; *Semana*, September 20, 1947, p. 5.
76 *El Siglo*, September 20, 1947, p. 1.
77 *El Tiempo*, December 19, 1947, p. 4.
78 *Semana*, January 31, 1948, p. 8.
79 *El Siglo*, January 6, 1948, p. 4.
80 *Semana*, January 31, 1948, p. 7.
81 *Eco Nacional*, January 9, 1948, p. 4.
82 Ibid., January 14, 1948, p. 4.

83 *Semana,* August 16, 1947, p. 6.
84 Ibid., December 13, 1947, p. 9.
85 *El Tiempo,* December 7, 1947, p. 5.
86 Ibid., December 23, 1947, p. 5.
87 *Jornada,* March 4, 1948, p. 1.
88 Alfonso López Michelsen, *Cuestiones colombianas* (México: Impresiones Modernas, 1955), p. 341.
89 *El Liberal,* April 1, 1948, p. 4.
90 *El Siglo,* January 21, 1948, p. 4.
91 Ibid., January 22, 1948, p. 1.
92 Ibid., January 29, 1948, p. 4.
93 Ibid., March 16, 1948, p. 4.
94 Interview 22 with Joaquín Estrada Monsalve, Conservative minister of education at the time the programs were reorganized, November 9, 1979. The program schedules of La Voz de Colombia and, after May 5, 1946, of Radio Nacional, were published daily in *El Siglo.*
95 *Jornada,* February 19, 1948, p. 4.
96 *El Tiempo,* December 24, 1947, p. 4.
97 Azula Barrera, *De la revolución al orden nuevo,* p. 336.
98 *Semana,* January 31, 1948, p. 5.
99 Ibid., November 22, 1947, p. 8.
100 *Eco Nacional,* January 30, 1948, p. 4.
101 *Semana,* Februray 28, 1948, p. 6.
102 Mario Fernández de Soto, *Una revolución en Colombia—Jorge Eliécer Gaitán y Mariano Ospina Pérez: un libro sobre Iberoamérica* (Madrid: Ediciones Cultura Hispánica, 1951), p. 68.
103 Osorio Lizarazo, *Gaitán,* p. 268.
104 José María Córdoba, *Jorge Eliécer Gaitán: tribuno popular de Colombia* (Bogotá: Litografías Cor-Val, 1952), pp. 121–22.
105 For a discussion of the role of silence in demonstrations, see George Mosse, *The Nationalization of the Masses: Political Symbolism and Mass Movements in Germany from the Napoleonic Wars through the Third Reich* (New York: New American Library, 1975), pp. 167–76.
106 Peña, *Gaitán íntimo,* pp. 18–19.
107 Ibid.
108 Jorge Eliécer Gaitán, "La oración de la paz," in Villaveces, *Mejores discursos,* p. 506.
109 Gaitán's speech and the spectacle on this occasion are remembered more than any other, not only by Gaitán's most intimate followers, but by regular Liberals and Conservatives as well. A conversation about Gaitán with almost anybody who lived through those years turns invariably to the Manifestación del Silencio. For Gaitán's followers it was a moment of singular pride. For those who opposed him, Gaitán's control of the crowd was an awesome demonstration of his power. Many who believe that Gaitán's assassination was ordered by leading Liberals and Conservatives remain convinced that the *convivialistas* reached their fateful decision because of the demonstration.

110 *El Siglo,* February 7, 1948, p. 4.
111 *Semana,* February 24, 1948, p. 7.
112 *Jornada,* March 5, 1948, p. 4; *Semana,* March 6, 1948, p. 5.
113 *Semana,* February 28, 1948, pp. 8–9.
114 *El Tiempo,* March 17, 1948, p. 1.
115 *Semana,* March 13, 1948, p. 5.
116 *Jornada,* March 18, 1948, p. 4.
117 *El Tiempo,* March 18, 1948, p. 1.
118 *Semana,* February 28, 1948, p. 9.
119 *El Tiempo,* March 19, 1948, p. 4.
120 *Jornada,* March 19, 1948, p. 1.
121 *El Tiempo,* March 20, 1948, p. 4.
122 *Semana,* March 6, 1948, pp. 5–8.
123 Azula Barrera, *De la revolución al orden nuevo,* p. 305.
124 *Semana,* March 27, 1948, p. 4.
125 Ibid.
126 *El Tiempo,* April 2, 1948, p. 7; *Semana,* December 6, 1947, p. 18, and March 6, 1948, p. 13.
127 *El Siglo,* November 16, 1947, p. 4.

Chapter 6

1 Rafael Azula Barrera, *De la revolución al orden nuevo: proceso y drama de un pueblo* (Bogotá: Editorial Kelly, 1956), p. 274.
2 Three weeks after the provincial daily published its statement, Gaitán defied the death threat and traveled to Montería. *Jornada,* January 14, 1948, p. 4.
3 Proceso Gaitán (PROG), vol. 21B, folio 450 (testimony of José María Córdoba).
4 *Jornada,* February 6, 1948, p. 4, and February 14, 1948, p. 9.
5 PROG, vol. 8B, ff. 109–20 (testimony of Virgilio Barco).
6 PROG, vol. 5, ff. 45–46 (testimony of Judge Pedro P. Pérez Sotomayor).
7 Interview 21 with Luis Eduardo Ricaurte, November 2, 1979; interview 37 with Guillermo Vargas, November 28, 1979.
8 Interview with Ricaurte.
9 In reconstructing the events of April 9, 1948, in Bogotá, I have used the sources left by those closest to the scene of the events. Wherever possible, I allow the actors to speak for themselves. At various points in the narrative, I extend the physical limits and the cultural context in which the participants themselves have placed their actions in order to draw conclusions, not about their recollections, but about the patterns that underlay their behavior. I thus seek to uncover the "deeper," more socially and historically conditioned meaning of their actions.

I have taken greater liberties in describing the changing moods and motivations of the crowds. This was inevitable, because the crowd members remain largely anonymous. At times I use the recollections of individuals who claim to have been part of them. At other times I use the interpretations of those who witnessed the actions.

Additional testimony from elite participants, leftists, and Gaitanistas can be found in Arturo Alape, *El Bogotazo: memorias del olvido* (Bogotá: Fundación Universidad Central, 1983). The author uses many of the same sources employed here and some forty interviews, including one with Fidel Castro. Alape has strung these testimonies together, presenting extracts from the written and oral material he uses. There is unfortunately no analysis of the events. Neither Alape nor I were able to get the testimony of looters and others in the crowds that spearheaded the destruction of the city.

10 Jorge Eliécer Gaitán, "Defensa del Teniente Cortés" (April 8–9, 1948), in Jorge Villaveces, ed., *Los mejores discursos de Gaitán* (Bogotá: Editorial Jorvi, 1968), pp. 535–44.

11 Interview 8 with José María Córdoba, July 15, 1979.

12 Jorge Padilla, "Historia de un disparo," *El Espectador (Magazin Dominical)*, April 7, 1968, p. 2.

13 According to *Semana*, February 28, 1948, p. 9, Mendoza Neira was given the task of stalking Gaitán in an effort to smooth over the differences and keep open the lines of communication between the *caudillo* and the Liberal leaders. *Semana* thought this no easy task, given Gaitán's difficult personality. He was neither "accessible nor governable" and surrounded himself with hostile defenses.

The relationship between Gaitán and Mendoza Neira had never been easy. Gaitán had left his mother's wake to go to Congress to defend Mendoza Neira from Carlos Lleras Restrepo's verbal onslaught when Mendoza Neira was comptroller general in 1937. See Gaitán, "En defensa de Plinio Mendoza Neira," (March 24, 1937), in Villaveces, *Mejores discursos*, pp. 216–36. In the early 1940s, however, the two men were hardly on speaking terms, and older Gaitanistas never felt that Mendoza Neira was part of the movement. Interview 42 with Gabriel Muñoz Uribe, December 1, 1979.

14 Richard E. Sharpless, *Gaitán of Colombia: A Political Biography* (Pittsburgh: University of Pittsburgh Press, 1978), p. 173.

15 PROG, vol. 24A, f. 91 (testimony of Plinio Mendoza Neira).

16 PROG, vol. 1B, f. 85 (testimony of Alejandro Vallejo).

17 PROG, vol. 1B, f. 143 (testimony of Pedro Eliseo Cruz).

18 PROG, vol. 1A, f. 5 (testimony of Carlos Alberto Jiménez Díaz).

19 PROG, vol. 5, f. 1 (testimony of Ciro Efraín Silva González).

20 PROG, vol. 1A, ff. 9–10.

21 PROG, vol. 5, f. 1 (testimony of Ciro Efraín Silva González).

22 PROG, vol. 1B, f. 36 (testimony of Elías Quesada Anchique, an employee of the drugstore).

23 Felipe González Toledo, "El nueve de abril de 1948 a nivel del pavimento," *El Tiempo*, April 9, 1968, p. 20.

24 Luis A. Bermúdez V., *Gaitán y el crimen que costó 300 mil muertos* (Caracas: Editorial Latina, 1967), p. 143.

25 PROG, vol. 25, ff. 39–43 (testimony of José Jaramillo Gaviria).

26 PROG, vol. 1B, f. 46 (testimony of eyewitness Hernando Oviedo Albarracín).
27 PROG, vol. 2, f. 128 (testimony of eyewitness Luis Eduardo Peñafor); vol. 4, f. 1 (testimony of former police officer Alfonso Castro González).
28 PROG, vol. 1B, f. 52 (testimony of Josué Gómez Eslava).
29 PROG, vol. 19, f. 60 (testimony of Marino López Lúcas); Francisco Fandiño Silva, *La penetración soviética en América Latina y el nueve de abril* (Bogotá: Editorial ABC, 1949).
30 *La Razón*, April 14, 1948, p. 1.
31 Natalie Bergson Carp, "Window Seat on a Revolution," reprinted as evidence in PROG, vol. 21, ff. 49–59. The author was an American citizen living in Bogotá.
32 The behavior of those who surrounded the body during the rest of the afternoon —doctors, politicians, Gaitanistas, nurses, and publicity-seekers—bordered on the macabre. Endless pictures of the cadaver were taken, and everybody wanted to be immortalized in them. In one picture a doctor holds up Gaitán's head so that it will be clearly visible. A man in black reaches out to touch Gaitán's face. Nurses, barely visible in the background, strain to be included. Other pictures show Gaitán's heavily bandaged head and his bullet-punctured back. An artist rapidly made a death mask from the impression of Gaitán's face. The artist apparently forgot to replace Gaitán's upper bridge, so that the death mask makes Gaitán look more like a docile *civilista* than an agressive *caudillo*. See Gonzalo Orrego Duque, *Nueve de abril fuera de Palacio* (Bogotá: Editorial Patria, 1949), p. 50. This book offers the reader a gland by gland account of the autopsy.

The autopsy created unusual interest, for everybody wanted to be part of it and to be responsible for having determined the cause of Gaitán's death. Two Conservative doctors, Juan Uribe Cualla and Juan Llinás, both of the Department of Legal Medicine, were called on to perform it, but neither could be found. According to one commentator, Uribe Cualla was at the Jockey Club when Gaitán was shot and was so afraid of being recognized on the streets that he had himself transported home in a coffin. See Sebastian Cifuentes, "Lo que se ignora del nueve de abril," in *Sábado*, January 22, 1949, p. 1.

There was so much publicity-seeking that two autopsies were produced. The first one was short, uninformative, and not very technical. It was written by Dr. Yezid Trebert Orozco, with the assistance of the Gaitanista activist Julio Ortiz Márquez, and signed by all the doctors present except Luis Guillermo Forero Nougués. It was witnessed by Judge Pedro P. Pérez Sotomayor, and three little-known politicians, Julio Enrique Santos Forero, Eudoro González de la Torre, and Luis Eduardo del Castillo. This "autopsy" was rushed to the press. A copy of this document is in PROG, vol. 1A, ff. 9–13. It also figures prominently in Julio Ortiz Márquez's memoirs, *El hombre que fue un pueblo* (Bogotá: Carlos Valencia Editores, 1978), pp. 175–77.

The real autopsy was performed some hours later by Drs. Forero Nougués and Angel Alberto Romero Torres. Forero Nougués remembered that others were carefully listening to his conversation with Romero Torres and presumed that the first autopsy report was taken by others from that informal talk. See Forero

Nougués's testimony in PROG, vol. 19, ff. 19–49. Dr. Trebert Orozco, who had written the first report, later admitted that there might have been more than one document, "because everybody there wanted to dictate one." See his testimony in PROG, vol. 19, ff. 82–87.

33 Two of the more complete accounts of the *bogotazo* are based almost entirely on the authors' recollections of the radio broadcasts. See Roberto Restrepo, *Nueve de abril: quiebra cultural y política* (Bogotá: Tipografía Bremen, 1948), and Gonzalo Canal Ramírez, *Nueve de abril 1948* (Bogotá: Litografía y Editorial "Cahur," 1948).

34 It is widely believed to this day that the radio broadcasters played a key role in instigating the riot. Liberal and Conservative commentators agree on this, though the latter have emphasized it more. The belief is that the announcers acted irresponsibly, inciting the crowds to loot and destroy. Even Gaitanistas and members of the crowd, although more skeptical of the role played by the radio in their actions, believe that it may have had an impact on those who looted and destroyed later. This idea has been repeated by the Conservative journalist and historian Arturo Abella in his popular pictorial account, *Así fue el nueve de abril* (Bogotá: Ediciones Internacional de Publicaciones, 1973), pp. 33–36.

Little has been written about the slogans and the orders issued by Liberals and leftists. There are two accounts. The first is in Canal Ramírez, *Nueve de abril,* pp. 9–22, published in 1948. The other was provided eight years later by Azula Barrera in his *De la revolución al orden nuevo,* pp. 359–65. Canal claims to have heard the announcers himself, and Azula Barrera asserts that he received transcriptions of the tapes from the minister of communications, José Vicente Dávila Tello. In addition, a small fragment of a speech by Gerardo Molina is on a recording of events that took place before, during, and after the riot, *El crimen de abril.* Neither Azula (interview 12, July 31, 1979) nor Dávila Tello (interview 30, November 19, 1979) remembers what happened to the tapes and the transcriptions. Abella (interview 15, August 18, 1979) remembers taking from already published sources the quotations that appear in his book.

There is little reason to doubt that Canal Ramírez's and Azula Barrera's versions are generally accurate, albeit shortened and synthetic, versions of what was actually said over the radio. Azula Barrera's version of Molina's speech roughly coincides with the taped fragment, and Molina acknowledges that he may have said what has been attributed to him (interview 19, September 25, 1979).

35 Alfonso López Michelsen, *Cuestiones colombianas* (México: Impresiones Modernas, 1955), p. 350. The author claims that those radio stations that called for order represented large corporate interests, but he does not name those interests.

36 Interview with Molina.

37 One such person was Ana María E. vda. de Cagua, a young woman who, as soon as she heard the news about Gaitán, began to worry about her husband, Jorge, a Gaitanista who worked for the railroads. He did not come home that night, and the next day she discovered that he had been killed, apparently by a stray bullet. Interview 29, November 18, 1979.

38 See the testimony in PROG vol. 1A, f. 64, by Encarnación Sierra de Roa, mother of Juan Roa Sierra, who is believed to be Gaitán's assassin. "All the people started to dress in mourning because of the death of Gaitán, and I also was going to do that." Her testimony may have been an attempt to save herself from reprisals by Liberals and Gaitanistas. Nonetheless, it seems likely that many did change their clothing. After order was reestablished, those who wore black on the streets of the city were beaten up by soldiers.

39 Isaac Gutiérrez Navarro, *La luz de una vida* (Bogotá: Editorial ABC, 1949), p. 576.

40 Interview with Córdoba.

41 Interview with Muñoz Uribe.

42 PROG, vol. 33, ff. 25, 32–33 (testimony of Lázaro Amaya).

43 Interview with Ricaurte.

44 PROG, vol. 28, f. 262 (testimony of Julio César Turbay Ayala).

45 PROG, vol. 19, f. 14 (testimony of Julio Enrique Santos Forero).

46 In his testimony in PROG, Lázaro Amaya claims that he and Eduardo Lozano went as far as the Plaza de Bolívar, but then went into a nearby café for a few drinks when the crowds became too much for them. The testimony may well have been self-serving, designed to head off possible prosecution for having participated in the riot. PROG, vol. 33, f. 32.

47 Interview with Ricaurte.

48 Jesús Delgadillo Morales testified that he started dragging the body after the procession had reached the Plaza de Bolívar. PROG, vol. 33, f. 25.

49 Jaime Quijano Caballero, in *El Tiempo,* April 16, 1948, p. 16.

50 PROG, vol. 1B, f. 64 (testimony of Gabriel Restrepo Botero, a Gaitanista who joined the march).

51 Quijano Caballero, *El Tiempo,* April 16, 1948, p. 11.

52 Ibid.

53 Interview 31 with Hernando Restrepo Botero, November 19, 1979. Restrepo Botero, a leading Gaitanista labor leader who attempted to organize the Gaitanistas throughout the afternoon, claims that cutting the telephone wires would have been easy, as would entering the Palace through the manholes. (In fact, the latter would certainly have been more difficult.) According to Restrepo Botero, the idea never came up in the many conversations he held with Gaitanistas throughout the afternoon, nor did he think of these options himself.

54 Mariano Ospina Pérez, "Las horas dramáticas en el Palacio Presidencial," in *El Tiempo (Lecturas Dominicales),* April 8, 1973, p. 1. The account was continued in *El Tiempo* on the following day, April 9, 1973, p. 1-B.

55 Ibid.

56 Ibid.

57 Untitled, MS account by Bertha Hernández de Ospina Pérez, in the files of the author, p. 1; interview 33 with Bertha Hernández de Ospina Pérez, November 22, 1979.

58 Hernández de Ospina Pérez, MS, p. 4.

59 Azula Barrera, *De la revolución al orden nuevo,* pp. 347–52.

60 Interview with Dávila Tello.

61 Joaquín Estrada Monsalve, *El nueve de abril en Palacio: horario de un golpe de estado* (Bogotá: Editorial "Cahur," 1948), pp. 8–12; interview 22 with Joaquín Estrada Monsalve, November 9, 1979.

62 Interview 25 with Msgr. Arturo Franco Arango, November 11, 1979; *El Siglo,* April 9, 1973, p. 1.

63 Estrada Monsalve, *Nueve de abril,* p. 22; Hernando Jaramillo Ocampo, *1946-1950: De la unidad nacional a la hegemonía conservadora* (Bogotá: Editorial Pluma, 1980), p. 98.

64 Estrada Monsalve, *Nueve de abril,* p. 22; Quijano Caballero in *El Tiempo,* April 16, 1948, p. 11.

65 Abelardo Forero Benavides, "Viaje al fondo de la noche: lo que ví en la revolución," in *Sábado,* May 1, 1948, p. 1.

66 Darío Echandía, "La historia también es con los muertos," interview with Gabriel Gutiérrez, *El Tiempo (Lecturas Dominicales),* April 8, 1973, p. 1.

67 PROG, vol. 28, ff. 138–41 (testimony of Carlos Lleras Restrepo).

68 PROG, vol. 1B, f. 111 (testimony of Dr. Alfonso Bonilla Mar).

69 Gonzalo Orrego Duque, *Nueve de abril fuera de Palacio,* p. 61.

70 González Toledo, "Nueve de abril de 1948," p. 20.

71 Darío Samper, "La trágica proyección del nueve de abril," in *El Tiempo,* April 9, 1968, p. 5.

72 Echandía, "La historia," p. 1.

73 Forero Benavides, "Viaje," p. 1.

74 Carlos Lleras Restrepo, interviewed by Antonio Montaña, in *El Tiempo,* April 8, 1973, p. 1.

75 Forero Benavides, "Viaje," p. 1.

76 Ibid.; Echandía, "La historia," p. 1; Lleras Restrepo interview in *El Tiempo,* April 8, 1973, p. 1.

77 Ortiz Márquez, *El hombre,* p. 180.

78 Forero Benavides, "Viaje," p. 1.

79 Samper, "Trágica proyección," p. 1.

80 PROG, vol. 28, f. 141 (testimony of Carlos Lleras Restrepo).

81 Interview with Molina, and interview 65 with Antonio García, December 19, 1979.

82 Forero Benavides, "Viaje," p. 1.

83 Interview with Molina.

84 Interview with Muñoz Uribe.

85 Interview 49 with Agustín Utrera, December 5, 1979.

86 One of the best-stocked hardware stores in the city, the Ferretería Vergara, was located close to that corner, just west of the Carrera 9 on the Calle 14. Its manager was Herbert Braun, the author's father. As soon as Braun realized what was going on in the street outside his store, he ordered the employees to return to their homes, closed the gates, and walked home. The thought that the store might be looted never seriously crossed his mind, but he knew that the crowds would be active throughout the afternoon and that he would be doing very little business. The store was looted, but the losses were not appreciable. Interview 1 with Herbert Braun, October 8, 1978. The subject of the *bogotazo,* of course,

crept into many conversations in the author's home over the years. H. W. Meyer, a friend of the family, owned his own hardware store and defended it from looters by locking himself inside for the entire night. Interview 4 with H. W. Meyer, March 14, 1979.

87 Abella, *Así fue*, pp. 24–30.

88 PROG, vol. 25, ff. 39–43 (testimony of José Jaramillo Gaviria).

89 Abella, *Así fue*, p. 29.

90 Abella, for example, remains convinced that the rains helped to save the city. Interview with Abella.

91 Interview with Muñoz Uribe.

92 PROG, vol. 25, ff. 39–43 (testimony of José Jaramillo Gaviria); vol. 5, f. 76 (testimony of Agustín Linares Flórez). Linares Flórez was the commander of the second police station mentioned here. He lost control over the policemen in his precinct, and most left after the attack on the station; vol. 25, f. 42 (testimony of José Jaramillo Gaviria).

93 Ospina Pérez, "Horas dramáticas," p. 1.

94 Azula Barrera, *De la revolución al orden nuevo*, pp. 352–57.

95 U.S. Department of State (USDS), Decimal File 821.00/5-1147. Incoming telegram no. 320, April 9, 1948.

96 Ospina Pérez, "Horas dramáticas," p. 1.

97 Interview with Bertha Hernández de Ospina Pérez.

98 Interview with Estrada Monsalve; Estrada Monsalve, *Nueve de abril en Palacio*, p. 13.

99 Azula Barrera, *De la revolución al orden nuevo*, pp. 354, 364, and 380.

100 Ospina Pérez, "Horas dramáticas," p. 1; Azula Barrera, *De la revolución al orden nuevo*, pp. 353–54.

101 Interviews with Bertha Hernández de Ospina Pérez, Estrada Monsalve, Azula Barrera, and Abella.

102 Interview 58 with Benito Rojas, December 8, 1979.

103 USDS, Decimal File 821.00/4-948. Incoming telegram no. 196. In the telegram, which was received at 8:49 in Washington, Beaulac claimed that Radio Nacional was on the air again after four hours of silence.

104 Canal Ramírez, *Nueve de abril*, p. 57.

105 Joaquín Estrada Monsalve, *Nueve de abril en Palacio*, p. 37.

106 Ibid., p. 24.

107 Ibid., p. 12.

108 USDS, Decimal File 821.00/4-948. Incoming telegram no. 197, April 10, 1948, 8:31 a.m.

109 PROG, vol. 8B, ff. 107–13 (testimony of Virgilio Barco).

110 Interview 62 with Daniel Ramos Ramos, December 13, 1979.

111 USDS, Decimal File 821.00/4-948. Incoming telegrams no. 192, 4 p.m., and no. 195, 8:11 p.m., both April 9, 1948; no. 197, 8:31 a.m., April 10, 1948.

112 Interview with Bertha Hernández de Ospina Pérez.

113 Interview with General Rafael Sánchez Amaya by Abelardo Forero Benavides, *Sábado*, June 12, 1948, p. 1; *Semana*, April 24, 1948, p. 16; *El Tiempo*, April 15, 1948, p. 2.

Chapter 7

1 Interview 44 with Sergio Céspedes, injured Gaitanista sympathizer and eyewitness, December 2, 1979.
2 Interview 45 with Euclides Londoño, casual eyewitness, December 3, 1979.
3 Interview 38 with Heliodoro Africano, November 28, 1979.
4 Roberto García Peña, "Memorias aproximadas del nueve de abril," in *El Tiempo (Lecturas Dominicales),* April 8, 1973, p. 5.
5 *El Espectador,* April 16, 1948, p. 2.
6 Interview 5 with Pío Nono Barbosa Barbosa, April 9, 1979.
7 Interview 21 with Luis Eduardo Ricaurte, November 2, 1979. Ricaurte asserts that he could not recognize anybody, and that he even went up to people he thought he knew only to realize that he was talking to strangers.
8 The notion of reversal crowds comes from Elias Canetti, *Crowds and Power* (New York: Seabury Press, 1978), pp. 58–62 and 303–33.
9 Interview 61 with José Vicente García, December 13, 1979.
10 Interview 31 with Hernando Restrepo Botero, November 19, 1979.
11 Interview 32 with Luis Cano Jacobo, November 21, 1979.
12 Many of the Gaitanistas interviewed identified the same Gaitanista leader when they made this charge. Gilberto Vieira, secretary general of the Communist party, also identified him (interview 28, November 17, 1979). I do not believe that any useful historical purpose would be served by giving his name here.
13 Natalie Bergson Carp, "Window Seat on a Revolution," printed as evidence in the Proceso Gaitán (PROG), volume 21, folios 49–59.
14 Most of the reasons the crowd drank during the *bogotazo* became clear as I began to understand the character of the uprising. This motive, however, did not occur to me but was suggested by Luis Eduardo Ricaurte and Pío Nono Barbosa Barbosa during interviews and in the various conversations I held with them. Both claimed to have taken only an occasional swig.
15 Interview with Ricaurte. Ricaurte claims that members of the crowd virtually forced everybody in sight to drink, shouting epithets at those who refused.
16 Felipe González Toledo, "El nueve de abril de 1948 a nivel del pavimento," *El Tiempo,* April 9, 1968, p. 20.
17 Interview 43 with Ezequiel Benavides (pseudonym), injured Gaitanista sympathizer, December 2, 1979.
18 Interview 57 with José Vicente Espinosa, December 8, 1979.
19 González Toledo, "Nueve de abril de 1948," p. 20.
20 *El Tiempo,* April 16, 1948.
21 Interview 26 with Msgr. Antonio Afanador Salgar, then the parish priest of Egipto, whose life was saved, November 14, 1979.
22 There is no evidence that the priests were in fact the ones who shot into the crowds from the church steeples. This remains one of the biggest controversies surrounding the *bogotazo* and is still the subject of heated discussions. The fact that the rumor continues to be fervently believed by many is an indication of the suspicion in which the priests in Bogotá were held. Put another way, many in Bogotá at the time would not have been greatly surprised had this in fact been the case.

23 For a view of the differences between Catholicism and crowds, see Canetti, *Crowds and Power*, pp. 154–58.

24 Interview 25 with Msgr. Arturo Franco Arango, November 11, 1979.

25 Arturo Franco Arango," "La destrucción del Palacio de los Arzobispos el día nueve de abril; actuación del Ilustre Arzobispo en tal emergencia," unpublished ms in the possession of Msgr. Franco Arango.

26 Arquidiócesis de Bogotá, Gobierno Eclesiástico, Tesorería, *Relación de las pérdidas sufridas en el saqueo e incendio del Palacio Arzobispal en el día nueve de abril de 1948*, unpublished report. The report is in the files of the Junta de Daños y Perjuicios, the official body set up by the government to investigate losses in property, commerce, and industry and repay the owners. The files are in the possession of Francisco Sáenz Arbeláez, the lawyer who headed the Junta with meticulous care and dedication.

27 *Datos históricos de la Comunidad de las Monjas Concepcionistas Franciscanas de Bogotá* (Bogotá: n.p., 1948), pp. 5–22. The report was written by one of the sisters of the order and approved by the abbess, Sor María Magdalena de San José. The document was found in the files of the Junta de Daños y Perjuicios; see also *El Catolicismo*, April 23, 1948, p. 2.

28 Mariano Ospina Pérez, "Las horas dramáticas en el Palacio Presidencial," in *El Tiempo (Lecturas Dominicales)*, April 8, 1973, p. 1; this account of the events was continued in the newspaper on the following day. See also Rafael Azula Barrera, *De la revolución al orden nuevo: proceso y drama de un pueblo* (Bogotá: Editorial Kelly, 1956), pp. 357–58.

29 Arturo Abella, *Así fue el nueve de abril* (Bogotá: Ediciones Internacional de Publicaciones, 1973), p. 32.

30 Interview with Barbosa Barbosa.

31 None of the Gaitanistas I interviewed admitted to having had a lot to drink. Although many could well understand why so many did, they all claimed that it was an outbreak of the *pueblo*, of primary instincts that were unleashed by Gaitán's death and the lack of law enforcement. For most of them, the intoxication of the crowd was the end of the political revolt, and many of them did what they could to stop the rioters from drinking. They must have been treated rather badly for their efforts.

32 Jacques Aprile Gniset estimates that fifty-two blocks were affected, with thirty suffering serious damage. He uses aerial maps and the lists of damaged buildings that appeared in the press after the riot rather than the archive of the Junta de Daños y Perjuicios. See his *El impacto del nueve de abril sobre el centro de Bogotá* (Bogotá: Centro Cultural Jorge Eliécer Gaitán, 1983), pp. 35–37, 55–170. He also presents an interesting account of the effect of the riot on real estate values and city planning (pp. 55–120).

33 Interview with Ricaurte. Ricaurte recalls that some of the bravest and most vocal members of the crowd were the women of the markets.

34 Interview 36 with Octavio López, November 28, 1979.

35 The information on losses in property, commerce, and industry comes from the final reports of the Junta de Daños y Perjuicios, *Registro definitivo de los certificados expedidos sobre pérdidas en propiedad raíz* and the *Registro definitivo de los certificados expedidos sobre pérdidas en comercio, industrias,*

etc. While most of the claims made to the government were inflated, the figures I have given are those finally agreed to by the Junta, which was extremely careful to be as impartial as possible. For example, one owner of a shoe store claimed an amount that Sáenz Arbeláez felt was out of proportion. He went to the store himself, took a look at its dimensions, measured a shoe box, asked what the average price of a pair of shoes was, and told the owner that the value of his stolen stock was less than the sum he had claimed. The owner did not protest. Interview 9 with Francisco Sáenz Arbeláez, July 17, 1979. According to Aprile Gniset, *El impacto*, p. 36, 136 buildings were affected.

36 *El Liberal*, April 12, 1948, p. 2; *Semana*, April 24, 1948, p. 22.

37 Bergson Carp, in PROG, vol. 21, ff. 49–59.

38 Photographs of the crowds in the *bogotazo* show many people in suits and hats throwing rocks, carrying machetes, and walking away with the loot.

39 This is the kind of behavior that most upper- and middle-class commentators at the time expected from crowds and the kind that would confirm their view of the *pueblo* and of collective behavior within an urban setting. Many Gaitanistas would not disagree with this view.

40 Abelardo Forero Benavides, "Viaje al fondo de la noche: lo que ví en la revolución," *Sábado*, May 1, 1948, p. 1.

41 Interview with Céspedes.

42 Interview with Benavides (pseudonym).

43 Interview 14 with Adelmo Toro, August 16, 1979.

44 Interview 54 with Daniel Rodríguez Rodríguez, December 6, 1979.

45 Interview 53 with Leo Matíz, December 6, 1979.

46 Interview 46 with Aníbal Turbay Ayala, notary public in Bogotá, December 3, 1979.

47 Interview with Ricaurte. In its first edition on April 12, *El Espectador* stated that Felipe Lleras Camargo had been slightly injured in the leg and was convalescing in the home of a friend.

48 U.S. Department of State (USDS), Decimal File 821.00/4-948. The telegram was unnumbered. This is not to say that the Americans were not nervous. At three o'clock the embassy sent a telegram (no. 190) stating that a bomb had exploded on the ground floor of the building that housed the offices of the American delegation. The ambassador was caught in the streets and had quite a scare before he made it back to the embassy. In his memoirs he recalled that the second floor of the building was sacked but that they had little difficulty keeping the looters from coming up to the third floor. Willard L. Beaulac, *Career Ambassador* (New York: Macmillan, 1951), p. 247. Nevertheless, they had much to reassure them at the same time. Beaulac informed Washington that a Senator Galves (probably Joaquín Tiberio Galvis) of the "Revolutionary Junta of Liberals" had called the embassy to offer the new revolutionary government's assurances that neither the American nor other foreign delegations would be molested. (Decimal File 821.00/4-948, incoming telegram no. 196, April 9, 1948). See also the memoirs of then aide and interpreter to Marshall, Vernon A. Walters, *Silent Missions* (New York: Doubleday, 1978), pp. 150–69.

49 *New York Times*, April 11, section 4, p. 10.

50 Interview 3 with Fernando Tamayo, December 22, 1978. See also a brief men-

tion of his exploits in *El Liberal,* April 13, 1948, p. 6.

51   Interview 16 with Dr. Alberto Vejarano Laverde, September 21, 1979.

52   There are many pictures of bodies lying in a row in the Cemeterio Central as others look down at them. See also *El Liberal,* April 15, 1948, p. 8, for a story.

53   American Red Cross, Bogotá Disaster Files, Historical Division, American Red Cross National Headquarters, Washington, D.C. Memo from James T. Nicholson, executive vice president, American Red Cross, to Basil O'Connor, April 15, 1948; memo from Melvin A. Glasser, assistant director, International Activities, Foreign Operations, to Phillip E. Ryan, April 14, 1948; incoming cablegram from Ambassador Beaulac to Secretary of State, DELBOG 84, April 16.

54   American Red Cross, Bogotá Disaster Files, Maurice R. Reddy to Melvin A. Glasser, April 17, 1948.

55   American Red Cross, Bogotá Disaster Files, *Report of the American Red Cross Assistance to the Colombian Red Cross Following the Revolution of April 9, 1948.* The report was written by Reddy, and directed to Glasser. It has no date, but was written after April 27. Reddy concluded his report by stating that he "left Bogotá on the morning of April 27 with a feeling that the American Red Cross had left an imprint of good will that will never be forgotten by Colombian people of all classes." This prophecy has been borne out. Many Bogotanos with whom I spoke remember the work of the American and Colombian Red Cross with awe, especially because they knew that they could seek help at the Red Cross without fear of political persecution. According to Guillermo Montaña Cuéllar, president of the Red Cross in 1978, that organization got off the ground because of the work it was forced into on April 9 and subsequent days and months. Interview 2 with Guillermo Montaña Cuéllar, December 17, 1978.
    Reddy's statement about the excellent care that the injured were receiving in the hospitals and clinics cannot be overemphasized. Colombian doctors worked long hours and gave selflessly of their time and knowledge to save many hundreds who had been injured. During my research in Bogotá I did not hear a single criticism of any doctor's performance.

56   American Red Cross, Bogotá Disaster Files, memo from Mary Lightle, administrative assistant, International Activities, to Melvin A. Glasser, April 16, 1948. Lightle interviewed Soper in his office after he was evacuated from Bogotá.

57   Paul Oquist, *Violencia, conflicto y política en Colombia* (Bogotá: Instituto de Estudios Colombianos, Biblioteca Banco Popular, 1978), p. 235.

58   *El Espectador,* May 10, 1948, p. 1; *El Tiempo,* May 11, 1948, p. 1.

59   Bogotá (Colombia), Departamento de Estadísticas e Investigación Social, *Anuario municipal de estadística de Bogotá, 1948* (Bogotá: Imprenta Nacional, 1949). See "Servicio de Cementerios, Inhumación Año 1948," p. 91. These figures include burials in the three largest public cemeteries in the city, the Cemeterio Central, the Cementerio de Chapinero, and the Cementerio del Sur, plus another category that includes the British, German, Hebrew, and Christian Brothers cemeteries. None of the last-named cemeteries, as we might expect, show an increase in burials during the month of April. According to *Anuario,* the average number of burials in the eleven months of 1948 excluding April was 712.6. The number of registered burials for April was 1,043, or 330.4 over the average.

60 Other lists of the dead and injured can be found in *El Liberal*, April 12, 1948, p. 7; April 13, 1948, p. 6; April 13, 1948, p. 4; April 15, 1948, p. 3; *El Tiempo*, April 15, 1948, p. 3; and *El Espectador*, April 12, 1948, p. 1.

61 On April 9, 1978, I spoke to an elderly man who has been working at the Cementerio Central in many different capacities since before April 9, 1948. He asked not to be identified. He showed me the place on the western fringes where the common pit was dug and where the dead of the *bogotazo* were buried. The bodies have since been disinterred. He remembers that there was no central authority at the cemetery and that "cadavers came and went." This has been confirmed by Dr. Alberto Vejarano Laverde, interview 16.

62 Interview with Msgr. Antonio Afanador Salgar. Afanador Salgar, the parish priest of Egipto at the time of the riot, told me that he did not know whether many bodies were buried in his barrio after the riot, but that he was certain that in others many were buried without the knowledge of state or church. This was confirmed by many Gaitanistas, and especially by Pío Nono Barbosa Barbosa, interview 5, and by Guillermo Vargas, interview 37, November 28, 1979.

63 See Cruz Roja Nacional, Archivo Emergencia 9 de abril, 1948. The records of the Colombian Red Cross are divided into the following categories: Libro de registro censo de personas desaparecidas; Estadística de elementos para rehabilitación del trabajo; Estadística de arrendamientos; Estadística elementos de alcoba; Estadística de ropa personal; Estadística de comedor y cocina. The archive also contains a record of doctors' visits to homes of injured or sick individuals during the three weeks after the riot. I am especially grateful to Daniel Martínez Quijano for finding this archive in the old building of the Colombian Red Cross. Martínez Quijano, a young volunteer in the fledgling Red Cross, spent the days after the riot attempting to organize the headquarters and accompanying doctors to homes of the injured in outlying areas of the city. He has been with the Red Cross ever since, and has dedicated his life to humanitarian causes throughout the Caribbean. He is now a delegate to the League of the Society of the Red Cross. Interview 68, January 5, 1980.

64 *Semana*, April 24, 1948, p. 5. The fact that the brewery workers did not participate in the riot was emphasized in both the Liberal and the Conservative press. According to the Gaitanista organizer Manuel José Valencia, who passed by the brewery on his way downtown to participate in the riot, many of the workers did leave the brewery and joined the crowds. Interview 67, January 2, 1980.

65 This description of the rioters has been compiled from the interviews, especially from the recollections of the Gaitanistas. Ricaurte (interview 21) especially remembers the role played by the *marchantas* of the market, who he claims were more attached to Gaitán than anyone else.

Chapter 8

1 *La Razón*, April 23, 1948, p. 1; *El Liberal*, April 10, 1948, p. 8.
2 Rafael Azula Barrera, *De la revolución al orden nuevo: proceso y drama de un pueblo* (Bogotá: Editorial Kelly, 1956), p. 360.

3 Interview 12 with Rafael Azula Barrera, July 31, 1979.

4 Hernando Tellez B., *Cincuenta años de radiodifusión colombiana* (Medellín: Editorial Bedout, 1974), pp. 90–91. A few days later Cristóbal Páez was killed in the outskirts of Bogotá. *El Tiempo*, April 16, 1948, p. 1.

5 Interview 19 with Gerardo Molina, September 25, 1979.

6 Proceso Gaitán (PROG), volume 20, folios 29–42 (testimony of Jorge Zalamea Borda); *El Tiempo*, April 17, 1948, p. 15.

7 Interview with Molina; Carlos Restrepo Piedrahita, "La junta revolucionaria de Bogotá," *Sábado*, April 9, 1949, p. 3.

8 *El crimen de abril;* Azula Barrera, *De la revolución al orden nuevo*, p. 361; Arturo Abella, *Así fue el nueve de abril* (Bogotá: Ediciones Internacional de Publicaciones, 1973), p. 34. The most complete version of the radio broadcasts appears in Azula Barrera's book. Molina's precise words are on the record *El crimen de abril.* Azula Barrera has correctly recorded them but attributed to Molina an introduction to his statements made by somebody else, as well as some statements at the end that are not Molina's. All in all, however, it appears that Azula Barrera faithfully transcribed the tapes of these broadcasts that he claimed to have received from then Minister of Communications Dávila Tello. Molina acknowledged that he said most but not all of what Azula Barrera attributes to him. Interview with Molina.

9 *El crimen de abril;* Restrepo Piedrahita, "Junta revolucionaria," p. 3.

10 Azula Barrera, *De la revolución al orden nuevo*, p. 362.

11 Interview with Molina.

12 Interview 24 with Adán Arriaga Andrade, November 10, 1979.

13 Roberto García-Peña, "Memoria aproximada del nueve de abril," *El Tiempo (Lecturas Dominicales)*, April 8, 1973, p. 5; Darío Samper, "La trágica proyección del nueve de abril," *El Tiempo*, April 9, 1968, p. 5.

14 PROG, vol. 20, ff. 93–94 (testimony of Antonio García).

15 Interview 65 with Antonio García, December 19, 1979.

16 Interview 42 with Gabriel Muñoz Uribe, December 1, 1979.

17 Interview 49 with Agustín Utrera, December 5, 1979. Utrera did not know how many men he had found.

18 Interview 31 with Hernando Restrepo Botero, November 19, 1979.

19 Interview 36 with Octavio López, November 28, 1979.

20 Interview 61 with José Vicente García, December 13, 1979.

21 Interview 59 with Clímaco Aldana, December 11, 1979.

22 Interview 21 with Luis Eduardo Ricaurte, November 2, 1979.

23 Interview 66 with Carlos J. Sánchez, January 2, 1980.

24 Interviews 51 and 52 with Valerio and Bernardo Valverde, December 6, 1979.

25 Interview 28 with Gilberto Vieira, November 17, 1979.

26 Carlos Franqui, *Diario de una revolución* (París: Ediciones Ruedo Ibérico, 1976), pp. 21–22.

27 Ibid., pp. 22–26.

28 Abelardo Forero Benavides, "Viaje al fondo de la noche: lo que ví en la revolución," *Sábado*, May 1, 1948, p. 1; *Semana*, April 24, 1948, p. 12.

29 Forero Benavides, "Viaje," p. 1; *Semana*, April 24, 1948, p. 11.

30 Darío Echandía, "La historia también es con los muertos," interview with Gabriel Gutiérrez, *El Tiempo (Lecturas Dominicales)*, April 8, 1973, p. 1.

31 García-Peña, "Memoria approximada," p. 5. That these were the instructions coming from the Fifth Police Precinct is confirmed by the U.S. Embassy. USDS, Decimal File 821.00/4-948. Incoming telegram no. 196, 8:49 p.m., April 9, 1948.

32 The Conservatives, the victors of the "political struggle" have been much more willing to disclose the details of the conversation than the Liberals. The first account was in Estrada Monsalve, *El nueve de abril en Palacio: horario de un golpe de estado* (Bogotá: Editorial "Cahur," 1948), published just weeks after the events. The most complete account from the Liberal side is Abelardo Forero Benavides, "Viaje." Forero Benavides, however, was not present at the conversation and bases his account on what the participants told him shortly afterwards. The Liberal protagonists have offered few details. Both Carlos Lleras Restrepo and Darío Echandía refused my request for an interview.

The best and most complete version of the conversation is in Azula Barrera, *De la revolución al orden nuevo*, pp. 367–74. It has no major differences from Estrada Monsalve's version. Nor are there any sharp differences between Azula Barrera's version and that given by Forero Benavides. The most recent recounting of the conversation is in Arturo Abella, *Así fue el nueve de abril*. It is based on interviews with some of the Conservative protagonists, and adds some interesting new information. Otherwise, it too relies heavily on Azula Barrera. Also illuminating is the president's version, "Las horas dramáticas en el Palacio Presidencial," *El Tiempo (Lecturas Dominicales)*, April 8, 1973.

33 Estrada Monsalve, *Nueve de abril en Palacio*, p. 30.

34 Ospina Pérez, "Horas dramáticas," p. 1; for an account of the reaction to Gaitán's assassination outside Bogotá, see Gonzalo Sánchez G., *Los días de la revolución: Gaitanismo y nueve de abril en provincia* (Bogotá: Centro Cultural Jorge Eliécer Gaitán, 1983); and Carlos Eduardo Jaramillo, *Ibagué: conflictos políticos de 1930 al nueve de abril* (Bogotá: Centro Cultural Jorge Eliécer Gaitán, 1983).

35 Interview with Arriaga Andrade.

36 Azula Barrera, *De la revolución al orden nuevo*, pp. 385–86.

37 Ospina Pérez, "Horas dramáticas," p. 1.

38 Ibid., p. 1; Echandía, "La historia," p. 1; Carlos Lleras Restrepo, interview with Antonio Montaña, *El Tiempo*, April 8, 1973, p. 1; Forero Benavides, "Viaje," p. 1.

39 Echandía, "La historia," p. 1; Lleras Restrepo interview, p. 1; Forero Benavides, "Viaje," p. 1; Ospina Pérez, "Horas dramáticas," p. 1.

40 Echandía, "La historia," p. 1; Ospina Pérez, "Horas dramáticas," p. 1.

41 Ospina Pérez, "Horas dramáticas," p. 1; Echandía, "La historia," p. 1.

42 *Semana*, April 24, 1948, p. 14.

43 Forero Benavides, "Viaje," p. 1.

44 *Semana*, May 8, 1948, pp. 18–19.

45 Ibid., January 24, 1948, p. 6, and April 24, 1948, p. 15.

46 This information was given to me by Doña Amparo Jaramillo vda. de Gaitán in

the months of November and December 1978. Doña Amparo did not wish to be interviewed, but she graciously received me in her home on various occasions. I did not take notes during our talks.

47 *El Liberal*, April 11, 1948, p. 1.

48 Interview 5 with Pío Nono Barbosa Barbosa, April 9, 1979.

49 USDS, Bogotá Consular Files, 800, Colombian Revolution, Beaulac to Secretary of State, telegram no. 248, April 14, 1948.

50 Ibid., Beaulac to Secretary of State, telegram no. 258, April 15, 1948.

51 *El Liberal*, April 10, 1948, p. 1.

52 Decree no. 1239, April 10, 1948, in *Diario Oficial*, vol. 2, 1948, p. 289.

53 Interview 35 with police officer Salvador Millán, November 27, 1979, and interview 38 with Heliodoro Africano, November 28, 1979.

54 USDS, Decimal File 821.00/5.748, dispatch from Beaulac to Secretary of State, May 7, 1948, p. 7.

55 Interview with Arriaga Andrade.

56 *El Liberal*, April 1948, p. 1; *El Tiempo*, April 16, 1948, p. 1.

57 Juan Roa Sierra is widely believed to be the assassin. He was a poor, usually unemployed man from Bogotá without any deep political convictions who had apparently boasted of his intention to kill Gaitán. Although the investigation into Gaitán's murder, which lasted twenty-five years (1948–1973) and was only made public in 1978, never fully established a motive for the crime, few convincing alternative leads were uncovered. A man named César Bernal Cordovéz (*"el flaco"*) might have been an accomplice, but he was never questioned, even though he spent many years in a mental hospital. PROG, vol. 24B, ff. 422–36 (1959).

A man named Roa Sierra had requested an interview with Gaitán, and a man generally resembling Roa Sierra was seen loitering outside Gaitán's office in the company of another man. A group of investigators barely managed to take the fingerprints of a nude man with a tie hanging around his neck, lying outside the *palacio* around two-thirty, moments after the guard cleared the street. (PROG, vol. 1A, ff. 5–6, 6–17.) The next day a similarly nude body, but with two ties, was found in the Cementerio Central, where many of the dead were transported by the marines. (Interview 16 with Alberto Vejarano Laverde, September 21, 1979.) The heavily mutilated body was identified by the investigators who had taken fingerprints the day before as the one they had seen in front of the *palacio*. The body was positively identified as that of Juan Roa Sierra by his lover, his mother, and his three brothers. (PROG, vol. 1A, ff. 37–64; vol. 1B, ff. 48, 111–17, 170–71.) It was also identified by Dr. Jorge Cavelier, who had performed an appendectomy on Roa Sierra in 1941. (PROG, vol. 1A. f. 16.) The gun was also traced to Roa Sierra. There is little evidence to implicate anyone else, or to suggest that he had connections with high politicians or with communists. At most, Roa Sierra may have been egged on by opponents of Gaitán who knew of his sinister intentions.

For the views of the first legal prosecutor, see Ricardo Jordán Jiménez, *Dos viernes trágicos* (Bogotá: Editorial Horizontes, 1968). Jordán includes the work of the special team sent by Scotland Yard at the behest of Ospina Pérez and

Zuleta Angel (pp. 173–221). The investigators found little, in large measure because they did not know Spanish. Their original mission had been to help reorganize the police. For their final report see PROG, vol. 32, ff. 191–200.

58 República de Colombia, *El Gobierno de Unión Nacional*, 5 vols. (Bogotá: Imprenta Nacional, 1950), 5: 403–10.

59 Ibid., pp. 405–6, 409.

60 *Avante*, July 11, 1948, p. 1; PROG, vol. 24B, ff. 314–15 (testimony of Mariano Ospina Pérez).

61 The idea that the rioters were ashamed of their actions is part of the "official" history of the *bogotazo*. Most of my own information on the riot comes from that official history and from interviews with leading Gaitanistas. I am convinced that they were all sincere when they told me that they had not participated in the destruction and the looting, larely because of their strong commitment to order and morality. The Gaitanistas I interviewed all felt, however, that the riot was the result of the worst instincts within the *pueblo*, which they were unwilling either to condemn outright or to defend.

62 All the Gaitanistas interviewed scoffed at the idea that the riot had been communist-inspired, and that Gaitán had been killed as part of an international conspiracy, and that the *pueblo* had been manipulated by foreigners. They all understood that the leaders of both parties were attempting to place the guilt elsewhere. Doña Amparo reacted angrily to such suggestions in the days immediately following her husband's assassination. She was convinced, and remains so today, that the Conservative regime was responsible for Gaitán's death and was seeking to place the blame elsewhere. Nevertheless, when I probed the issue with Gaitanistas, many readily admitted that it was possible that the rioters had been manipulated by communists. At the time of the interviews, it seemed to me that many had seriously thought about the possibility before.

63 USDS, Decimal File 821.00/4.948. Incoming telegram no. 197, April 9, 1948, 10 p.m.; *La Razón*, April 13, 1948, p. 1.

64 *New York Times*, April 16, 1948, p. 1. For attempts to pin the blame on communists see Alberto Niño H., *Antecedentes y secretos del nueve de abril* (Bogotá: Editorial Pax, 1949); José María Nieto Rojas, *La batalla contra el comunismo en Colombia* (Bogotá: Empresa Nacional de Publicaciones, 1956); Francisco Fandiño Silva, *La penetración soviética en América Latina y el nueve de abril* (Bogotá: Editorial ABC, 1949); Raúl Andrade, *La internacional negra en Colombia y otros ensayos* (Quito: Editorial Quito, 1954); USDS, Bogotá consular files, 800, Colombian revolution, SC, confidential memos no. 311, May 20, 1948, and unnumbered, May 21, 1948.

The only person found guilty of treason was Captain José Phillips, but this was because he was a military officer. He was sentenced to two years in prison. (Interview 47 with José Phillips, December 4, 1979; *El Tiempo*, June 18, 1948, p. 8) One other military officer, Captain Elías Escobar Salamanca, was brought to trial, but he was absolved. (Interview 39 with Elías Escobar Salamanca, November 29, 1979.) Three Liberals went into exile in Venezuela: Joaquín Tiberio Galvis, Hernando Vega Escobar, and Guillermo Benavides. While scores of Liberals were threatened with persecution, and many even spent months in jail, none were actually tried. Rómulo Guzmán was picked up at least three times before Congress resumed and he was granted immunity.

65 *New York Times*, April 13, 1948, p. 4.
66 USDS, Decimal File 821.00/4.948. Incoming telegrams no. 192, 4:00 p.m., and 193, 5:53 p.m.
67 *New York Times*, April 11, 1948, section 4, p. 10.
68 Ibid., April 11, 1948, p. 37.
69 Ibid., April 13, 1948, p. 1.
70 Actually, the break in diplomatic relations was not made official until May 3, 1948. (Ibid., April 13, 1948, pp. 1, 26; May 4, 1948, p. 1.) During the interval nobody, including Soviet diplomats, knew whether relations had or had not been broken off.
71 Ibid., April 16, 1948, p. 1.
72 Ibid., April 23, 1948, p. 1.
73 Ibid., April 14, p. 10; April 15, pp. 1, 17; April 17, 1948, p. 7; *El Tiempo*, April 18, 1948, p. 1.
74 Conversations with Doña Amparo Jaramillo vda. de Gaitán, November 1978.
75 *Jornada*, April 20, 1948, p. 4.
76 This is the figure cited in the national press. It is the same as that reported for the February 7 silent demonstration. Before the funeral the *New York Times* reported that a hundred thousand mourners were expected (April 18, 1948, p. 25). However, the U.S. newspaper concluded that only twenty thousand actually attended (April 21, 1948). The *convivialistas* were not experienced at estimating crowd numbers and had a stake in claiming a large turnout. It may be that many refused to attend the Liberal-sponsored ceremony or were afraid of recurring violence.
77 Interview with Ricaurte.
78 The speech is printed in *El Tiempo*, April 21, 1948, p. 13. Emphasis added.
79 Ibid.
80 Ibid., April 19, 1948, p. 9.
81 Pío Nono Barbosa Barbosa, who claimed not to have left the house from April 10 to April 21, told the author that he had never seen such a deep hole. The vault was lined with cement, and Gaitán's coffin was incased in a three-layered zinc container. *El Tiempo*, April 21, 1948, p. 16; *New York Times*, April 21, 1948, p. 16.
82 Conversations with Doña Amparo Jaramillo vda. de Gaitán, November 1978.
83 Forero Benavides, "Gaitán," in *Sábado*, April 24, 1948, p. 1.
84 Forero Benavides, "El país nacional," *Sábado*, June 19, 1948, p. 1; see also his "A los hombres de buena voluntad," *Sábado*, May 8, 1948, p. 1; and "Los enemigos de la normalidad," *Sábado*, May 15, 1948, p. 1.
85 It is not possible to attribute to any single person the notion that the *bogotazo* split the nation's history. The idea filled the air immediately after April 9 and found ample expression in the writings of both Liberals and Conservatives. Much of the discussion and the anguish revolved around the cliché "*aquí no pasa nada*" ("nothing happens here in Colombia"), which leaders of both parties

used throughout the years of *convivencia*. The statement reflected both their incredulousness at the fact that nothing—that is, no social revolution or uprising—took place in the face of the inequities they were painfully aware of, and their abiding fear that something might. On April 9 something did, confirming their worst fears.

Examples of this thinking can be found in Luis López de Mesa, *Perspectivas culturales* (Bogotá: Talleres Ediciones Universidad Nacional, 1949), pp. 70–73: "we were an American *pueblo* proud of its history. We had the honor of living our republic honestly . . . and it was a delight of the spirit to travel to the world of western culture with the name of Colombia in one's passport. . . . (We) broke the nation's history, for from today on, and for another generation at least, nobody in the world will sincerely believe in our national culture." See also Augusto Ramírez Moreno, "La tragedia nacional del nueve de abril," in *El Tiempo*, July 10, 1948, p. 4, and Silvio Villegas, "Aventura y reconstrucción" in *Sábado*, May 8, 1948, p. 3. The most complete interpretation of the *bogotazo* along these lines in Roberto Restrepo, *Nueve de abril: quiebra cultural y política* (Bogotá: Tipografía Bremen, 1948). More recently this idea has been continued by Arturo Abella in his *Así fue el nueve de abril*.

Within academic circles the idea has also gained adherents. José Gutiérrez, for example, concludes that "the total failure of the politicians on that day constituted the rude begining of a historic change" in the customs of the political elite: thereafter they sought power for the sake of power. See his *La rebeldía colombiana* (Bogotá: Ediciones Tercer Mundo, 1962), p. 65.

86   *El Siglo*, May 22, 1948, p. 4.

87   *Semana*, June 26, 1948, p. 5.

88   *Semana*, May 29, 1948, pp. 5–6.

89   *Jornada*, April 17, 1948, pp. 1–3; April 19, 1948, p. 4; *El Tiempo*, April 16, 1948, p. 4; for similar views in the Conservative press, see *El Siglo*, April 27, 1948, p. 4; April 30, 1948, p. 4; and May 1, 1948, p. 4.

90   Luis López de Mesa, *Perspectivas*, pp. 77–78. For the Conservatives' agreement with López de Mesa's views, see the article by Aurelio Angarita Cárdenas in *El Siglo*, August 27, 1948, p. 4.

91   Gerardo Molina, *Las ideas liberales en Colombia de 1935 a la iniciación del Frente Nacional* (Bogotá: Ediciones Tercer Mundo, 1977), p. 215.

92   Gilberto Vieira, *Nueve de abril: experiencia de un pueblo* (Bogotá: Ediciones Suramérica, 1973), pp. 24–28.

93   Luis Carlos Pérez, *Los delitos políticos: interpretación jurídica del nueve de abril* (Bogotá: Distribuidora Americana de Publicaciones, 1948), esp. pp. 148–49. Luis Vidales also presented a thorough attack on the black legend, and especially the views presented by López de Mesa. See his *La insurrección desplomada: el nueve de abril, su teoría, su praxis* (Bogotá: Alberto Estrada, 1979). The work was first published in 1948.

94   Most of the Gaitanistas interviewed revealed a clear understanding of the reasons that led the leaders of both political parties to blame communists and outside infiltrators. Most considered it an attempt to shift the blame to outsiders. Yet when pressed, many grudgingly admitted that "foreigners" might have led

the *pueblo* astray. The seeds of doubt had been planted, it seems, and many have in fact wondered over the years whether their own actions were entirely of their own making.

95 Otero Silva's poem "La chusma de Jorge Eliécer Gaitán," was reprinted in *Jornada*, May 9, 1948, and in *Sábado*, May 15, 1948, p. 13. It was originally published in *El Nacional*, of Caracas, Venezuela. Samper's "Los muertos del pueblo" is in *Jornada*, April 25, 1948, p. 2. Samper makes a careful distinction between the "bandits" who burned and looted and the *pueblo* that filled the streets to protest against the death of their leader. For a rhythmic condemnation of the *pueblo*, see José María Vivas Balcázar's poem "Después de la vergüenza," in *Revista de las Indias*, no. 103, June 1948: 5–7.

96 *La Iglesia* (journal of the archdiocese of Bogotá) 2 (1948): 90–92.

97 Interview 20 with Msgr. Carlos Vargas Umaña, October 31, 1979, and interview 26 with Msgr. Antonio Afanador Salgar, November 14, 1979.

98 Interview with Ricaurte and interview 37 with Guillermo Vargas, November 28, 1979.

99 After much controversy among the Liberal and Conservative members of the new cabinet, the entire police force of Bogotá was finally dismissed on May 1, with the last members leaving the force on May 6, 1948. *El Tiempo*, May 2, 1948, p. 1; interview with Millán.

100 Decree no. 1839 of June 2, 1948, *Diario Oficial*, vol. 2, 1948, p. 1040. The argument against *chicha* is presented by Jorge Bejarano, *La derrota de un vicio: origen e historia de la chicha* (Bogotá: Editorial Iqueima, 1950).

101 Most of those interviewed, as well as others in Bogotá, were asked whether such a monument existed. The invariably incredulous responses revealed that the thought of such a monument had never crossed their minds.

102 See Alexander W. Wilde, "Conversations Among Gentlemen: Oligarchical Democracy in Colombia," in Juan Linz and Alfred Stepan, eds., *The Breakdown of Democratic Regimes, vol. 3: Latin America* (Baltimore: Johns Hopkins University Press, 1978), p. 47.

103 *El Tiempo*, April 18, 1948, p. 9. The declaration was signed by the following Liberals: Carlos Lleras Restrepo, Jorge Uribe Márquez, Plinio Mendoza Neira, Julio Roberto Salazar Ferro, Víctor Julio Silva, Alberto Arango Tavera, Alberto Galindo, Darío Samper and Julio Ortiz Márquez. For the Conservatives, the following leaders signed: Guillermo León Valencia, Luis Navarro Ospina, Roberto Urdaneta Arbeláez, Augusto Ramírez Moreno, Silvio Villegas, Joaquín Estrada Monsalve, Juan Uribe Cualla, José Elías del Hierro, and Lúcio Pabón Núñez.

104 *El Tiempo*, April 19, 1948, p. 4.

105 *Eco Nacional*, July 12, 1948, p. 1, and July 13, 1948, pp. 1, 4; *Avante*, July 11, 1948, p. 7; *Derechas*, August 4, 1948, p. 1.

106 For a rich and nuanced account of the break, see Wilde, "Conversations," esp. pp. 51–58. See also Guillermo Fonnegra Sierra, *El parlamento colombiano* (Bogotá: Gráficas Centauro, 1953), pp. 213–76.

107 Ibid., p. 213; *Semana*, May 28, 1949, pp. 5–7.

108 *Semana*, October 1, 1949, pp. 5–6.

109   Wilde, "Conversations" p. 53.
110   *Semana*, October 29, 1949, p. 5.
111   Carlos Lleras Restrepo, *De la república a la dictadura* (Bogotá: Editorial ARGRA, 1955), p. 212.
112   Paul Oquist, *Violencia, conflicto y política en Colombia* (Bogotá: Instituto de Estudios Colombianos, Biblioteca Banco Popular, 1978), p. 17.
113   For the view of a participant in that exodus, see Eduardo Franco Isaza, *Las guerrillas del llano* (Bogotá: Editorial Librería Mundial, 1959). A social history of the guerrilla movement is Gonzalo Sánchez and Donny Meertens, *Bandoleros, gamonales y campesinos: el caso de la Violencia en Colombia* (Bogotá: El Áncora Editores, 1983).

Conclusion

1   The term *bogotazo* has traditionally been used in Colombia by those who want to give the events an international dimension. Although Latin American in its roots, the term was also catchy enough to appeal to the international press. It caught on slowly, however, for the events were referred to as *"el nueve de abril"* for quite a few years in Colombia. Conservatives and especially *El Siglo* have done the most to promote the term in order to give the impression that the events were hatched elsewhere. It still strikes many Colombians today as sensationalist.

2   These different memories were brought home to me in the interviews conducted for this study. At first I only wanted to study the riot, but the Gaitanistas I talked to only wanted to remember Gaitán. It was indeed difficult to get them to talk about the events that took place upon his assassination. Conversely, the *convivialistas* I spoke to were eager to talk about the riot and felt that my developing interest in Gaitán was of lesser consequence.

3   The idea that *la Violencia* in the countryside was caused by the violent, passionate, and barbaric character of the *pueblo* has long been part of the official interpretation. On January 31, 1948, the moderate Liberal weekly *Semana*, opened its pages to a debate on the causes of *la Violencia*. Fighting between rank-and-file Liberals and Conservatives had taken on a particularly virulent character in the department of Santander, and especially in the towns of Cucutilla and Arboledas, whose inhabitants were said to be naturally prone to violence. In the pages of *Semana*, a twenty-eight-year-old medical doctor gave a measure of scientific support to the idea. In his view the region" is inhabited by descendants of the most fearful Indians that in remote times populated Colombia. We need only study them superficially to know what we are dealing with. They live in extremely marshy (*palúdico*) lands and are friends of alcohol in the extreme. When they get drunk, the toxins begin to affect them and they become crazy. . . . the only thing that matters to them is killing, and they do it without a second thought" (pp. 15–16).

   On April 1, 1949, one year after Gaitán's assassination, the Liberal leadership offered an explanation of *la Violencia* that was not much different from the doctor's. "To the shame of our political culture, it just so happens that in some regions of the country there are towns (*poblaciones*) where *la Violencia* has acquired, in different periods, permanent and systematic characteristics. . . . Political sectarianism, and on occasion interests and passions even lower, have created in specific regions of the country an environment of lawlessness that returns us to the most primitive forms of social life." *El Tiempo*, April 2, 1949, p. 1.

The idea still has adherents. According to Joaquín Estrada Monsalve, *la Violencia* was an "inexplicable thing . . . a cancer. The country went crazy. After April 9 the *pueblo* learned to kill." In his mind *la Violencia* was simply an expression of the *Pueblo's* "thirst for blood." (Interview 22, November 9, 1979.) Another Conservative, Arturo Abella, expressed a similar view. "It is simply that we cannot say that we are among angels, nor among civilized people, or Anglo-Saxons, Swedes, or Danes or whatever. This *pueblo* is a very difficult *pueblo* and . . ." (Interview 15, August 18, 1979.)

4   Rafael Azula Barrera, *De la revolución al orden nuevo: proceso y drama de un pueblo* (Bogotá: Editorial Kelly, 1956), p. 365; Joaquín Estrada Monsalve, *El nueve de abril en Palacio: horario de un golpe de estado* (Bogotá: Editorial "Cahur," 1948), p. 24; Mariano Ospina Pérez, "Las horas dramáticas en el Palacio Presidencial," *El Tiempo (Lecturas Dominicales)*, April 8, 1973, p. 1, and April 9, 1973, p. 1-B.

5   Gerardo Molina, *Las ideas liberales en Colombia de 1935 a la iniciación del Frente Nacional* (Bogotá: Ediciones Tercer Mundo, 1977), p. 212; *Semana*, April 24, 1948, p. 12; Abelardo Forero Benavides, "Viaje al fondo de la noche: lo que ví en la revolución," in *Sábado*, May 1, 1948, p. 1.

6   U.S. Department of State, Decimal File 821.00/4-948. Incoming telegram no. 195, April 9, 1948, 8:11 p.m.

7   Darío Echandía, "La historia también es con los muertos," interview with Gabriel Gutiérrez, *El Tiempo (Lecturas Dominicales)*, April 8, 1973, p. 1; Forero Benavides, "Viaje," p. 1; Carlos Lleras Restrepo, "Carlos Lleras Restrepo relata la jornada del nueve de abril," interview with Antonio Montaña, *El Tiempo*, April 8, 1973, p. 1.

8   The letter is reproduced in Doña Bertha Hernández de Ospina Pérez's unpublished personal account, pp. 7–9, in the author's files.

9   Arturo Abella, *Así fue el nueve de abril* (Bogotá: Ediciones Internacional de Publicaciones, 1973), p. 42.

10 The reaction of the Colombian government stands in marked contrast to the reaction of the U.S. government after the racial riots of the late 1960s, which spawned investigation upon investigation into the identity, motives, and psychological characteristics of the rioters. The only question that seemed to be of any interest, either to the government or to anyone else, was who killed Gaitán. The official investigation into his death lasted a full thirty years. It was sporadic, repetitive in the extreme, and far from enlightening. Its conclusions were finally made public in a ceremony headed by then President Alfonso López Michelsen on April 9, 1978, at the Casa Museo Jorge Eliécer Gaitán, where the thirty-nine bound volumes of testimony are now housed.

The investigation, known as the Proceso Gaitán (PROG), was more a reflection of the prevailing political pressures than a serious effort to get to the bottom of the issue. The investigation virtually ceased functioning during the military dictatorship of Gustavo Rojas Pinilla (1953–1957). Its activity was feverish during the first years of the Frente Nácional, when the leaders of the two traditional parties were attempting to reassert their control over public life, this time by formally dividing up its offices and positions rather than competing for them. The two sides attempted to find evidence that might bolster their respective positions. When Fidel Castro came to power in Cuba in January 1959, his participation in the riot, which had already been dealt with at some length between 1948 and 1950, was again a topic of interest. The Conservatives were delighted at this fortunate turn of events. In the mid-1960s, as Rojas Pinillas' Alianza Nacional Popular (ANAPO) gained in popularity, the old general became the center of the investigation's interest.

All search for evidence ended in March 1973, although the investigation was not officially declared completed until the presiding judge, Hellyda Hincapié Arboleda, had reviewed all the evidence once again in March 1976 and concluded that no further leads existed. At the last moment some Gaitanistas, most notably Rafael Galán Medellín, attempted to have the case reopened (interview 11, July 26, 1979).

One of the most interesting aspects of the investigation was the secrecy surrounding it. It engendered a host of myths surrounding Gaitán's assassination and kept sundry conspiracy theories alive over the years. Yet, the great bulk of the information collected was in the public record. Most of those who testified freely gave their views to the press. None of those who testified incriminated themselves.

The search for clues bordered on the bizarre. On June 6, 1960, the body of Gaitán was exhumed. Graphic descriptions of the odor that filled what was once the dead man's living room fill the pages of the investigation. The investigators were searching for the lost bullet. They found it between the seventh and eighth dorsal vertebrae. It came from the same gun as the other bullets. There was only one assassin. (PROG, vol. 30, ff. 171–75). The man who had disturbed so many in his lifetime was not allowed to rest in peace.

Bibliography

Archives

American Red Cross. Bogotá Disaster Files, 1948. Historical Division, American Red Cross National Headquarters, Washington, D.C.

Cruz Roja Nacional. Archivo Emergencia Nueve de Abril, 1948, Cruz Roja Nacional, Bogotá.

Gaitán Papers (GP). Documents, files and correspondence of the Gaitanista movement, 1933–1948, Casa Museo Jorge Eliécer Gaitán, Bogotá.

Junta Informadora de Daños y Perjuicios. Findings of the body organized by President Mariano Ospina Pérez to determine the extent of the losses incurred as a result of the *bogotazo*. In the offices of the junta's director, Francisco Sáenz Arbeláez, Bogotá.

National Archives of the United States, Department of State, Colombian revolution files (1948) and Bogotá consular reports (1946–1948), Washington, D.C.

Proceso Gaitán (PROG). Official investigation into the assassination of Jorge Eliécer Gaitán, Casa Museo Jorge Eliécer Gaitán, Bogotá.

Official Documents

Bogotá. Departmento de Estadísticas e Investigación Social. *Anuario Municipal de Estadísticas de Bogotá (1948)*. Bogotá: Imprenta Nacional.

Colombia. Departamento Administrativo Nacional de Estadística. "Tendencias electorales, 1935–1968." *Boletín Mensual de Estadística* (December 1969).

Colombia. Presidente. 1934–1938 (López Pumarejo). *La política oficial: mensajes, cartas y discursos del presidente López.* 5 vols. Bogotá: Imprenta Nacional, 1942.

Colombia. Presidente. 1946–1950 (Ospina Pérez). *El gobierno de Unión Nacional.* Bogotá: Imprenta Nacional, 1950.

Colombia. Presidente. 1946–1950 (Ospina Pérez). *El gobierno de Unión Nacional y los acuerdos patrióticos.* Bogotá: Presidencia de la República, 1948.

Colombia. Presidente. 1946–1950 (Ospina Pérez). *La oposición y el gobierno del nueve de abril de 1948 al nueve de abril de 1950.* Bogotá: Imprenta Nacional, 1950.

Unpublished Manuscripts

Arquidiócesis de Bogotá, Gobierno Eclesiástico, Tesorería. *Relación de las pérdidas sufridas en el saqueo e incendio del Palacio Arzobispal en el día nueve de abril de 1948.*

Datos históricos de la Comunidad de las Monjas Concepcionistas Franciscanas de Bogotá. Report written by one of the sisters of the order and approved by the abbess, Sor María Magdalena de San José.

Monseigneur Arturo Franco Arango. *La destrucción del Palacio de los Arzobispos el día nueve de abril: actuación del Ilustre Arzobispo en tal emergencia.* Rome, 1949.

Hernández de Ospina Pérez, Bertha (wife of President Mariano Ospina Pérez). Untitled personal account of the *bogotazo* as seen from inside the walls of the Presidential Palace.

Recordings

Caudillos y muchedumbres. Edited by Jorge Eduardo Girón Barrios. Medellín: Discos Fuentes, 1975.
    Vol. 1: Jorge Eliécer Gaitán.
    Vol. 2: Jorge Eliécer Gaitán.
    Vol. 6: Jorge Eliécer Gaitán.
El crímen de abril.
Jorge Eliécer Gaitán: yo no soy un hombre, soy un pueblo. 2 vols.

Books and Articles

Abella, Arturo. *Así fue el nueve de abril.* Bogotá: Ediciones Internacional de Publicaciones, 1973.

Alape, Arturo. *El Bogotazo: memorias del olvido.* Bogotá: Fundación Universidad Central, 1983.

Andrade, Raul. *La internacional negra en Colombia y otros ensayos.* Quito: Editorial Quito, 1954.

Andrade de Pombo, Helena. *Tres godos en aprietos.* Bogotá: Editorial Santa Fé, 1956.

Aprile Gnizet, Jacques. *El impacto del nueve de abril sobre el centro de Bogotá.* Bogotá: Centro Cultural Jorge Eliécer Gaitán, 1983.

Arciniegas, Germán. "La academia, la taberna y la universidad." *Revista de las Indias* 58 (October 1943): 5–15.

Arciniegas, Germán. *Este pueblo de América.* México: Fondo de Cultura Económica, 1945.

Arciniegas, Germán. *Memorias de un congresista.* Bogotá: Editorial Cromos, 1933(?).

Arendt, Hannah. *The Human Condition.* Garden City, N.Y.: Doubleday Anchor Books, 1959.

Arendt, Hannah. *Totalitarianism.* New York: Harcourt, Brace and World, 1968.

Ariès, Philippe. *Western Attitudes Toward Death: From the Middle Ages to the Present.* Baltimore: Johns Hopkins University Press, 1979.

Arrubla, Mario, et al. *Colombia hoy.* Bogotá: Siglo XXI, 1978.

Azula Barrera, Rafael. *De la revolución al orden nuevo: proceso y drama de un pueblo.* Bogotá: Editorial Kelly, 1956.

Bautista, Ramón. *La muerte del caudillo (nueve de abril de 1948).* Bogotá: Editorial Patria, 1948.

Beaulac, Willard L. *Career Ambassador.* New York: Macmillan, 1951.

Becker, Ernest. *The Denial of Death.* New York: Free Press, 1973.

Bejarano, Jorge. *La derrota de un vicio: origen e historia de la chicha.* Bogotá: Editorial Iqueima, 1950.

Bergquist, Charles W. *Coffee and Conflict in Colombia, 1886–1910.* Durham: Duke University Press, 1978.

Bergquist, Charles W. *Workers in the Making of Modern Latin American History: Capitalist Development and Labor Formation in Chile, Argentina, Venezuela, and Colombia.* Stanford: Stanford University Press, 1985.

Bermúdez V., Luis A. *Gaitán y el crimen que costó 300 mil muertos.* Caracas: Editorial Latina, 1967.

Berry, R. Albert, Ronald G. Hellman, and Mauricio Solaún, eds. *Politics of Compromise: Coalition Government in Colombia.* New Brunswick, N.J.: Transaction Books, 1980.

Bierck, Harold A., Jr. *Selected Writings of Bolívar.* Compiled by Vicente Lecuna. New York: Colonial Press, 1951.

Billington, James H. *Fire in the Minds of Men: Origins of the Revolutionary Faith.* New York: Basic Books, 1980.

Blanco Núñez, José María. *Memoria de un gobernador: el nueve de abril de 1948.* Barranquilla: Tipografía Dorel, 1968.

Burns, James MacGregor. *Leadership.* New York: Harper and Row, 1978.

Bushnell, David. *The Santander Regime in Gran Colombia.* Newark: University of Delaware Press, 1954.

Caballero Calderón, Eduardo. *Historia privada de los colombianos.* Bogotá: Antares, 1969.

Caballero Calderón, Lucas. *Figuras políticas de Colombia.* Bogotá: Editorial Kelly, 1945.

Canal Ramírez, Gonzalo. *Nueve de abril 1948.* Bogotá: Litografía y Editorial "Cahur," 1948.

Canetti, Elias. *Crowds and Power.* New York: Seabury Press, 1978.

Carnicelli, Américo. *Historia de la masonería colombiana, 1833–1940.* 2 vols. Bogotá: Talleres de la Cooperativa Nacional de Artes Gráficas, 1975.

Conniff, Michael L., ed. *Latin American Populism in Comparative Perspective.* Albuquerque: University of New Mexico Press, 1982.

Córdoba, José María. *Jorge Eliécer Gaitán: tribuno popular de Colombia.* Bogotá: Litografías Cor-Val, 1952.

Cuéllar Vargas, Enrique. *Trece años de violencia.* Bogotá: Editorial SIPA, 1960.

Dealy, Glen Caudill. *The Public Man: An Interpretation of Latin American and Other Catholic Countries.* Amherst: University of Massachusetts Press, 1977.

Deas, Malcolm. "Algunas notas sobre la historia del caciquismo en Colombia." *Revista de Occidente* (Madrid), no. 127 (October 1972): 118–40.

Delpar, Helen. *Red Against Blue: The Liberal Party in Colombian Politics, 1863–1899.* University, Ala.: University of Alabama Press, 1981.

Díaz, Antolín. *Los verdugos del caudillo y su pueblo.* Bogotá: Editorial ABC, 1948.

Dix, Robert H. *Colombia: The Political Dimensions of Change*. New Haven: Yale University Press, 1967.

Douglas, Mary. *Natural Symbols: Explorations in Cosmology*. New York: Vintage Books, 1973.

Estrada Monsalve, Joaquín. *El nueve de abril en Palacio: horario de un golpe de estado*. Bogotá: Editorial "Cahur," 1948.

Falk Moore, Sally, and Barbara G. Myerhoff, eds. *Secular Ritual*. Assen: Van Gorcum, 1977.

Fandiño Silva, Francisco. *La penetración soviética en América Latina y el nueve de abril*. Bogotá: Editorial ABC, 1949.

Fernández de Soto, Mario. *Una revolución en Colombia—Jorge Eliécer Gaitán y Mariano Ospina Pérez: un libro sobre Iberoamérica*. Madrid: Ediciones Cultura Hispánica, 1951.

Ferri, Enrico. *Criminal Sociology*. New York: Agathon Press, 1967.

Ferri, Enrico. *The Positive School of Criminology*. Edited by Stanley E. Grupp. Pittsburgh: Pittsburgh University Press, 1968.

Figueredo Salcedo, Alberto, ed. *Colección Jorge Eliécer Gaitán: documentos para una biografía*, vol. 1. Bogotá: Imprenta Nacional, 1949.

Fitzgibbon, Russell H., and Julio A. Fernández. *Latin America: Political Culture and Development*. 2d ed. Englewood Cliffs, N.J.: Prentice-Hall, 1981.

Fonnegra Sierra, Guillermo. *El parlamento colombiano*. Bogotá: Gráficas Centauro, 1953.

Foucault, Michel. *The History of Sexuality, Vol. I: An Introduction*. New York: Vintage Books, 1980.

Franco Isaza, Eduardo. *Las guerrillas del llano*. Bogotá: Editorial Librería Mundial, 1959.

Franqui, Carlos. *Diario de una revolución*. París: Ediciones Ruedo Ibérico, 1976.

Gaitán, Aquilino. *Por qué cayó el partido conservador*. Bogotá: n.p., 1955.

Gaitán, Miguel Angel. *El por qué de un asesinato y sus antecedentes*. Bogotá: Editorial Minerva, 1949.

Galvis Gómez, Carlos. *Por qué cayó López*. Bogotá: Editorial ABC, 1946.

García, Antonio. *Gaitán y el camino de la revolución colombiana*. Bogotá: Ediciones Camilo, 1974.

García, Antonio. *Gaitán y el problema de la revolución colombiana*. Bogotá: M.S.C., 1955.

García, J. J. *Epocas y gentes*. Bogotá: Ediciones Tercer Mundo, 1977.

García, J. J. *Política y amigos*. Bogotá: Ediciones Tercer Mundo, 1975.

García Márquez, Gabriel. *One Hundred Years of Solitude*. New York: Avon Books, 1971.

García Ortiz, Laureano. "Los cachacos de Bogotá." *Boletín de la Academia Colombiana de Historia* (1936): 126–29.

Germani, Gino. *Authoritarianism, Fascism, and National Populism*. New Brunswick, N.J.: Transaction Books, 1978.

Giraldo Londoño, Pedronel. *Don Fernando: juicio sobre un hombre y una época*. Medellín: Editorial Granamérica, 1963.

Gómez, Laureano. *Comentarios a un régimen*. Bogotá: Editorial Minerva, 1934.

Gómez, Laureano. *El cuadrilátero*. Bogotá: Editorial Central, 1939.

Gómez, Laureano. *Discursos.* Bogotá: Colección Populibro, no. 1, Editorial Revista Colombiana, 1968.

Gómez, Laureano. *Interrogantes sobre el progreso de Colombia: conferencias dictadas en el Teatro Municipal de Bogotá.* Bogotá: Populibro, 1970.

Gómez, Laureano. *Obras selectas.* Bogotá: Cámara de Representantes, Colección Pensadores Políticos Colombianos, 1981.

Gómez Aristizábal, Horacio. *Gaitán: enfoque histórico.* Bogotá: Editorial Cosmos, 1975.

Gómez Correa, Pedro. *El nueve de abril.* Bogotá: Editorial Iqueima, 1951.

Guía de Bogotá. Sucesos colombianos, no. 4. Bogotá: Librería Colombiana Camacho Roldán, 1948.

Gutiérrez, José. *De la pseudo-aristocracia a la autenticidad: psicología social colombiana.* Bogotá: Ediciones Tercer Mundo, 1961.

Gutiérrez, José. *Idiosincracia colombiana y nacionalidad.* Bogotá: Editorial Colombiana, 1966.

Gutiérrez, José. *La rebeldía colombiana.* Bogotá: Ediciones Tercer Mundo, 1962.

Gutiérrez Navarro, Isaac. *La luz de una vida.* Bogotá: Editorial ABC, 1949.

Henderson, James D. *Cuando Colombia se desangró: un estudio de la Violencia en metropoli y provincia.* Bogotá: El Áncora Editores, 1984.

Hirschman, Albert O. *Journeys Toward Progress.* New York: Twentieth Century Fund, 1963.

Hirschman, Albert O. *The Passions and the Interests: Political Arguments for Capitalism before Its Triumph.* Princeton: Princeton University Press, 1977.

Hirschman, Albert O. *Shifting Involvements: Private Interest and Public Action.* Princeton: Princeton University Press, 1982.

Jaramillo, Carlos Eduardo. *Ibagué: conflictos políticos de 1930 al nueve de abril.* Bogotá: Centro Cultural Jorge Eliécer Gaitán, 1983.

Jaramillo Ocampo, Hernando. *1944-1950: de la unidad nacional a la hegemonía conservadora.* Bogotá: Editorial Pluma, 1980.

Jaramillo Uribe, Jaime, ed. *Antología del pensamiento político colombiano.* 2 vols. Bogotá: Publicaciones del Banco de la República, 1970.

Jaramillo Uribe, Jaime, ed. *El pensamiento colombiano en el siglo XIX.* Bogotá: Editorial Temis, 1964.

Jordán Jiménez, Ricardo. *Dos viernes trágicos.* Bogotá: Editorial Horizontes, 1968.

Lasch, Christopher. *The Culture of Narcissism.* New York: W. W. Norton, 1978.

Latorre Cabal, Hugo. *Mi novela: apuntes autobiográficos de Alfonso López.* Bogotá: Ediciones Mito, 1961.

Laun, John I. *El reclutamiento político en Colombia: los ministros de estado, 1900-1975.* Bogotá: Universidad de los Andes, 1976.

Leal Buitrago, Francisco. *Análisis histórico del desarrollo político nacional, 1930-1970.* Bogotá: Ediciones Tercer Mundo, 1973.

Léndez, Emilio. *¿Por qué murió el capitán?* Bogotá: Tipográfico Escorial, 1948.

Lleras Camargo, Alberto. *Mi gente.* Vol. 1. Bogotá: Ediciones Banco de la República, 1975.

Lleras Restrepo, Carlos. *Borradores para una historia de la república liberal.* Bogotá: Editorial Nueva Frontera, 1975.

Lleras Restrepo, Carlos. *De la república a la dictadura.* Bogotá: Editorial ARGRA, 1955.

López, Alejandro. *Idearium liberal.* París: Ediciones La Antorcha, 1931.

López, Francisco. *La política del miedo.* Bogotá: Editorial Iqueima, 1961.

López Botero, Iván. *El asesinato de Gaitán y la "operación x": análisis espectral de un crímen del imperialismo.* Bogotá: L. Martel, 1973.

López de Mesa, Luis. *De cómo se ha formado la nación colombiana.* Bogotá: Editorial Bedout, 1970.

López de Mesa, Luis. *Perspectivas culturales.* Bogotá: Talleres Ediciones Universidad Nacional, 1949.

López Giraldo, Fermín. *El apóstol desnudo, o dos años al lado de un mito.* Manizales: Editorial Arturo Zapata, 1936.

López Michelsen, Alfonso. *Cuestiones colombianas.* México: Impresiones Modernas, 1955.

López Michelsen, Alfonso. *Los elegidos.* Bogotá: Ediciones Tercer Mundo, 1967.

López Michelsen, Alfonso. *Esbozos y atisbos.* Bogotá: Antares, 1980.

López Pumarejo, Alfonso. *Obras selectas.* 2 vols. Bogotá: Cámara de Representantes, Colección Pensadores Políticos Colombianos, 1979.

Lozano y Lozano, Juan. *Ensayos críticos—Mis contemporáneos.* Reprint ed. Bogotá: Biblioteca Colombiana de Cultura, 1978.

Madrid-Malo, Néstor. *Ensayos y variaciones.* Bogotá: Biblioteca Colombiana de Cultura, 1978.

Mannheim, Hermann, ed. *Pioneers of Criminology.* London: Stevens and Sons, 1960.

Manrique, Ramón. *A sangre y fuego: un dramático reportaje del nueve de abril en todo Colombia.* Barranquilla: Librería Nacional, 1948.

Martínez Zelada, Eliseo. *Colombia en el llanto: crónica auténtica del movimiento popular de abril de 1948.* México: Editorial B. Costa-Amic, 1948.

Marx, Karl. *Capital.* Vol. 1. New York: International Publishers, 1967.

Marx, Karl, and Frederick Engels. *Selected Works in One Volume.* New York: International Publishers, 1968.

Mazuera Villegas, Fernando. *Cuento mi vida.* Bogotá: Canal Ramírez, 1972.

McGreevey, William Paul. *An Economic History of Colombia, 1845–1930.* Cambridge: Cambridge University Press, 1971.

Medina, Medófilo. *Historia del partido comunista de Colombia.* Vol. 1. Bogotá: Editorial Colombia Nueva, 1980.

Mendoza Neira, Plinio, and Alberto Camacho Angarita. *El liberalismo en el gobierno, 1930–1946.* 3 vols. Bogotá: Editorial Antena, 1946–1949.

Mitchell, Christopher. *The Legacy of Populism in Bolivia: From the MNR to Military Rule.* New York: Praeger, 1977.

Molina, Felipe Antonio. *Laureano Gómez: historia de una rebeldía.* Bogotá: Editorial Voluntad, 1940.

Molina, Gerardo. *Las ideas liberales en Colombia, 1915–1934.* Vol. 2. Bogotá: Ediciones Tercer Mundo, 1974.

Molina, Gerardo. *Las ideas liberales en Colombia de 1935 a la iniciación del Frente Nacional.* Bogotá: Ediciones Tercer Mundo, 1977.

Montaña Cuéllar, Diego. *Colombia: país formal y país real.* Bogotá: Ediciones Suramérica, 1963.

Moreno, David. *Trayectoria del pensamiento político de Gaitán.* Bogotá: Centro Cultural Jorge Eliécer Gaitán, 1983.

Moreno, Francisco José. *Legitimacy and Stability in Latin America: A Study of Chilean Political Culture.* New York: New York University Press, 1969.

Mosse, George L. *The Nationalization of the Masses: Political Symbolism and Mass Movements in Germany from the Napoleonic Wars Through the Third Reich.* New York: New American Library, 1975.

Mount, Ferdinand. *The Theater of Politics.* London: Wiedenfeld and Nicholson, 1972.

Naranjo Villegas, Abel. *Generaciones colombianas.* Bogotá: Banco de la República, 1974.

Nieto Rojas, José María. *La batalla contra el comunismo en Colombia.* Bogotá: Empresa Nacional de Publicaciones, 1956.

Niño H., Alberto. *Antecedentes y secretos del nueve de abril.* Bogotá: Editorial Pax, 1949.

Ocampo, José Fernando. *Colombia siglo XX: estudio histórico y antología política, 1886-1934.* Vol. 1. Bogotá: Ediciones Tercer Mundo, 1980.

Oquist, Paul. *Violencia, conflicto y política en Colombia.* Bogotá: Instituto de Estudios Colombianos, Biblioteca Banco Popular, 1978.

Orrego Duque, Gonzalo. *Nueve de abril fuera de Palacio.* Bogotá: Editorial Patria, 1949.

Ortega y Gasset, José. *The Revolt of the Masses.* New York: W. W. Norton, 1957.

Ortiz Márquez, Julio. *El hombre que fue un pueblo.* Bogotá: Carlos Valencia Editores, 1978.

Osorio, Abraham T. *Por qué mataron a Gaitán.* Bogotá: Editorial Minerva, 1949.

Osorio Lizarazo, José Antonio. *Colombia: donde los Andes se disuelven.* Santiago: Editorial Universitaria, 1955.

Osorio Lizarazo, José Antonio. *El día del odio.* Buenos Aires: Ediciones López Negri, 1952.

Osorio Lizarazo, José Antonio. *Gaitán: vida, muerte y permanente presencia.* Reprint ed. Bogotá: Carlos Valencia Editores, 1979.

Osorio Lizarazo, José Antonio. *Novelas y crónicas.* Edited by Santiago Mutis Durán. Bogotá: Instituto Colombiano de Cultura, 1978.

Palacios, Marco. "La clase más ruidosa." *Eco,* no. 254 (December 1982): 113–56.

Palacios, Marco. *Coffee in Colombia, 1850-1970: An Economic, Social, and Political History.* Cambridge: Cambridge University Press, 1980.

Palacios, Marco. *El populismo en Colombia.* Bogotá: Ediciones el Tigre de Papel, 1971.

Palacios, Marco, ed. *La unidad nacional en América Latina: del regionalismo a la nacionalidad.* México: El Colegio de México, 1983.

Palza, Humberto. *La noche roja en Bogotá: páginas de un diario.* Buenos Aires: n.p., 1949.

Pareja, Carlos H. *El monstruo.* Buenos Aires: Editorial Nuestra América, 1955.

Payne, James L. *Patterns of Conflict in Colombia*. New Haven: Yale University Press, 1968.

Pecaut, Daniel. *Política y sindicalismo en Colombia*. Bogotá: La Carreta, 1973.

Peña, Luis David. *Gaitán íntimo*. Bogotá: Editorial Iqueima, 1949.

Pérez, Luis Carlos. *Los delitos políticos: interpretación jurídica del nueve de abril*. Bogotá: Distribuidora Americana de Publicaciones, 1948.

Pérez, Luis Carlos, ed. *Jorge Eliécer Gaitán, su obra científica*. 4 vols. Bogotá: Ministerio de Educación Nacional, 1952.

Pérez, Luis Carlos. *El pensamiento filosófico de Gaitán*. Bogotá: Editorial de los Andes, 1954.

Perry, Oliverio. *Quién es quién en Colombia, 1948*. Bogotá: Editorial Oliverio Perry, 1948.

Ramírez Moreno, Augusto. *La crisis del partido conservador*. Bogotá: Tipografía Granada, 1937.

Ramírez Moreno, Augusto. *Los leopardos*. Bogotá: Editorial Santa Fé, 1935.

Reich, Wilhelm. *The Mass Psychology of Fascism*. New York: Farrar, Straus and Giroux, 1973.

Restrepo, Roberto. *Nueve de abril: quiebra cultural y política*. Bogotá: Tipografía Bremen, 1948.

Restrepo Posada, José. *La iglesia en dos momentos difíciles en la historia patria*. Bogotá: n.p., 1935.

Rippy, J. Fred. *British Investments in Latin America, 1822–1949*. Minneapolis: University of Minnesota Press, 1959.

Rippy, J. Fred. *Globe and Hemisphere*. Westport: Greenwood Press, 1972.

Ritter, Alan. *The Political Thought of P. J. Proudhon*. Princeton: Princeton University Press, 1969.

Robinson, J. Cordell. *El movimiento gaitanista en Colombia*. Bogotá: Ediciones Tercer Mundo, 1976.

Rodríguez Garavito, Agustín. *Gabriel Turbay: un solitario de la grandeza*. Bogotá: Ediciones Prócer, 1966.

Rodríguez Garavito, Agustín. *Gaitán: biografía de una sombra*. Bogotá: Ediciones Tercer Mundo, 1979.

Rueda Vargas, Tomás. *Escritos*. 3 vols. Bogotá: Antares, 1963.

Sánchez G., Gonzalo. *Los días de la revolución: Gaitanismo y nueve de abril en provincia*. Bogotá: Centro Cultural Jorge Eliécer Gaitán, 1983.

Sánchez, Gonzalo, and Donny Meertens. *Bandoleros, gamonales y campesinos: el caso de la Violencia en Colombia*. Bogotá: El Áncora Editores, 1983.

Sanín Echeverri, Jaime. *Ospina supo esperar*. Bogotá: Editorial Andes, 1978.

Santos, Eduardo, *Las etapas de la vida colombiana: discursos y mensajes, 1938–1942*. Bogotá: Imprenta Nacional, 1946.

Santos Forero, Julio Enrique. *Yo sí vi huir al verdadero asesino de Jorge Eliécer Gaitán*. Bogotá: Gráficas Atenas, 1959.

Santos Montejo, Enrique (Calibán). *La danza de las horas y otros escritos*. Bogotá: Libros del Cóndor, 1969.

Schafer, Stephen. *Theories in Criminology*. New York: Random House, 1969.

Sennett, Richard. *The Fall of Public Man: On the Social Psychology of Capitalism*. New York: Vintage Books, 1978.

Sharpless, Richard E. *Gaitán of Colombia: A Political Biography*. Pittsburgh: University of Pittsburgh Press, 1978.

Soboul, Albert. *The Sans-Culottes: The Popular Movement and the Revolutionary Government, 1793–1794*. New York: Anchor Books, 1972.

Socarrás, José Francisco. *Laureano Gómez: psicoanálisis de un resentido*. Bogotá: Editorial ABC, 1942.

Stein, Steve. *Populism in Peru: The Emergence of the Masses and the Politics of Social Control*. Madison: University of Wisconsin Press, 1980.

Taylor, William B. "Between Global Process and Local Knowledge: An Inquiry into Early Latin American Social History, 1500–1900." In Olivier Zunz, ed., *Reliving the Past: The Worlds of Social History*. Chapel Hill: University of North Carolina Press, 1985.

Teeters, Negley K. *Penology from Panama to Cape Horn*. Philadelphia: Temple University Press, 1946.

Tellez B., Hernando. *Cincuenta años de radiodifusión colombiana*. Medellín: Editorial Bedout, 1974.

Tirado Mejía, Alvaro. *Aspectos políticos del primer gobierno de Alfonso López Pumarejo, 1934–38*. Bogotá: Instituto Colombiano de Cultura, 1981.

Torres, Mauro. *Gaitán: grandeza y limitaciones psicológicas*. Bogotá: Ediciones Tercer Mundo, 1976.

Torres García, Guillermo. *Historia de la moneda en Colombia*. Bogotá: Imprenta del Banco de la República, 1945.

Turner, Victor. *Dramas, Fields and Metaphors: Symbolic Action in Human Society*. Ithaca: Cornell University Press, 1974.

Turner, Victor. *The Ritual Process: Structure and Anti-Structure*. Ithaca: Cornell University Press, 1969.

Turner, Victor. "Variations on a Theme of Liminality." In Sally Falk Moore and Barbara G. Myerhoff, eds., *Secular Ritual*, pp. 36–52. Assen: Van Gorcum, 1977.

Uribe Uribe, Rafael. *Obras selectas*. 2 vols. Bogotá: Cámara de Representantes, Colección Pensadores Políticos Colombianos, 1979.

Urrutia, Miguel. *The Development of the Colombian Labor Movement*. New Haven: Yale University Press, 1969.

Urrutia, Miguel. *El sindicalismo en Colombia*. Bogotá: Ediciones Universidad de los Andes, 1969.

Urrutia Montoya, Miguel, and Mario Arrubla, eds. *Compendio de estadísticas históricas de Colombia*. Bogotá: Universidad Nacional, 1970.

Valencia, Luis Emiro, ed. *Gaitán: antología de su pensamiento económico y social*. Bogotá: Ediciones Suramérica, 1968.

Vallejo, Alejandro. *Bogotá: ocho de junio*. Bogotá: Publicaciones de la Revista *Universidad*, 1929.

Vallejo, Alejandro. *Diario de la palabra encadenada, o antes del nueve de abril y después*. Bogotá: Editorial Minerva, 1949.

Vallejo, Alejandro. *Políticos en la intimidad*. Bogotá: Ediciones Antena, 1936.

Van Gennep, Arnold. *The Rites of Passage*. Chicago: University of Chicago Press, 1960.

Velasco, Hugo. *Ecce homo: biografía de una tempestad*. Bogotá: Editorial ARGRA, 1950.

Véliz, Claudio. _The Centralist Tradition in Latin America._ Princeton: Princeton University Press, 1980.

Véliz, Claudio, ed. _Obstacles to Change in Latin America._ London: Oxford University Press, 1965.

Vidales, Luis. _La insurrección desplomada: el nueve de abril, su teoría, su praxis._ Bogotá: Editorial Iqueima, 1948. Reprint ed., Bogotá: Alberto Estrada, 1979.

Vieira, Gilberto. _Nueve de abril: experiencia de un pueblo._ Bogotá: Ediciones Suramérica, 1973.

Villaveces, Jorge, ed. _Los mejores discursos de Gaitán._ Bogotá: Editorial Jorvi, 1968.

Villegas, Silvio. _No hay enemigos a la derecha._ Manizales: Editorial Arturo Zapata, 1937.

Walters, Vernon. _Silent Missions._ Garden City, N.Y.: Doubleday, 1978.

Weiss, Anita. _Tendencias de la participación electoral en Colombia, 1935-1966._ Bogotá: Universidad Nacional, Departamento de Sociología, 1968.

Wiarda, Howard J. _Corporatism and National Development in Latin America._ Boulder: Westview Press, 1981.

Wiarda, Howard J., ed. _Politics and Social Change in Latin America: The Distinct Tradition._ Amherst: University of Massachusetts Press, 1974.

Wilde, Alexander W. "Conversations Among Gentlemen: Oligarchical Democracy in Colombia." In Juan Linz and Alfred Stepan, eds., _The Breakdown of Democratic Regimes, Vol. 3: Latin America,_ pp. 28–81. Baltimore: Johns Hopkins University Press, 1978.

Willner, Ann Ruth. _The Spellbinders: Charismatic Political Leadership._ New Haven: Yale University Press, 1984.

Zapata Olivella, Manuel. _La calle diez._ Bogotá: Ediciones Casa de la Cultura, 1960.

Zuleta Angel, Eduardo. _El presidente López._ Medellín: Ediciones Alba, 1966.

Newspapers, Magazines and Journals

Acción Liberal (Bogotá), 1932–1933.

Avante (Bogotá), 1948.

Avanzada (Bogotá), 1948.

Batalla (Bogotá), 1944–1945.

El Catolicismo (Bogotá), 1948–1949.

Clarín (Bogotá), 1948.

El Debate (Bogotá), 1929–1930.

Derechas (Bogotá), 1948.

Diario Oficial (Bogotá), 1948–1949.

Eco Nacional (Bogotá), 1948.

El Espectador (Bogotá), 1936, 1948, 1968, 1973, 1978.

El Fígaro (Bogotá), 1929–1930.

La Iglesia (Bogotá), 1948.

Jornada (Bogotá), 1947–1949.

Life Magazine (New York), 1948.

El Liberal (Bogotá), 1946–1948.

New York Times (New York), 1948.
Lo Nuevo (Bogotá), 1948.
La Razón (Bogotá), 1945–1948.
Reconquista (Bogotá), 1948.
La República (Bogotá), 1959, 1961.
Revista de las Indias (Bogotá), 1948.
Revista de Medicina Legal de Colombia (Bogotá), 1948.
Sábado (Bogotá), 1948–1949.
Semana (Bogotá), 1946–1949.
El Siglo (Bogotá), 1944–1949, 1959, 1968, 1973, 1978.
El Tiempo (Bogotá), 1928–1949, 1968, 1973, 1978.
Unirismo (Bogotá), 1933–1934.
Universidad (Bogotá), 1928–1929.

Major Articles on the *Bogotazo*

Caballero Calderón, Eduardo. "Antes y después del nueve de abril." *Sábado*, December 18, 1948, p. 1.

Cifuentes, Sebastian. "Lo que se ignora del nueve de abril." *Sábado*, January 22, 1949, p. 1.

Dangond Uribe, Alberto. "Laureano Gómez y el nueve de abril." *El Espectador*, April 14, 1968, p. 10A.

Echandía, Darío. "La historia también es con los muertos." (Interview with Gabriel Gutiérrez.) *El Tiempo (Lecturas Dominicales)*, April 8, 1973.

Estrada Monsalve, Joaquín. "Las causas del nueve de abril." *Sábado*, June 5, 1948, p. 7.

Forero Benavides, Abelardo. "A los hombres de buena voluntad." *Sábado*, May 8, 1948, p. 1.

Forero Benavides, Abelardo. "Gaitán." *Sábado*, April 24, 1948, p. 1.

Forero Benavides, Abelardo. "Los enemigos de la normalidad." *Sábado*, May 15, 1948, p. 1.

Forero Benavides, Abelardo. "El país nacional." *Sábado*, June 19, 1948, p. 1.

Forero Benavides, Abelardo. "Refutación a López de Mesa." *Sábado*, August 14, 1948, p. 1.

Forero Benavides, Abelardo. "Viaje al fondo de la noche: lo que ví en la revolución." *Sábado*, May 1, 1948, p. 1.

García-Peña, Roberto. "Memoria aproximada del nueve de abril." *El Tiempo (Lecturas Dominicales)*, April 8, 1973, p. 5.

González Toledo, Felipe. "El nueve de abril de 1948 a nivel del pavimento." *El Tiempo*, April 9, 1968, p. 20.

Lleras Restrepo, Carlos, "Carlos Lleras Restrepo relata la jornada del nueve de abril." (Interview with Antonio Montaña.) *El Tiempo*, April 8, 1973, p. 1.

López, Alfonso. "El mensaje de Alfonso López sobre el nueve de abril." *Sábado*, June 5, 1948, p. 4.

Ospina Pérez, Mariano. "Las horas dramáticas en el Palacio Presidencial." *El Tiempo (Lecturas Dominicales)*, April 8, 1973, p. 1, and April 9, 1973, p. 1B.

Ramírez Moreno, Augusto. "La tragedia nacional del nueve de abril." *El Tiempo,* July 10, 1948, p. 1.

Restrepo Piedrahita, Carlos. "La junta revolucionaria de Bogotá." *Sábado,* April 9, 1949, p. 3.

Royo, Rodrigo. "Lo que se ignora del nueve de abril." *Sábado,* January 29, 1949, p. 9.

Samper, Darío. "La trágica proyección del nueve de abril." *El Tiempo,* April 9, 1968, p. 5.

Villegas, Silvio. "Aventura y reconstrucción." *Sábado,* May 8, 1948, p. 3.

Zapata Olivella, Manuel. "El nueve de abril: interpretación comunista." *Sábado,* April 9, 1949, p. 5.

Interviews (all held in Bogotá)

1. Herbert Braun, Bogotá hardware store manager at the time of the *bogotazo;* author's father. October 8, 1978, and subsequent conversations.
2. Guillermo Montaña Cuéllar, president, Colombian Red Cross. December 17, 1978.
3. Fernando Tamayo, physician in charge of the Hospital de San José during the *bogotazo* and subsequent days. December 22, 1978.
4. H. W. Meyer, Bogotá hardware store owner at the time of the *bogotazo.* March 14, 1979.
5. Pío Nono Barbosa Barbosa, Bogotá carpenter and stonemason; leading working-class Gaitanista; member of the Cundinamarca assembly. April 9, 1979, and subsequent conversations.
6. Jorge Corredor, Gaitanista, member of the committees that organized the Manifestación del Silencio; participant in the *bogotazo.* April 9, 1979.
7. Julio E. Pereira, Gaitanista, organizer of working-class neighborhoods. April 9, 1979.
8. José María Córdoba, general secretary of the Gaitanista movement, 1944–1948; historian of the movement. July 15, 1979.
9. Francisco Sáenz Arbeláez, director of the Junta Informadora de Daños y Perjuicios, body commissioned by the Ospina Pérez government to determine losses incurred in the *bogotazo.* July 17, 1979, and subsequent conversations.
10. Daniel Bello, general secretary of the JEGA after the death of Gaitán, 1948–1949. July 21, 1979.
11. Rafael Galán Medellín, leading Gaitanista; mayor of Girardot, 1947–1948; first lawyer to represent the Gaitán family in the investigation into Gaitán's assassination; expert on the investigation, the Proceso Gaitán. July 26, 1979.
12. Rafael Azula Barrera, secretary to President Mariano Ospina Pérez, 1946–1949; participant in the *palacio* conversations on the evening of the *bogotazo;* noted Conservative historian. July 31, 1979.
13. Diógenes Parra, Gaitanista organizer. August 13, 1979.
14. Adelmo Toro, Gaitanista sympathizer, participant in the attack on the Presidential Palace during the *bogotazo;* injured by the military. August 16, 1979.

15. Arturo Abella, editor of the Conservative daily *El Siglo* during the *bogotazo;* Conservative historian of the riot. August 18 and 19, 1979.
16. Alberto Vejarano Laverde, marine physician commissioned by the army to clean Bogotá's streets of the cadavers on April 9 and 10, known as *"el enterrador de régimen"* ("the regime's gravedigger"). September 21, 1979.
17. Andrés Holguín Holguín, Prefecto Nacional de Seguridad for the Conservative regime after the *bogotazo.* September 25, 1979.
18. Pascual del Vecchio, Gaitanista organizer on the northern coast, primarily in Barranquilla; financial consultant to the Gaitanista movement. September 25, 1979.
19. Gerardo Molina, Marxist rector of the Universidad Nacional, leader of the protesters, and president of the Executive Committee of the Revolutionary Junta of Government during the *bogotazo;* leading historian of the Liberal party. September 25, 1979.
20. Msgr. Carlos Vargas Umaña, defender of the palace of the archbishop during the *bogotazo.* October 31, 1979.
21. Luis Eduardo Ricaurte, known as *"el coronel"* and *"el chiquito";* Gaitán's trusted bodyguard and leader of the first march on the Presidential Palace during the *bogotazo.* November 2, 1979, and subsequent conversations.
22. Joaquín Estrada Monsalve, member of the Ospina Pérez cabinet; participant in the *palacio* conversation on the evening of the *bogotazo;* historian of the riot. November 9, 1979.
23. Guillermo Hernández Rodríguez, leftist intellectual and occasional advisor to Gaitán. November 9, 1979.
24. Adán Arriaga Andrade, Liberal Turbayista leader; governor of Chocó during the *bogotazo* and leader of the Liberal rebels at the Fifth Police Precinct, April 9–12, 1948. November 10, 1979.
25. Msgr. Arturo Franco Arango, defender of the palace of the archbishop; trusted advisor to Archbishop Ismael Perdomo; historian of the *bogotazo.* November 11, 1979.
26. Msgr. Antonio Afanador Salgar, parish priest of the barrio El Egipto, whose church was defended from the rioters by the women of the barrio. November 14, 1979.
27. Presbítero Julio César Orduz, editor of *El Catolicismo* during the *bogotazo.* November 17, 1979.
28. Gilberto Vieira, general secretary of the Communist party during the *bogotazo.* November 17, 1979.
29. Ana María E. vda. de Cagua, wife of Jorge Cagua, railroad worker killed in the *bogotazo.* November 18, 1979.
30. José Vicente Dávila Tello, Conservative minister of communications in the Ospina Pérez administration, 1946–1949; participant in the *palacio* conversation on the evening of the *bogotazo.* November 19, 1979.
31. Hernando Restrepo Botero, Gaitanista labor leader; participant in the *bogotazo.* November 19, 1979.
32. Luis Cano Jacobo, Gaitanista lawyer and politician. November 21, 1979.

33. Bertha Hernández de Ospina Pérez, wife of President Ospina Pérez; hostess to the *palacio* conversation on the evening of the *bogotazo*. November 22, 1979.

34. David Luna Serrano, member of the Gaitanista movement; consultant to Gaitán on legal matters. November 27, 1979.

35. Salvador Millán, policeman, Eighth Precinct, imprisoned by the army after the *bogotazo*. November 27, 1979.

36. Octavio López, Gaitanista, secretary to Gaitán during his mayoralty, 1936–1937; participant in the *bogotazo*. November 28, 1979.

37. Guillermo Vargas, Gaitanista leader of the barrio Perseverancia; participant in the *bogotazo*. November 28, 1979.

38. Heliodoro Africano, police sergeant, detained after the *bogotazo*. November 28, 1979.

39. Elías Escobar Salamanca, army captain in Manizales who took over the municipal building in the name of the Liberal party; later court martialed and found innocent. November 29, 1979.

40. Felipe González Toledo, well-known *El Tiempo* journalist, eyewitness, participant, and historian of the *bogotazo*. November 29, 1979.

41. Eduardo Fajardo Motta, police commander of the Ninth Precinct during the *bogotazo*. November 30, 1979.

42. Gabriel Muñoz Uribe, Gaitanista lawyer and leader of the protesters during the *bogotazo*. December 1, 1979, and subsequent conversations.

43. Ezequiel Benavides (pseudonym), Gaitanista sympathizer, injured in the *bogotazo*. December 2, 1979.

44. Sergio Céspedes, Gaitanista sympathizer, injured in the *bogotazo*. December 2, 1979.

45. Euclides Londoño, eyewitness to the burning of *El Siglo*. December 3, 1979.

46. Aníbal Turbay Ayala, notary public during the *bogotazo*. December 3, 1979.

47. Captain José Phillips, Gaitanista sympathizer and legal aide to Gaitán; leader of the protesters; court martialed and found guilty for his actions during the riot. December 4, 1979.

48. José Luis Cueto, Bogotá lawyer and eyewitness to the *bogotazo*. December 4, 1979.

49. Agustín Utrera, Bogotá barber, Gaitanista organizer and participant in the first march on the Presidential Palace. December 5, 1979.

50. Leslie Donald, amateur filmmaker and eyewitness to the *bogotazo*. December 5, 1979.

51, 52. Valerio and Bernardo Valverde, Gaitanista organizers of the barrio El Vergel, participants in the *bogotazo*. December 6, 1979.

53. Leo Matíz, professional photographer, injured during the *bogotazo*. December 6, 1979.

54. Daniel Rodríguez Rodríguez, dean of Bogotá photographers; eyewitness to the *bogotazo*. December 6, 1979.

55. Manuel Jiménez, Gaitanista whose son was run over by a car as he was laying a wreath of flowers at the site of Gaitán's assassination a year after the *bogotazo*. December 7, 1979.

56. Jaime Célis, Gaitanista, participant in the *bogotazo*. December 7, 1979.

57. José Vicente Espinosa, defender of the Museo Colonial; eyewitness to the sack of the Palacio de San Carlos during the *bogotazo*. December 8, 1979.

58. Benito Rojas, cavalry soldier sent from Usaquén to Bogotá to take over Radio Nacional; injured as battalion proceeded to the *palacio* during the *bogotazo*. December 8, 1979.

59. Clímaco Aldana, Gaitanista librarian of the Consejo de Bogotá; secretary of the movement and historian of Gaitanismo. December 11, 1979.

60. Arturo Céspedes, Gaitanista, participant in the *bogotazo*. December 13, 1979.

61. José Vicente García, Gaitanista, participant in the *bogotazo*. December 13, 1979.

62. Daniel Ramos Ramos, commander of the Bogotá fire department, Eleventh Police Precinct, during the *bogotazo*. December 13, 1979.

63. Hipólito Mora, chef of the Gun Club, injured on the evening of the *bogotazo*. December 14, 1979.

64. Luis E. Botero Jaramillo, physician at the Clínica Central during the *bogotazo*. December 19, 1979.

65. Antonio García, leftist organizer and economist; economic and political advisor to Gaitán; leader of the protesters during the *bogotazo;* noted historian of Colombia and the Third World. December 19, 1979.

66. Carlos J. Sánchez, Gaitanista, participant in the *bogotazo*. January 2, 1980.

67. Manuel José Valencia, Gaitanista, participant in the *bogotazo*. January 2, 1980.

68. Daniel Martínez Quijano, Red Cross volunteer during the *bogotazo*. January 5, 1980.

Index